THE KLUWER INTERNATIONAL SERIES ON INFORMATION RETRIEVAL

Series Editor

W. Bruce Croft
University of Massachusetts, Amherst

Also in the Series:

MULTIMEDIA INFORMATION RETRIEVAL: Content-Based Information Retrieval from Large Text and Audio Databases, *by Peter Schäuble;* ISBN: 0-7923-9899-8

INFORMATION RETRIEVAL SYSTEMS: Theory and Implementation, *by Gerald Kowalski;* ISBN: 0-7923-9926-9

CROSS-LANGUAGE INFORMATION RETRIEVAL, *edited by Gregory Grefenstette;* ISBN: 0-7923-8122-X

TEXT RETRIEVAL AND FILTERING: Analytic Models of Performance, *by Robert M. Losee;* ISBN: 0-7923-8177-7

INFORMATION RETRIEVAL: UNCERTAINTY AND LOGICS: Advanced Models for the Representation and Retrieval of Information, *by Fabio Crestani, Mounia Lalmas, and Cornelis Joost van Rijsbergen;* ISBN: 0-7923-8302-8

DOCUMENT COMPUTING: Technologies for Managing Electronic Document Collections, *by Ross Wilkinson, Timothy Arnold-Moore, Michael Fuller, Ron Sacks-Davis, James Thom, and Justin Zobel;* ISBN: 0-7923-8357-5

AUTOMATIC INDEXING AND ABSTRACTING OF DOCUMENT TEXTS, *by Marie-Francine Moens*; ISBN 0-7923-7793-1

ADVANCES IN INFORMATIONAL RETRIEVAL: Recent Research from the Center for Intelligent Information Retrieval, *by W. Bruce Croft*; ISBN 0-7923-7812-1

INFORMATION RETRIEVAL SYSTEMS: Theory and Implementation, Second Edition, *by Gerald J. Kowalski and Mark T. Maybury;* ISBN: 0-7923-7924-1

PERSPECTIVES ON CONTENT-BASED MULTIMEDIA SYSTEMS

by

Jian Kang Wu
Kent Ridge Digital Labs, Singapore

Mohan S. Kankanhalli
National University of Singapore

Joo-Hwee Lim
Kent Ridge Digital Labs, Singapore

Dezhong Hong
Kent Ridge Digital Labs, Singapore

SPRINGER SCIENCE+BUSINESS MEDIA, LLC

Library of Congress Cataloging-in-Publication Data

Perspectives on content-based multimedia systems / Jian Kang Wu... [et al.].
p. cm. -- (The Kluwer international series on information retrieval; 9)
Includes bibliographical references and index.
ISBN 978-1-4757-7361-3 ISBN 978-0-306-47033-2 (eBook)
DOI 10.1007/978-0-306-47033-2

1. Multimedia systems. I. Wu, Jian-Kang, 1947- II. Series.

QA76.575.P485 2000
006.7--dc21

00-060508

Printed on acid-free paper.

Contents

Preface

Due to the rapid advances in computing and communication technologies, human beings are constantly being inundated by information in form of text, image, audio, video and spatial data. There is an overwhelming need for an integrated multimedia system to reduce the work and information overload for people. The technologies for handling multimedia data are most important and most challenging: our society is increasingly generating vast amount of multimedia data by means of cameras, satellites, etc.; the complexity and variety of multimedia data are beyond one's imagination.

It is quite natural for us human beings to recall multimedia information by content. We recognize our friends by their appearances. The story of one video may remind us of the ones similar to that. Therefore, content-based access to multimedia is of primary importance. This book deals with various aspects of content-based multimedia systems.

Formalization of the whole paradigm of content-based retrieval to bring it to a sufficient level of consistency and integrity is essential to the success of the field. After introduction, we will discuss the formalism of content-based multimedia systems, which is proposed and developed by the authors of the book. With the formalism, a reconfigurable retrieval engine can be developed.

For the content-based retrieval of a large multimedia database, a unified feature space (referred to as vector space in information retrieval community) is desirable. In such a unified feature space, data items can be represented and measures of similarity can defined.

Unlike conventional databases, where primary data types are well handled by standard query languages such as SQL, the retrieval of multimedia databases is approximate, and is not likely able to be handled by a single language like SQL. In the fourth chapter, we will present methods for content-based indexing for visual browsing, fuzzy retrieval method, customizable similarity retrieval, and case-based reasoning.

As show cases, three application examples will be presented. A face database is a typical image database where each data item share the same structure. Many concepts can be demonstrated using this system. Because of the diversity of the trademarks, the retrieval of conflicting trademarks relies on several properties of those trademarks. These include the word, phonetics, shape and interpretation of the trademark image. The system retrieval engine should be able to find feature spaces to accommodate those properties in order to define proper similarity functions. The medical database example is used to illustrate case-based reasoning. Digital photo album is a very practical application as digital cameras become popular.

This book covers the research results supported by Kent Ridge Digital Labs (KRDL), Singapore and funded by Real World Computing Partnership (RWCP), Japan. The authors sincerely appreciate the support and help given by the management and colleagues from these two organizations.

The following people made contributions to the book: Chian Prong Lam (Chapter 10 and 11), Fuchun Shang (Chapter 4, 7 and 12), Xinding Sun (Chapter 5), Bin Wang (Chapter 6), and Harro Stokman (Chapter 7). We would also like to thank Ms. Anuradha Srinivasan for the proofreading help.

Jian-Kang WU

Chapter 1

Introduction

One of the lasting legacies of the twentieth century is the pervasive impact of digital techniques in explicit as well as embedded forms. The implications of the new "digital age" are still being explained by scientists, engineers, sociologists and philosophers[1,2,4]. Depending upon our perspective, we all are intrigued by many perplexing questions. What is the most remarkable change that this digital age brings to our life? What type of roles multimedia indexing and retrieval technology can play? As multimedia researchers, we believe that the transformation of media information from the analog form to digital form is having a significant impact.

For example, digital cameras are becoming affordable and popular. We can view the result while taking photographs. The photos can be kept forever without worrying about degradation. We can share photos with relatives or friends who are far away over Internet with great ease. What about our photo album? There is an unmet need for a digital photo album[3], where indexing and retrieval of images[4] can be done flexibly.

Our television is going to be digital[5,6]. Interactive TV allows us to see whatever of interest whenever we like. There is no more worry about missing a favourite TV program. How can we find programs of our interest? Here again, content-based indexing and retrieval plays a very important role.

Music CD constitutes one of the largest markets in the world. Now digital music is available. Instead of buying CDs, people can obtain their favourite songs from the Internet. To protect the interest of recording industries, the Secure Digital Music Initiatives (SDMI)[7] has proposed secure hardware MP3[8] player standard to prevent piracy. To music consumers, convenient tools and functions to find and use music data are

testing sets for Bayes classifier contain 2/3 and 1/3 of the images. The performance is quite consistent with visual perception although there are some misclassification among certain categories.

Virage

Virage Inc. has its roots in the research done at University of California at San Diego. Their technology of image retrieval is built around a core module called the Virage Engine [23]. Virage Engine is an open, portable and extensible architecture to incorporate any domain specific schema. Virage applies three levels of information abstraction for images: the raw image(the image representation level), the processed image(the image object level) and the user's feature of interest (the domain object level). The computed visual features are named by Virage as "primitives", which are either global or local. According to Virage, a primitive should be meaningful for perception, compact in storage, efficient in computation, accurate in comparison and should be indexable. Several "universal primitives" given by Virage include global color, local color, structure and texture. These primitives are universal in the sense that they are useful in most domain- independent applications and they can be automatically computed by Virage Engine. The user can choose to mix and match these primitives in conjunction with domain specific primitives to build a particular application, such as medical or multimedia application. Its extensible architecture enables the user to "plug-in" domain optimized algorithms to solve specific problems. Virage Engine is delivered as a statistically or dynamically linkable library for various platforms (Sun, SGI, Windows and MAC). The library accommodates different types of databases and application frameworks. Databases such as Oracle, Sybase or image- manipulation and processing tool like Photoshop, CorelDraw could use the Virage Engine for image search and management. An Internet search engine like WebCrawler or InfoSeek can extend their capabilities with image finding in the network and thus help building a searchable image storage system distributed over the WWW.

KRDL's CORE

CORE, a COntent-based Retrieval Engine, for multimedia databases, was developed by RWC Lab of KRDL [19]. CORE provides functions in multimedia information systems for multimedia objects creation, analysis, storage and retrieval. Some salient techniques in CORE include: multiple feature extraction methods, multiple content- based retrieval methods, a novel content-based indexing on complex feature measures using self-organizing neural networks and a new technique for fuzzy retrieval of multimedia information. CORE has three main modules:

1. Multimedia data analysis module (Analysis),
2. Query module (Retrieval and Indexing),
3. Customization module (Training).

CORE provides elementary multimedia classes as building blocks for application system development. Its image representation scheme consists of four levels from bottom to top: gray/color image, segmented image, descriptions and features, interpretation. CORE provides three types of segmentation functions, namely, color segmentation, morphological segmentation, and segmentation by boundary extraction. Feature extraction functions are invoked to compute feature measures on segmented objects/regions. These functions include: principal component analysis, moment invariant, shape measure by Fourier descriptors, projections, shape parameters, texture energy, color feature measures etc. CORE's content-based indexing is located between feature and interpretation level. It utilizes the concept of tree classifier and content-based indexing, and uses LEP (Learning based on Experiences and Perspective) neural network model to provide a solid theoretical basis and to be able to fuse composite feature measures. This is used to generate self-organizing nodes for content-based index tree of complex and composite feature measures. This indexing scheme has been implemented in CORE to support similarity retrieval. It can also be used for fuzzy indexing on multi-variate fuzzy membership functions. There are four types of retrieval methods in CORE, namely, visual browsing, similarity retrieval, fuzzy retrieval and text retrieval. Similarity retrieval provides access to multimedia objects through feature measures, while fuzzy retrieval and text retrieval provide access through the interpretation of multimedia objects. User feedback is often necessary for effective retrieval. By using feedback functions, user can select one or more objects from current query results, which he/she thinks are very close to the desired one. Feedback function then finds the information from the selected objects and refines the query. Feedback function in CORE assumes that feedback objects are selected in a sequence such that the most desired one is selected first, and the selection will be based on the most similar features among those selected objects. CORE has been used in the development of two application systems: Computer-Aided Facial Image Inference and Retrieval (CAFIIR)

[20] and System for Trademark Archival and Registration (STAR) [19]. In addition, a medical image database system for computer-aided diagnosis and surgery is under development using this engine. CORE has rich and comprehensive functionalities. However, each application has its domain specific problems so domain expertise must be added to customize the indexing and retrieval module. That is, training is a crucial step in the application development. We have developed our research using useful results and functions provided by CORE.

1.3 Challenges and solutions

In general, existing research and commercial systems perform image retrieval on global or local similarity based on visual features (color, texture, shape, spatial location/relation). They often perform image segmentation or region extraction to generate locally salient image regions for future retrieval or classification. Some try to categorize images into predefined classes to facilitate management and search. Others let the user refine their query through interactive interface. In many cases, their results are satisfactory according to visual perception but sometimes the findings are nearly totally irrelevant in content, mostly occurring in global retrieval. This suggests that simple comparison of global features may not be a robust method for mission critical applications. Content-based indexing and retrieval calls for functions and features at the object level. The reason is very simple, the content of media are its objects.

The challenges of content-based indexing and retrieval of images and video are due to extreme complexity of the data in nature:

- Video and images are primitive signals. They often need several steps of processing (pre-processing, segmentation, analysis, and recognition) and human interaction as well in most cases to derive interpretations. Video and images are also multi-dimensional. The richness of the multi-dimensional signal results in a variety of features[2]: color, texture, shape, spatial property, and object specific features such as human eyes in face images. This makes the processing extremely difficult. For example, automatic segmentation of a body organ from ultra-sonic images is still questionable because there is too much noise and the boundaries are seriously blurred.

- Interpretations of video and images are subjective and can have several levels and different aspects. For example, large eyes from a

Japanese view point can be interpreted as medium or small for an Indian.

- There is almost no exception to the truism that objects of interest are embedded in a background or noise. Segmentation of objects from this background/noise has been a challenging research topic in the field of computer vision from the very beginning. Here, the definition of signal and noise is also relative. When we want to segment a specific person from an image, all other persons as well as the surroundings are considered as background or noise.

- An object can vary from image frame to frame, with respect to size, location, attitude, orientation, and even the appearance. Object itself may change as well. For example, a person can change his/her clothes, hair style, and get fatter/thinner etc.

Content representation is a fundamental issue in the field of indexing and retrieval of multimedia information. There are two main approaches: signature-based and object-based. The former is a rather new approach inspired by information processing methods, the latter attempts to identify salient objects for indexing.

Two terms appear frequently in the literature: feature-based and content-based. The former is about low level (sometimes called "syntactic") characteristics of the data, e.g., image texture or color histogram. Content based, however, are about properties of the entities in the data, sometimes called "semantic" characteristics. To go from feature-based to content-based, the necessary condition is that the feature must be object-based. This is because the content of a video or an image is about objects. For example, the color histogram of an image does not provide a hint to the content of the image, whereas the color histogram of individual objects in the image does.

There are two ways to obtain the object-based representation in feature/vector space. One is to directly identify objects first, and then to extract feature measures for their recognition/cataloging. Therefore, we refer it as object-based. This is a straight forward method, and can create high level interpretations for descriptive querying. On other hand, this approach is based on video and image understanding technologies, and is very difficult to implement for general applications. Although video and image understanding area is not yet mature, the object-based approach can create very useful representations to guide the search for relevant video clips and images.

The signature-based approach, on the other hand, looks into content representation issue from another perspective. Rather than viewing the world as individual objects, it sees video and images data as signatures of objects. Signatures consists of aspects such as color, intensity gradient, motion, texture, and their changes. Variances in these signatures correspond to certain objects at certain states. By keeping track of those signatures, we should be able to represent the content and retrieve relevant video and images.

1.4 Layout of the Book

Chapter 2 describes a generic framework for content-based indexing and retrieval of multimedia data. The framework governs the structure and principles to be presented in the rest of the book. In this chapter, the formalism is presented for application system design, development and tuning.

Chapter 3 and 4 discuss feature extraction methods for color, texture and motion, respectively. These feature measures serve as primitives for the object level.

The first step for object-oriented description is object segmentation. Chapter 5 describes methods for video segmentation and summary while Chapter 6 deals with object segmentation. People have a central role in media content for many applications. Chapter 7 is dedicated to human face detection and description.

Two special retrieval methods are treated in Chapter 8 and 9. Chapter 10 describes a signature-based approach, visual keywords, for image and video. It touches the methods of deriving visual keywords for an application, and learning of semantics. Our description of media content has been never exact. Chapter 10 presents a fuzzy retrieval method.

Three applications, face database, trademark archival & retrieval and digital home photo album, are presented in Chapter 10, 11 and 12. Finally, Chapter 13 deals with performance evaluation issues.

References

1. D. Crevier, R. Lepage, "Knowledge-based Image Understanding Systems: A Survey", Computer Vision and Image Understanding, Vol. 67, No. 2, pp. 161-185, 1997
2. J. R. Smith, "Integrated Spatial and Feature Image Systems: Retrieval, Analysis and Compression", Thesis of PhD, Graduate School of Arts and Science,

Columbia University, 1997

3. D. Hong, S. Singh, Y. W. Zhu, J. K. Wu, "Customisable Image Categorisation and Retrieval with Interactive User Interface", Intern. Conf on Multimedia Modeling, Ottawa, Canada, pp. 441-462, 1999
4. M. D. Marsicoi, L. Cinque, S. Levialdi, "Indexing Pictorial Documents by Their Content: A Survey of Current Techniques", Image and Vision Computing, vol. 15, pp. 119-141, 1997
5. Advanced Television Systems Committee, http://www.atsc.org/
6. The Digital Television Group, http://www.dtg.org.uk/
7. The Secure Digital Music Initiative Website, http://www.sdmi.org/
8. MP3 Website, http://www.mp3.com/
9. Home site of the JPEG and JBIG committees, http://www.jpeg.org/
10. The MPEG Home Page, http://drogo.cselt.it/mpeg/
11. EBU/SMPTE Task Force, http://www.edlmax.com/TaskForce.html
12. DVB Service Information, http://www.ebu.ch/
13. Information Society Standardization System, http://www.cenorm.be/ISSS/
14. W. Niblack, et.al, "The QBIC project: Querying Image by content using color, texture and shape", SPIE: Storage and Retrieval for Images and Video Database, San Jose , 1993
15. J. Yang and A. Waibel, "A Real-Time Face Tracker", Proceedings of Third IEEE Workshop on Applications of Computer Vision, Sarasota, Florida, pp. 142-147, 1996
16. A. Pentland, R. Picard, S. Sclaroff, "Photobook: Content-based Manipulation of Image Databases", Int. Journal of Computer Vision, vol. 18, no. 3, pp. 233-254, 1996
17. P. Brodatz, "Texture: A Photographic Album for Artists and Designers", Dover: New York, 1966
18. S. Belongie and C. Carson and H. Greenspan and J. Malik, "Recognition of Images in Large Databases Using a Learning Framework", Computer Science Division, University of California, Berkeley, Technical Report, No. 939, 1997
19. J. K. Wu, A. D. Narasimhalu, B. M. Mehtre, C. P. Lam, Y. J. Gao, "CORE: A content-based retrieval engine for multimedia information systems", ACM Multimedia Systems, Vol. 3, pp. 3-25 , 1995
20. J. K. Wu, Y. H. Ang, C. P. Lam, A. D. Narasimhalu, "Inference and retrieval of facial images", ACM Multimedia Journal, Vol. 2, No. 1, pp. 1-14, 1994
21. T. P. Minka and R. W. Picard, Interactive learning using a "society of Models", Media Lab, Massachusetts Institute of Technology, Technical Report, No. 349, 1995
22. R. Smith, S.-F. Chang, "Querying by color Regions using the VisualSEEK Content-based visual query system", M. T. Maybury, Intelligent Multimedia Information Retrieval, 1997
23. A. Gupta, "Visual information retrieval technology: A Virage Perspective", May, 1996
24. V. Guigueno, L'identite de l'image: expression et syst. emes documentaires, IRIT rapport d'option, Ecole polytechnique, Palaiseau, France, Juilet, 1991

mation in form of text, graphics, image, audio, video and spatial data (by multimedia, we refer to all these types of information). There is an overwhelming need for an integrated media system to reduce the work and information overload for people.

Recently, there is an increasing research interest on *intelligent agents.* The Apple Newton with its agent software and General Magic's messaging agents are evidences of this trend. Although the agent terminology is confusing and some people have reservation about it, the basic idea of agent research is to develop software system which engage and help all types of end users. Minsky is one of those people who initiated the terminology "agent". He said: "The idea was to use the word 'agent' when you want to refer to a machine that accomplishes something, without your needing to know how it works." [19]

Reducing the work and information overload can be achieved by implementing a new style of man-machine interaction. Current dominant interaction metaphor is *direct manipulation.* It requires the user to initiate all tasks explicitly and to monitor all events. By agent concept, the metaphor is referred to as *personal assistant.* The assistant is collaborating with the user to initiate communication, monitor events and perform tasks. The assistant becomes more effective as it learns the user's interests, preferences, and connections.

As the computing paradigm has been shifted from scientific computation to services. And the users are no longer professional. They may be layman users. Therefore, the technical challenges would be the user-centric retrieval. The key research issues have emphasized heavily on users' needs. The query languages should be able to anticipate users' needs and assist the user in formulating precise requests, and the interfaces should be capable of adapting to user preferences, limitations and behavior.

That is to say, the retrieval engine of the information bases should be user-centered; i.e be able to be adapted to users' needs and ready to incorporate users' perception into the retrieval. In order to do so, we propose a new formalism for user-centered content-based retrieval, object recall.

2.2 Content-based Multimedia Information System

According to Webster's New World Dictionary, *media* refers to "all the means of communication". *Multimedia* then is "a combination of communication media, such as television, newspapers, and radio." It is commonly recognized that image, video, graphics, 1-D signal (speech, sound, ECG, etc.), text and symbols are all different facets of multimedia information. From a computer science perspective, multimedia information can be represented using data structures or object classes.

Now we define important terms and outline the research scope of multimedia information systems.

2.2.1 Definitions

Multimedia information system

A *Multimedia Information System* should offer functions for multimedia object creation, storage, management, retrieval, processing, presentation, and utilization. In order to create a multimedia object, its data set needs to be processed, feature measures are extracted, and meanings are assigned. When using multimedia information to reach a reasonable decision, case-based reasoning or logical reasoning must be invoked. So a multimedia information system is more than a database.

A model for multimedia object

A *MultiMedia Object* (MOB) can be defined using a six tuple $O_{mob} = \{U, F, M, A, O^p, S\}$, where

- U is mUltimedia data component. It can be *null*, or may have one or more multimedia components, such as image and video. In the case of a trademark object, U is a trademark image.

- $F = \{F^1, F^2, ...\}$ represents a set of features derived from data. A feature F^i can either be numerically characterized by feature measures in feature space $F_1^i \times F_2^i \times ... \times F_n^i$, or conceptually described by their interpretations.

- $M^i = \{M_1^i, M_2^i, ...\}$ represents the interpretation of feature F^i.

  For example, in a facial image there are visual features such as hair, eyes, eyebrows, nose, mouth and outline shape. To characterize eyes, we need to extract measures such as area and fitting parameters to a deformed template. These feature measures are vectors and can be considered as points in feature spaces. Eyes can also be described by a set of concepts such as big eyes, medium eyes, or small eyes. The concepts big, medium, and small are interpretations of facial feature eyes.

- A stands for a set of attributes or particulars of O_{mob}. For example, a trademark can have attributes like trademark number, trademark owner and date of registration.

- O^p is a set of pointers or links, and is expressed as, $O^p = \{O^p_{sup}, O^p_{sub}, O^p_{other}\}$. There are three type of pointers/links pointing/linking to super-objects, sub-objects, and other objects, respectively. This leads to object hierarchies and links to other objects. With the hierarchy and links, the user can browse through types of objects, down to objects of a type and then into details of an object.

- S represents a set of *states* of O_{mob}. It takes values s_p -persistent, s_{np} - non-persistent, s_c - completely defined (with all slots assigned values), s_{uc} - incomplete.

Data, feature measures and concepts

Data, feature measures and concepts (interpretation) form a three layer hierarchy as shown in Figure 2.1. The two bottom-up mappings are very important.

Mapping from data set to feature measures is performed by feature extraction, and is denoted by $\Gamma_f : U \to F$. For a data set, several feature measures can be extracted. Different applications may require different set of feature measures from the same input data. This is a phenomenon of focus of attention and can be formulated as a one-to-many mapping from data to feature measures. On other hand, different data sets may share the same property which is captured as similar feature measures. This suggests many-to-one mapping from data sets to feature measures.

Mapping from data sets to feature measures is many-to-many. This is true in many multimedia information systems. Looking at a picture of a garden in a video information system, one user may be interested in a person in the garden, and therefore ask to search all video segments of this person. The style of the garden may motivate the interest of another user, and he/she may want video segments of similar gardens.

Similarly, mapping from feature measures to concepts is written as $\Gamma_c : F \to C$. It is also many-to-many. For a given set of multi-spectral images of a land area obtained by satellite, people from agriculture may be interested in estimation of crop production, while geologists may be interested in earth quake studies.

There are mainly two methods which are commonly used to perform mapping Γ_c. One is based on pattern recognition techniques which tries to optimally assign conceptual labels $M^i = \{M^i_1, M^i_2, ...\}$ to "patterns"

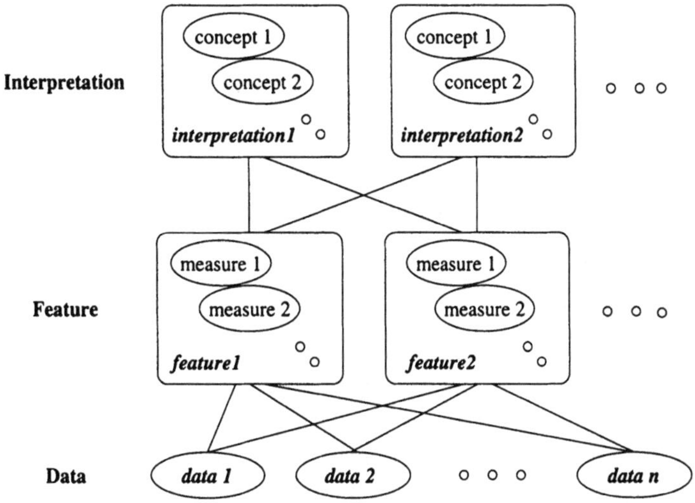

Figure 2.1: Three layers (data, feature and interpretation) hierarchy.

characterized by feature measures $F^i = \{F_1^i, F_2^i, ...\}$. The other is based on fuzzy theory. Here concepts $M^i = \{M_1^i, M_2^i, ...\}$ are treated as fuzzy sets, fuzzy membership functions $m_{M_j^i}(F^i), j = 1, 2, ...$ is used for mapping from F^i to M^i.

It is also true that automatic mappings of Γ_f and Γ_c are very difficult. In some applications, direct assignment of meaning to a data set is preferable. For example, in trademark system, automatic recognition of certain objects such as crown is impossible. It is then mandatory to let the trademark officer do manual assignment.

Content-based retrieval

From computer vision community's perspective, content-based retrieval is synonymous with the feature-based retrieval. In this case, the *content of a multimedia object* is actually the content of its data component U, which is restricted to a certain set of features of the object and is characterized by some feature measures $F^i, i = 1, 2, ...$ and is described by some concept sets $M^i, i = 1, 2, ...$

Content-based information retrieval comes from the study of human perception. We recall information by its content. The memory used for this purpose is referred to as *content-addressable memory*. Content-addressable memory is also called *associative memory* and has been extensively studied in the field of neural networks. The capability of content-addressable memory is achieved through association. There are two types of associations: auto-association and hetero-association. Auto-association is defined when a piece of information is associated with itself in the process of its storage. In the retrieval phase, one can recall the information through a partial or lower resolution version of the original information. With hetero-association, a piece of information is associated with another piece of information. These two pieces of information can have relationships such as having similar (or opposite) meaning/appearance and being closely related. When two pieces of information are stored using hetero-association, one piece of information can be used to recall another.

Content-based retrieval of multimedia information system can be classified into three categories corresponding to auto-association, hetero-association, and a combination of both. These three categories of retrieval are: searching within one object class, browsing among object classes, and partial matching of complex objects or *cases*.

Queries to find the best matches within one object class can be formally defined as:
For a given query object O^q, find an ordered set of objects $O^1, O^2, \ldots$ from the same object class in the database such that

$$\begin{aligned} sim(O^q, O^1) &= \max_{O \in DB} sim(O^q, O) \\ sim(O^q, O^2) &= \max_{O \in (DB - O^1)} sim(O^q, O) \\ \ldots &= \ldots \end{aligned} \tag{2.1}$$

where $sim(O_q, O)$ is the similarity measure between query object O_q and any object O from database DB. Depending on a given query object, retrieval can be of several types:

- *Visual browsing.* Quite often, multimedia information is either visual or audio. Confirmation of query results is carried out interactively. Instead of forming query object, user may want to just browse through the collection of the data to find desired ones. In this case, a content-based index is useful.

- *Similarity retrieval.* The query object is given as $O^q_{mob} = \{U, \emptyset, \emptyset, A^*, \emptyset, s_{np}\}$, where A^* represents partially defined set of attributes. The interpretation is "find objects whose data are most similar to O^q_{mob}'s and whose attributes match A^*". Usually, the similarity evaluation is carried out via feature measures in feature space. In the database, all feature measures are pre-computed and indexed. When processing a query, feature measures of the query object are computed at runtime. Using these feature measures, the query processing module searches the database by traversing the index tree.

- *Fuzzy retrieval.* When the query object is given as $O_q = \{\emptyset, \emptyset, M^*, A^*, \emptyset, s_{np}\}$, where M^* represents partial defined interpretations in terms of concepts, it is then best to process the query by fuzzy retrieval technique. These concepts can be represented by fuzzy sets and the query is processed by fuzzy reasoning in fuzzy space.

- *Text retrieval.* When the interpretation is given in terms of text in query object $O_q = \{\emptyset, \emptyset, M^*, A^*, \emptyset, s_{np}\}$, text retrieval method, such as free text retrieval, can be applied.

Browsing among object classes is achieved by hetero-association and internal links of composite objects $O^p = \{O^p_{sup}, O^p_{sub}, O^p_{other}\}$. These links are supported by object-oriented functionalities of the system.

A multimedia object $O_{mob} = \{U, F, M, A, O^p, S\}$ can represent complex objects in real world. Complex object consists of sub-objects and links among them. In query involving complex object, the query object is given as $O^q = \{U^*, F^*, M^*, A^*, O^{p*}, s_{np}\}$, where data, feature, interpretation, attributes and pointers can be partially defined. Retrieval of complex objects is then the partial matching between query object and objects in the system. Successful retrieval of similar complex objects implies recognition or problem solution. For example, in a medical information system for diagnosis and therapy planning, medical cases are complex composition of elementary objects such as images, test signals, text, and graphics. Doctors' experiences are represented as historical cases. Retrieval of suitable past cases will help to make diagnosis and plan therapy for the current patient. Another example of complex multimedia object query is model-based Recognition. After processing, one view of a 3-D scene is represented by a complex query object with sub-objects representing faces and links representing edges. Querying the 3-D model base using this complex query object completes the 3-D object recognition.

2.2.2 Challenges in content-based retrieval

The challenges in content-based retrieval are due to the nature of multimedia object (MOB). Some of the properties include:

- MOBs are complex entities and are difficult to describe. Hence they are less than completely represented when a query is submitted.

and descriptions/measures are created to maintain associations among them. Access to any level of the representation is facilitated with such bi-directional links and propagation function supported by the retrieval engine.

Segmented image consists of labeled regions, which clearly define the locations and boundaries of the regions and retain spatial fidelity. Because regions are labeled, the labels will be used to link region and their descriptions/feature measures.

Feature measures are directly derived from the regions of image by invoking feature extraction procedures. The descriptions can be text, describing the contents of the region, which is usually given by the user. The descriptions can also be interpretations generated by classification algorithms using feature measures. For example, when a radiologist is reading a CT image of a patient, he sees a tumor, and draws a contour on the image, enters text such as "small tumor indicating early stage of cancer", and then invokes a measurement tool to measure the area and diameter of the tumor. The contour he draws is represented in segmented image, the text he enters and the measurements he creates are captured in the description/measure level. However, within this level, only visual features of the image are characterized by descriptions and feature measures in terms of region. The description of a region may include spatial relationships among regions, which are inherently represented by segmented image.

Interpretation level is the highest level. It contains global and domain-specific interpretations of the image.

These four levels form a general representation scheme. As a matter of fact, several images can be taken for one patient, and one medical image may be interpreted by several doctors. These multiple links will be created and maintained by the retrieval engine.

2.2.4 Multimedia data analysis

Multimedia data analysis is aimed to process the data of multimedia object so as to produce feature measures, derive interpretation, and fill up attributes of the object. The object creation process is thus completed. Then, we need to build up links either to construct a complex object or to build relationship among objects.

The multimedia data analysis module has following functions:

- **Data acquisition** interacts with either local or remote data acquisition device/file to get data into the main memory as non-persistent object.

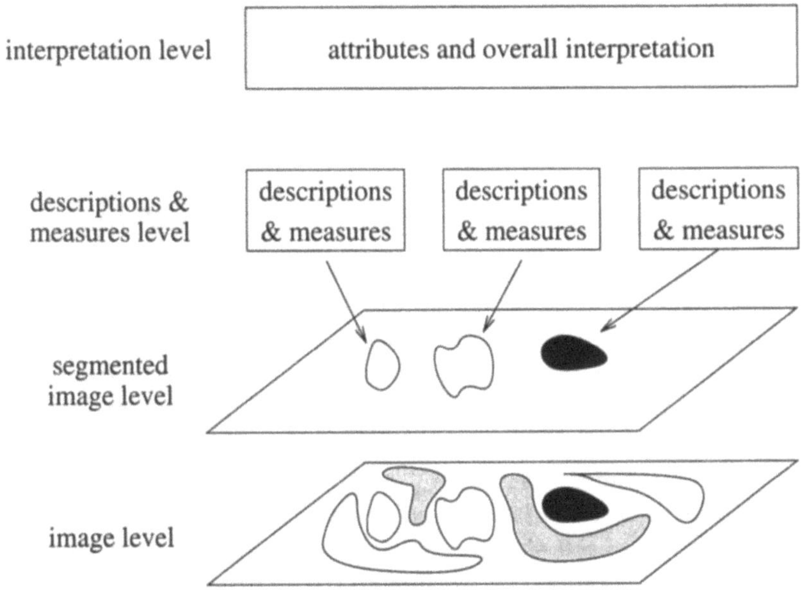

Figure 2.2: Image Representation Scheme

- **Data preprocessing** performs processing such as noise reduction, normalization, geometric and grey scale transformation to correct any distortions and scale variations for images, etc.

- **Segmentation** separates meaningful data entities or region-of-interest from original data. In the case of images, this module provides three types of segmentation functions, namely, color segmentation, morphological segmentation, and segmentation by boundary extraction. Segmentation procedures written by users can also be incorporated into the module. Interactive editing after segmentation facilitates a set of functions like selection of component, region of interest definition, draw/edit any shape of regions and link regions with interpretations.

- **Feature extraction** functions are invoked to compute feature measures on segmented objects/regions. Due to the complexity of real world objects, feature extraction has been a hard problem for the last two decades. As a solution, multiple feature extraction procedures must be provided to meet the various needs of different applications. Examples include: principal component analysis, moment invariants, shape measure by fourier descriptors, projections, shape parameters (area, elongation, etc.), texture energy, color feature measures etc. for images and video.

- **Text Editor** provides the facility for entering and editing of attributes of objects.

2.3 Object Recall - A New Formalism for Content-Based Retrieval

Although there have been a lot of R&D effort on content-based multimedia databases from both academic and national research laboratories [8, 23, 15] and companies (IBM, NTT, Hitachi, Siemens, and Virage), the state of the art is now still at the level of extracting the most effective feature measures with respect to shape, texture, color, and spatial relationships. There is a lack of unified formalism. "Formalization of the whole paradigm of content-based retrieval to bring it to a sufficient level of consistency and integrity is essential to the success of the field. Without this formalism it will be hard to develop sufficiently reliable and mission critical applications that are easy to program and evaluate."[1]

2.3.1 Need for formalism of content-based retrieval

Content-based retrieval is basically "finding something similar". "Finding something similar" is a natural phenomenon in people's life, just as "finding something different". There is a formalism, *pattern classification*, for "finding something different". We propose to define a formalism, *object recall*, for "finding something similar". Current multimedia databases are feature-based. The techniques in this field provide tools to store, process, and analyze the data. Feature measures are derived from the data items using these tools. Retrieval of data is done solely by evaluating the similarity using simple distance or correlation between feature measures of the data items. "A is similar to B" is subjective, and depends on human perception. The feature-based retrieval is objective. It is not necessarily to represent the right interpretation of users. By "content", we mean the users' interpretation of the data for certain applications. Existing techniques in multimedia databases are all feature-based. In order to go from feature-based to content-based, we need a formalism to build a bridge, as shown in Figure 2.3. The formalism must have capability of learning/training to incorporate human perception as pattern recognition has.

Let us have a look at a few examples.

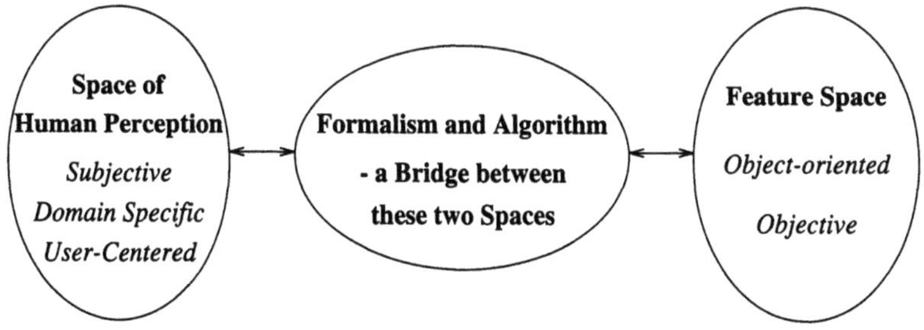

Figure 2.3: Feature-based retrieval represents the current state of the art. It is objective, not necessarily represent the users' interpretation for certain applications. Fully content-based retrieval must have user/application in the loop. A formalism is needed to build a bridge in order to go from feature-based to content-based.

Case study is very important for lawyers and doctors. It is routine work for them to find some cases which are similar to the one they are working at. They then pick up one or few of the most similar cases as references. In what sense do they consider A is more similar to B than to C? What features do they use in their judgement, and what type of similarities do they employ? Further more, how do we model this process of finding the most similar cases so that we can implement it as a computer system?

Another example would be buying textiles. You may have found one which is nearly to your satisfaction, and would like to see something similar to choose from. Here again, we need to define similarity from your perception.

A technical example can be road tracing in images. At each position, a set of feature measures can be extracted. By knowing the feature measures of previous positions, evaluation of candidates of next position is carried out to find the most appropriate one in terms of similarity between the current position and the candidates. Here, the problems would be: are feature measures effective and adequate enough for similarity evaluation?

These three examples are "finding something similar". There is a need of formalism to formally define the similarity, and to provide mechanisms to evaluate the effectiveness and adequateness of feature measures with respect to applications and users; requirements. Based on the formalism, algorithms will be developed, applications can be implemented.

In following sections, we will first outline the differences between the formalism of content-based retrieval and the pattern recognition, which is the sister discipline of content-based retrieval. *Object recall - the formalism for content-based retrieval* will be described in three parts: content-based navigation, content-based retrieval by fuzzy concepts, and content-based similarity retrieval.

2.3.2 Contrast to pattern classification

Since both content-based retrieval and classical pattern classification rely on feature measures and similarity matching (or distance metric), the following questions would come to one's mind: Can we directly apply pattern classification techniques to solve the problems in content-based retrieval? In particular, can we use separability measure in pattern classification to evaluate the feature measures for content-based retrieval?

Our answer is negative. Pattern classification [2] is concerned with the partition of the feature space into subspaces, possibly disjoint, for distinct pattern classes. Class boundaries (or decision boundaries), which are at the centerstage in pattern classification, are defined by discrimination functions which are mostly nonlinear. Under this context, feature selection aims to map the feature space into a new space where the patterns are most separable, i.e. the inter-class distances are maximized and the inner class distances are minimized. A central issue is to determine the discriminant functions. Very often, similarity functions such as Euclidean distances and correlation are used. Learning of pattern classifiers, which is usually done before operation, concerns the estimation of parameters in the discriminant functions (in parametric approaches) or the selection of prototypes (in non-parametric approaches). In general, the definitions and algorithms are class-oriented.

On the other hand, in content-based retrieval, individual objects play a central role. There is no class boundary at all. Although some memory-based approach such as nearest neighbor method in pattern classification also utilize training samples directly in classification decision, they are treated as varying representatives in each class to provide supporting evidence rather than the final goal by themselves. Therefore, in content-based retrieval, the choice of similarity function is crucial as it is used to evaluate the similarity between any two objects which can be employed to rank retrieved objects for a query object from the most similar one to the least similar one. Feature evaluation is then to find the most effective measures which can best relate similar objects. Feature measures which can best distinguish among classes in pattern classification may not be appropriate for similarity matching in content-based retrieval.

Moreover, unlike pattern classification, content-based retrieval is an interactive and iterative process. Users' feedback must be respected and incorporated to refine the retrieval results in successive iterations until the user is satisfied with the retrieved results. Last but not least, in content-based retrieval, users' perception of similarity is implicit and subjective. Up to now, not much research has been done in learning a user's preference for similarity matching. Our work reported in this section would represent a first attempt in this direction.

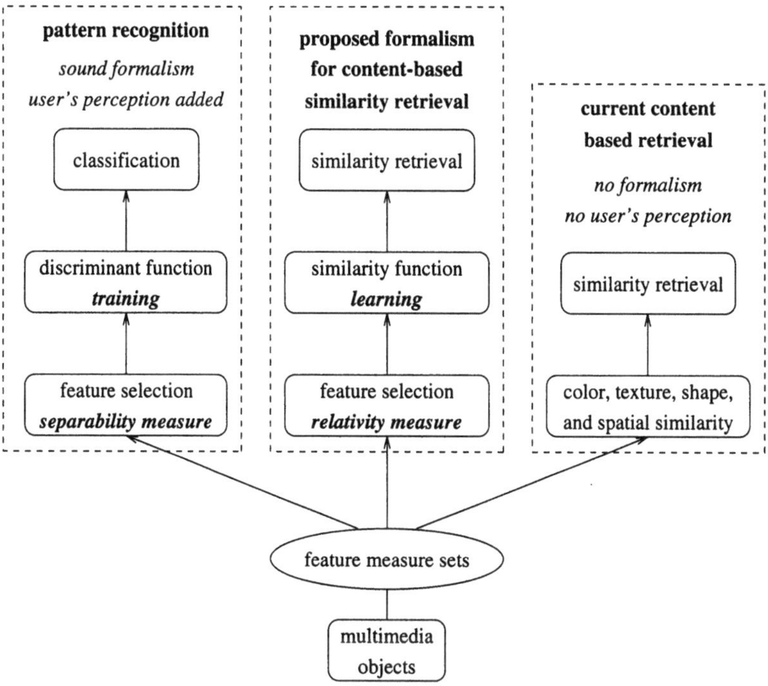

Figure 2.4: Formalism for content-based retrieval with comparison to pattern classification and current content-based similarity retrieval

As shown in Figure 2.4, the objective of pattern classification is to partition the patterns into disjoint classes. It has sound theoretical foundation. Algorithms to find the discriminant functions are very well defined. Users' perception can be incorporated by supervised learning on a selected training data set. There are several separability measures available to evaluate the effectiveness of the feature measures, and to map the feature vectors onto the new coordinate system where the best class separation can be achieved.

Quite unlike pattern classification, similarity retrieval in content-based retrieval is to find something similar. It is true that simple similarity functions such as distance and correlation are used very often in pattern classification. It is used by assuming that patterns within the same class

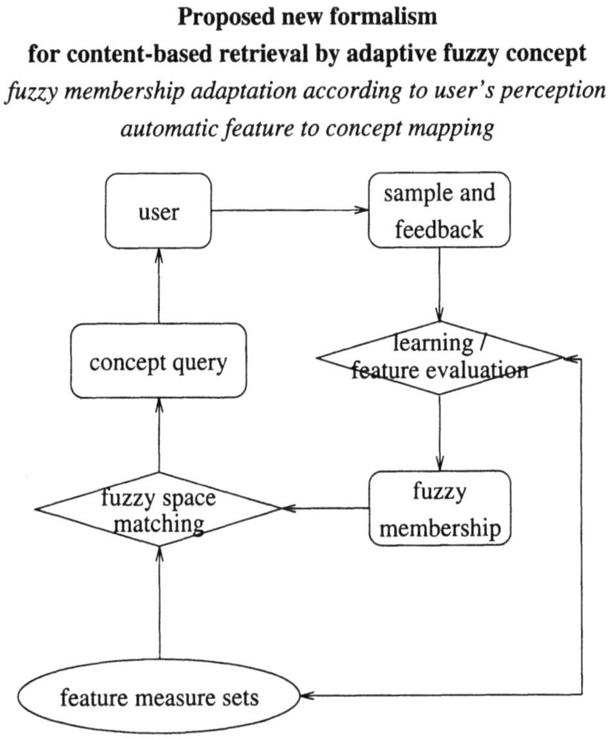

Figure 2.6: Formalism for content-based retrieval by fuzzy concept.

As shown in Figure 2.6, the central point here is to incrementally adapt the fuzzy membership function to users' perception.

Building a formalism for content-based multimedia systems is essential for the development of reliable and mission critical applications. This chapter represents such an attempt to formalize the content-based retrieval paradigm for multimedia systems. While classical pattern classification theory may provide useful ingredients for developing a content-based retrieval formalism, we feel that a radically different and fresh perspective is necessary as fundamental differences do exist in both research areas. Our formalism will provide a generic framework and criterion for describing and evaluating content-based retrieval applications. Based on the framework and criterion, we propose novel learning methods to customize the retrieval engine. With the proposed learning methods, using the user's feedback, the system is able to adapt its similarity matching function to improve on subsequent retrievals. The experimental results on using our learning aproach to mimick a user's perception of similarity measure in face retrieval have demonstrated the validity of the our proposed formalism and learning algorithms.

Although there has been a lot of R&D effort on content-based multimedia databases from both research laboratories (e.g. [8, 23, 10, 6]) and private companies (IBM [7], Hitachi, Siemens, and Virage), the state of the art is still at the level of extracting the most effective feature measures with respect to shape, texture, color, and spatial relationships. There is a lack of unifying formalism. As pointed out in [1],a formalization of the whole paradigm of content-based retrieval to bring it to a sufficient level of consistency and integrity is essential to the success of the field. Without this formalism it will be hard to develop sufficiently reliable and mission critical applications that are easy to program and evaluate.

2.4 A Content-Based Similarity Retrieval Formalism

Following the definition in the previous sections, the query object is given as $O^q_{mob} = \{U, \emptyset, \emptyset, A^*, \emptyset, s_{np}\}$, where we are given a raw data and partially defined set of attributes. Following the multimedia description hierarchy, objects need to be segmented and feature measures for those objects be extracted and formed, and similarity function be defined to measure the similarity between the query object and objects in the database. Let us now start from the similarity function. Like the discriminant function in pattern recognition, similarity function plays the central role in content-based retrieval.

2.4.1 Feature measures and similarity functions

In content-based database, objects are characterized by a set of features $F^1, F^2, ..., F^m$. A multimedia object "facial image", for example, is characterized by facial features such as chin, eyes, nose, and mouth. A feature F^i can be numerically represented by feature measures $\{F^i_1, F^i_2, ...\}$. For simplicity, let us just consider one feature and its measures, and omit the superscript: $F_1, F_2, ...$ Here, F_i is one type of feature measures for a feature. For example, the size of eyes can be a measure of the feature "eye", and color and orientation can be the other two. Each type of feature measure forms a feature vector which consists of several components:

$$F_i = (f_{i1}, f_{i2}, ... f_{iN})^T \tag{2.2}$$

The similarity function for object retrieval can be written as

$$S = g(h_1(f_{11}, f_{11}^s; f_{12}, f_{12}^s; ...), h_2(f_{21}, f_{21}^s; f_{22}, f_{22}^s; ...), ...) \quad (2.3)$$

where h_i is the similarity function for feature measure F_i, and g is the overall similarity measure. f^s stands for feature measures of the sample query object s presented to the database to retrieve similar objects from the database. Notice here, neither h nor g are explicitly defined. h can be distance, correlation, or more complicated functions. g is a function which fuses similarity functions on different type of feature measures. The simplest similarity function is the linear combination of feature measures:

$$S = w_{11}\Delta f_{11} + w_{12}\Delta f_{12} + ... + w_{21}\Delta f_{21} + w_{22}\Delta f_{22} + ... \quad (2.4)$$

where Δf_{ij} stands for $|f_{ij} - f_{ij}^s|$.

Equation 2.3 plays a central role in content-based retrieval. We can see, from this equation, that there are two main issues. The first is the effectiveness of feature measures, which is reflected in three levels of granularity: elements in a feature vector (f_{ij}), feature measure (F_i), and multiple feature vectors (F_i^k). The second is the suitability of the similarity functions g and h's for a given application.

In other words, the similarity retrieval should mimic the domain expert's view on similarity. To achieve that, first, the feature space defined by the feature vectors chosen should be rich enough to represent human's perceptual space of the objects. In the case of similar face retrieval, the saliant features which human beings use to compare faces should be captured and well represented in the feature space. Now the question would be: do we have the criterion and method to evaluate those feature measures to see if they effectively represent those saliant features (consistency), and if all saliant features have been represented by the feature measures extracted (completeness).

Assume that we have the right feature space, the second issue would be to find the right similarity function.

In practice, these two problems are usually mixed up. The ultimate criterion is the retrieval results. We will define a *loss function* as a criterion for evaluation of content-based retrieval.

2.4.2 Training data set and loss function

Ideal Recall: For a given query sample, the result of the ideal recall should exactly follow the user's perception of similarity - all items which are similar to the sample must be recalled and ordered from the most similar to the least similar according to the user's perception of similarity matching.

To represent the ideal recall, the training data set can be written as
$s_1 : d_{11}, d_{12}, ...; s_2 : d_{21}, d_{22}, ...; ...$
where s_i $(i = 1, 2, \cdots, N)$ is the query sample presented to the retrieval engine, and d_{ij} $(j = 1, 2, \cdots, K)$ is the desired retrieval sequence for the sample s_i in a proper order.

In reality, the retrieval results are different from the ideal one, and the target sequences produced by the retrieval engine could be written as
$s_1 : t_{11}, t_{12}, ...; s_2 : t_{21}, t_{22}, ...; ...$

Having compared the retrieval results with the ideal one, we found that some retrieval objects should appear more to the front, and some should move more to the rear. We refer these absolute position shifts as *mis-rank*. Then we have a mis-rank sequence:
$s_1 : m_{11}, m_{12}, ...; s_2 : m_{21}, m_{22}, ...; ...$

If we assign a unit loss to a mis-rank, the total loss of the retrieval would be:

$$L = \frac{\sum_{ij} m_{ij}/K}{K}$$

where K is the length of retrieval sequence, and the average loss of the retrieval would be:

$$\widehat{L} = \frac{L}{N}$$

where N is the number of mis-rank sequences in the training data set.

After defining the loss function, we can evaluate the retrieval and consequently the similarity function and feature measures. The learning algorithms can be developed based on the minimization of the loss function or the equivalent of it.

2.5 Learning of Similarity Function

2.5.1 Problem statement

In this section, we focus on the learning of similarity function in the similarity retrieval engine using the mis-rank feedback on query results from the user. The objective of learning is to mimic his or her perception of similarity matching and thus reduce the loss function in a particular content-based retrieval application.

More specifically, a user presents a sample query object to the system. The system responds with an ordered sequence of retrieved objects. The user reorders the sequence according to his or her perception of similarity matching. The mis-rank information (i.e. m_{ij}) derived from the difference between the retrieved (i.e. target) sequence (i.e. t_{ij}) and the desired sequence (i.e. d_{ij}) is feedbacked as error signal to the system for learning.

There are two possible types of learning problems. The first type involves short-term learning using only a single mis-rank sequence i. The aim here is to learn user's perception of similarity matching from this sequence. The intention is that the system will be able to produce a new retrieval sequence that is closer to user's perception of similarity matching for query refinement. That is, the new mis-rank and loss function will be reduced. The probable consequence is that objects considered similar by the user but not retreived previously are now retrieved or ordered more to the front of the retrieved sequence and objects considered dissimilar by the user but retreived previously are now not retrieved or ordered more to the rear of the retrieved sequence.

The second type of learning (long-term learning) is more ambitious. Its objective is to capture a user's perceptual consistency in similarity matching. Learning requires the user's mis-rank feedback on a number (say N) of retrieval sequences corresponding to N sample query objects. The intention is that the system will be able to learn the regularities in the user's perception of similarity matching for the multimedia objects in the target application domain. After the learning, a new query sample will produce retrieval sequence with less mis-rank and loss function, as compared to the one without learning.

2.5.2 Related works

Although we are using error-correcting supervised learning for both types of learning mentioned above, it is neither similar to conventional supervised learning for pattern classification [2] nor adaptive Information Retrieval (IR) [3].

To train a pattern classifier, N training samples of the form, (X_i, d_i) where X_i is a feature vector and d_i is the desired class label for X_i, are presented to the classifier. For each X_i, the classifier will ouput a target class label t_i. The difference between d_i and t_i is treated as an error $E_i = d_i - t_i$ which can be used to modify the parameters in the classifier towards less erroneous classification performance.

In our approach described in this chapter, the training patterns and objectives are quite different. First, the input vectors for learning are not feature vectors, but similarities (or distances) between the feature vectors of two multimedia objects. Second, the output vectors for learning are not desired and target class labels, but mis-rank information. Last but not least, the learning process modifies the representation of the similar function which is fundamental in comparing two multimedia objects for retrieval purpose, instead of some discrimination function used in defining the class or decision boundaries.

While learning in content-based multimedia retrieval is new [5], adaptive IR has been an active research area [3]. In fact, Fabio & Rijsbergen [3] have given a comprehensive and up-to-date survey of past works in adaptive IR in their chapter. We shall not repeat the review here but would like to point out some important observations.

First in IR, the feacture vectors are mainly binary vector representation of query and document descriptors (i.e. index terms). But in multimedia CBR, the feature vectors are usually real vectors. They are much richer to capture color, shape, texture, and even spatial information. In fact, due to their complex nature, they are best described in multi-level structure. Second, learning in IR typically uses relevance feedback directly in the form of class labels (graded class labels if non-binary feedback is allowed) as in the case of supervised learning for pattern classification. In this chapter, error has to be derived indirectly from the mis-rank information provided by the user. Last but not least, adaptive IR, as typified by the approach described in [3], attempts to acquire application domain knowledge by learning the association between the queries (or actually the query descriptors) and the documents (or actually the document descriptors) into a query adaptation or expansion function. The latter can then be used to modify a query for matching (by a "Matcher" [3]) with documents in the database during retrieval. However, in our approach, it is the similarity function (i.e. "Matcher") that gets adapted using mis-rank feedback.

In short, the uniquenss in our approach surrounds a common notion of relativity: since the similarity function is the function that determines the relative closeness between any two multimedia objects, it is the focus of adaptation. In the same token, the input and supervised information for learning are also computed and presented in relative sense, namely similarities between pairwise feature vector elements of query and retrieved objects and ranking error of retrieved sequence with respect to ideal sequence respectively.

2.5.3 Learning of simple similarity functions

We start with learning of a simple similarity function as in equation (2.4). In this case, the similarity function is simply a linear combination of feature measures f_j:

$$S = \sum_j w_j \Delta f_j \tag{2.5}$$

where Δf_j stands for $|f_j - f_j^s|$. Here, the learning is to find the proper weights w_j in the similarity function.

Assume that after one retrieval, the user rearranges the retrieval sequence (say $t_1, t_2, ..., t_K$) into the desired sequence (say $d_1, d_2, ..., d_K$) according to his or her perception of similarity matching. From this pair of sequences, we can generate a mis-rank sequence: $m_1, m_2, ..., m_K$ as a training sequence in the training data set. Note that m's are absolute positional shifts. A forward shifting means that the distance measure between the sample and this retrieved object is smaller than what it should be. A backward shift means that the distance measure is larger than what it should be.

For a forward shift mis-rank m_i, the learning should increase the weights by

$$\Delta w_j = \alpha \Delta_j m_i \tag{2.6}$$

where α is a parameter to control the learning rate. Similarly, for a backward shift mis-rank m_i, the learning should decrease the weights using the same equation (2.6). Care should be taken in the selection of the learning rate. A large α will lead to oscillation and a small α will hardly show any effect in learning. Since there are forward shifts and backward shifts, the final amount of modification to a weight w_j will be the summation of all relevant adjustments.

2.5.4 Learning of multi-level similarity functions

Similar to discriminant function in pattern classification, similarity function in content-based retrieval can be very complex and non-linear. As shown in equation (2.3), the similarity function should initially consist of sufficiently rich set of primitives (i.e. h_i) before any customization or learning can take place. More often than not, the similarity function is multi-level (or hierarchical), where similarity matching at level k is defined in terms of similarity matching at level $k+1$ until the most primitive distance measures or correlation metrics are used at the leaf level. The multi-level structure reflects the application domain knowledge used in characterizing the multimedia objects in terms of features, feature measures, and feature vectors etc. An illustration of such a similarity matching tree is shown in Figure 2.7.

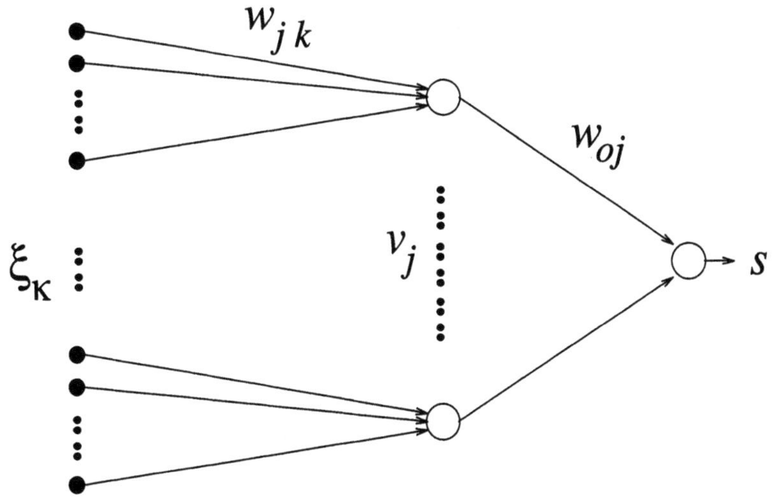

Figure 2.7: A multi-level similarity function

The learning rule (equation (2.6)) given previously assumes a simple similarity function (i.e. linear combination of distance measures). It does not lend itself immediately to a multi-level similarity function. To allow learning in such similarity function and to derive learning rule for each level uniformly from a global error function, we can treat the similarity matching tree as a feedforward neural network and apply the Backpropagation (BP) learning rule for multi-layer perceptrons [4]. However, the BP learning rule cannot be applied directly as the error function in our case is different.

In standard BP learning, the error measure or cost function is defined as ([4], pp. 117)

$$E = \frac{1}{2}\sum_{\mu}(\zeta^{\mu} - s^{\mu})^2 \tag{2.7}$$

where ζ^{μ} is the desired value (i.e. supervised label) of the output node for the μth training pattern and s^{μ} is the actual (or target) value of the output node for the μth training pattern which is defined as (assuming only one hidden layer as in Figure 2.7)

$$\begin{aligned} s^{\mu} &= g(\sum_{j} w_{oj} v_j^{\mu}) \\ &= g(\sum_{j}\{w_{oj} g(\sum_{k} w_{jk}\xi_k^{\mu})\}) \end{aligned} \tag{2.8}$$

where μ indexes the μth training pattern, v_j^μ is the output of the jth hidden node, w_{oj} is the weight connecting the jth hidden node to the output node, ξ_k^μ is the kth element of the input vector $\vec{\xi}^\mu$, w_{jk} is the weight connecting the kth input node to the jth hidden node, and g is a nonlinear transfer function at the hidden and output nodes.

In our case, the user does not provide the relevance feedback as the desired value for the output node directly. Instead, based on the actual outputs s^μ, which are the similarity values between the retrieved objects and the query object, the system produces a target sequence in descending order of s^μ. The user rearranges the relative positions of the target sequence into a desired sequence for ideal recall. There is no information about the desired values for each s^μ though their desired relative ranking information is available. Thus, one way to define the error function could be:

$$
\begin{aligned}
E &= \frac{1}{2}\sum_\mu (d^\mu - t^\mu)^2 \\
&= \frac{1}{2}\sum_\mu (E^\mu)^2 \qquad (2.9)
\end{aligned}
$$

where μ indexes the μth training pattern, $E^\mu = d^\mu - t^\mu$ is the error contribution of $\vec{\xi}^\mu$, d^μ is the desired rank given by the user, t^μ is the target rank actually obtained by the system.

Now using gradient descent as in BP learning rule and the chain rule, we have

$$
\begin{aligned}
\Delta w &= -\eta\frac{\partial E}{\partial w} = -\eta\frac{\partial E}{\partial s}\cdot\frac{\partial s}{\partial w} \\
&= -\eta\sum_\mu \frac{\partial E}{\partial s}\Big|_{s^\mu}\cdot\frac{\partial s}{\partial w}\Big|_{s^\mu} \qquad (2.10)
\end{aligned}
$$

$$
\text{and,}\quad \frac{\partial E}{\partial s}\Big|_{s^\mu} = -(d^\mu - t^\mu)\frac{\partial t}{\partial s}\Big|_{s^\mu} \qquad (2.11)
$$

Now, since t^u is the rank of a retrieved multimedia object, it is integral and hence discrete. Therefore t is not differentiable in general. Without further information, we assume that ∂t is inversely proportional to ∂s since the obtained rank of a retrieved object will always improve (i.e. reduce in value) with an increase in its similarity value s. Hence we heuristically replace the term $\frac{\partial t}{\partial s}$ in equation (2.11) with a negative number $-\kappa$ (κ is a positive constant). Then, equation (2.10) becomes:

$$
\Delta w = -\kappa\eta\sum_\mu m^\mu \frac{\partial s}{\partial w}\Big|_{s^\mu} \qquad (2.12)
$$

since $m^\mu = (d^\mu - t^\mu)$, the mis-rank for the μth training pattern. Combining all the constants into one and simply call it η, we get

$$\Delta w = -\eta \sum_\mu m^\mu \frac{\partial s}{\partial w} |_{s^\mu} \tag{2.13}$$

where η the learning rate, is a small positive number.
More precisely,

$$\Delta w_{oj} = -\eta \sum_\mu m^\mu \, g'(h^\mu) \, v_j^\mu \tag{2.14}$$

where $h^\mu = \sum_j w_{oj} \, v_j^\mu$.

$$\Delta w_{jk} = -\eta \sum_\mu m^\mu \, g'(h^\mu) \, w_{oj} \, g'(h_j^\mu) \, \xi_k^\mu \tag{2.15}$$

where $h_j^\mu = \sum_k w_{jk} \, \xi_j^\mu$. In our experiments conducted, we have scaled m^u by $\tanh(m^u)$ to fall within [-1,1].

2.6 Experimental Results

2.6.1 The data set

The data set for the experiments comprises of face images taken from the NIST Special Database 18: Mugshot Identification Database (MID). The details of MID can be found at `http://www.nist.gov/`. Only those candidates who have 3 or more photographs have been selected for our data set. Ordered sequences of images were prepared from this data set as follows. Each sequence contains three or more images of the same individual. Within every ordered sequence, the images are sorted according to their similarity to the first image. This means that second image is more similar to the first image, than the third image is to the first image; as perceived by the person ranking them. Of course, the first image is most similar to itself. This procedure of ranking images according to their similarity was done manually by one individual.

The learning algorithm in our experiments will attempt to mimick the individual's perception of similarity matching using these ordered sequences. We have 130 such sequences in our data set.

2.6.2 Feature extraction

Every face image is marked with a set of 17 points called landmarks. These points are a subset of anthropometric landmarks of the face. They identify salient points of the face like corners of eyes, tip of nose, chin, etc. Using these landmarks as anchor points, six different regions each containing one of the six facial features namely, eye, nose, mouth, eyebrow, hair and chin are extracted from each image. These six regions are then individually subject to principle component analysis (K-L transform) and 16 components corresponding to the 16 largest eigenvalues are extracted. Hence in all, we have 96 features.

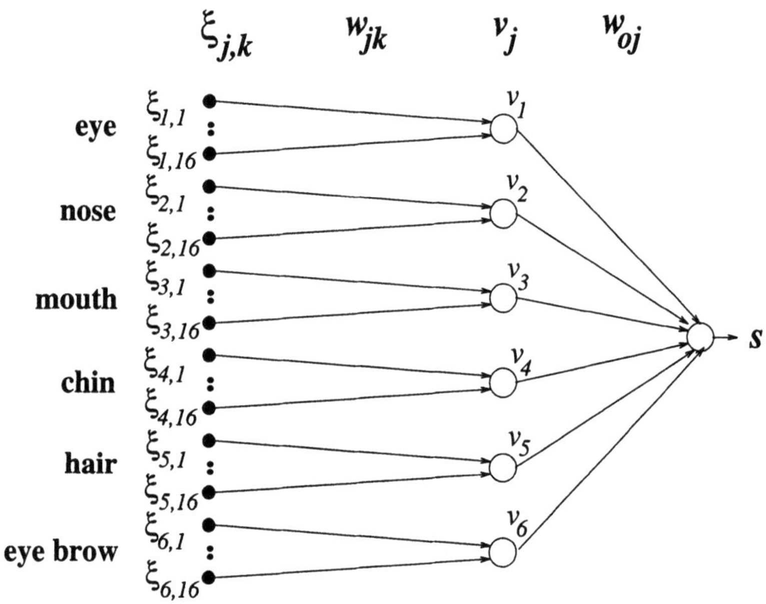

Figure 2.8: A multi-level similarity function for face retrieval

Let the features be represented by $f_{j,k}$ where $j \in \{1, 2 \cdots, 6\}$ represents one of the facial features and $k \in \{1, 2 \cdots, 16\}$ represents one of the 16 principle components. Each image is represented by its corresponding feature vector $\vec{f}$. Then the input $\vec{\xi}^{u,v}$ to a multi-level similar function (which can be viewed as a feedforward multi-layer neural network as shown in Figure 2.8) is given by

$$\begin{aligned} \xi_{j,k}^{u,v} &= 1 - \left| \frac{z_{j,k}^{u,v}}{\lambda_j} \right| \qquad and \qquad (2.16) \\ z_{j,k}^{u,v} &= f_{j,k}^{u} - f_{j,k}^{v} \end{aligned}$$

where u and v represent the two images which are to be compared for similarity, and λ_j is a normalizing constant for facial feature j given by

$$\lambda_j = \max(|\max(\vec{z}_j^{u,v})|, |\min(\vec{z}_j^{u,v})|) \tag{2.17}$$

taken over all pairs (u, v) where $\vec{z}_j^{u,v}$ is the vector $\{z_{j,1}, z_{j,2}, \cdots, z_{j,16}\}$ Note that $\vec{\xi}^{u,v}$ is a measure of similarity between images u and v. We shall alternately refer to this vector as *similarity vector.*

Input vectors $\vec{\xi}^{u,v}$ are calculated for each of the 130 ordered sequences as follows. Consider an ordered sequence $\{u_1, u_2, \cdots, u_n\}$. The image pairs obtained from this sequence are $\{u_1, u_1\}, \{u_1, u_2\}, \cdots \{u_1, u_n\}$. The input vectors generated from this ordered sequence will be the n similarity vectors comparing all images in the list with the first image. We have in all, 449 such similarity vectors from the 130 ordered sequences.

2.6.3 Within-sequence learning

This set of experiments concerns short-term learning. Using only a single mis-rank sequence, the system will modify its similarity function to tune its target sequence towards the user's desired sequence. In the experiments, each of the 130 ordered sequences obtained from the NIST MID is treated as an independent training set for learning. The results reported here are averages over the 130 training sets and each set was run for 20 times with different initial weights.

	$\widehat{L}$
Before learning	0.20
After learning	0

Table 2.1: Results of short-term learning on simple similarity function.

Table 2.1 shows the experimental results of short-term learning using equation (2.6) for simple similarity function. The table shows that the learning is able to correct the mis-rank errors in each of the 130 sequences, thus reducing the average loss to zero. The average number of training iterations is 22.9 and the learning rate $\alpha = 0.08$.

Table 2.2 shows the experimental results of short-term learning using equation (2.13). The neural network architecture parallels the one shown in Figure 2.8. The table shows the mean squared error (MSE) and the average loss ($\widehat{L}$) before and after learning. Once again, the errors in each

	MSE	$\widehat{L}$
Before learning	0.400	0.20
After learning	0	0

Table 2.2: Results of short-term learning on multi-level similarity function.

of the 130 target sequences are corrected to the desired sequences after learning. The average number of training iterations is 25.9 and the learning rate $\eta = 0.008$.

From these two tables, we can see that both learning rules given by equations (2.6) and (2.13) are effective for short-term learning of user's perception of similarity matching.

2.6.4 Across-sequence learning

This set of experiments deals with long-term learning. To capture a user's perceptual consistency in similarity matching, the learning looks across the ordered sequences in a training set, built from the 130 sequences prepared using the NIST MID, and modify the system's similarity function accordingly.

Since the learning rule of equation (2.6) does not have satisfactory convergence results for long-term learning, we shall only report the results of long-term learning using equation (2.13) on multi-level similarity function.

We will report on two types of experiments that investigated the learning and generalization capabilities of our learning approach respectively.

Learning capability

In these experiments, learning was conducted on all the 130 sequences as training set. Table 2.3 shows the average results of long-term learning using equtaion (2.13) over 20 runs (with different initial weights). The table shows the mean squared error (MSE) and the average loss ($\widehat{L}$) before and after learning for two different neural network architectures. The "partly connected" label indicates the network architecture of Figure 2.8 and "fully connected" means full connection is allowed between the input and hidden layers. While the partly connected network architecture incorporates the domain knowledge of the problem in the form of a multi-level similarity matching tree, a fully connected network is treated as a black box function mapping. The average numbers of training iterations are 837.0 (partly connected) and 258.5 (fully connected) respectively. The learning rates η are set as 0.01 (partly connected) and 0.005 (fully connected) respectively. The stopping condition for training is $MSE \leq 0.01$.

	partly connected		fully connected	
	MSE	$\widehat{L}$	MSE	$\widehat{L}$
Before learning	0.180	0.0821	0.180	0.0819
After learning	0.007	0.0028	0.007	0.0029

Table 2.3: Results (on trg set) of long-term learning on multi-level similarity function.

The results in Table 2.3 show that long-term learning based on equation (2.13) is able to reduce the mis-rank errors in the training set significantly by mimicking the similarity matching in the training set.

Generalization capability

Since our data set is relatively small, we have used the leave-one-out method to evaluate how well our learning algorithm generalizes. 130 experiments were conducted with partly connected and fully connected neural network architectures as described above. In each experiment, a unique sequence was chosen as test set and the other 129 sequences as training set. Table 2.4 shows the mean squared error (MSE) and the average loss ($\widehat{L}$) before and after learning on the test set over 130 runs. The average numbers of training iterations are 983.2 (partly connected) and 385.2 (fully connected) respectively. The learning rates η are set as 0.01 (partly connected) and 0.005 (fully connected) respectively. The stopping condition for training is $MSE \leq 0.01$.

The results in Table 2.4 show that the errors (MSE and $\widehat{L}$) on unseen queries after long-term learning of similarity function from the training set have been reduced by 21.7% to 27.8%.

In another set of experiments, learning was conducted on a subset of the 130 sequences as training set and tested on the rest of the 130 sequences as test set to examine the effect of generalization with respect to their relative sizes. The results are averaged over 20 runs (with different initial weights and different training/test set sampling) and summarized

	partly connected		fully connected	
	MSE	$\widehat{L}$	MSE	$\widehat{L}$
Before learning	0.178	0.0821	0.180	0.0819
After learning	0.132	0.0643	0.130	0.0634

Table 2.4: Results (on test set) of long-term learning on multi-level similarity function.

in Figure 2.9 for both partly connected and fully connected network architectures.

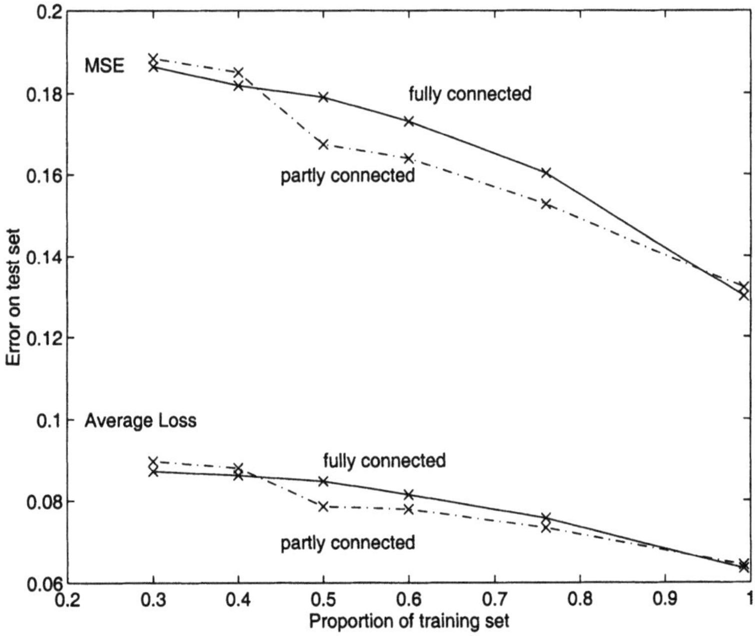

Figure 2.9: Generalization with respect to training and test proportions

As expected from the theory of neural network learning, the errors on test set decrease with the (relative) size of the training set, for both partly connected and fully connected network architectures although the generalization capability of the fully connected network seems to be slightly better when more training data is available.

2.7 Conclusions

In this chapter, a new formalism for content-based retrieval multimedia systems is proposed to provide a generic framework and criterion for describing and evaluating content-based retrieval applications. In particular, we have proposed novel methods to customize the similarity-based retrieval engine via learning based on ranking feedback from users. From our preliminary experimental results in face retrieval, the system is able to adapt its similarity function to improve on subsequent retrievals, in both short-term and long-term senses. While the perceptual consistency in similarity matching of a single user can be captured by our long-term learning approach as suggested by the experimental results and thus can be exploited to build *personalized* multimedia search engine, it is still uncertain that the same perceptual consistency can be extended to multiple users.

References

1. P. Aigrain, H.J. Zhang, D. Petkovic, "Content-Based Representation and Retrieval of Visual Media: a State of the Art Review", Multimedia Tools and Applications, Vol. 3, No. 3, pp. 179-202, 1996
2. R.O. Duda, P.E. Hart, "Pattern Classification and Scence Analysis", John Wiley & Sons, 1973
3. F. Crestani, C.J. van Rijsbergen, "A Model for Adaptive Information Retrieval", Journal of Intelligent Information Systems, Vol. 8, pp. 29-56, 1997
4. J. Hertz, A. Krogh, R.G. Palmer, "Introdunction to the Theory of Neural Computation", Addison-Wesley Publishing Company, 1991.
5. R. Jain, "Infoscopes: multimedia information systems", Multimedia Systems and Techniques, Kluwer Academic Publishers, pp. 217-253, 1996
6. T. Kato, "Database Architecture for Content-Based Image Retrieval", SPIE Image Storage and Retrieval Systems, Vol. 1662, pp. 112-122, 1992
7. W. Niblack et.al., "The QBIC Project: Querying Images by Content using Color, Texture, and Shape", SPIE Conf.: Storage and retrieval for image and video databases, San Jose, USA, pp. 173-181, 1993
8. A. Pentland, R.W. Picard, S. Sclaroff, "Photobook: Tools for Content Based Manipulation of Image Databases", SPIE Conf.: Storage and Retrieval of Image and Video Databases II, Vol. 2185, pp. 6-10, 1994
9. S. Santini, R. Jain, "Similarity matching", IEEE Trans. on Pattern Analysis and Machine Intelligence, 1998
10. J.K. Wu et.al. "Content-Based Retrieval for Trademark Registration", Multimedia Tools and Applications, Vol. 3, No. 3, pp. 245-267, 1996
11. J.K. Wu, "Recognition by Recall", RWC Symp. 97.

12. J.K. Wu, "Content-based Indexing of Multimedia Databases", IEEE Trans. Knowledge and Data Engineering, 1996
13. J.K. Wu, A.D. Narasimhalu, "Fuzzy Content-Based Image Database", Information Processing and Management, 1997
14. W. Niblack et.al, "The QBIC project: Querying images by content using color, texture, and shape", Storage and retrieval for image and video databases, San Jose, USA, pp173-181, SPIE, 1993
15. T. Kato, "Learning of Personal Visual Impression for Image Database Systems", Proc. of International Conference on Document Analysis and Recognition, 1993
16. S. Kaski, T. Honkela, K. Lagus, T. Kohonen, "Creating an order in digital libraries with self-organizing maps." Proceedings, WCNN'96, San Diego, 1996
17. H. Rheingold, "An Interview with Don Norman", The Art of Human-Computer Interface Design, Reading, MA: Addison-Wesley Publishing Company, 1990
18. M. Wooldridge, N. R. Jennings, "Intelligent Agents: Theory and Practice", Knowledge Engineering Review, 1996
19. M. Minsky, D. Riechen, "A conversation with Marvin Minsky about Agents", Communications of ACM, Vol. 37, No. 7, pp. 22-29, 1996
20. J. K. Wu, et.al., "Facial Image Retrieval, Identification, and Inference System", ACM Multimedia Journal, Vol. 2, pp. 1-14, 1994
21. J. K. Wu, et.al., "Evaluation of Feature Measures and Similarity Measures for Content-Based Retrieval", SPIE Symposium on Digital Image Storage and Archiving Systems, Philadelphia, Vol. 2606, 1995
22. G. A. Carpenter and A. H. Tan, "Rule extraction: From neural architecture to symbolic representation", Connection Science, Vol. 7, No. 1, pp. 3-27, 1995
23. J. K. Wu et.al, "CORE: A Content-based Retrieval Engine for Multimedia Databases", ACM Multimedia Systems, Vol. 3, pp. 3-25, 1995
24. J. K. Wu, et.al, "Evaluation of Feature Measures and Similarity Measures for Content-Based Retrieval", SPIE Symposium on Digital Image Storage and Archiving Systems, Vol. 2606, 1995
25. G. Senthilkumar, J. K. Wu, "Content-based retrieval using fuzzy interactive and competitive neural network", SPIE Symposium on Digital Image Storage and Archiving Systems, Vol. 2606, 1995
26. R. Picard, "A society of models for video and image libraries, Media Lab", Technical Report, Massachusetts Institute of Technology, No. 360, 1996

Chapter 3

Color Feature Extraction

Color is an important and the most straight-forward feature that humans perceive when viewing an image. Human vision system is more sensitive to color information than gray levels so color is the first candidate used for feature extraction. Color histogram is one common method used to represent color contents. The algorithms follow a similar procession: Selection of a color space, representation of color features, and matching algorithms.

3.1 Color Spaces Selection

There are several color spaces used internationally. Each of those color spaces were designed for certain applications and based on certain considerations.

3.1.1 *RGB* color space

RGB color space is the most common one used for images on computer because the computer display is using the combination of the primary colors (red, green, blue) to display any perceived color. Each pixel in the screen is composed of three points which is stimulated by red, green and blue electron gun separately. However, *RGB* space is not perceptually uniform so the color distance in *RGB* color space does not correspond to color dissimilarity in perception. Therefore we prefer to transform image data in *RGB* color space to other perceptual uniform space before feature extraction.

3.1.2 Munsell color system

The Munsell color system organizes the colors according to natural attributes. It represents three color primitives (hue, intensity and saturation) by a sphere like 3 dimensional spatial model and names them as *hue*, *value* and *chroma*. Its advantage is that it is a discrete system and gives a finite set of colors by perceptual similarities over an intuitive three dimensional space. Because of its perceptual uniformity, Munsell color system is used widely for color design. The disadvantage is that there does not exist a simple transformation from RGB color space and often requires a lookup table to convert.

3.1.3 CIE color systems

The CIE (Commission Internationale de I' Eclairage) in 1976 defined the CIE 1976 ($L^*u^*v^*$) and CIE 1976 ($L^*a^*b^*$) two color spaces for the perceptual uniformity. They are produced by linear transformation from RGB to XYZ color space first, then followed by one of two non-linear transformations to CIE 1976 ($L^*u^*v^*$) and CIE 1976 ($L^*a^*b^*$) respectively [1].

$$\begin{bmatrix} X \\ Y \\ Z \end{bmatrix} = \begin{bmatrix} 0.430 & 0.342 & 0.178 \\ 0.300 & 0.590 & 0.110 \\ 0.020 & 0.130 & 0.939 \end{bmatrix} \begin{bmatrix} R \\ G \\ B \end{bmatrix}$$

$$\begin{aligned}
L^* &= 116(Y/Y_0)^{1/3} - 16 && \text{for } Y/Y_0 > 0.008856 \\
L^* &= 903.3(Y/Y_0) && \text{for } Y/Y_0 <= 0.008856 \\
u^* &= 13L^*(u - u_0) \\
v^* &= 13L^*(v - v_0) \\
u &= 4X/(X + 15Y + 3Z) && u_0 = 4X_0/(X_0 + 15Y_0 + 3Z_0) \\
v &= 6Y/(X + 15Y + 3Z) && v_0 = 6Y_0/(X_0 + 15Y_0 + 3Z_0) \\
a^* &= 500[(X/X_0)^{1/3} - (Y/Y_0)^{1/3}] \\
b^* &= 200[(Y/Y_0)^{1/3} - (Z/Z_0)^{1/3}]
\end{aligned}$$

Where (X_0, Y_0, Z_0) are the tristimulus values of an appropriate reference white, the *perfect reflecting diffuser* (100% diffuse reflectance at all visible wavelengths), illuminated by CIE standard illumination (eg. D65). The total color difference are given respectively by:

$$\Delta E_{CIE}(L^*, u^*, v^*) = [(\Delta L^*)^2 + (\Delta u^*)^2 + (\Delta v^*)^2]^{1/2}$$

$$\Delta E_{CIE}(L^*, a^*, b^*) = [(\Delta L^*)^2 + (\Delta a^*)^2 + (\Delta b^*)^2]^{1/2}$$

The CIE color spaces are perceptually uniform but they are inconvenient for existing non-linear transformation between them and RGB color spaces.

3.1.4 HSV color space

Commonly used in Computer Graphics, HSV color space [1], which represents color by *hue, saturation* and *value* components, is natural and approximately perceptually uniform. HSV color space can be visualized as a cone (see Fig. 3.1). The long axis represents *value*: blackness ($v = 0$) to whiteness ($v = 1$). Distance from axis represents *saturation*: amount of color present ($s = 0 \sim 1$). The angle around the v-axis is the *hue*: tint or tone. In the *hue* circle, red, green, blue are separated by 120 degrees: red ($0^o C$), yellow ($60^o C$), green ($120^o C$), cyan ($180^o C$), blue ($240^o C$), magenta ($300^o C$). All coordinates range from 0 to 1. The Cartesian coordinates of points in the cone is $(sv\cos(2\pi h), sv\sin(2\pi h), v)$. Since the HSV color space is nearly perceptually uniform, the similarity of two colors (h_i, s_i, v_i) and (h_j, s_j, v_j) is determined by their Euclidean distance in Cartesian coordinates.

$$
\begin{aligned}
d_{ij} &= |(s_i v_i \cos(2\pi h_i), s_i v_i \sin(2\pi h_i), v_i) - (s_j v_j \cos(2\pi h_j), s_j v_j \sin(2\pi h_j), v_j)| \\
&= \sqrt{[s_i v_i \cos(2\pi h_i) - s_j v_j \cos(2\pi h_j)]^2 + [s_i v_i \sin(2\pi h_i) - s_j v_j \sin(2\pi h_j)]^2 + [v_i - v_j]^2}
\end{aligned}
$$

Transformation from RGB to HSV

For $r, g, b \in [0,1], h, s, v \in [0,1]$ is given by the following algorithm:

h=undefined if s=0

(1) v=max(r,g,b)

(2) let x=min(r,g,b)

(3) s=(v-x)/v; if s=0 return;

(4) let r'=(v-r)/(v-x), g'=(v-g)/(v-x), b'=(v-b)/(v-x);

(5) if r=v then 6h=b'-g';
else if g=v then 6h=2+r'-b';
else if b=v then 6h=4+g'-r';

(6) if h¡0 then h=h+1;

Transformation from HSV to RGB

For $h, s, v \in [0,1], r, g, b \in [0,1]$ is given by the following algorithm:

(1) if s=0 then r=g=b=v; return;

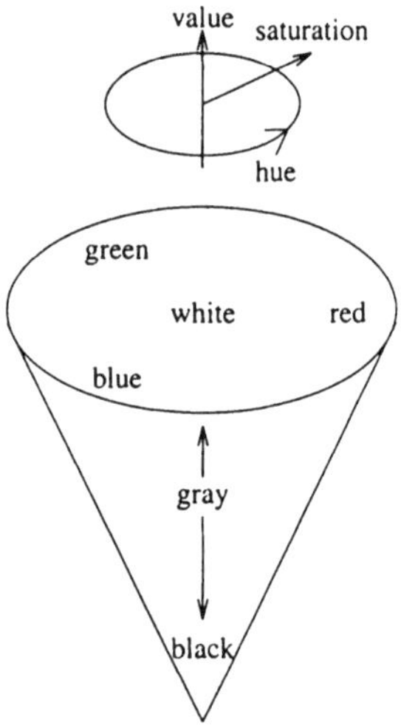

Figure 3.1: *HSV* color cone.

(2) if h=1 then h=0
else h=6h;

(3) f=h-round(h);

(4) let m=v*(1-s), n=v*(1-(s*f)), k=v*(1-(s*(1-f)))

(5) switch(round(h))
case 0: (r,g,b)=(v,k,m)
case 1: (r,g,b)=(n,v,m)
case 2: (r,g,b)=(m,v,k)
case 3: (r,g,b)=(m,n,v)
case 4: (r,g,b)=(k,m,v)
case 5: (r,g,b)=(v,m,n)

The transformation between *RGB* and *HSV* color space is non-linear, but easily implemented. Thus, *HSV* color space will be used in this research for color representation.

3.2 Color Measures

For content-based retrieval, color is considered to be an important feature. Color does form a vital component of our perception and moreover the color content does not change much if there is object motion. Therefore it provides an important cue for retrieving objects which have significant color information. The motivation for developing effective color features is to provide better methods for visual information retrieval. This is required in image and video databases and visual information systems like multimedia databases, trademarks databases, face image databases etc. In this section, we will talk about color features with an emphasis on image retrieval systems. But it should be clear that these measures are useful for any visual information system such as video databases or animation sequences. The problem can be defined as follows: assume that we have a large number of color images in the database. Given a query image, we would like to obtain a list of images from the database which are most "similar" in color to the query image. For solving this problem, we need two things – first, a feature which represents the color information of the image and second, a similarity measure to compute the similarity between features of two images.

Each pixel in a color image is specified by a point in the 3-dimensional space, for example, the RGB color space. Similarity between two images can be based on the extracted color features as well as the spatial location of color components in the images. Here spatial information denotes the positions of pixels having a similar color. Normally, the spatial locations of the color components are not considered but we will show subsequently that it is easy to incorporate this information. Initially, we briefly review some of the color features and then we will present a few color features in detail.

3.2.1 A brief review of color features

In a discrete color space, such as RGB and LUV, the color histogram, $h(x, y, z)$, is obtained by computing the number of pixels having the same color. This histogram can be used as a color feature. Swain and Ballard[16] have proposed a similarity measure based on color histogram intersection. The underlying concept is to compute:

$$Sim(I_1, I_2) = \frac{\sum_{i=1}^{b} \min(I_{1_i}, I_{2_i})}{\sum_{i=1}^{b} I_{2_i}} \tag{3.1}$$

where $Sim(I_1, I_2)$ is the match value between images I_1 and I_2 respectively, and I_{1_i} and I_{2_i} are the number of pixels in ith bin of images I_1 and I_2 respectively. Here b denotes the number of bins which can range from 2 to 2^{24} for RGB color space assuming each of the RGB components are in the range [0-255]. A bin is a cube in the 3-dimensional color space. Any two points in a bin are assumed to represent the same color. Note that the match value between exactly similar images is 1. A similar technique has been employed in [5,11] as a color similarity measure. This similarity measure depends on the bin resolution. This approach does not take into account the similarity of colors in the neighborhood bins. In general, the colors of two neighboring bins are perceptually similar but this is not captured in this similarity measure. Consider the three two dimensional histograms, $h_1(x,y), h_2(x,y)$ and $h_3(x,y)$. Histogram 2 is obtained by shifting one column of histogram 1. The match value between these histograms, i.e., Sim, is 0.0. The match value between histograms 1 and 3 is also same. But the colors associated with the neighborhood bins are more similar compared to colors in distant bins. It is clear that histograms 1 and 2 are more similar compared to histograms 1 and 3. But this approach is not able to bring out this fact.

Ioka[7] has developed a generalized similarity measure which considers the correlation among colors. This similarity measure is given by:

$$Sim_1(I_1, I_2) = \sum_{i=1}^{b}\sum_{j=1}^{b} a_{ij}(I_{1_i} - I_{2_j})(I_{1_i} - I_{2_j}) \tag{3.2}$$

Here weight a_{ij} defines the similarity between i^{th} and j^{th} colors. This reduces to Euclidean distance if $a_{ij} = 0, \forall i \neq j$ and $a_{ii} = 1, \forall i$. The computational complexity of this approach is $O(b^2)$ and in a typical case, the number of bins is in the range $1024 - 4096$. This means, we need to perform 1 to 16 million computations for finding similarity between two images.

Stricker and Orengo [15] have proposed a color feature based on the first three moments of each color channel of an image. If the value of the ith color channel at the jth image pixel is p_{ij}, then the feature is defined by these three moments for each channel (i.e. R, G and B):

$$E_i = \frac{1}{N}\sum_{i=1}^{N} p_{ij} \tag{3.3}$$

$$\sigma_i = \left(\frac{1}{N}\sum_{i=1}^{N}(p_{ij} - E_i)^2\right)^{\frac{1}{2}} \tag{3.4}$$

$$s_i = \left(\frac{1}{N}\sum_{i=1}^{N}(p_{ij} - E_i)^3\right)^{\frac{1}{3}} \tag{3.5}$$

where N is the number of pixels in the image. For two images, Q and I, with r color channels, the distance measure is defined as:

$$d(Q,I) = \sum_{i=1}^{r} w_1|E_i^Q - E_i^I| + w_2|\sigma_i^Q - \sigma_i^I| + |w_3|s_i^Q - s_i^I| \quad (3.6)$$

Thus this method is based on the dominant features of the color distribution of images.

We will now describe three color features in detail.

3.2.2 The distance method

As seen earlier, the histogram intersection technique takes into account every color bin of the 3-D color histogram of the two images compared and it does a very detailed comparison. However, for many images like trademark images, flags, textile design patterns etc., there are large regions of uniform color. Therefore the 3-D histogram will have a few dominant peaks and the rest of the bins do not capture much color information of the image. Hence a detailed comparison for such images is not required. Also, it has been observed that there is some noise introduced during the process of scanning color images. Hence, a fine comparison is not necessary and may even produce incorrect results. The distance method [12] therefore does a coarse comparison of the color histograms of the query and model images.

The feature used for capturing the color information is the mean value, μ, of the 1-D histograms of each of the three color components of the image. These components could be R, G and B for the RGB representation or the three opponent color axes – rg, by and wb [16] given by:

$$rg = R - G; \; by = 2 * B - R - G; \; wb = R + G + B \quad (3.7)$$

Therefore, the feature vector $\overline{\mathbf{f}}$ for characterizing a RGB image will be:

$$\overline{\mathbf{f}} = (\mu_R, \mu_G, \mu_B) \quad (3.8)$$

The histogram can be normalized by considering the relative fraction of pixels (compared to the total number of pixels in the image) in each bin of the histogram. A distance measure can then be used to compute the similarity or match value for a given pair of images. Depending on the type of the distance measure used – Manhattan (city block) or Euclidean, the following measures can be used:

$$D_{q,i}^{M} = |\overline{\mathbf{f_q}} - \overline{\mathbf{f_i}}| = \sum_{R,G,B} |\mu_q - \mu_i| \tag{3.9}$$

$$D_{q,i}^{E} = \sqrt{(\overline{\mathbf{f_q}} - \overline{\mathbf{f_i}})^2} = \sqrt{\sum_{R,G,B} (\mu_q - \mu_i)^2} \tag{3.10}$$

where $D_{q,i}^{M}$ is the Manhattan distance between the query image and a database image, $D_{q,i}^{E}$ is the Euclidean distance between the query image and a database image, $\overline{\mathbf{f_q}}$ is the color feature vector of the query image and $\overline{\mathbf{f_i}}$ is the color feature vector of the database image. Note that a similar feature and distance measures can be deduced for color images using any other representation scheme, like the opponent color axes. It is obvious that the distance of an image from itself is zero.

3.3 Reference Color Table Method

The distance method computes a coarse feature measure and uses a relative distance measure for a given pair of images. It involves less computation and gives fast and reasonably accurate results. The histogram intersection method is highly granular and it carries out a detailed comparison of all the histogram bins in the 3D color representation but is susceptible to noise. The Reference Color Table method [12] can be considered as an intermediate approach to the distance method and histogram intersection approaches, which reduces the detail of histogram matching yet retains the speed and robustness of the distance method.

In the Reference Color Table method, a set (table) of reference colors is defined. This set of colors is selected such that all the colors in the database are approximately covered perceptually. Table 3.1 shows a typical color table which we can be used. For every image in the database, we can compute a histogram for this set of colors, 27 in this example. For this purpose, each pixel in the color image is classified against the colors in the color table and assigned the nearest color. A simple city-block distance is used to compute the nearest color in the reference table. Then the histogram of the pixels with the newly assigned colors is computed. If the color table selected is good, the 'new image' after assigning the nearest color from the table, will perceptually be the same as the original image. So, for this method, the color feature chosen is this reduced color

Color	R	G	B	Color	R	G	B
Black	0	0	0	SlateBlue	128	128	255
DarkBlue	0	0	128	LawnGreen	128	255	0
Blue	0	0	255	PaleGreen	128	255	128
DarkGreen	0	128	0	LightCyan	128	255	255
Turquoise	0	128	128	Red	255	0	0
SkyBlue	0	128	255	Maroon	255	0	128
Green	0	255	0	Magenta	255	0	255
SpringGreen	0	255	128	Orange	255	128	0
Cyan	0	255	255	Pink	255	128	128
Brown	128	0	0	LightMagenta	255	128	255
Violet	128	0	128	Yellow	255	255	0
MarineBlue	128	0	255	LightYellow	255	255	128
OliveDrab	128	128	0	White	255	255	255
Grey	128	128	128				

Table 3.1: Reference Color Table

histogram based on the colors of the reference table. Therefore,

$$\overline{\mathbf{f}} = (\lambda_1, \lambda_2, ..., \lambda_n) \tag{3.11}$$

where λ_i is the relative pixel frequency (with respect to the total number of pixels) for the ith reference table color in the image. The size of the reference color table is n. This feature is computed for all the images in the database.

For a particular query image, the reference color histogram feature described above is first computed. Then, the image is matched against all images in the database to obtain the similarity measure with each image in the database. For computing the similarity, a weighted distance measure is used:

$$D_{q,i} = \omega\sqrt{(\overline{\mathbf{f_q}} - \overline{\mathbf{f_i}})^2} \tag{3.12}$$

which leads to:

$$D_{q,i} = \sum_{i=1}^{n} \omega_i \sqrt{(\lambda_i^Q - \lambda_i^I)^2} \text{ where } \omega_i = \begin{cases} \lambda_i^Q & \text{if } \lambda_i^Q, \lambda_i^I > 0 \\ 1 & \text{if } \lambda_i^Q \text{ or } \lambda_i^I = 0 \end{cases} \tag{3.13}$$

where $\mathbf{f_q}$ and $\mathbf{f_i}$ are the color features of the query image and database image respectively. Note that λ_i^Q and λ_i^I are the ith reference color relative pixel frequency of the query and database images respectively. n is the number of colors in the reference color table. Note ω is the weight factor used. For a particular color, if both of the histogram bins are non-zero, then the weight ω_i used is λ_i^Q since we want to take the relative proportion of color i in that image. If either of the corresponding histogram bins have a value of zero (which means that color is missing), then ω_i is taken to be unity. In this case the relative difference of the two bins is used as a *push factor* to separate the two images in the similarity measure. Again, it is obvious here that the distance of an image from itself is zero.

3.3.1 The color clustering-based method

A comparison of the histogram intersection, distance and reference color methods has been given in [12]. The reference color table method was found to be the best in terms of retrieval efficiency. However, the drawback of this method is that it requires a pre-defined set of reference colors which can approximately cover all colors in the application. While this condition may be satisfied in some applications, in situations where there are ongoing additions/deletions to the database and where knowledge of colors in the images is not available before-hand, such a technique will not give good results. The reference color table method requires a representative sample of all images stored in the database in order to select the reference color table. For example, such a priori knowledge is impossible to obtain in a trademarks database [18]. Another color similarity technique based on clustering [9] which does not need any knowledge about the colors in the images to be handled is discussed next.

The cluster feature

The pixels of a color image can be regarded as points in the 3-D color space. Their coordinates are the values of the pixels. The chroma of synthesized color images (also for natural images with a few dominant colors) show continuity in the color space. Usually, since the number of objects in an image is limited, the reflection characteristics of each object in natural light tends to be consistent and results as clusters in the color space. If we perform clustering in the 3-D color space, we would obtain a few clusters, each cluster corresponding to one of the dominant colors in the image. We can take a representative sample (e.g. the mean color) of all such clusters and define a new color feature representing the color information

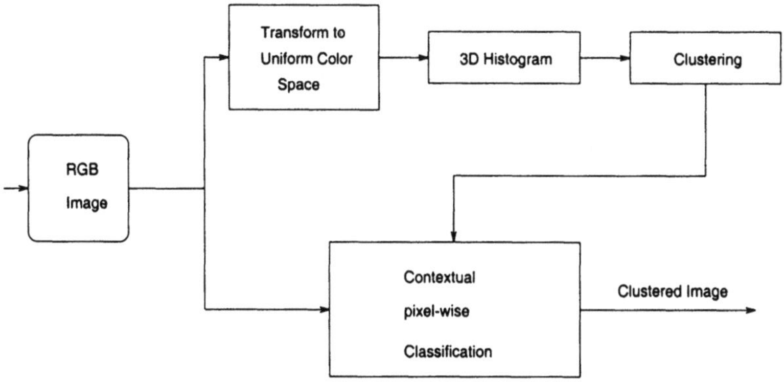

Figure 3.2: Block Schematic of the Clustering Algorithm

of the image. We also propose a new distance measure to compute the color similarity between two images based on this feature. But before we give the formal definition of our color feature and similarity measure, we present the clustering algorithm which can be used to perform clustering in color space. This algorithm is based on the method proposed in [17]. An alternative method for clustering is [3].

The clustering algorithm

A block diagram of the clustering algorithm is shown in Figure 3.2. The input images are in RGB representation. Color image pixels can be regarded as points in the 3-D color space. Now consider images such as trademark images (basically images with a few dominant colors). The number of components in such an image is small and each component is represented by one color, and the optical reflection characteristics of each component tends to be consistent. Thus, the color of each component appears as one cluster in the color space. Color clustering can be used to find out these clusters and to assign a representative color to each of these clusters.

Unfortunately, for a given set of color images, there is not enough information about the number and population of clusters. Moreover, training data is usually not available. Therefore, we make the assumption that each color cluster has normal distribution with one peak and there is sufficient distance between every two color clusters. In this case, the clustering operation can be simplified to a method for finding peaks and estimating distribution parameters.

The distance measure is very important in clustering. The measure should be consistent with the visual resolution and should also be uniform in all directions in the entire color space. If we use the CIE 1976 uniform color system (L^*, u^*, v^*), the distance between two colors can be calculated by the Euclidean distance:

$$d(L^*, u^*, v^*) = [(\Delta L^*)^2 + (\Delta u^*)^2 + (\Delta v^*)^2]^{\frac{1}{2}} \tag{3.14}$$

We now describe the initial clustering algorithm which does the peak finding in the 3-D color space:

1. Compute the RGB color histogram.
2. Find all the color peaks (6-neighborhood maxima in the 3-D color space) using the histogram.
3. A peak corresponds to a color cluster. For each cluster, note the RGB values and population from the histogram.
4. Sort the peaks in the descending order, based on the cluster population.
5. Determine the number of peaks which do not have a very small population.
6. If the number of peaks found in step 5 is less than in step 3, merge the very small clusters to their nearest color clusters. The nearest cluster is computed based on the color-distance metric in (L^*, u^*, v^*) space. The representative color for this merged cluster is the weighted mean of the two original clusters.
7. For each pixel, compute the color distance to the different clusters. Assign the pixel to the cluster for which color distance is minimum. Thus every pixel gets assigned to one of the clusters.

We now describe in detail the two major problems in reducing the classification error: the design of the classification method, and the utilization of spatial information.

Design of classification method

We have obtained the number of classes (clusters), the coordinates of center of each class, and the corresponding amplitude value through the initial cluster analysis in the color space. For more accurate classification, Bayes classifier is not applicable because the covariance matrices are not available. We can use the minimum distance classifier. Minimum distance classifier makes an implicit assumption that all classes have the same population. It is very often that within an image, the difference in number of pixels for different colors is quite large. In this case, the minimum distance classifier will result in large classification errors. Hence, we use a classifier which takes care of population differences in the color space. Suppose we have N samples to classify into M clusters: $\omega_1, \omega_2, \ldots, \omega_M$; each cluster being Gaussian distributed $N(m_i, \sigma_i)$, containing N_i samples. All clusters have the same covariance matrix. With the assumption that $N_i >> 1$, we have the optimal decision rule:

$$d(\mathbf{x}, \mathbf{m}_j) - 2log[p(\omega_j)] = \min_i\{d(\mathbf{x}, \mathbf{m}_i) - 2log[p(\omega_i)]\} \qquad (3.15)$$

where $d()$ is the Euclidean distance from the sample to the center of class ω_i calculated in the uniform color space. The ratio of the population of class ω_i to the total samples, $p(\omega_i)$, can be calculated by the ratio of the corresponding i^{th} amplitude value to the total value, N_i/N, obtained by clustering in the 3-D color space.

Use of spatial correlation information

There has been a lot of research to improve the image classification accuracy through the use of spatial information [19]. These methods fall into three main categories:

1. Relaxation Methods, which represent spatial correlation information by consistency coefficients.

2. Contextual Classifiers, which directly make use of spatial information.

3. Use of image texture measure, together with the spectral data.

The first two methods are very complicated and computation-intensive. The third method does not seem to be applicable here. Therefore a predictive classifier based on the Markov random field model of image data can be used. In the first order Markov random field, a pixel is closely related to its two neighbors (top and left). It means that the probability that a pixel and its neighbors belong to the same color class is relatively high. The following decision procedure is then applicable:

> Perform classification using equation 3.15 in a raster scan order. For the current pixel,

- Record the class label of top and left neighbor pixels ω_t and ω_l and compute corresponding distance measures $d_t()$ and $d_l()$ (i.e. the distance of the pixel from the class mean).
- Calculate the decision function $d_c()$ which measures the distance between the present pixel and its current class ω_c. This distance $d_c()$ is used for deciding the new label for the current pixel. Then, if $|d_t - d_c| < \theta$ then the pixel is assigned class ω_t, otherwise class ω_l is given the same consideration. If the pixel can not be classified to either class ω_t or class ω_l, it is classified using equation 3.15.

This method makes use of spatial correlation property of image data. It also reduces the effect of noise in the clustering and saves considerable computational time.

Cluster matching

Suppose we have an image I of size N pixels and assume that a clustering operation on the image obtains m color clusters. Each cluster C_i is defined as follows:

$$C_i = \{R_i, G_i, B_i, \lambda_i\} \text{ where } i = 1, 2, \ldots, m \tag{3.16}$$

where (R_i, G_i, B_i) is the representative color of the cluster (we use the mean) and λ_i is the fraction of the pixels in that cluster as compared to the total number of pixels, i.e.

$$\lambda_i = \frac{\text{Number of pixels } \epsilon\ C_i}{N}. \tag{3.17}$$

Now, we can define the color feature of image I as:

$$\bar{\mathbf{f}}_I = \{C_i \mid i = 1, 2, 3 \ldots m\} \tag{3.18}$$

C_i refers to a cluster in the color space computed by some clustering algorithm. Now this feature vector can be computed for every image and stored in the database.

The similarity between a pair of images Q and I is given by a distance function, $d(Q, I)$. It is not necessarily true that the two images to be compared have similar or same number of colors. Assume that image Q has m clusters and image I has n clusters and that $m \leq n$ (the reverse case can be similarly handled). We first compute the permutation function P for Q which maps every cluster i of Q to the closest cluster (in color space) $P(i)$ of image I. This permutation can be very easily computed, as follows:

1. Form the distance matrix $G = [g]_{pq}, 1 \leq p \leq m, 1 \leq q \leq n$ where $g_{pq} = \text{coldis}(C_p^Q, C_q^I)$.

2. Find the minimum entry g_{xy} in G.

3. $P(x) \;=\; y$.

4. Delete row x and column y (but do not change the index numbers of the rows & columns of matrix G).

5. If G is empty (all rows and columns have been deleted) then stop else go to step 2.

The color distance in the above algorithm can be the simple euclidean distance:

$$\text{coldis}(C_p^Q, C_q^I) \;=\; [(R_p^Q - R_q^I)^2 \;+ (G_p^Q - G_q^I)^2 \;+ (B_p^Q - B_q^I)^2]^{\frac{1}{2}} \qquad (3.19)$$

If desired, the RGB representation could be converted to the 1976 CIE color representation and the distance can be computed in the CIE space using equation 3.14. The CIE space distance is perceptually a better distance measure than the RGB space.

For computing the similarity, we use a weighted distance measure:

$$D(Q, I) \;=\; \omega\sqrt{(\overline{\mathbf{f}_\mathbf{q}} - \overline{\mathbf{f}_\mathbf{i}})^2} \qquad (3.20)$$

which leads to:

$$D(Q, I) \;=\; \sum_{i=1}^{\min(m,n)} \omega_i\sqrt{(\lambda_i^Q - \lambda_{P(i)}^I)^2} \;+\; \sum_{i=1}^{\min(m,n)} \text{cdist}(C_i^Q, C_{P(i)}^I) \qquad (3.21)$$

where:

$$\omega_i \;=\; \begin{cases} \lambda_i^Q & \text{if } \lambda_i^Q, \lambda_{P(i)}^I > 0 \\ 1 & \text{otherwise} \end{cases} \qquad (3.22)$$

and

$$\text{cdist}(C_i^Q, C_{P(i)}^I) \;=\; \begin{cases} \text{coldis}(C_i^Q, C_{P(i)}^I) & \text{if } \lambda_i^Q, \lambda_{P(i)}^I > 0 \\ 1 & \text{otherwise} \end{cases} \qquad (3.23)$$

where $\mathbf{f_q}$ and $\mathbf{f_i}$ are the color features of the query image Q and database image I respectively. Note that λ_i^Q and $\lambda_{P(i)}^I$ are the ith cluster's relative pixel frequency of the query and database images respectively. If the number of clusters is not the same, the value of $\lambda = 0$ is assumed for the corresponding cluster of any unmatched cluster in the image with the larger number of clusters.

The distance formula has two factors – the relative frequency of the pixels of the corresponding clusters as well as the color distance between the two clusters. Note that ω is the weight factor used. For a pair of corresponding clusters, if both the histogram bins are non-zero, then the weight ω_i used is λ_i^Q since we want to take the relative proportion of color i in that image. If either of the corresponding histogram bins have a value of zero (which means that it is an unmatched cluster), then ω_i is taken to be unity. In this case the relative difference of the two bins is used as a *push factor* to separate the two images in the similarity measure. Therefore the first term (relative frequency term) represents the proportion of each individual color in the image. This factor in the distance expression helps to rank the images based on color similarity when the retrieved images have either an unequal number of colors (more or less number of colors) or a different mix of proportions of the individual colors than the query image. If the two corresponding clusters have exactly the same relative frequency, then the color distance becomes the primary factor in deciding the distance. It is obvious here that the distance of an image from itself is zero.

As far as the computational complexity is concerned, both the cluster method and the reference color table method require $O(m^2)$ time for a $m \times m$ image for the feature computation (which is done only once). For the matching part, the reference color table requires $O(L)$ time where L is the size of the reference color table. The cluster method requires $O(pq)$ time for the matching, where p and q are the number of clusters respectively in the two matched images. The actual time taken is not very high since the number of dominant colors in an image is usually very small.

3.3.2 Experimental results

We have implemented the cluster-based color matching algorithm in an image information system and tested it on two databases. We first used one database of 100 airline trademark images and then tested on another database of 70 flag images of different countries.

We designed the tests in this manner: we picked 10 query images each

Matching Method	Airlines DB				Flags DB			
	T=5	T=10	T=15	T=20	T=5	T=10	T=15	T=20
Hist. Intersection	0.547	0.645	0.713	0.771	0.475	0.625	0.778	0.868
Distance Method	0.880	0.925	0.986	0.993	0.612	0.837	0.958	0.983
Ref. Color Table	0.930	0.987	0.987	1.000	0.943	0.986	0.988	1.000
Cluster Matching	0.912	0.968	0.986	0.997	0.919	0.967	0.979	1.000

Table 3.2: Average Efficiency of different methods over 10 queries.

for both the databases which represented the population well. For each of these query images, we manually listed the similar images found in the database. Then we applied the techniques to each query image against all the images in the database to obtain *short lists* of similar images. The summary of results are presented in table 3.2. For any query, we define the efficiency of retrieval, η_T, for a given short list of size T as follows:

$$\eta_T = \begin{cases} \frac{n}{N} & \text{if } N \leq T \\ \frac{n}{T} & \text{if } N > T \end{cases} \tag{3.24}$$

where n is the number of similar images retrieved in the short list and N is the total number of similar images in the database. Table 3.2 represents the retrieval efficiency, η_T, for both the methods, averaged over 10 queries. We have presented the results for short list sizes of $T = 5,\ 10,\ 15$ and 20. It can be seen from table 3.2 that the efficiency of the clustering method is superior to that of the histogram intersection and the distance method. While the efficiency of the reference color method is better than the clustering method, both are almost of the same order. This shows that if we have a priori knowledge of the colors in the database, then one can use a suitable reference color table to obtain good retrieval efficiency. However, in case where such information is not available, the clustering method is very good since it can give almost a similar efficiency. Figure 3.3 shows a sample query image with the retrieved images for the airline database with a short list of size $T = 9$ using the clustering method. The image on the lower-right is the query image and the results of the query are presented as a 3×3 grid of image icons. The images are ranked from most similar to least similar in a left-to-right and top-to-bottom scan order. Any of these icons can be clicked in the system and the corresponding image is displayed on the lower-left area.

3.3.3 Remarks

We have presented a brief review of color features for the purpose of image retrieval. Three features were then described in detail. These meth-

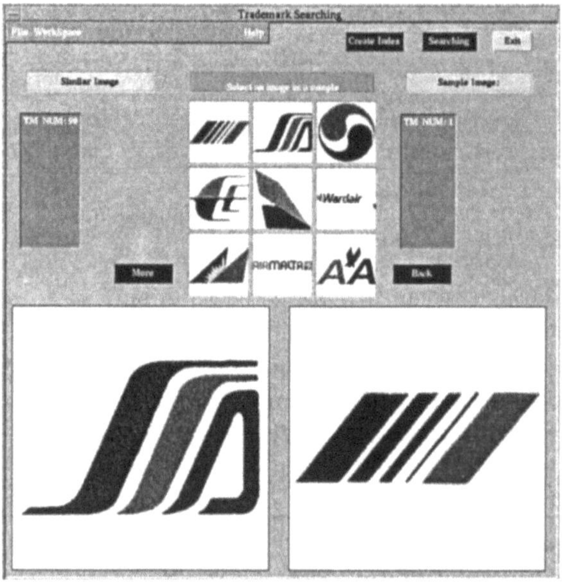

Figure 3.4: Retrieval Results for a Sample Query Image

ods although not invariant to lighting condition, are not very sensitive to it. As long as the light is white light, variations in intensity should not matter. This is because white light will ensure the same proportionality of chromal reflection, and hence preserve the color information. The cluster-based method has the additional advantage that it can be used for building efficient indexes [2]. This is because clustering can be viewed as a generalized form of indexing [6]. Moreover, it can be naturally combined with shape measures [13]. Finally, by noting the spatial coordinates (say by the centroid) of the objects (corresponding to a blob of contiguous pixels belonging to the same color cluster), spatial information can also be easily incorporated in this method [10]. This color feature is being incorporated in our Trademarks image database which uses shape, text and phonetics as other features [18].

References

1. J.K.Wu, "Digital Image Processing", Communication Press of China, Beijing, 1989
2. G.P. Babu, B.M. Mehtre, M.S. Kankanhalli, "Color Indexing for Efficient Image Retrieval", Multimedia Tools and Applications, Vol. 1, No. 4, pp. 327-348,

November 1995

3. M. Celenk, "A Recursive Clustering Technique for Color Picture Segmentation", Proc. Conference on Computer Vision and Pattern Recognition, pp. 437-444, 1988
4. J. Foley, A.V. Dam, S.K. Feiner, J.F. Hughes, "Computer Graphics: Principles and Practice", Addison-Wesley, 1990
5. Y. Gong, H. Zhang, H. C. Chuan, M. Sakauchi, "An image database system with content capturing and fast image indexing abilities", Proc. IEEE International Conference on Multimedia Computing and Systems, pp. 121-130, 1994
6. W.I. Grosky, R. Mehrotra, "Image Database Management", Advances in Computers, Vol. 352, pp. 237-291, 1992
7. M. Ioka, "A method for defining the similarity of images on the basis of color information", Technical Report RT-0030, IBM Tokyo Research Lab, Japan, 1989
8. A. K. Jain, R. C. Dubes, "Algorithms for Clustering Data", Prentice-Hall, Englewood, Cliffs, NJ, 1988
9. M. S. Kankanhalli, B. M. Mehtre, J. K. Wu, "Cluster-based color matching for image retrieval", Pattern Recognition, Vol. 29, No. 4, pp. 701-708, 1996
10. M. S. Kankanhalli, B. M. Mehtre, H. Y. Huang, "Color & Spatial Feature for Content-based Image Retrieval", ISS Technical Report, 1996
11. H. Lu, B. C. Ooi, K. L. Tan. "Efficient image retrieval by color contents", Applications of Databases, First International Conference ADB-94, Lecture Notes in Computer Science, Vol. 819, pp. 95-108, 1994
12. B.M. Mehtre, M.S. Kankanhalli, A.D. Narasimhalu, G.C. Man, "Color matching for image retrieval", Pattern Recognition Letters, Vol. 16, pp. 325-331, March 1995
13. B.M. Mehtre, M.S. Kankanhalli, W.F. Lee, "Content-based Image Retrieval Using a Composite Color-Shape Approach", Information Processing and Management, Vol. 34, No. 1, pp. 109-120, 1998
14. W. Niblack, R. Barber, W. Equitz, M. Flickner, E. Glasman, D. Petkovic, P. Yanker, C. Faloutsos, G. Taubin, "The QBIC Project: Querying Images by colour, texture and shape", Proc. of SPIE, Vol. 1908, pp. 173-187, 1993
15. M. Stricker, M. Orengo, "Similarity of Color Images", Proc. SPIE Conference on Storage and Retrieval for Image and Video Databases III, SPIE Vol. 2420, pp. 381-392, 1995
16. M. J. Swain, D.H. Ballard, "Color indexing", International Journal of Computer Vision, Vol. 7, No. 1, pp. 11-32, 1991
17. J.K. Wu, "Color coding of images", Signal Processing (Official Journal of ASSP, China), Vol. 3, pp. 1-17, 1987
18. J.K. Wu, B.M. Mehtre, Y.J. Gao, C.P. Lam, A.D. Narasimhalu, "STAR - A Multimedia Database System for Trademark Registration", Applications of Databases, First International Conference ADB-94, Lecture Notes in Computer Science, 819:109–122, 1994
19. T.Y. Young, K.S. Fu, "Handbook of Pattern Recognition and Image Processing", Academic Press, 1986

Chapter 4

Texture Feature Extraction

Texture is an important element of human vision. Texture has been found to provide cues of scene depth and surface orientation[1]. In computer graphics people often map textures onto 3D surface to achieve the stereo effect. Texture analysis has been studied for at least 35 years and applied to problems of texture classification, discrimination and segmentation. What is texture? We recognize it when we see it, but it is difficult to describe. For different domain textures have different appearance. So far no one has given a universally accepted definition of texture. Figure 4.1 shows some of the examples of Brodatz texture images [2] widely used in texture analysis literature. These textures may be considered as structured or random placement of texture primitives[5]. But in unconstrained home photos, textures often lack these primitives. In general, texture refers to the presence of visual patterns or spatial arrangement of pixels that regional intensity or color alone does not sufficiently describe. Texture may have statistical properties, structural properties or both. Conceptually, it is difficult to make a concise definition for any texture. It is also difficult to obtain general mathematical model for various textures. For example, sky seems to be homogeneous with little texture, grass land and trees seem almost random but have different scale of granularity and complexity, while buildings have very strong structural characteristics and water exhibits prominent orientation.

Even though extensive research work on texture has been done and many technologies[6] have been proposed and developed for the last three decades, none has produced very clear solutions for the problem of texture analysis and classification[7]. The existing texture analysis methods can be categorized into statistical methods, signal processing methods, model based methods and structural methods. There are also some other

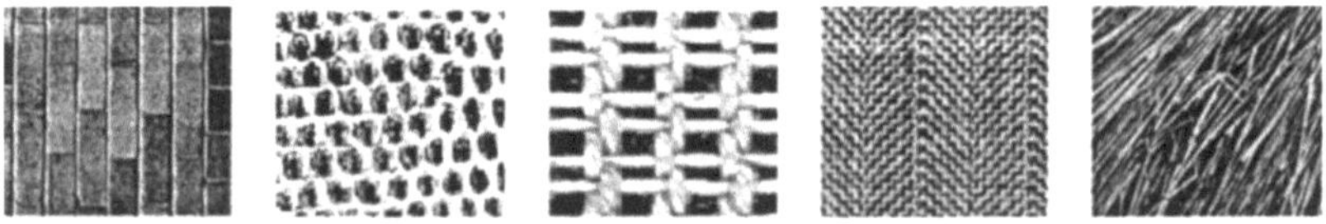

Figure 4.1: Some examples of Brodatz texture images

methods such as multi-resolution analysis and Wold decomposition[8, 9] which are difficult to categorize.

4.1 Discrete Cosine Transformed Texture

4.1.1 Discrete cosine transform

The first method we used in our research to extract texture features was the discrete cosine transform (DCT)[10]. DCT is a traditional and useful method in image processing. 2-dimensional cosine transformation is defined by:

$$F(u,v) = \frac{2C(u)C(v)}{N} \sum_{j=0}^{N-1} \sum_{k=0}^{N-1} f(j,k) \cos\frac{(2j+1)u\pi}{2N} \cos\frac{(2k+1)v\pi}{2N} \quad (4.1)$$

$$f(j,k) = \frac{2}{N} \sum_{u=0}^{N-1} \sum_{v=0}^{N-1} C(u)C(v) \cos\frac{(2j+1)u\pi}{2N} \cos\frac{(2k+1)v\pi}{2N} F(u,v) \quad (4.2)$$

where,

$$C(u), C(v) = \begin{cases} \frac{\sqrt{2}}{2} & \text{u,v=0} \\ 1 & \text{otherwise} \end{cases}$$

Here we use block DCT because we are only interested in image regions, and not the whole image. Due to the irregular edges of regions the block size selected cannot be too large, and if the block size is too small it will not cover the sufficient area including texture elements. Here the block size is 16×16. Figure 4.3 shows the block DCT of the images in Figure 4.2. From these figures we found strong directionality in the DCT of buildings and water - multi-direction for buildings and uni-direction for 1D water wave texture. For grassland, trees and sky there is no obvious directionality in their DCT. Sky has less high frequency components comparing to grass land and trees.

Figure 4.2: Images of various textures

Figure 4.3: Block DCT of images in Figure 4.2.

4.1.2 Texture feature based on discrete cosine transform

Let $F(u,v)$ denote DCT of each block. Set $F(u,v) = 0$ to discard the average gray scale since we are only interested in changes in pixel intensity along with spatial positions. The three feature measures are given below:

1. **Texture Energy Measure**

$$ENERGY = \sum_{u=0}^{M-1} \sum_{v=0}^{M-1} |F(u,v)| \tag{4.3}$$

2. **Directionality Measure**

$$DIR = \sum_{u=0}^{M-1} \sum_{v=0}^{M-1} \tan^{-1}(v/u)|F(u,v)|/ENERGY \tag{4.4}$$

   If there is a horizontal strip in transformed space, the value of DIR is close to 0^oC; if there is a vertical strip, the value is close to 90^oC; therwise it is about 45^oC.

3. **Directional Dispersion Measure**

$$DISP_\theta = -\int_0^{\frac{\pi}{2}} P_F(\theta) \log P_F(\theta) d\theta \tag{4.5}$$

where,

$$P_F(\theta) = \int_0^R |F(r,\theta)|dr/ENERGY \tag{4.6}$$

If there is obvious directionality in the transformed space, $DISP_\theta$ approximates 0 otherwise it approximates maximum.

4. **Frequency Dispersion Measure**

$$DISP_r = \int_0^R P_F(r)\log P_F(r)dr \tag{4.7}$$

where,

$$P_F(r) = \int_0^{\frac{\pi}{2}} |F(r,\theta)|d\theta/ENERGY \tag{4.8}$$

4.1.3 Feature vector formation

If μ denotes mean and σ denotes standard variation, in each image region we form the feature vector as $[\mu_{ENERGY}, \mu_{DIR}, \sigma_{DIR}, \mu_{DISP_\theta}, \sigma_{DISP_\theta}]$. For the images in Figure 4.2, feature vectors are:

$$\begin{array}{l} [0.2575 \quad 47.0012 \quad 3.4588 \quad 0.7502 \quad 0.0239] \\ [2.0237 \quad 48.9369 \quad 2.2217 \quad 0.7547 \quad 0.0118] \\ [2.4423 \quad 44.7535 \quad 11.0113 \quad 0.6935 \quad 0.0652] \end{array}$$

Obviously, the value of DIR of buildings is about 45^oC, and $DISP_\theta$ is small. It indicates that the DCT of buildings has strong directionality, but it does not have uniform directions, such as in Figure 4.3. In contrast, the texture of water has a prominent direction.

4.1.4 Test results

For these feature vectors the divergence measure between any two categories is calculated and illustrated in Figure 4.4.

	light sky	*blue sky*	*grass land*	*trees*	*buildings*	*water*
light sky	0	3.0538	99.5934	241.2954	219.4390	40.0931
blue sky	3.0538	0	120.0989	304.3823	310.5818	43.5437
grass land	99.5934	120.0989	0	6.6850	83.9279	37.4276
trees	241.2954	304.3823	6.6850	0	169.9698	145.7518
buildings	217.4390	310.5818	83.9279	169.9698	0	52.3426
water	40.0931	43.5437	37.4276	145.7518	52.3426	0

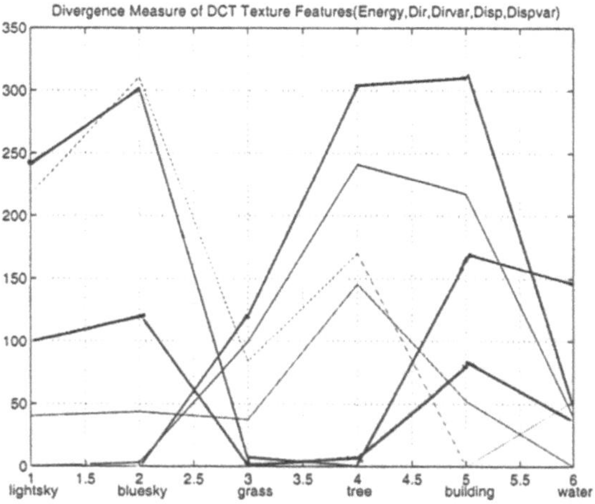

Figure 4.4: Divergence measure for DCT texture features.

Using back propagation feed-forward neural network as the classifier, training 500,000 iterations, sum of square error is around 14, momentum constant is 0.95. The classification results for test images is:

	light sky	*blue sky*	*grass land*	*trees*	*buildings*	*water*	*percent*
light sky	45	27	0	0	0	6	57.7
blue sky	28	51	0	0	0	1	63.8
grass land	1	0	12	3	1	0	70.6
trees	0	0	7	24	1	0	75.0
buildings	0	0	2	0	24	0	92.3
water	0	7	4	1	3	19	55.9

The classification results of all the images are listed below:

	light sky	*blue sky*	*grass land*	*trees*	*buildings*	*water*	*percent*
light sky	80	32	0	0	0	6	67.8
blue sky	30	88	0	0	0	2	73.3
grass land	1	0	32	3	1	0	86.5
trees	0	0	7	44	1	0	84.6
buildings	0	0	2	0	44	0	95.7
water	0	7	5	1	3	38	70.4

From these data we find DCT texture feature can extract structure information for buildings and water and their correct classification rate is relatively high. But for water it is still not good enough. This may be because water surface is normally calm and has no waves at all.

4.2 Wavelet Transformed Texture Feature

4.2.1 Wavelet Transform

Multi-resolution analysis techniques such as Gabor and wavelet models[11, 12] are most aligned with the mechanisms of human vision and have attracted great attention in recent years. They often outperform traditional methods. Multi-resolution analysis, as implied by its name, analyzes the signals at different frequencies with different resolutions. Wavelet transform[3] is the transformation which decomposes a signal with a set of real orthonormal bases $\psi_{s,l}(x)$ obtained through translation and dilation of a kernel function $\psi(x)$ known as the *mother wavelet*,

$$\psi_{s,l}(x) = 2^{-s/2}\psi(2^{-s}x - l) \tag{4.9}$$

where s and l are integers. The scale index s indicates the wavelet's width and the location index l gives its position. The function $\psi(x)$ must satisfy the admissibility condition

$$\int_{-\infty}^{\infty} \frac{|\Psi(\xi)|^2}{\xi} d\xi < \infty \tag{4.10}$$

where $\Psi(\xi)$ is the Fourier transform of $\psi(x)$. Due to the orthonormal property, the wavelet coefficients of a signal $f(x)$ can be easily computed via

$$c_{s,l} = \int_{-\infty}^{+\infty} f(x)\psi_{s,l}(x)dx \tag{4.11}$$

and the synthesis formula

$$f(x) = \sum_{s,l} c_{s,l}\psi_{s,l}(x) \tag{4.12}$$

can be used to reconstruct $f(x)$ from its wavelet coefficients. Thus, the continuous wavelet transform was computed by changing the scale of the analysis window, shifting the window in position, multiplying by the signal, and integrating over all times. In discrete case it is convenient to regard discrete wavelet transformation as passing a signal through a pair of filters H and G with impulse responses $h(n)$ and $g(n)$ and downsampling the filtered signals by two. The pair of filters H and G correspond to the halfband lowpass and highpass filters, respectively, and are called the *quadrature mirror filters* (QMF) in the signal processing literature. The halfband filtering halves the resolution, but leaves the scale unchanged. Then the filtered signal is downsampled by two since half the number of samples is redundant. The scale will be doubled after the downsampling. One important property of the discrete wavelet transform is the relation between the impulse responses of the lowpass and highpass filters. They are related by the equation $g(L-1-n) = (-1)^n h(n)$, where L is the filter length. The two filtering and downsampling operations can be expressed by

$$y_H(k) = \sum_n x(n) \cdot g(2k-n) \tag{4.13}$$

$$y_L(k) = \sum_n x(n) \cdot h(2k-n) \tag{4.14}$$

Of the many family of wavelets the most important one is that of compactly supported orthogonal wavelets. In the discrete wavelet transform, compactly supported wavelets correspond to FIR filters. Two popular families of compactly supported wavelets are the Daubecheis wavelets and Coifman wavelets [3]. A major disadvantage of compactly supported wavelets is their asymmetry. This property translates into nonlinear phase in the associated FIR filters. In computing a DWT using a nonlinear phase wavelet filters with finite-length data, a periodic "wrap-around" extension is often used. This may cause artifacts at the borders due to the discontinuity in the "wrap-around" borders. These artifacts can be avoided if the linear phase wavelet filters and a "flip-over" data extension are used. The linear phase means the wavelet must be symmetric, which can be obtained only if we are willing to give either compact support or orthogonality. If both the symmetry and the compact support are wanted, biorthogonal wavelets are inducted. When using biorthogonal wavelets, the QMF used to compute a DWT are no longer an orthogonal pair. They are, however, orthogonal to another QMF pair that are used to compute the inverse DWT. The perfect reconstruction property is still preserved.

4.2.2 Feature vector formation

The filters designed by Ingrid Daubechies [3] are widely used, and have been used in this research. Some Daubechies wavelet coefficients are listed in Table 4.1. For 2D image signal, separable QMF filter bank is used to decompose images. By iterating the four channel 2D QMF filter bank on the output of the low frequency, a pyramid-structured QMF filter bank is constructed and a 3 scales 2D pyramid wavelet QMF filter bank diagram is given in Figure 4.5. In the figure H_{xy} denotes filter, and the first subscript denotes horizontal direction highpass(H) or lowpass(L) filtering, the

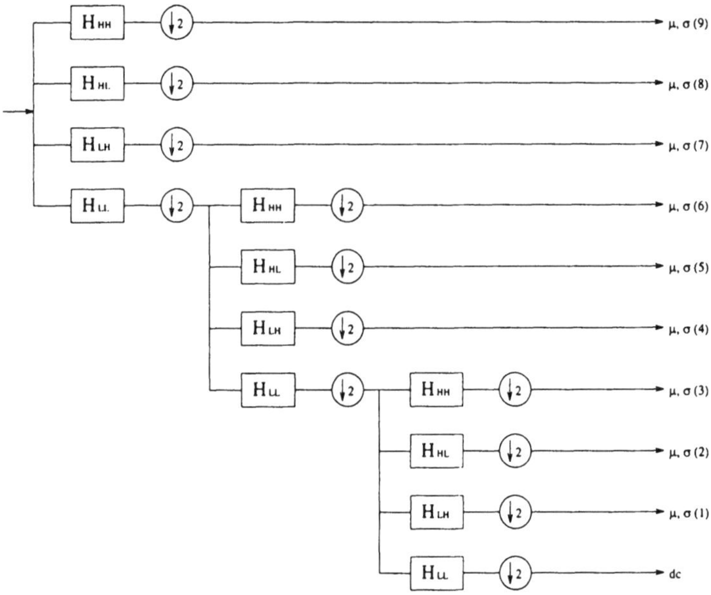

Figure 4.5: 2D pyramid-structured wavelet QMF filter bank.

second subscript denotes vertical direction highpass(H) or lowpass(L) filtering. $\downarrow 2$ means downsampling by 2. Figure 4.6 shows a 2-scales wavelet transformed image. The original image is decomposed into a low resolution subimage(top left) and a series of detailed subimages. The low resolution subimage is obtained by iteratively lowpass filtering the original image and information lost in this process is retained in the detail subimages. From the output of 9 channels a texture vector is computed for each pixel by the magnitude of filter outputs. The feature vector of interested region is represented by the mean and standard deviation of the texture vector. The wavelet transforms of the images in Figure 4.2 are shown in Figure 4.8. Here we use the Daubechies wavelet transform and the order is 4. The coefficients of the lowpass filter $h(n)$ is shown in Table 4.1 and the coefficients of the highpass filter $g(n)$ is calculated by the equation $g(L-1-n) = (-1)^n h(n)$. The frequency responses of these two filters are shown in Figure 4.7.

	n	h(n)
	0	0.48296291314453
N = 2	1	0.83651630373781
	2	0.22414386804201
	3	-0.12940952255126
	0	0.33267055295008
	1	0.80689150931109
N = 3	2	0.45987750211849
	3	-0.13501102001025
	4	-0.08544127388203
	5	0.03522629188571
	0	0.23037781330890
	1	0.71484657055291
	2	0.63088076792986
N = 4	3	-0.02798376941686
	4	-0.18703481171909
	5	0.03084138183556
	6	0.03288301166689
	7	-0.01059740178507
	0	0.16010239797419
	1	0.60382926979719
	2	0.72430852843777
	3	0.13842814590132
N = 5	4	-0.24229488706638
	5	-0.03224486958464
	6	0.07757149384005
	7	-0.00624149021280
	8	-0.01258075199908
	9	0.00333572528547
	0	0.11154074335011
	1	0.49462389039847
	2	0.75113390802111
	3	0.31525035170919
	4	-0.22626469396546
N = 6	5	-0.12976686756727
	6	0.09750160558732
	7	0.02752286553031
	8	-0.03158203931749
	9	0.00055384220116
	10	0.00477725751095
	11	-0.00107730108531
	0	0.07785205408500
	1	0.39653931948188
	2	0.72913209084617
	3	0.46978228740518
	4	-0.14390600392850
	5	-0.22403618499382
N = 7	6	0.07130921926683
	7	0.08061260915107
	8	-0.03802993693501
	9	-0.01657454163067
	10	0.01255099855610
	11	0.00042957797292
	12	-0.00180164070405
	13	0.00035371379997

	n	h(n)
	0	0.05441584224316
	1	0.31287159091460
	2	0.67563073629788
	3	0.58535468365452
	4	-0.01582910525678
	5	-0.28401554296218
	6	0.00047248457376
N = 8	7	0.12874742662055
	8	-0.01736930100187
	9	-0.04408825393086
	10	0.01398102791741
	11	0.00874609404741
	12	-0.00487035299346
	13	-0.00039174037338
	14	0.00067544940645
	15	-0.00011747678412
	0	0.03807794736386
	1	0.24383467461245
	2	0.60482312368978
	3	0.65728807805103
	4	0.13319738582515
	5	-0.29327378327878
	6	-0.09684078322279
	7	0.14854074933806
N = 9	8	0.03072568147935
	9	-0.06763282906126
	10	0.00025094711484
	11	0.02236166212366
	12	-0.00472320475775
	13	-0.00428150368246
	14	0.00184764688305
	15	0.00023038576352
	16	-0.00025196318894
	17	0.00003934732032
	0	0.02667005790036
	1	0.18817680007634
	2	0.52720118892804
	3	0.68845903944926
	4	0.28117234366018
	5	-0.24984642432293
	6	-0.19594627437333
	7	0.12736934033662
	8	0.09305736460365
N = 10	9	-0.07139414716568
	10	-0.02945753682166
	11	0.03321267405906
	12	0.00360655356690
	13	-0.01073317548326
	14	0.00139535174704
	15	0.00199240529517
	16	-0.00068585669495
	17	-0.00011646685513
	18	0.00009358867032
	19	-0.00001326420289

Table 4.1: The filter coefficients $h(n)$(low-pass filter) for Daubechies wavelets

Figure 4.6: A wavelet transformed image.

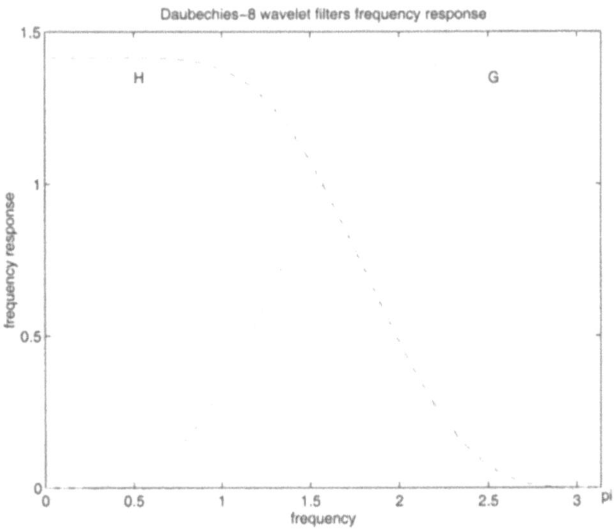

Figure 4.7: Daubechies-8 wavelet filters frequency responses.

Figure 4.8: Pyramid-structured wavelet transforms of images in Figure 4.2.

4.2.3 Performance evaluation and test results

Divergence measure for wavelet transformation mean value of each channel is given below and shown in Figure 4.9. Obviously, the mean values alone have very poor separability:

	light sky	*blue sky*	*grass land*	*trees*	*buildings*	*water*
light sky	0	8.3746	53.9699	48.9877	57.1450	21.4631
blue sky	8.3746	0	41.7469	46.6598	74.8930	18.5271
grass land	53.9699	41.7469	0	7.5863	26.8283	14.1671
trees	48.9877	46.6598	7.5863	0	12.8378	15.6996
buildings	57.1450	74.8930	26.8283	12.8378	0	29.5271
water	21.4631	18.5271	14.1671	15.6996	29.5271	0

Using variation of each channel as the feature vector the divergence measure is calculated and illustrated in Figure 4.10. It is not unusual that the divergence measures between classes light sky and blue sky, grass land and trees are relatively small because they are similar in perception respectively.

	light sky	*blue sky*	*grass land*	*trees*	*buildings*	*water*
light sky	0	29.7	355.2	284.0	420.7	207.3
blue sky	29.7	0	1045.2	766.5	1058.9	433.2
grass land	355.2	1045.2	0	39.0	74.6	61.4
trees	284.0	766.5	39.0	0	196.0	132.4
buildings	420.7	1058.9	74.6	196.0	0	189.9
water	207.3	433.2	61.4	132.4	189.9	0

Combination of mean value and variation can improve the separability and the divergence measure is illustrated in Figure 4.11.

	light sky	*blue sky*	*grass land*	*trees*	*buildings*	*water*
light sky	0	52.0	585.1	464.9	694.4	345.2
blue sky	52.0	0	1503.4	1124.6	1404.1	521.4
grass land	585.1	1503.4	0	88.0	217.2	117.2
trees	464.9	1124.6	88.0	0	319.7	223.0
buildings	694.4	1404.1	217.2	319.7	0	355.7
water	345.2	521.4	117.2	223.0	355.7	0

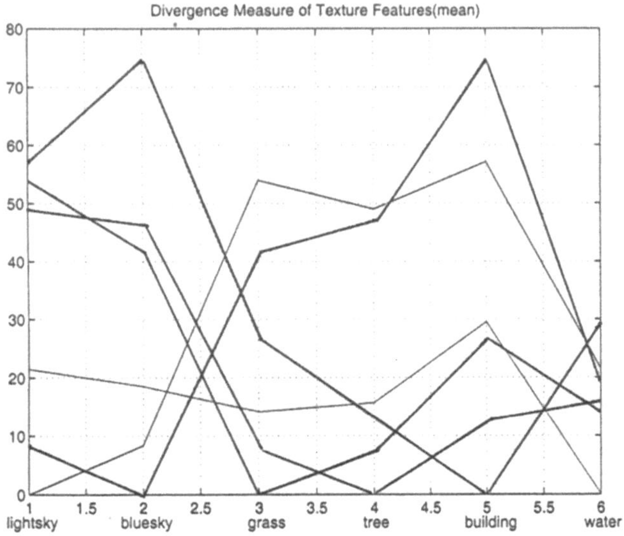

Figure 4.9: Divergence measure for DWT texture features(mean).

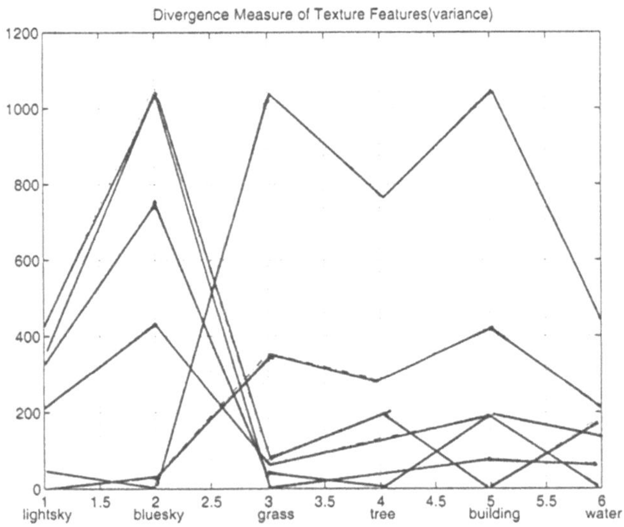

Figure 4.10: Divergence measure for DWT texture features(variation).

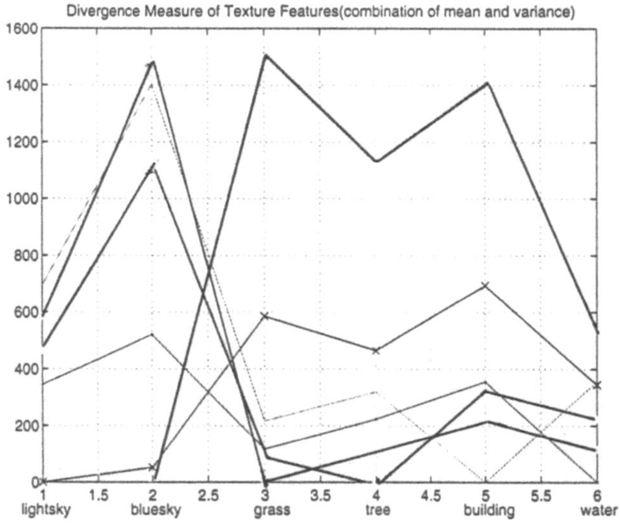

Figure 4.11: Divergence measure for DWT texture features(combination of mean and variation).

Only the variation is used as the feature vector. After 500,000 training iterations, the sum of square error is close to 5, and the momentum constant is about 0.9. The classification results for the test images are as follows:

	light sky	*blue sky*	*grass land*	*trees*	*buildings*	*water*	*percent*
light sky	45	10	0	3	0	0	77.6
blue sky	9	49	1	0	1	0	81.7
grass land	0	0	10	6	0	1	58.8
trees	0	0	3	19	0	0	86.4
buildings	1	0	0	1	20	4	76.9
water	0	2	0	0	2	20	83.3

If all the images including training data are classified, the classification results are listed below:

	light sky	*blue sky*	*grass land*	*trees*	*buildings*	*water*	*percent*
light sky	104	10	0	3	0	1	88.1
blue sky	10	108	1	0	1	0	90.0
grass land	0	0	30	6	0	1	81.1
trees	0	0	3	49	0	0	94.2
buildings	1	0	0	1	40	4	87.0
water	1	2	0	0	2	49	90.7

When using the combination of mean and variation as the feature vector, the neural network converges very slow and there is no improvements in the performance. Therefore, we discard the mean measures.

4.3 Texture Features Based on Second Moment Matrix

A texture description proposed by Serge Belongie et al [4] models texture as a cone like HSV color space. The basic idea is to extract texture features based on information obtained from the *windowed image second moment matrix.* The first step is to compute the gradient, denoted by ∇I, using the first difference approximation along each dimension. Then the windowed image second moment matrix $M_\sigma(x, y)$ is computed via the expression $M_\sigma(x,y) = G_\sigma(x,y) * (\nabla I)(\nabla I)^T$ where $G_\sigma(x, y)$ is a 9×9 separable binomial approximation to a Gaussian smoothing kernel with variance σ^2. At each pixel location, $M_\sigma(x, y)$ is a 2×2 symmetric positive semidefinite matrix; thus it provides us with three pieces of information about each pixel. Rather than work with the raw entries in M_σ, it is more common to deal with its eigenstructure. Consider a fixed σ and pixel location, let λ_1 and λ_2 $(\lambda_1 \geq \lambda_2)$ denote the eigenvalue of M_σ at that location, and let ϕ denote the argument of the principal eigenvector. When λ_1 is large compared to λ_2, the location neighborhood possesses a dominant orientation, as specified by ϕ. When the eigenvalues are comparable, there is no preferred orientation, and when both eigenvalues are negligible, the local neighborhood is approximately constant. The polarity is a measure of the extent to which the gradient vectors in a certain neighborhood all point in the same direction. The polarity is defined as

$$p = \frac{|E_+ - E_-|}{E_+ + E_-} \tag{4.15}$$

where,

$$E_+ = \sum_{(x,y)\in\Omega} G_\sigma(x,y)[\nabla I \cdot \hat{n}]_+ \tag{4.16}$$

and

$$E_- = \sum_{(x,y)\in\Omega} G_\sigma(x,y)[\nabla I \cdot \hat{n}]_- \tag{4.17}$$

$[q]_+$ and $[q]_-$ are the rectified positive and negative parts of their argument, $\hat{n}$ is a unit vector perpendicular to ϕ, and Ω represents the neighborhood under consideration. We can think of E_+ and E_- as measures

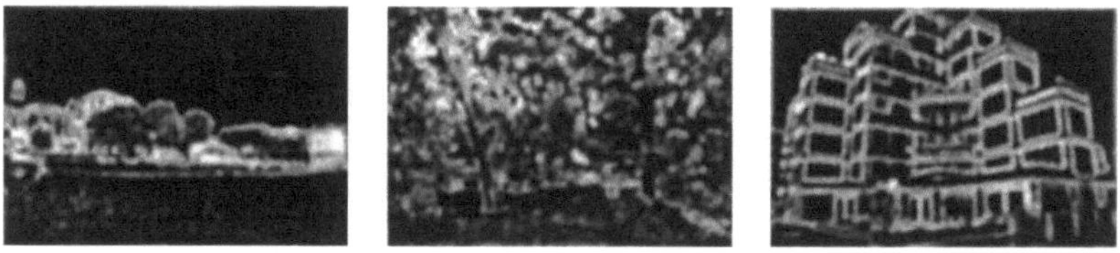

Figure 4.12: Gradient of images in Figure 4.2.

of the number of gradient vectors in Ω are on the "positive side" and "negative side" of the dominant orientation, respectively. Once a scale σ is selected, each pixel is assigned four texture descriptors: the polarity p, anisotropy $1 - \lambda_2/\lambda_1$, normalized texture contrast $2\sqrt{\lambda_1 + \lambda_2}$ and the doubled orientation 2ϕ. The mean and variation of these descriptors in interested region form the feature vector. The gradient of images in Figure 4.2 is shown in Figure 4.12.

4.3.1 Performance evaluation and test results

Using theses features the divergence measure is as follows and shown in Figure 4.13. We notice that the dissimilarities between less texture and rich texture classes are high, and small among those textureless classes or rich texture classes.

	light sky	*blue sky*	*grass land*	*trees*	*buildings*	*water*
light sky	0	65.6	512.8	626.4	1009.3	100.8
blue sky	65.6	0	544.8	610.3	1155.5	131.2
grass land	512.8	544.8	0	25.3	24.5	34.6
trees	626.4	610.3	25.3	0	64.6	76.7
buildings	1009.3	1155.5	24.5	64.6	0	76.7
water	100.8	131.2	34.6	76.7	58.1	0

Following are the classification results for test images using UCB texture feature, training 500,000 iterations, sum of square error is around 15, momentum constant is 0.9:

	light sky	*blue sky*	*grass land*	*trees*	*buildings*	*water*	*percent*
light sky	49	15	0	0	0	0	76.5
blue sky	5	60	0	0	0	1	90.9
grass land	0	0	17	2	0	0	89.5
trees	0	1	1	23	0	0	92.0
buildings	0	0	0	2	16	1	84.2
water	0	1	1	1	1	23	85.2

If all the images including training data are classified, the classification results are listed below:

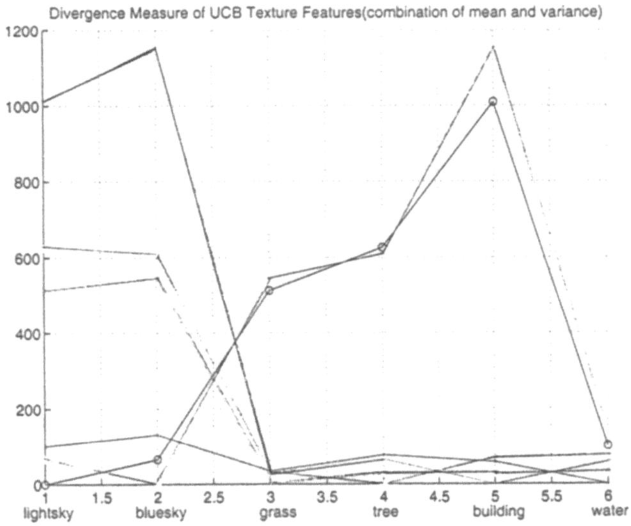

Figure 4.13: Divergence measure for UCB texture features.

	light sky	*blue sky*	*grass land*	*trees*	*buildings*	*water*	*percent*
light sky	100	17	0	0	0	1	84.8
blue sky	5	114	0	0	0	1	95.0
grass land	0	2	29	3	1	2	78.4
trees	0	0	3	40	9	0	76.9
buildings	0	1	0	12	32	1	69.6
water	0	1	0	0	12	41	75.9

4.4 Comparative Study

4.4.1 Comparison based on classification

Individual method is always good at some aspects and bad at other aspects. When they are combined, they may complement each other.

4.4.2 Multiple features - combination of color and texture

As described in the previous sections, using these feature alone can achieve the good results. It is natural to think that integration of these features will achieve the better results[6,13]. Here we simply concatenate the respective features to form a 36 dimensional feature vector. The divergence

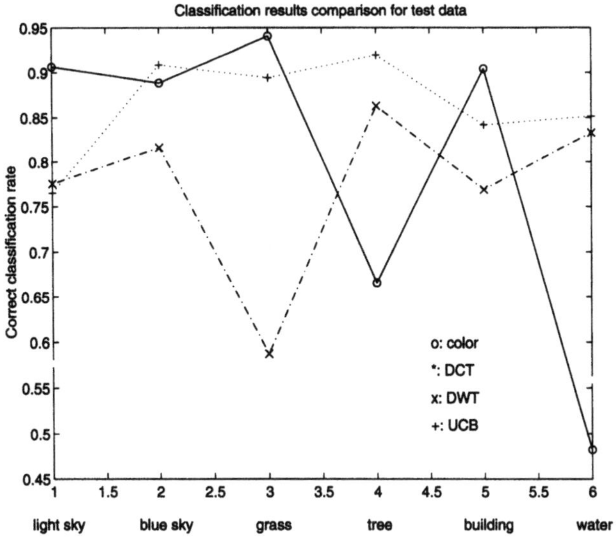

Figure 4.14: Correct classification rate comparison for test data.

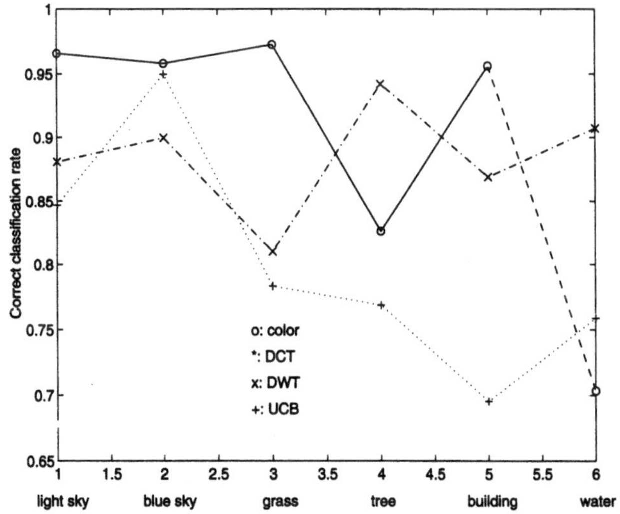

Figure 4.15: Correct classification rate comparison for all images.

measure for this new feature is as follows:

	light sky	*blue sky*	*grass land*	*trees*	*buildings*	*water*
light sky	0	5307	9071609	77401	28764	15907
blue sky	5307	0	229840	3830	6460	1462
grass land	9071609	229840	0	60389	181697	60125
trees	77401	3830	60389	0	3826	1382
buildings	28764	6460	181697	3826	0	2075
water	15907	1462	60125	1382	2075	0

Because we use neural network as classifier we need not care about the weights for each component of the features. The network is four layer feed-forward neural net, training 20,000 iterations, sum of square error is around 1, momentum constant is 0.65, and the classification results for the test images are:

	light sky	*blue sky*	*grass land*	*trees*	*buildings*	*water*	*percent*
light sky	54	4	0	0	0	0	93.1
blue sky	0	57	3	0	0	0	95.0
grass land	0	0	16	1	0	0	94.1
trees	0	1	7	20	0	0	74.1
buildings	0	0	0	0	21	0	100
water	1	1	0	1	1	25	86.2

If all the images including training data are classified, the classification results are listed below:

	light sky	*blue sky*	*grass land*	*trees*	*buildings*	*water*	*percent*
light sky	114	4	0	0	0	0	96.6
blue sky	0	117	3	0	0	0	97.5
grass land	0	0	36	1	0	0	97.3
trees	0	0	7	45	0	0	86.5
buildings	0	0	0	0	46	0	100
water	1	1	0	1	1	50	92.6

We find the results are reasonably good. Let's find out which component is more important in the feature vector by the following method. If w_{ij} denotes the weight which connects the ith node of the input layer and the jth node of the first hidden layer, the following measure will indicate the relative importance of components in the feature vector.

$$W_i = \sum_j |w_{ij}| \tag{4.18}$$

For the above mentioned feature vector, the W_is are: {**87.0620, 103.2220, 91.6286, 88.3103, 81.3325, 81.6909, 28.8563, 37.2881, 28.7674, 24.2144, 29.1575, 42.3105,** 24.5813, 21.9015, 49.0700, 28.8029, 31.1959, 60.8104, 32.0128, 34.7012, 70.9183, *23.4881, 104.9990, 25.9556, 89.5466, 23.3044, 112.9968, 25.6335,* 40.7322, 133.5153, 141.4547, 177.2955, 28.4189, 283.2264, 337.2077, 168.1983}. The first 12

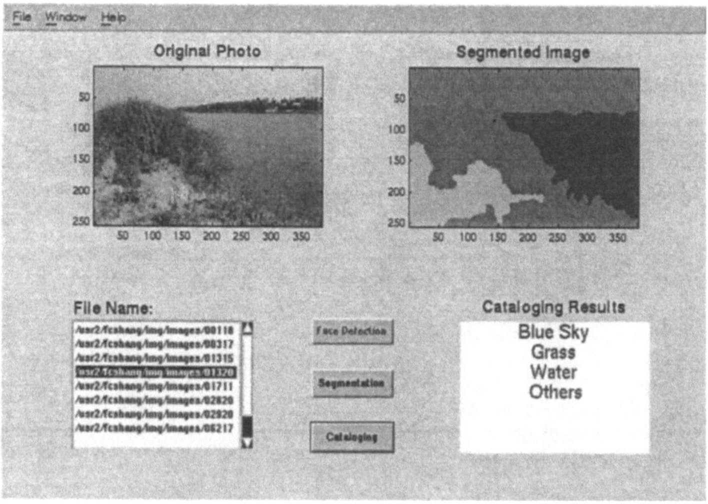

Figure 4.16: Automatic cataloging results.

components are color features, and the next 9 components are wavelet features, the next 7 components are discrete cosine transform features, and the last 8 components are windowed image second moment matrix features. These figures give two clues: one is that windowed image second moment matrix components play a more important role than others; and the other is that the mean measure is a bit more important than variation measure.

4.4.3 Retrieval test

Based on the multiple features mentioned above, two prototypes are implemented and tested on a database containing 2400 digital home photos. The first one is an automatic cataloging system as shown in Figure 4.16 and Figure 4.17. A segmented image is presented to the system. For each segment in the image multiple features are extracted, then the features are fed into the trained classifier to automatically catalogue the segment into one of the predefined categories. If no category exists, it assumes the segment doesn't belong to any of the predefined categories and "unknown" is returned.

The second one is an object-based image retrieval prototype, which support queries by high level concept (images of my family on a grass

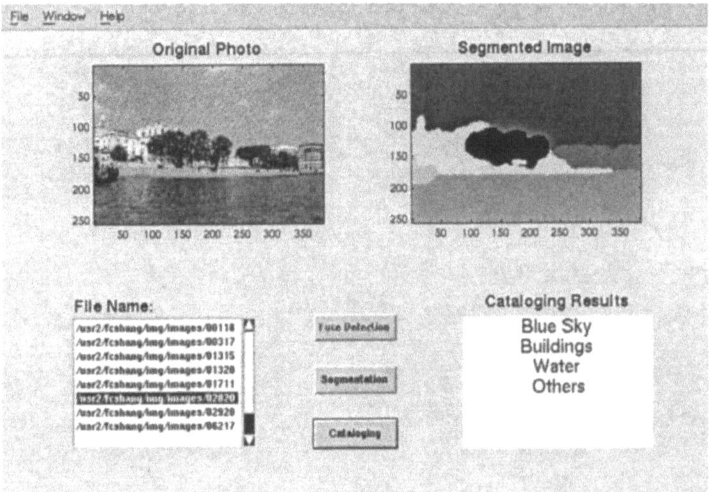

Figure 4.17: Automatic cataloging results.

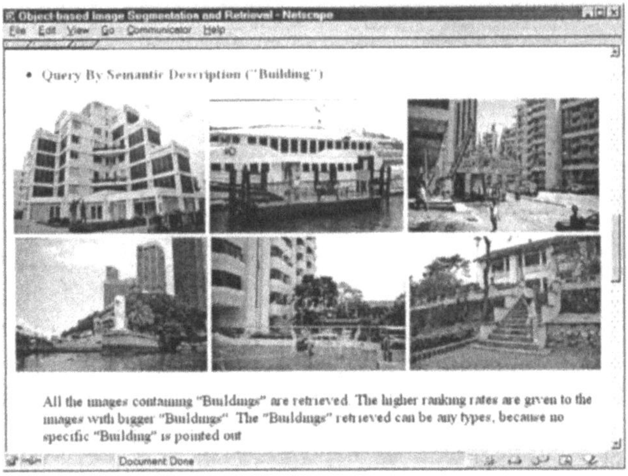

Figure 4.18: Query results by semantic descriptions.

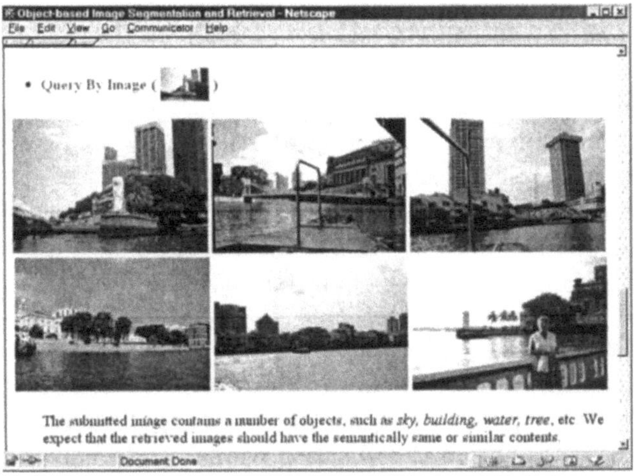

Figure 4.19: Query results by images.

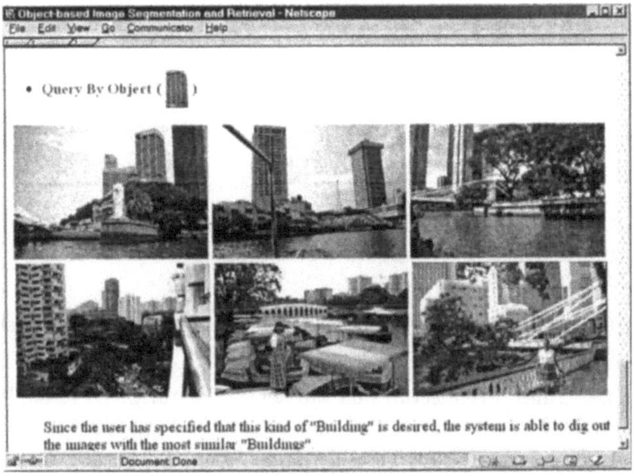

Figure 4.20: Query results by visual objects.

land), and query by similar image content (in terms of object categories and appearance). The preliminary experimental results presented here are based on the six defined objects: *Tree, Sky, Water, Field, Mountain* and *Building.* In this experiment, users submit the queries in three ways:

1. Query by semantic descriptions: Users submit queries by one or a few semantic descriptions that describe the desired contents in images. The valid semantic descriptions are the object category titles already defined in the system. From the vague instructions, it is unlikely to accurately estimate the actual needs of the users due to the variant appearances of objects(shown in Figure 4.18).

2. Query by images: Users submit queries by one or a few images. By examining the contents in the image(s), the system is able to estimate the requirements of the users more specifically. As no specific object is located, the estimation of the users' requirements is not accurate(shown in Figure 4.19).

3. Query by visual objects: Users submit queries by pointing out one or a few visual object(s) presented in images, which represent more specific contents for the image retrieval. By the information extracted from the visual object(s), the system is able to understand the particular query requirements more accurately(shown in Figure 4.20).

References

1. T. R. Reed, J. M. Hans du Buf, "A Review of Recent Texture Segmentation and Feature Extraction Techniques", CVGIP: Image Understanding, Vol. 57, No. 3, pp. 359-372, 1993

2. P. Brodatz, "Textures: A photographic album for artists and designers", Dover Publications, New York, 1966

3. I. Daubechies, "Ten lectures on wavelets", Capital City Press, Montpelier, Vermont, 1992

4. S. Belongie, C. Carson, H. Greenspan, J. Malik, "Color- and Texture-based Image Segmentation Using EM Algorithm and Its Application to Content-Based Image Retrieval", International Conference on Computer Vision, Bombay, India, 1998

5. S. Livens, et al, "Wavelet for Texture Analysis: What is Texture.", http://wcc.ruca.ua.ac.be/livens/WTA/textu.html

6. J. R. Smith, "Integrated Spatial and Feature Image Systems: Retrieval, Analysis and Compression", Thesis of PhD, Graduate School of Arts and Science, Columbia University, 1997

7. F. Liu, "Modeling Spatial and Temporal Textures", Thesis of PhD, Media Arts and Sciences, School of Architecture and Planning, MIT, 1997

8. F. Liu, W. Picard, "Periodicity, Directionality, and Randomness: Wold Features for Image Modeling and Retrieval", IEEE Trans. on PAMI, Vol. 18, No. 7, pp. 722-733, 1996

9. R. Picard, F. Liu, "A new Wold Ordering for Image Similarity", IEEE Trans. on Image Processing, Vol. 5, No. 5, 771-779, 1996

10. I. Pitas, "Digital Image Processing Algorithms", Prentice Hall, 1993

11. T. Chang, C. J. Kuo, "Texture Analysis and Classification with Tree Structured Wavelet Transform", IEEE Trans. on Image Processing, Vol. 5, No. 5, 771-779, 1996

12. P. P. Raghu, B. Yegnanarayana, "Segmentation of Gabor-Filtered Textures Using Deterministic Relaxation", IEEE Trans. on Image Processing, Vol. 5, No. 12, pp. 1625-1639, 1996

13. S. Belongie, C. Carson, H. Greenspan, J. Malik, "Recognition of Images in Large Databases Using a Learning Framework", Technical Report Rep. 939, Computer Science Division, University of California, Berkeley, 1997

Chapter 5

Video Processing

Among the media delivered through the Internet, digital video is playing an increasingly important role. Digital TV has been mandated as the future of television in many countries. The most important is the United States, where all TV broadcasts will be digital by 2006. HDTV broadcasts will start soon, and consumer HDTV sets are already selling in the US. In recent years, the development of compression and networking technology has enabled the creation of a large amount of digital video content. Owing to the rapid increase in the size of digital video databases, users are being provided with a very broad selection of video content, and thus they require more flexible as well as powerful video handling tools. Therefore, development of advanced video data management tools is a very important area of research.

From the video production process to the storage of video data, video data management is diverse and covers almost every aspect of audio, image, text and other medium processing technique. For example, given a video sequence, we can recompile it or attach it to another video. Both image and audio content of the video could be manipulated using image processing and audio processing techniques to obtain special results. Also, image and audio content of interest could be extracted based on the retrieval technique. Other kinds of manipulation include data protection, data compression etc. In this chapter, we focus on the indexing of digital video and its application on video retrieval.

Because of the temporal redundancy of video frames, segmentation of video sequence into small partitions is always the first step of video indexing. This is also the basis of most of the other processes. Since the video data is very large, and with redundancy, it is very important to select one image to represent a series of images having very similar content. Based on the conventional video production process, we can divide video into scenes and shots which represent periods of continuous camera action.

Content based image retrieval systems like Core[33], QBIC[11] and Virage[4] have focused on the static low level features of images in a large image and video database. While some other systems, Video-Book[17], for example, have incorporated the motion feature, all of them stay at the low-level feature stage. To advance to a level higher, video frame structure should be analyzed. In this chapter, we will also talk about our indexing method for this purpose. The main aim of our feature based indexing work is to get the key points on each representative frame and cluster them according to their motion features. Building a video retrieval system based on such indexing method is our on-going work.

In this chapter, the video data characteristics and related techniques are discussed in section 1. An overview of the state of the art of current research on video data management is presented in this section as well. Section 2 presents a new method on content based representative frame extraction. The criterion, the extraction process with experimental results are described. The applications of video summary are also demonstrated.

5.1 Review of Video Processing Techniques

In this section, we will discuss the background of video processing techniques and review the state-of-the-art of video processing techniques. Since video processing covers a wide range of research topics, it is impossible to discuss it in detail in this chapter. Therefore, we only concentrate on the software related topics.

When we talk about video processing, the first question we should answer is "What is video?" While we focus on the visual content of video data, the video is a medium which has both visual and audio content. In this chapter, video refers to the visual content unless explicitly pointed out.

5.1.1 Video features

Video is very different from other media like text, audio, etc. These unique features make watching a video generally more enjoyable. So, we base our research on these features.

One feature of video is that it is a kind of non-alphanumeric data, which can not be defined by a finite set of symbols. This can be seen from its primitive production process. Using a video camera to record a scene or using an audio recorder to record an audio signal does not usually require text or numeric representation. Therefore, description and representation of video data usually go with similarity measurement. Actually, the information existing in it is so large that it is almost impossible to describe it using a finite set of words. This is a common feature of multimedia. As far as this work is concerned, the objective of video analysis is to use limited "words" to describe unlimited video content.

Another feature of video lies in its large volume. This large volume requires a large space to store it, a large bandwidth to transfer it and a long time to manipulate it. Therefore, video data usually exists in a compressed manner. Video standards like MPEG, H.261 etc. consider the compression aspect as the most important part.

The third feature of video comes from its multi dimensional components. Not taking audio content into account, if we regard the video frames as two dimensional signal, then video is three-dimensional with the third dimension coming from time. Because of its multi-dimensional feature, video content is much richer than its components and thus provides more information than them.

5.1.2 Video applications

Video has such a wide range of applications that today it is a part of our daily life. Although researchers have tried to provide a general approach to process video, because of the limitation of the available techniques, most of them still provide solutions restricted to a special domain with typical features. A model would usually be constructed to process a special domain video. The solutions are usually ad hoc, but they are suitable for some practical applications. Therefore, it is necessary for us to understand the class of a given video. The class of a video determines its production process, content features, application areas and processing methods.

Transport video, security video, etc. have been successfully developed for scientific usage for a long time. The production process of these videos is very largely with a fixed camera position. Their production is passive. Video content is also constrained and fairly well defined. For example, the content of transport video mainly contains cars detected by a camera when passing by it, the content of a security video mainly contains people within the range of a camera. Unique background, few objects and simple motion styles make object analysis easier for these videos than for other kinds of videos.

The content of sports video and news video has a wider range, but it is still highly structured. For example, soccer video would have a grass field as background, the lines and gates in fixed positions, the players wearing conforming clothes. News video does not have fixed background, but it is temporally structured. Each part of news video has anchor-person(s) sitting in a fixed position. The structural content is very suitable for model based content analysis.

The feature film video is much more complex in content. Its main purpose is to provide entertainment for people. Feature film video has subjects, plots and story units which convey information of high level. We can also further classify the video into different categories, like war movies, western movies etc. Since the theme of this kind of video is to reflect human activities, it is featured with limited number of roles. As a result, automatic searching of people in this kind of video is very important for indexing.

5.1.3 Research areas

The emergence of video is due to the development of several closely related research areas. Video processing is a combination of techniques of signal processing, data compression, computer vision, networking, etc. In this chapter, we emphasize on the software aspect. Here, we classify video processing into the following five areas:indexing and retrieval, data management, representation,interaction and data compression.

Indexing and Retrieval. We always begin the video data analysis by dividing it into small partitions. This makes it easier to access video data. Therefore, devising a fast algorithm to partition video is a very important issue. On the other hand, how to organize the indexed data into a proper database is also important. Because it will determine the way of accessing the data. With the indexed data, diverse retrieval methods could be implemented. The underlying issue here is how to measure the similarity of images, sequences, etc and how to present retrieval results.

Data Management. Editing of video data is part of video production process. Before the video data is finally assembled, data insertion, data cutting and effect processing are usually needed. We can group the management of indexing and retrieval data into this area as well. A powerful video data management system is the basis of other video applications.

Representation. Once the content of the video is indexed, it is necessary to represent it. The representation of video data could be icons, text, or other kinds of content transformations. Semantic summarization of video plots, story units also belong to this issue. Whether transforming video content into a different domain or not, representation of video data is to describe it in a more compact way, temporally, spatially or both.

Interaction. With the interactive tools, users can fully utilize the video data. The function of user interface is as important as the function of video data itself. The user interface includes the ways a user plays or browses a video. It can also include the ways of querying and representing video content. By interacting with video systems, users can be more active in accessing video data.
Compression. Data compression technique is always an important issue in video processing. When we talk about data compression techniques, we refer not only to the compressing of large amount of data, but also to the processing of video data in the compression domain. The objective of the latter is to improve the processing speed by avoiding the decoding process. This approach is receiving more and more attention recently.

5.1.4 State of the art review

In this section we will discuss about the state of the art of the research areas related to video processing.

Video segmentation

While Sun [25] developed an algorithm to extract representative frames without shot detection, most other researchers have focused on shot detection. The basic assumption of shot detection is that low level features of frames at shot boundaries would change abruptly and high above those in other places.

Techniques involved in shot detection are pixel differences, statistical differences, histogram comparisons, edge differences, compression differences and motion vectors. Comparison of these techniques could be found in [6].

Zhang [38], Shahraray[23] and Hampapur [13] applied the pixel difference technique between two consecutive frames as metric to detect shot boundaries. The differences were computed upon individual pixels, or image regions, or chromatic images of the two frames. When the difference exceeded a threshold, a cut or shot boundary was declared. The method was sensitive to camera motion. In [18], images were broken into regions and the statistical measures of those regions were compared to get frame differences. This method tolerates noise, but it was slow and might generate a lot of false positives. Nagasaka [21], Swanberg [28], Zhang [38], Ueda [31], applied histogram comparison technique to detect shot boundaries. The bin-wise difference between the color or gray level histograms of two frames was computed in different ways in their work. Threshold was also set for detection.

Little [19], and Arman [2] detect shot boundaries in the compression domain. Difference in the size of compressed frames and coefficients were used to detect change. This method avoids the need to decompress video frames, so the detection process can be speeded up.

Zabih [36] use edge detection technique to detect different kinds of video boundaries. Since the method detect the edge feature of images, it is less sensitive to motion and scaling.

Zhang [38], Ueda [31] and Shahraray[23] applied motion vectors in their shot detection work. Because motion vector information can be obtained from MPEG videos, this method will also speedup processing. However, because the MPEG video use a strategy which may lead to wrong motion estimation, the performance of block matching is not very good.

Video indexing

Our primary concern of the indexing technique is with the retrieval of video information. We classify related techniques into high level, low level and model based areas.

The high level indexing techniques like those of Davis[10] and Davenport [9] provided global representations and archives for retrieval of video content in a layered or annotated way. Bimbo [5] also developed a symbolic language to represent spatial relationship between objects.

The low level indexing techniques utilize the segmentation techniques mentioned above to index image sequences. In the system of [14], the motion properties of objects was adopted for indexing. Motion vectors were mapped into spatio-temporal space and the relevant trajectories were used for vector groups. In the system of [2], one frame from each detected shots was extracted to index a video. Based on the so called R-frames, browsing and retrieval could be achieved. In [25], fixed percent of video frames were extracted to index the whole video. The frames could be extracted using different kinds of low level features.

Video retrieval

Retrieval of images from a video database is similar to the retrieval of images from a image database if we do not consider the dynamic feature of video content. Therefore, the techniques developed by systems like CORE[33], QBIC[11] and Virage[4] still work on video images. Some of their developers claim that their systems are for both images and videos.

In [1], [17], [15], etc. motion feature was considered. For example, in the Video-Book[17] system, low level image features as well as motion are used for the comparison of different video sequences. In [15], the motion trajectories are detected and indexed. The object motion styles could be retrieved based on the indexed data.

Video representation

Video frames can be sub-sampled or mixed to represent video content. If segmentation is for the indexing of video data, representation provides a concrete way to index or to describe video content. In the IMPACT[32], for example, a global structured view of a video document was introduced. In [30] and [16], automatic construction of images representing video content was proposed.

Video summary

A digital video is usually very long, therefore it is important to summarize its content for a variety of uses. In this chapter, we propose a method of summarizing which is based on our representative frame extraction technique. Representative frames plus its a number of following frames will provide a kind of summary with a dynamic feature. In [41] and [35], the methods of abstracting of video shots into similar clusters were proposed. Their objective was to describe the video content in structures. The ultimate objective of video summary is to provide semantic analysis of video content.

Video compressed domain manipulation

Manipulation of video data in compressed domain will speedup a video data processing because it will avoid the decoding of compressed data into the uncompressed domain.

Shen [26], Smith [27], Chiptprasert [8] and Chang [7] have proposed methods for processing video images in DCT domain. The methods could realize common image processing techniques like filtering, translation, scaling etc.

Zhang [39], Arman [2] and Yeung [35] have proposed methods of indexing video in compressed domain. Because the temporal segmentation of video frames is to find changes of content and the changes of content are reflected by the changes of the coefficients in the compressed domain, in [2] compression coefficients are used to detect shot boundaries. Since the indexing technique does not require exact image matching, some researchers, like [35], tried to speed up processing using degraded images by eliminating parts of coefficients.

5.2 Content-Based Representative Frame Extraction and Video Summary

A digital video is temporally very long, requiring a large storage capacity. Therefore, given a long video, a user would like to obtain a pre-determined fixed number of important frames to describe the video. This would help the user in getting an approximate idea of the video content. This number can be 5 or 10 percent of the total number of frames in the original video. Such a request is reasonable since a video normally contains much redundant information. The objective of this work is actually to temporally compress a digital video for a given length criterion. In this chapter, we will discuss how to achieve this objective by using our adaptive clustering method. We will also show its applications on content-based video browsing and summary.

5.2.1 Definition

While much work has been done on video indexing and browsing, the work of extracting a fixed number of important frames from a given video has not been addressed by researchers. Here, we term the important frames as *representative frames* (R-frames). Some researchers call them key frames as well[24,38]. The representative frames therefore should reflect the content changes of a video. Even now, automatic understanding of image and video content in terms of semantics is not possible. So video processing is still based on low-level features like color, motion, shape, texture etc.[40]. As a result, in this chapter we also base our analysis on these low-level features. However, unlike shot detection, our work is not based on the assumption that all kinds of low level features like color, motion, shape, texture, etc. change somewhat abruptly at shot boundaries. For extracting representative frames, our result depends on the selected low-level feature of interest. This is because each different low-level feature changes in a different manner even in the same video. For example, in a soccer game, the most dynamically changing low-level feature is motion and not color. The above requirements can be formally described as:

Given:

- an ordered set of input digital video sequence V with cardinality N. $V = F_1, F_2, ..., F_N$, where $F_1, F_2, ..., F_N$ are the frames of V.

- a ratio α such that $0 < \alpha < 1$.
- low-level content P of {color, motion, ...}.

To extract:
a set of output frames V' with cardinality of N'.

$$V' = \{R_{p1}, R_{p2}, ...R_{pN'}\} \tag{5.1}$$

where,

- $N' = N * \alpha$.
- $R_{p1}, R_{p2}, ..., R_{pN'} \in V$, are the representative frames of V with respect to feature P.
- $V' \in V$.

So, basically given a digital video V having N frames, we would like to extract an $N * \alpha$ cardinality subset of frames which best represents the content P of the video V.

5.2.2 Related work

An example of early work on video content analysis was carried out by Connor[22]. Specific object changes are detected for key frames. Mills [20] applied the temporal sub-sampling method in their "magnifier tool". Finkelstein [12] utilized a multi-resolution method for video browsing, which can both spatially and temporally subsample a video sequence.

After the development of shot detection techniques, researchers would select one frame(usually the first frame) from a shot to represent the entire shot. One example of such work is the content-browsing system by Arman [2]. Boreczky [6] compared shot boundary detection techniques such as pixel differences, statistical differences, compression differences, edge track tracking etc. Using shots as the basic unit is not enough for detailed video analysis, so other researchers have focused their work on finding representative frames.

In Zhang [40], color and motion features are utilized for key frame extraction based on shot detection. For the color feature based criterion, the first frame is used both as a reference frame and as a key frame in the beginning. The distances to this frame from the subsequent frames are computed. When the distance exceeds a given threshold, a new representative frame is claimed and the claimed frame serves as the new reference frame for the following frames. For the motion feature based criterion, mainly two types of motions – pans and zooms are detected. The first and the last frame of a zooming process are taken as key frames. For the panning process, key frames are extracted depending on the scale of panning. The aim of this work is not to solve the problem we put forward, but it is a large step beyond the usual one key frame per shot methods of video description.

Smith [24] have proposed a method of selecting key frames based on audio, image and text. The audio track is created based on keywords. The image frames are selected using a ranking system which regards faces or text as most important, static frames following camera motion the second important, etc. Though the integration of speech, language and image information is the best way to understand a video, the generation of key frames based on such a technique still requires manual intervention and there is a lot of scope for further improvement.

Until now, most of the previous work on video parsing was based on the shot detection technique. Detection of shot comes naturally from the video production process but it is difficult to accurately detect all shot boundaries in a video. While Hampapur [13] proposed using post production editing frames to detect shot boundaries, advanced video editing techniques can blur the shot boundaries as well. The morphing technique, for example, can process a video in a way that even humans cannot find the explicit shot boundaries in it. One example of such a video is employed in our experiment in section 3.2.4. Therefore, the question arises – can we effectively extract representative frames without detecting the shot boundaries?

To meet the above considerations, in out work we propose the *CBAC* technique that can extract a fixed number of representative frames from a video without shot detection. Different fractions of a video possessing different number of frames can thus be computed based on any desired low-level feature. When required, they can be retrieved and utilized for diverse applications.

5.2.3 Extraction of representative frames

Suppose a user is asked to select some important frames of a video based on a typical low-level content like color, motion, shape or texture. He will probably make the choice based on the amount of change of the low-level content. In the places where there are more changes he will choose more frames and will choose a lesser number of frames where there is less content change. In fact, the work of extracting representative frames is based on such an assumption.

Spatial feature of video frames

If we use an M-dimensional feature to analyze a video, each frame of the video maps to a point in the Euclidean space E_M. The visual similarity between any two frames is well reflected by the distance between the two corresponding points in the space. Thus the entire sequence of video frames maps to a set of points in the$M$-dimensional space. The temporal succession of the frames in the video traces a corresponding trajectory of points in the feature space. Thus the video begins from a point which corresponds to the first frame and the temporal sequence of frames subsequently traces a path through the points in the space. When the content of frames changes quickly, the path also moves quickly with a larger step size between the points. When the feature changes slowly, the points are also more closely spaced on the path. The feature could be color, motion, shape or texture. We base our work on color. As histogram is a good tool [38]for video processing, we describe our algorithm using histogram. However, it must be noted that our technique is more general and can be used with the other low-level content with appropriate feature measures.

Given two M bins color histograms of two images, the distance metric for image retrieval is as followed[11]:

$$D^2(X,O) = (X-O)^T A(X-O) = \sum_{i=1}^{M}\sum_{j=1}^{M} a_{ij}(X_i - O_i)(X_j - O_j) \quad (5.2)$$

where $A(a_{ij})$ is an $M * M$ matrix, and a_{ij}represents the proximity of the bin i and j; X_i and Ojdenotes the histogram value of X and O respectively. When A is an identity matrix, equation (5.2) yields the Euclidean distance.

In our implementation, to save computational time without degrading performance[38], we use the gray-level histogram city-block distance as the metric:

$$D_c(X,O) = \sum_{i=1}^{M-1} |X_i - O_i| \quad (5.3)$$

If we use the first frame of a video as the reference frame and compute the distances of this frame to all the subsequent frames, we can map all the frames to a one-dimensional discrete signal. This method is similar to [40], except that only the first frame of the whole video rather than the first frame of each shot is selected as the reference frame.

Suppose O is the histogram of the first frame of a video and we use it as the reference frame, X is the histogram of a randomly selected frame from the same video. Given a constant $\omega > 0$, if the video moves on a hyper-cube:

$$\sum_{i=1}^{M} |X_i - O_i| = \omega \tag{5.4}$$

then, such distance measurement can not detect any change. For the sake of simplicity, in Figure 5.1 we assume $M = 2$ and O, A, B, C are frames of a video. So all the points are located on the same plane. If we use O as a reference point, because $OB \perp AC$, on the line ABC we can not detect any distance change. Actually, we can see that the distance between A and C is even larger than that of OA. Figure 5.2 shows an example video

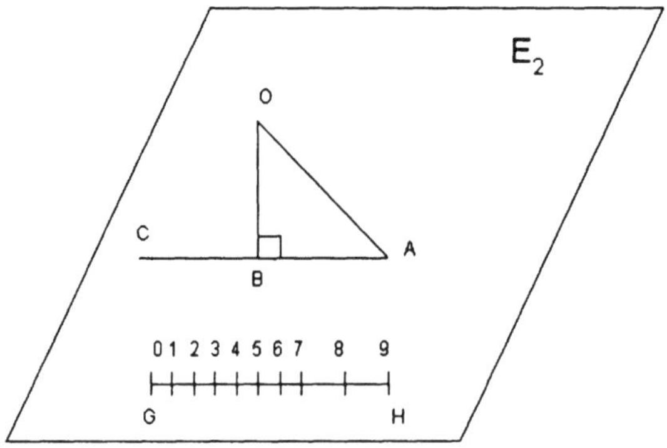

Figure 5.1: Examples of video trajectories in the feature space. $M = 2$.

with such a problem. A test video "skate" starts with a black picture whose histogram is $O = (S, 0, ...0)$, where S is the number of pixels of each frame. If we use the M-bin histogram for analysis, then according to equation (5.3) we can obtain:

$$D_c(X, O) = \sum_{i=0}^{M-1} |X_i - O_i| = 2S - 2X_0 \tag{5.5}$$

This will reflect changes only of the first bin of each frame. In the beginning, for more than 100 frames, X_0 is very similar, so the above distance will not detect change although the real content (and the value of other bins) changes a lot.

Similarly, we can also apply this analysis to the Euclidean distance measure (the problem occurs when the points corresponding to frames move on a hyper-sphere in the feature space) and equation (5.2). Although

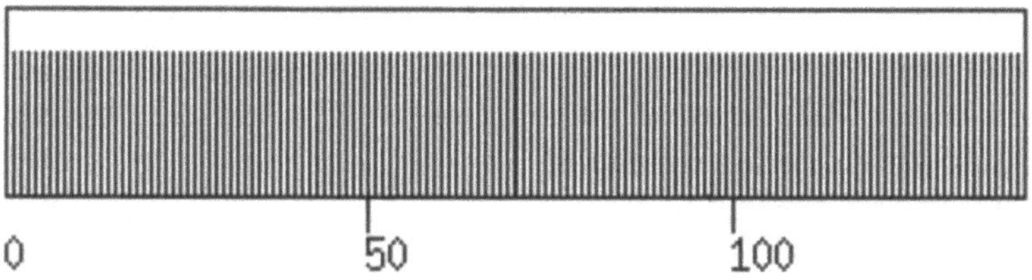

The Distances to the First Frame

Frame 0 Frame 60

Figure 5.2: Part of experiment result on "skate"

the severity of the above problem may vary with the metric selected, since a video is generally very long, the overall possibility of the problem occurring is still significant.

In [40], the first frame of each shot is used as the reference frame in the beginning and its distances to the subsequent frames are computed. When the distance exceeds a given threshold, a representative frame is claimed and the claimed frame serves as a new reference frame. By changing the reference frame intermittently, the errors due to the above problem may be limited. However, the above problem still persists. In the case we require a very small fraction of frames to be extracted, it will require a big threshold. So it is possible that this may introduce large errors.

Also, if we want to extract a fixed pre-determined number of frames from a video, then it will be very difficult to control the output number by controlling the threshold. Moreover, our aim is to extract representative frame without shot detection. Therefore, we would like to pursue other solutions which can avoid these difficulties.

Using clustering method for extraction of representative frames

As described earlier, the temporal sequence of frames of a video maps to a trajectory of points in the feature space. The nature of the spatial distribution of the points corresponding to a video can be described as clusters connected by abrupt or gradual changes. During most of the time, the trajectory will move around in a small cluster. It is impossible for all the frames in a video to be spatially far apart and thus have unrelated content, because the frames of a video work together to convey meaningful information. This nature of the distribution of points provides a sound basis for our clustering technique.

Clustering Criterion If we regard a video V as the set of N points in the multi-dimensional feature space, then the representative frames in fact divide V into N' clusters. We call such clusters *units* in the context. The units are temporally contiguous and they are delineated by the representative frames R_{p1} to $R_{pN'}$. According to equation (5.1), we can also use the units to describe V as:

$$V = U_1 \circ U_2 \circ \ldots \circ U_N' \tag{5.6}$$

where,

- $U_i = R_{pi}, R_{pi1}, \ldots, R_{p(i+1)}, i \in [1, N']$
- $\circ$ is the temporal concatenation operation

Since we are analyzing the feature-points trajectory of a video in temporally localized regions, it is possible to use the change between consecutive representative frames to represent the change within a unit. Given a unit U_i and a selected feature P, we define the *unit change* as following:

$$Change(U_i) = D_c(R_{pi}, R_{p(i+1)}) \tag{5.7}$$

From the optimization point of view, given a selected feature, the objective of representative extraction is to divide a video into units that have very similar unit changes. Our algorithm should thus try to make the unit changes as similar as possible. This can be described as to minimize:

$$\sum_{i=1}^{N'-1} \sum_{j=i+1}^{N'-1} |Change(U_i) - Change(U_j)| \tag{5.8}$$

Therefore, we base our algorithm on this criterion. We begin the algorithm with finely divided units which are classified into two clusters after each iteration. And then the units are modified by deleting redundant frames from the units of one of the clusters so as to make the unit changes similar. This clustering and deletion process is carried out several times. The algorithm thus iteratively converges to the desired number of units in an adaptive way based on the content change within units.

Adaptive extraction process The whole process of our clustering algorithm is shown in Figure 5.3. Here, we will provide the description.

For a given video V with length N, suppose we want to extract N' representative frames. The feature (in this work we use histogram) of each frame in V is computed first. This algorithm works in an iterative fashion. We start initially with all the frames of the video and iteratively drop frames till the desired result is obtained.

The sequence of the video frames is partitioned into small units whose length are all L. All the units are temporally consecutive. Figure 5.4 shows the partitioning with $L = 2$ and $L = 3$ respectively. The units for $L = 3$ are $\{(0,1,2),(2,3,4),(4,5,6),(6,7,8)\}$. In each unit, the unit change is computed, which is the distance between the first frame and the last frame of the unit. The computed changes stand for each unit and they construct an array of length $K = \lceil(N/(L-1)\rceil$. Because our objective is to extract representative frames according to frame content changes, the changes do reflect the actual degree of content change in all the units. This is because the distance metric is computed in a temporally localized region. By sorting the unit changes in an ascending manner, we get an array which represents the general content change of the video. The elements which are located in the beginning part of the array represent the frames where there are small changes, while the units in the later part consists of frames having large changes.

By selecting a ratio $0 < r < 1$ we cluster the array into two clusters according to the value of unit change. The first cluster comprises of the smallest elements of the array and its length is $K * r$, here we call it the *small-change cluster*. The rest of the elements comprise the *large-change cluster*.

If the change of a unit belongs to the currently large-change cluster, then we take all of its frames as part of the current extracted representative frames. If the change of a unit belongs to the small-change cluster, then we will delete all the frames except the first and the last frames from the unit. The first and the last frames are retained as part of the current extracted representative frames. After the deletion process, $K * r * (L-2)$ frames will be deleted.

Suppose the number of frames left is N''. If $N' \geq N''$, then our desired result is obtained and we can stop the algorithm. If it is not true, we can dynamically regroup all the retained frames as a new video and repeat the last procedure.

With the decrease in the number of frames for comparison, small units are consequently clustered together. A unit will physically span across more frames in the original video. So it will adaptively represent a larger range of frame changes in the original video. The smaller the number we

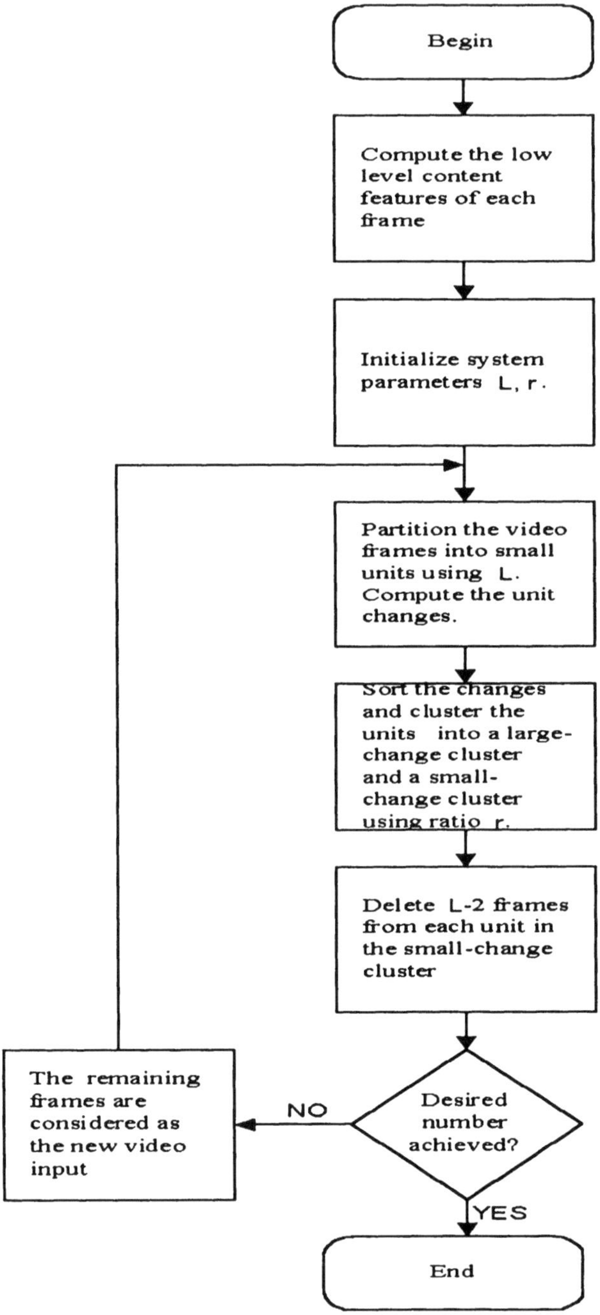

Figure 5.3: Adaptive clustering algorithm

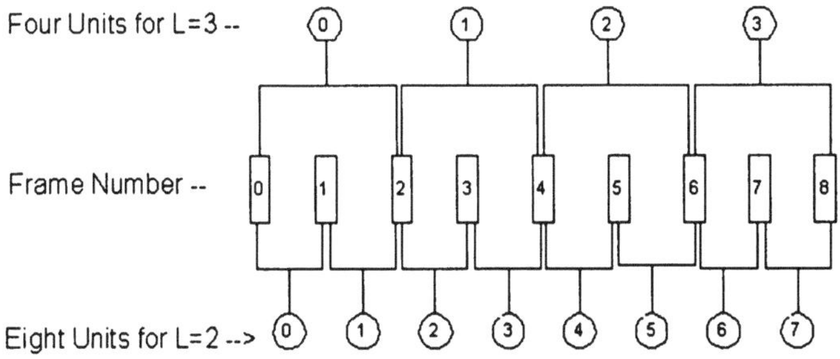

Figure 5.4: Sequence partitions

desire, the more times the algorithm would adaptively repeat the procedure. After each iterative process, there will be frames deleted from the sequence, so the overall number of frames left will decrease each time. Therefore, no matter how small a number may be required, the algorithm will adaptively and iteratively converge to the desired requirement.

Throughout the algorithm, shot boundaries do not need to be detected. The algorithm will automatically converge. So, an adaptive way of extracting is achieved.

Selection of Parameters

As the whole extraction process is basically unsupervised, the result will depend on the proper selection of the parameters L and r.

1) Selection of L

If $L = 2$, the distance is in fact consecutive frame difference. Consecutive frame difference has been successfully applied for shot detection, but it is not suitable for finding representative frames. As illustrated in Figure 5.1, assume on line GH are ten frames of a video. They are labeled 0 to 9. Their positions are shown as ticks on the line in the figure. Each step in 7 - 9 is larger than those in 0-7. Suppose we want to select 2 frames from G-H and use consecutive frame difference as measurement, we would delete all the frames in 0-7. However, the overall distance from 0-7 is actually even larger than that of 7-9, so we should extract at least one frame in 0-7. The failure of consecutive frame difference arises from the fact that it loses the cumulative change information in a video.

In general, if we use a large L, the algorithm will converge very fast and it will save a lot of computation time. In the beginning of the algorithm, a large L will not degrade result. However, if the required number is very small, the algorithm will iterate many times. With the iterations of the algorithm, the unit will in the end may physically span across many frames. Consequently, the smaller the L is, the better the result quality will be. Table 5.1 shows the frame numbers extracted from our test video "news". Its content is listed in Table 5.3. Required representative number is $N' = 330 * 0.05 \simeq 17$. When $L = 3$, the main information is indeed extracted by the algorithm but when $L = 5$, frames of section 4 are all missed. In practice, if a video is very short, then we use $L = 3$ in the algorithm. If the video is very long, then we use a variable L. In the beginning of algorithm, we let $L = 5$ and when the extracted number drops to no more than 20% of original video, we then change L to 3.

L	r	Nr	Representative Frames
3	0.3	16	0 67 68 78 109 110 114 118 169 170 258 259 265 300 306 307
5	0.3	17	0 67 68 69 70 113 114 115 116 168 265 299 300 301 305 306 307

Table 5.1: The extracted frames of "news", N'=17. Nr is the actually extracted number. The positions of the frames for $L = 3$ and $L = 5$ are displayed in Figure 5.9.e and 5.9.f respectively.

2) Selection of r

If $L = 3$ or 5, then 1 or 3 frames in each unit of the small-distance cluster will be deleted after the execution of one loop of the iterative algorithm. Accordingly, if before the iteration the retained number is N'', then after the iteration, around

$$\begin{aligned} N''/2 * r * 1 &= N'' * r * (1/2) \quad for \quad L = 3 \\ N''/4 * r * 3 &= N'' * r * (3/4) \quad for \quad L = 5 \end{aligned} \tag{5.9}$$

number of the frames will be deleted.

In many cases, it is really not critical that the number of extracted representative frames is strictly equal to the required number. Assume that the maximum allowed error is 20%. Then we can calculate that the maximum allowed r is

$$\begin{aligned} r &= 0.2/(1/2) = 0.4 \quad for \quad L = 3, \\ r &= 0.2/(3/4) \simeq 0.3 \quad for \quad L = 5 \end{aligned} \tag{5.10}$$

Since the bigger the ratio r, the faster the algorithm converges, we try to use the largest r that we can possibly use in our algorithm. In practice, we select a $r = 0.3$ in our work.

Experimental results

As our aim is to extract representative frames without shot detection, here we classify the videos into two types, one type is the video with explicit shot boundaries and the other is without explicit boundary. We provide experimental results on the two types of videos to see how the algorithm works effectively.

Section	Range	Content	Section	Range	Content
1	0-41	The first man's head is moving	4	148-205	The second man's head is moving
2	38-89	The first girl's head is moving	5	203-243	The third girl's head is moving
3	89-150	The second girl's head is moving			

Table 5.2: The content of "mjackson"

Section	Range	Content	Section	Range	Content
1	0-67	Two anchor persons are speaking	4	170-258	An official is commenting
2	68-109	The first girl is receiving award	5	259-306	The second girl is receiving award
3	110-169	A man is receiving award	6	307-329	The third girl is receiving award

Table 5.3: The content of "news"

1) Video without explicit shot boundaries

The content of our test video "mjackson" is shown in Table 5.2. The morphing technique has been used in the video sequence. The changes

Figure 5.5: The representative frames in Figure 5.8.e of "mjackson"

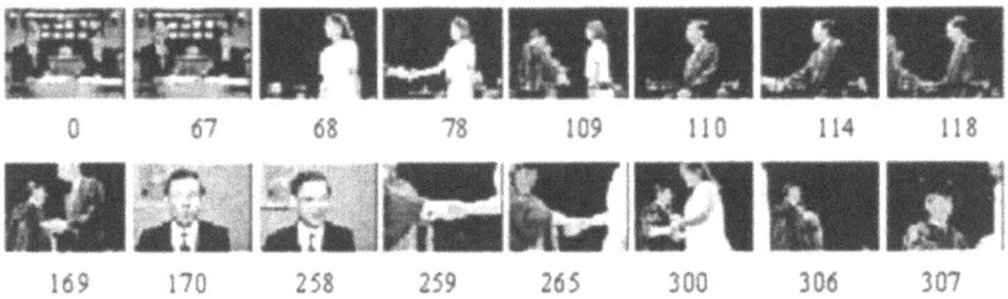

Figure 5.6: The representative frames of Figure 5.9.e in "news"

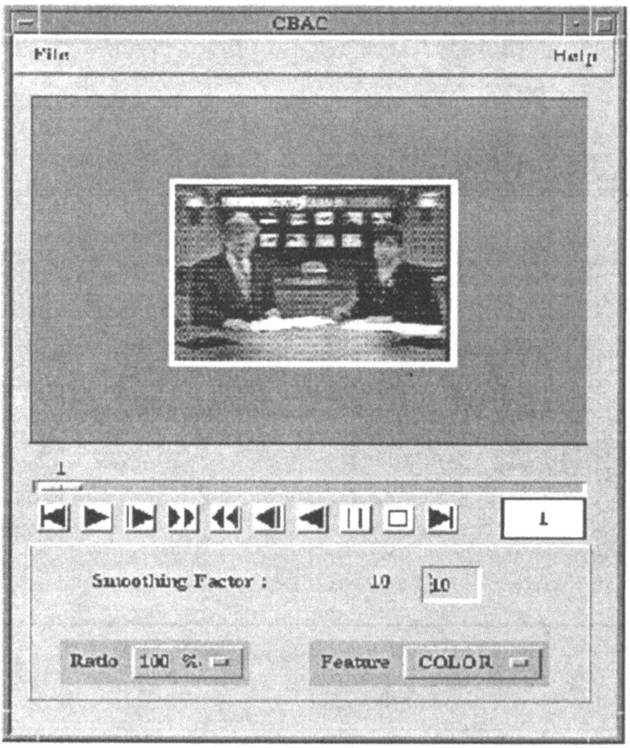

Figure 5.7: The CBAC MPEG video player

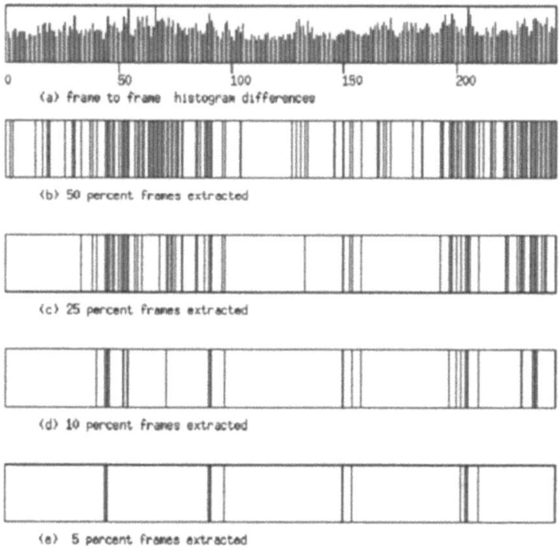

Figure 5.8: Experiment result on "mjackson". The vertical lines in b, c, d and e represent the positions of extracted representative frames. $L = 3, r = 0.3$

across the sections are gradual and it is very difficult even for human beings to define precisely where the shot boundaries exist. So, we only give a rough boundary in the table. There have been a lot of techniques proposed by researchers on video segmentation, yet none of them has claimed work on this kind of video. Figure 5.8.a shows the consecutive frame histogram differences of "mjackson". If we apply the threshold method proposed in Zhang [38], apparently we can not detect any shot boundary in it. However, using CBAC, we successfully extract representative frames from the video according to content changes. When required number reaches 5 percent length of the original video, the main information of the video is still captured very well in the representative frames.

2) Video with explicit shot boundaries

Table 5.3 shows the content of our test video "news". In section 1 and 4, there are only people speaking and the video content changes very little. This can also be seen in Figure 5.9.a which shows the distances to the first frame for all frames in the video. The result shows that though the two sections are much longer than other sections, the number of extracted representative frames from them are smaller than all other sections for all the fractions selected. Representative frames are extracted with respect to

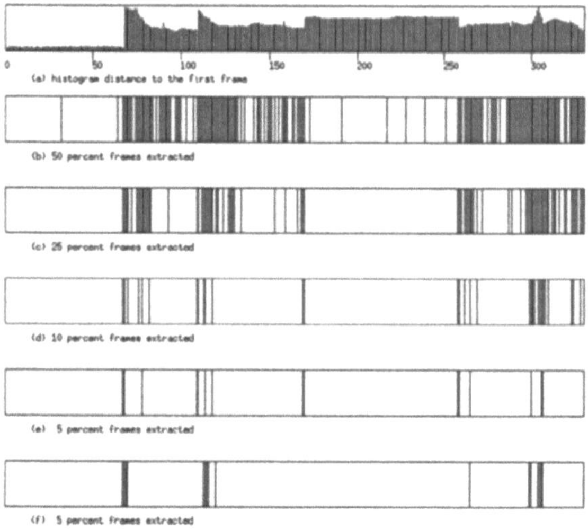

Figure 5.9: Experiment result on "news". The vertical lines in b, c, d and e represent the positions of extracted representative frames for $L = 3, r = 0.3$ The vertical lines in f represent the positions of extracted representative frames for $L = 5, r = 0.3$

the changes of content selected, shown in Figure 5.6. We can also see from the figure, that although we do not explicitly segment a video into shots, the algorithm automatically produces representative frames following the change of shots. Therefore, it can reflect the content of the video very well.

5.2.4 Application of representative frame extraction technique

To gather information from videos, we go back and forth between three stages: grazing, browsing and watching[29]. In the grazing stage, the user is passive, just waiting for interesting information to appear. In the browsing stage, a user interactively searches for information with no specific target in mind. In the watching stage, a user concentrates on understanding information. Since video data is usually very large, before starting a video and begin the understanding stage, it is worthwhile to spend some time getting a general idea about its content. After the extraction of representative frames, we obtain a subset which represents the important content of a video very well. It therefore provides a good basis for the development of video reviewing tools. Based on our content-based representative frame extraction technique, we have developed a CBAC video player system which has the functions of content based browsing and content-based video summary.

Content based video browsing

The functionality of content-based browsing is often compared to the function of a video cassette recorder(VCR). It is the next logical step beyond simple browsing using the fast-forward/rewind (FF/REW) buttons. After the development of shot detection techniques, many efforts have been made by researchers on how to provide an effective browsing tool. These efforts range from using a representative frame in a shot in Arman [2], to the clustering of shots by Yeung [34] and Zhong [40], to the clustering of story units of Yeung [35]. All of the development of such browsing techniques concentrates on providing a general structural description of a video.

In practice, a user mostly wants to use the VCR's fast forward and rewind functions. The user may just want to skip over some uninteresting sequence of frames when watching a video. Because within a shot there maybe many changes, skipping a shot will probably not meet the requirement of the user. The user in fact would like to skip to the next interesting part of a video.

Zhang [40] have proposed a way for extraction of frames from a video for content-based video browsing. But their work does not provide a way to obtain a fixed number of frames for video description. Based on our CBAC technique, we make such a function possible. As the representative frames with respect to a content have been computed and indexed, we can let the user select on-line his feature of interest and the percent of representative frames he would like to use for skipping. The user is thus provided with a very flexible tool.

Content-based video summary

Browsing tools provide interactive functions which help users to get hierarchical views of a video, from a global view to a detailed one. The interactive functionality of a browsing tool is very useful. However, the interaction process itself involves a lot of feedback between the user and the computer. There can be anywhere from 500 to 1000 shots per hour in a typical video program [3]. If one frame of each shot is selected from the video, it will compose a very large structure graph. So, traversing the graph is still very time consuming for many end users. Therefore, many users would prefer a grazing view over the traversal of a browsing structure.

Zhang [38] have proposed a way of finding representative frames within a shot. The extracted frames are output sequentially for video review. However, from the process of frames extraction we can see that these frames are of different content.

From our experiments we have found that if a sequence of unrelated pictures is output sequentially at the normal frame rate, the user will find it very difficult to grasp some information from it. In our content-based video summary, we use the *representative sequences* which is composed of a representative frame plus its several successive frames to describe a video. The length of the following frames is called the *smoothing factor* and can be tuned by a user to obtain a smooth output. If we use equation (5.1) to describe representative frames, then representative sequences can be described as :

$$\begin{aligned} V'' &= V_1 \circ V_2' \circ ...V_{N'}' \\ &= \{R_{p11}, R_{p12}, ..., R_{p1S}\} \circ \\ &\quad \{R_{p21}, R_{p22}, ..., R_{p2S}\} \circ ... \\ &\quad \{R_{pN'1}, R_{pN'2}, ..., R_{pN'S}\} \end{aligned} \tag{5.11}$$

where,

- $S > 0$, is the smoothing factor
- $V_i' = \{R_{pi}, R_{pi1}, ..., R_{piS}\}$, is the representative sequence of R_pi of feature P, $i \in [1, N']$
- $V_1', V_2', ..., V_{N'}' and V'' \in V$
- $\circ$ is the temporal concatenation operation

So, given a video V, we can obtain the representative frames by using CBAC with an appropriately specified ratio. These representative frames can be augmented by "S" successive frames and this entire concatenated sequence constitutes the summary video of V. If $S = 0$, then $V'' = V'$ and the result is the representative frame sequence. From our experiments, we find that to obtain a visually pleasing result, $S = 5$ is the smallest smoothing factor required.

MPEG video player

The video browsing and summary technique has been incorporated in our CBAC system. The system works on the Sun Solaris system and has been written in C using Motif (The software is written based on Brown's MPEG decoders, which is written around the Berkeley's decoders). The user interface of the system is shown in Figure 5.7.

The representative frames pre-computed at different percents and on different features are indexed for a given MPEG video. When a user opens a video file in the system, he has three choices: play, summary and browsing. If he only wants to play the video, he can set the "Ratio" to 100% and click the play button.

If the user wants to perform a content-based reviewing, then he has to select his content of interest by changing the "Feature" first, followed by selecting a ratio(0-1) of the representative frames he wants to use. When he wants to do content-based browsing, he may then just click on the FF/REW buttons to skip to the positions of his interest. Each time the user clicks the FF/REW button, the system will automatically jump to the next/last consecutive representative frame. If he wants a content-based video summary to be played, he has to select the smoothing factor as well. After the selection of a proper smoothing factor, he can press the play button and a representative sequence is displayed. The rightmost button on the top row displays the current frame number.

References

1. E. Ardizzone and M. L. Cascia, " Automatic Video Database Indexing and Retrieval", Multimedia Tools and Applications, 1996
2. F. Arman, R. Depommier, A. Hsu, M. -Y. Chiu, "Image Processing on Encoded Video Sequences", Multimedia Systems, Vol. 1, No. 5, pp. 211-219, 1994
3. P. Aigrain, H. J. Zhang, D. Petkovic, "Content-based Representation and Retrieval of Visual Media: A State-Of-the-Art Review", Multimedia Tools and Applications, Vol. 3, No. 3, pp. 179-202,1996
4. J. R. Bach, C. Fuller, A. Gupta, A. Hampapur, B. Horowitz, R. Humphrey, R. Jain, C. -F. Shu, "The Virage Image Search Engine:An Open Framework for Image Management." Proc. of the SPIE: Storage and Retrieval for Image and Video Databases IV, Vol. 2670, pp. 76-87, San Jose, CA, Feb. 1996.
5. A. D. Bimbo and E. Vicario, "A Logical Framework for Spatio Temporal Indexing of Image Sequences", Spatial Reasoning, 1993
6. J. S. Boreczky, L. A. Rowe, "Comparison of Video Shot Boundary Detection Techniques", Storage and Retrieval for Image and Video Databases IV, Proc.

of IS&T/SPIE 1996 Int'l Symp. on Elec. Imaging: Science and Technology, pp. 170-179, 1996

7. S. -F. Chang, W. -L Chen and D. G. Messerschmitt, "Video Compositing in the DCT Domain", IEE Workshop on Visual Signal Processing and Communications, pp. 138-143, 1992

8. B. Chitprasert and K.R. Rao, "Discrete Cosine Transform Filters", Signal Processing, Vol. 19, pp. 233-245, 1990

9. G. Davenport, T. A. Smith and N. Pincever, "Cinematic Primitives for Multimedia", IEEE Computer Graphics and applications, pp. 67-74, 1991

10. M. Davis, "Media Streams, An Iconic Visual Language for Video Annotation", IEEE Symposium on Visual Languages, pp. 196-202, 1993

11. G. Faloutsos, R. Barber, M. Flickner, J. Hafner, W. Niblack, D. Petkovic and W. Equitz, "Efficient and Effective Querying by Image Content", Journal of Intelligent Information Systems, Vol. 3, pp. 231-262, 1994

12. A. Finkelstein, C. E. Jacobs, D. H. Salesin, "Multiresolution Video", Proc. of SIGGRAPH'96, pp. 281-290, 1996

13. Arun Hampapur, R. Jain, T. Weymouth, "Digital Video Indexing in Multimedia Systems", Proc. Workshop on Indexing and Reuse in Multimedia Systems, American Association of Artificial Intelligence, 1994

14. M. Ioka and M. Kurokawa, "Estimation of Motion Vectors and their Application to Scene Retrieval", IBM Technical Report, 1993

15. M. Ioka and M. Kurokawa, "A Method for Retrieving Sequences of Images on the Basis of Motion Analysis", SPIE Storage and Retrieval Systems, Vol. 1662, pp. 35-46, 1994

16. M. Irani, P. Anandan, J. Bergen, R. Kumar and S. Hsu, "Mosaic Based Representations of Video Sequences and Their Applications", Image Communication Special Issue on Image and Video Semantics: Processing, Analysis and Applications, 1996

17. G. Iyengar and A. B. Lippman, "Video-Book: An Experimentation in Characterization of Video", Proc. of Inte. Conf. on Image Processing'96, 1996

18. R. Kasturi and R. Jain, "Dynamic Vision", Computer Vision: Principles, IEEE Computer Society Press, 1991

19. T. D. C. Little et.al, "A Digital on Demand Video Service Supporting Content-Based Queries", Proc. ACM Multimedia 93, pp. 427-436, 1993

20. M. Mills, J. Cohen, Y.Y. Wong, "A Magnifier Tool for Video Data", Proc. CHI'92, pp. 93-98, 1992

21. A. Nagasaka and Y. Tanaka, "Automatic Video Indexing and Full-Video Search for Object Appearances", Visual Database Systems 2, pp. 113-127, 1992

22. C. O'Connor, "Selecting Key Frames of Moving Image Documents: A Digital Environment for Analysis and Navigation", Microcomputers for Information Management, Vol. 8, No. 2, pp. 119-133, 1991

23. B. Shahraray, "Scene Change Detection and Content-Based Sampling of Video Sequences", Proc. SPIE Digital Video Compression:Algorithms and Technologies, Vol. 2419, pp. 2-13,1995

24. M. A. Smith, T. Kanade, "Video Skimming for Quick Browsing based on Audio and Image Characterization", Technical Report No. CMU-CS-95-186, School of Computer Science, Carnegie Mellon University, 1995

25. X. Sun, M. S. Kankanhalli, Y. Zhu and J. K. Wu, "Content Based Representative Frame Extraction for Digital Video", Proc. IEEE Multimedia Computing and Systems, 1998

26. B. Shen and C. B. Owen, "Inner-Block Operations on Compressed Images", Proc. ACM Multimedia 95, pp. 489-498, 1995

27. B. C. Smith and L. Rowe, "A New Family of Algorithms for Manipulating Compressed Images", IEEE Computer Graphics and Applications, 1993

28. D. Swanberg, C. F. Shu and R. Jain, "Knowledge Guided Parsing and Retrieval in Video Databases", Proc. Storage and Retrieval for Image and Video Databases, pp. 173-187, 1993

29. Y. Taniguchi, A. Akutsu, Y. Tonomura, H. Hamada, "An Intuitive and Efficient Access Interface to Real-Time Incoming Video Based on Automatic Indexing", Proc.ACM Multimedia 95, pp. 25-33, 1995

30. L. Teodosio, W. Bender, "Salient video stills: Content and context preserved", Proc. ACM Multimedia 93, pp. 39-46, 1993

31. H. Ueda, T. Miyatake and S. Yoshizawa, "IMPACT: An Interactive Natural-Motion-Picture Dedicated Multimedia Authoring System", Proc. CHI, pp.343-350, 1991

32. H. D. Wactlar, M. Christel, A. Hauptmann, T. Kanade, M. Mauldin, R. Reddy, M. Smith and S. Stevens, "Technical Challenges for the Informedia Digital Video Library", Proc. Int. Symp. on Digital Libraries, pp. 10-16, 1995

33. J. K. Wu, A. D. Narasimhalu, B. M. Mehtre, C. P. Lam, Y. J. Gao, "CORE: A Content-Based Retrieval Engine for Multimedia Information Systems", Multimedia Systems, Vol. 3, pp. 25-41, 1995 , 1995

34. M. M. Yeung and B. Liu, "Efficient Matching and Clustering of Video Shots", IEEE International Conference on Image Processing, pp. 338-341, 1995

35. M. M. Yeung, B. -L. Yeo, W. Wolf, B. Liu, "Video Browsing using Clustering and Scene Transitions on Compressed Sequences", IS&T/SPIE Multimedia Computing and Networking, 1995

36. R. Zabih, J. Miller and K. Mai, "A Feature-Based Algorithm for Detecting and Classifying Scene Breaks", Proc. ACM Multimedia 95, pp. 189-200, 1995.

37. H. J. Zhang et.al, "Automatic Parsing of News Video", Proc. of Multimedia Computing and Systems, pp. 45-54, 1994

38. H. J. Zhang, A. Kankanhalli, S. W. Smoliar, "Automatic Partitioning of Full-Motion Video", Multimedia Systems, Vol. 1, No. 1, pp. 10-28, 1993

39. H. J. Zhang, C. Y. Low, S. W. Smoliar, "Video Parsing and Browsing Using Compressed Data", Multimedia Tools and Applications, Vol. 1, No. 1, pp. 89-111, 1995

40. H. J. Zhang, J. H. Wu, D. Zhong and S. W. Smoliar, "An Integrated System for Content-Based Video Retrieval and Browsing", Pattern Recognition, Vol. 30, No. 4, pp. 643-658, 1997

41. D. Zhong, H. J. Zhang, S.-F. Chang, "Clustering Methods for Video Browsing and Annotation", SPIE Conference on Storage and Retrieval for Image and Video, 1996

Chapter 6

Object Segmentation

Object segmentation is the first step toward object-oriented representation. Formally, segmentation is to split an image into disjoint regions while each region represents a meaningful object or object part. Object segmentation is achieved by looking into uniformity of the region with respect to measurable properties such as brightness, color and texture.

In general, segmentation can be divided into two main types, supervised and unsupervised. In applications such as remote sensing, medical imaging and industrial automation the prior knowledge of the objects and backgrounds are known in advance so the segmentation can be executed in a supervised manner. For automatic indexing of images and video, we are dealing with variety of image and video content, about which we do not have any prior knowledge. In this case, the segmentation is unsupervised.

The challenge here is, it is expected that the segmentation should be object-oriented, but even the concept "object" itself is not well defined. For example, we define a person as an "object", but at the same time the face and clothes can also be referred to as "objects" because they have distinct visual properties. In this case what is the "ideal" segmentation becomes fuzzy. It depends on how many details are expected to be kept after the segmentation. There are some efforts [5] to define objective criteria but in most cases the results are subjectively evaluated based on perceptual or semantic meaning. Here, we will evaluate the segmentation subjectively and the evaluation will inevitably be influenced by context and personal preference.

As mentioned above, for unsupervised segmentation, the most important clue we can use is the homogeneous property of certain measurable image features(e.g. brightness, color, texture) within a region and diversity of these features among regions. The "homogeneity" itself is also application or domain dependent. Since our eventual goal is the cataloging of objects, the aim of our segmentation is to segment out major regions in an image or video frame for the following indexing procedure. The regions preferred to be segmented out may correspond to sky, tree, grass, water(sea, river, pool), road, building, field, human faces etc. Furthermore, it is preferred that the image is over-segmented than under-segmented, because in the latter case, the indexing task will be very difficult since different objects are mixed up.

The image feature utilized in our experiment will be color, texture or the combination of them. For better segmentation performance, distance in $CIE - L^*u^*v^*$ color space is used to measure the color similarity. Texture features are extracted by wavelet frame transform that generates an over-complete but shift-invariant representation which is demonstrated to be well suited to the segmentation application. Edge-preserved smoothing is carried out to smooth away noise and small variation within regions while keeping the salient edges between regions. After this procedure the feature vectors are ready to be taken as input for the segmentation algorithm.

For the segmentation algorithm, we propose an unsupervised statistical approach in which the image is modeled as a random field and the segmentation problem is posed as a maximum *a posteriori* (MAP) estimation problem. By using Bayes' theorem, the optimal segmentation is achieved by jointly optimizing two probability functions, corresponding to a region process modeled by Markov Random Field and a nearest neighbor clustering process in feature space respectively. We also propose a likelihood based approach to solve the cluster validation problem to make the algorithm fully automatic. In the above process parameters are set to obtain an over-segmented result in order to avoid any mixture of different objects. Following this we design a region merging procedure which merges small regions and regions sharing weak boundaries. The region merging procedure, which works by testing the boundary merit value, can compensate for the over-segmented result derived before and finally obtain a reasonably good segmentation. The advantage of such an approach is that both global feature properties and local spatial constraints are incorporated.

In this chapter, edge-preserved smoothing for color and texture features is presented in Section 6.1. Section 6.2 deals with segmentation algorithm based on feature space clustering and region merging. It includes the clustering algorithm, cluster validation problem, the spatial constraint using the Markov Random Field model, region labelling and region merging. Experiment results are given in Section 6.3, where the various aspects and the overall performance of the segmentation solution are tested and evaluated. The effect of various thresholds and parameters on the final result is investigated in the last section.

6.1 Edge-preserved smoothing of features

6.1.1 Principle of edge-preserved smoothing

It is highly preferred that adaptive smoothing on the color and texture features be performed before they are applied in the segmentation. Edge-preserved smoothing (EPSM) or adaptive smoothing [12, 13, 14] is a technique to smooth away the noise and small variation in a signal while preserving the major edges or discontinuity. It is achieved by repeatedly convoluting the signal with a very small average mask weighted by a measure of the signal continuity at each point. Two results can be obtained from the method: one is the sharpening of the strong edges and the other is the smoothing within regions. It can be applied in edge detection, range image feature extraction, image enhancement or stereo matching. We focus its application in image segmentation as a feature post-processing stage where color and texture features are involved.

The most common filter used in smoothing is the Gaussian filter. Gaussian filtering can be implemented by repeated convolutions with a small averaging filter. The degree of smoothing, or the σ of the Gaussian, is equivalent to the number of iterative convolutions. If the one dimensional signal is $f(x)$, the smoothing kernel is $S = [1\ 2\ 1]$, then the smoothing at $(t+1)th$ iteration is,

$$f^{(t+1)}(x) = \frac{1}{N}\sum_{i=-1}^{+1} f^{(t)}(x+i)S(i) \tag{6.1}$$

where,

$$N = \sum_{i=-1}^{+1} S(i) \tag{6.2}$$

The Gaussian smoothing implemented as above uses a fixed smoothing kernel. It smoothes the signal everywhere resulting in a blurred signal where the noises are averaged away and sharp edges also become smoothed. Adaptive smoothing requires that small variations are removed while major edges are kept. It can be implemented by setting the weights of the convolution mask to zero where the signal has a high contrast, so the smoothing of the signal near those discontinuities will not take into account the points belonging to the discontinuities. Since the smoothing kernel adopted is very small, data belonging to different regions separated by an edge will not be averaged. The repeated convolution will force it to be closer to one of the regions. At the points where the signal contrast is low, the weight of the smoothing kernel is high which means these points can be averaged. The discontinuity or contrast of the signal can be guessed from its gradient $g(x) = |\frac{df(x)}{dx}|$ and the weighting function can be any form of decreasing function $W(g(x))$ such that $W(0) = 1$ and $W(g(x)) \to 0$ as $g(x)$ increases. We choose the W to have the form of:

$$W(g) = e^{-\frac{g^2}{2\tau^2}} \tag{6.3}$$

Therefore the smoothing at $(t+1)th$ iteration is given as,

$$f^{(t+1)}(x) = \frac{1}{N_x^{(t)}} \sum_{i=-1}^{+1} f^{(t)}(x+i) W(g^{(t)}(x+i)) S(i) \tag{6.4}$$

where,

$$N_x^{(t)} = \sum_{i=-1}^{+1} W(g^{(t)}(x+i)) S(i) \tag{6.5}$$

For clarity, the above equation can be written in a simple convolution form:

$$f^{(t+1)} = \frac{f^{(t)} W(g^{(t)}) * S}{W(g^{(t)}) * S} \tag{6.6}$$

The algorithm is proved to converge in [12] and the parameter τ in Equation (6.3) determines the final result of the iteration. The edges whose gradient value is higher than τ will be kept and sharpened during the iterative smoothing while the small noises and variations with a gradient lower than τ will be smoothed away.

Figure 6.3 illustrates the effect of the algorithm on a 1D signal plotted in Figure 6.2, which is a horizontal slice taken from the red channel of the scenery image shown in Figure 6.1. In this experiment we do not fix the value of the parameter τ. Instead it is set adaptively according to the content of the signal. In each iteration, it is set to twice the mean value of the gradient of $f(x)$. Therefore at the beginning, the signal varies a lot so the τ is big. As the iteration evolves, the signal becomes smoother and

Figure 6.1: A scenery image

the τ decreases. The result in Figure 6.3 is generated with 20 iterations. It can be seen that the main structure of the original signal is kept after the adaptive smoothing. Those major features of the signal are well preserved and the important edges are sharpened while the small variation or noise within the regions are averaged away. For comparison, the result of the Gaussian smoothing performed on the same signal is shown in Figure 6.4. It is generated using the same smoothing kernel S but without adaptive weighting by W and the iteration is also performed 20 times in this case. It can be seen that some important structures in the original signal are lost.

It should be realized that the EPSM algorithm results in two effects. One is the sharpening of strong edges and the other is the smoothing within regions. The first one is achieved rather quickly while the smoothing converges rather slowly. In segmentation the main purpose for EPSM is its smoothing function so the slow converging speed may cause the processing time to be too long. Choosing the value of parameter τ adaptively can help to speed up the convergence. As mentioned before, the parameter τ determines what kind of content of the signal to keep and what to remove. If the τ is chosen to be very large then every part of the signal is smoothed so the effect is just the same as a normal Gaussian filtering. If τ is small then less smoothing will be carried out. Setting the

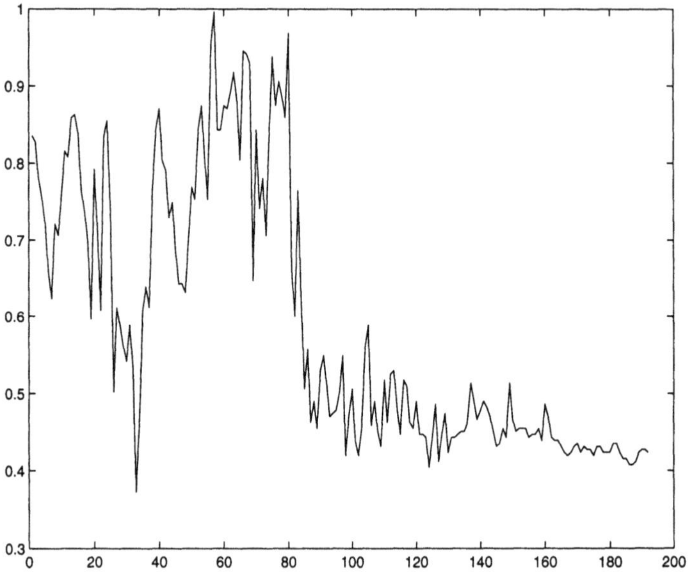

Figure 6.2: Original 1D signal

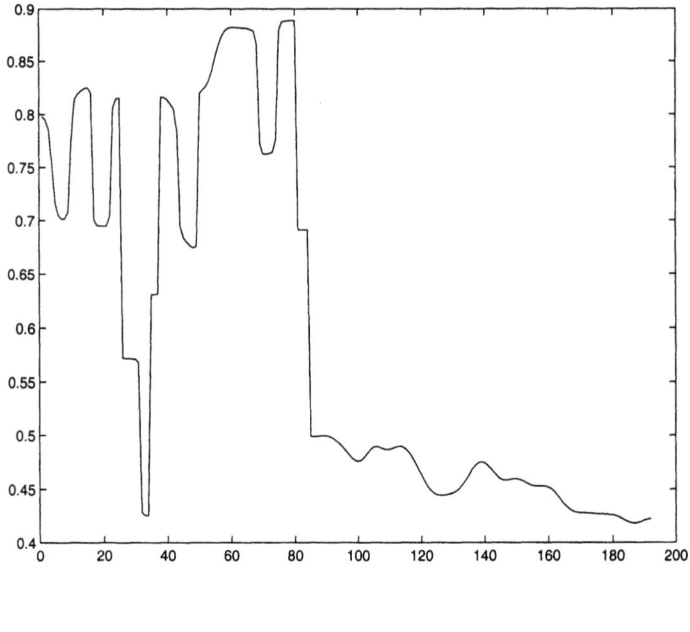

Figure 6.3: 1D signal after EPSM

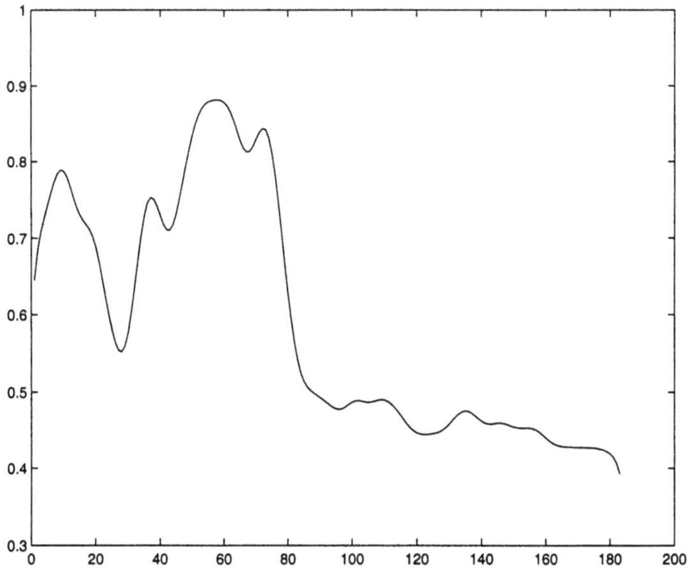

Figure 6.4: 1D signal after Gaussian smoothing

value of τ adaptively will make the smoothing converge more quickly at the beginning, saving some processing time.

6.1.2 EPSM for 2D signal

The adaptive smoothing can be applied to a 2D signal easily. For intensity image $f(x, y)$, the iteration becomes,

$$f^{(t+1)}(x,y) = \frac{1}{N_{xy}^{(t)}} \sum_{i=-1}^{+1} \sum_{j=-1}^{+1} f^{(t)}(x+i, y+j) W(g^{(t)}(x+i, y+j)) S(i,j) \quad (6.7)$$

where,

$$N_{xy}^{(t)} = \sum_{i=-1}^{+1} \sum_{j=-1}^{+1} W(g^{(t)}(x+i, y+j)) S(i,j) \quad (6.8)$$

and the $g^{(t)}(x, y)$ is the magnitude of the gradient $(\frac{\partial f^{(t)}(x,y)}{\partial x}, \frac{\partial f^{(t)}(x,y)}{\partial y})$. The averaging mask S adopted here is,

$$S = \begin{bmatrix} 1 & 2 & 1 \\ 2 & 4 & 2 \\ 1 & 2 & 1 \end{bmatrix} \quad (6.9)$$

Since S is a separable filter,

$$S = [1\ 2\ 1]^T[1\ 2\ 1] \tag{6.10}$$

The 2D convolution with S can be implemented by the cascade of two 1D filtering with [1 2 1] in horizontal and vertical directions consecutively.

6.1.3 Application in color feature

For a complex "vector" signal where data takes a multi-channel form, such as color imagery, the definition of gradient at a pixel level is not readily available. In this case we need a notion of "generalized gradient" so that the adaptive smoothing framework can be applied to these "vector" signal. We assume that the signal is defined over $\Re^2$ and takes value in $\Re^m$ (which means we restrict the signal to be the m-dimensional feature data of 2D image):

$$F(X) = F(x, y) = \{f_1(x, y), f_2(x, y) \dots f_m(x, y)\} \tag{6.11}$$

Assuming the signal can be Taylor expanded,

$$F(X + \Delta X) \approx F(X) + F'(X)\Delta X \tag{6.12}$$

where the higher order forms are omitted and $F'(x)$ is the $m \times 2$ Jacobian matrix of F,

$$F'(X) = J(X) = \begin{pmatrix} \frac{\partial f_1}{\partial x} & \frac{\partial f_1}{\partial y} \\ \frac{\partial f_2}{\partial x} & \frac{\partial f_2}{\partial y} \\ \vdots & \vdots \\ \frac{\partial f_m}{\partial x} & \frac{\partial f_m}{\partial y} \end{pmatrix} \tag{6.13}$$

$$dF = \|F(X + \Delta X) - F(X)\| = \|F'(X)\Delta X\| = \sqrt{\Delta X^T J^T J \Delta X} \tag{6.14}$$

The step direction which maximize dF is the eigenvector of $J^T J$ corresponding to its larger eigenvalue λ. The square root of the λ corresponds to the gradient magnitude g.

According to Equation (6.13),

$$dF = \sum_{i=1}^{2} \frac{\partial F}{\partial x_i} dx_i \tag{6.15}$$

so,

$$\|dF\|^2 = \sum_{i=1}^{2}\sum_{j=1}^{2} \left(\frac{\partial F}{\partial x_i} \cdot \frac{\partial F}{\partial x_j}\right) dx_i dx_j \tag{6.16}$$

since $\frac{\partial F}{\partial x_i} = \{\frac{\partial f_1}{\partial x_i} \cdots \frac{\partial f_m}{\partial x_i}\}$, we have,

$$\|dF\|^2 = \begin{bmatrix} dx_1 \\ dx_2 \end{bmatrix}^T \begin{bmatrix} g_{11} & g_{12} \\ g_{21} & g_{22} \end{bmatrix} \begin{bmatrix} dx_1 \\ dx_2 \end{bmatrix} \tag{6.17}$$

where,

$$g_{ij} = \sum_{k=1}^{m} \frac{\partial f_k}{\partial x_i} \frac{\partial f_k}{\partial x_j} \tag{6.18}$$

so the larger eigenvalue of $J^T J$ is,

$$\lambda = \frac{1}{2}\left(g_{11} + g_{22} + \sqrt{(g_{11} - g_{22})^2 + 4g_{12}^2}\right) \tag{6.19}$$

Now we have the "generalized gradient" for the color image. The original data in RGB space is transformed into $CIE - L^*u^*v^*$ space first. The "generalized gradient" of every pixel is calculated as above (equal to $\sqrt{\lambda}$) using the $CIE - L^*u^*v^*$ data and then smoothing is carried out in L, u and v channels using Equation (6.8).

The smoothing experiment has been done on the scenery image in Figure 6.1. The smoothing result shown in Figure 6.5, where the data in $CIE - L^*u^*v^*$ space is transform back to RGB for display, is obtained after five times iterations. It can be seen that the performance is satisfactory in preserving the main structure of the color image while removing the fine detail and noise.

6.1.4 Application in texture feature

Texture features extracted by the WFT can be treated as a m-channel image, where m is the dimension of the texture vector. Therefore the "generalized gradient" concept introduced in the previous section can be applied to texture smoothing as well. However color is a point property of an image while texture is defined over a neighborhood. The different wavelet subbands, or the texture feature channels, are obtained by convolution with filters of different support sizes. When derivatives $(\frac{\partial f_k}{\partial x}, \frac{\partial f_k}{\partial y})$ are computed, the scale of the subband k should be taken into account, i.e., the derivatives should be obtained by applying operators of appropriate magnitude and spatial support.

A synthetic texture mosaic image [17] is shown in Figure 6.6, where seven texture patterns are presented and every different texture pair shares at least one common border. The magnitude of the wavelet subbands obtained by the WFT is shown from Figure 6.7 to Figure 6.9. The

Figure 6.5: Color image after EPSM

$W(g)$ image calculated before any smoothing is displayed in Figure 6.10, where the dark color represents high gradient (g) and bright color represents low gradient. From these images it can be seen that although the raw texture features derived from the WFT are able to represent the properties of textures in different scales and orientations, they are not uniform within a single texture region. High texture gradients appear inside a uniform texture region rather than along the true texture boundary. The reason of this has been stated at the end of Section 6.3. Therefore if the raw texture features are used directly for segmentation the performance can not be expected to be satisfactory.

The EPSM is executed for 10 iterations and then the magnitude of these smoothed subbands is shown from Figure 6.11 to Figure 6.13. For comparison, the $W(g)$ image after smoothing is also displayed in Figure 6.14. Compared to the experiment of color smoothing, in this experiment we choose a smoothing kernel S with longer support to make the convergence faster. The parameter τ is also set larger for the same purpose. It can be observed that the texture features become much more uniform within the same texture region while the different features in two neighboring regions are not mixed together. The texture gradient within a texture region is low and the contrast between neighboring regions are preserved.

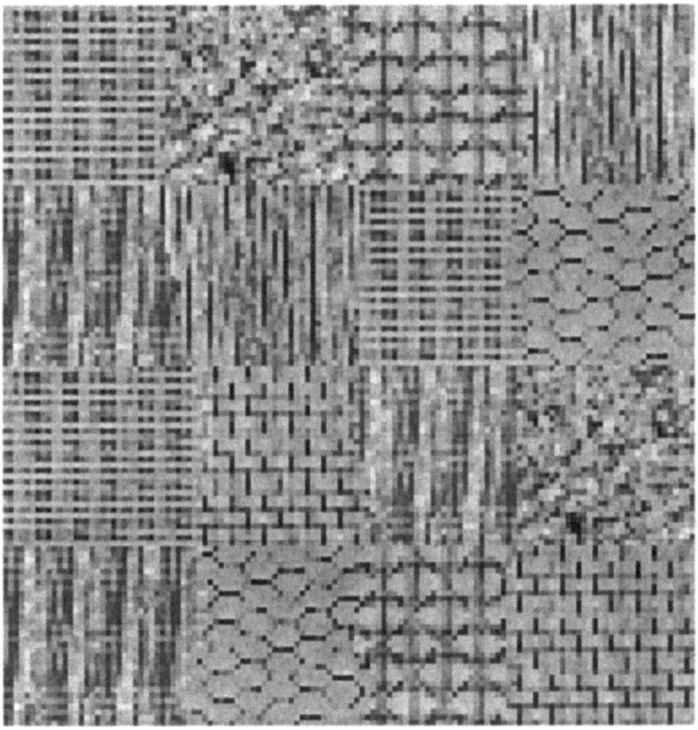

Figure 6.6: A synthetic texture image

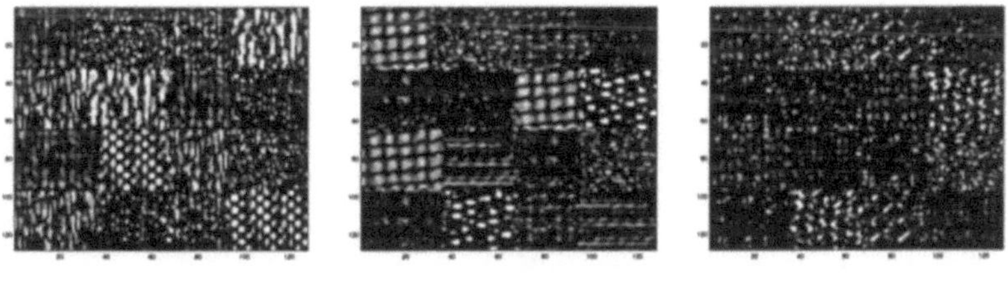

Figure 6.7: Wavelet subband image: scale 1

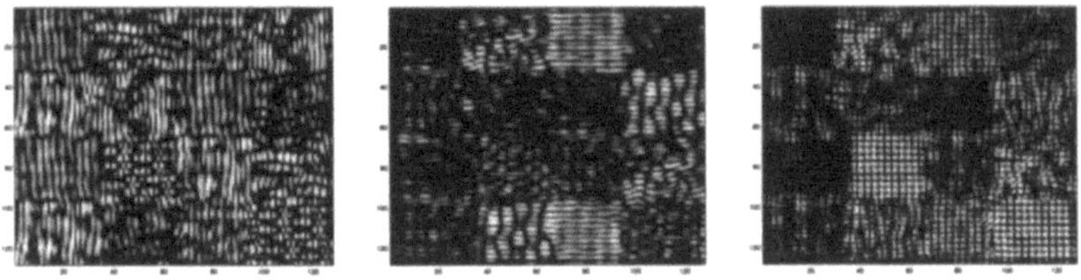

Figure 6.8: Wavelet subband image: scale 2

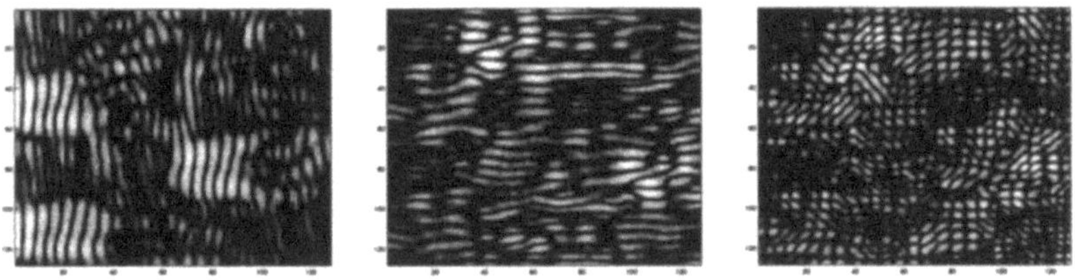

Figure 6.9: Wavelet subband image: scale 3

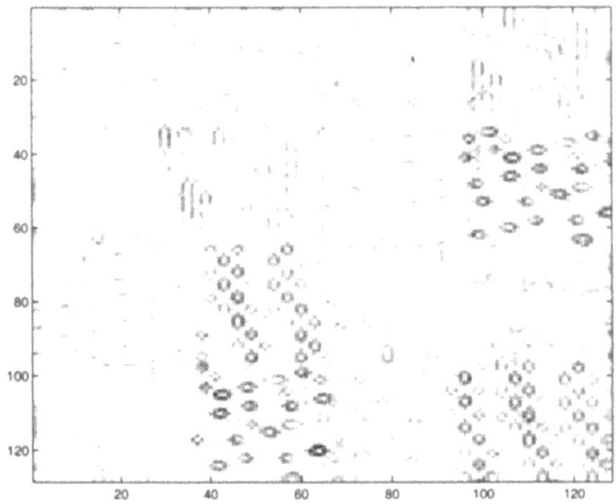

Figure 6.10: Texture gradient before smoothing

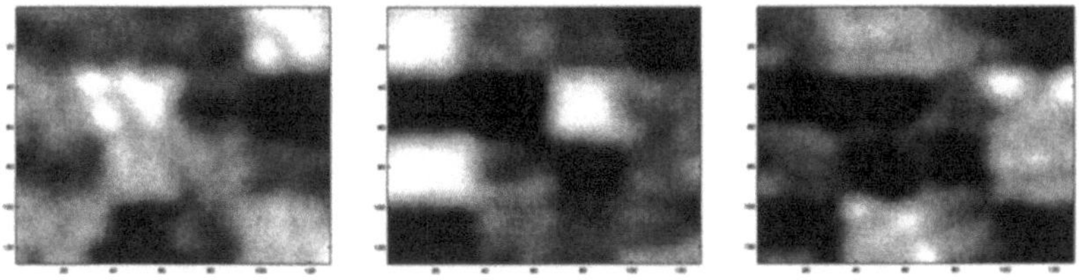

Figure 6.11: Wavelet subband image smoothed: scale 1

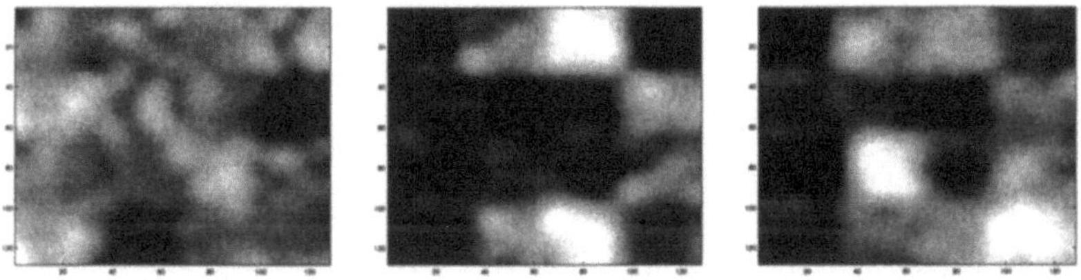

Figure 6.12: Wavelet subband image smoothed: scale 2

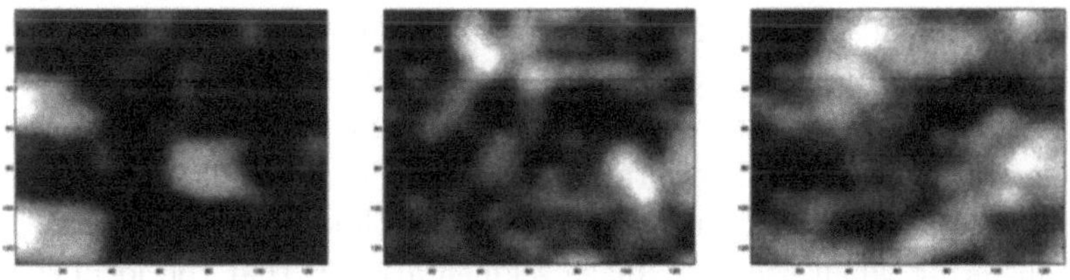

Figure 6.13: Wavelet subband image smoothed: scale 3

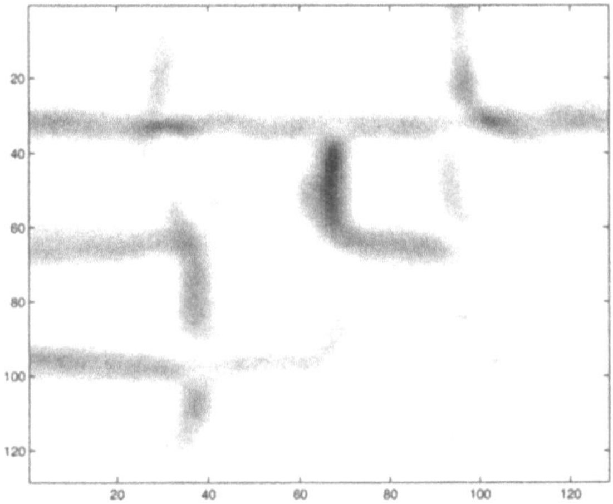

Figure 6.14: Texture gradient after smoothing

6.2 Segmentation algorithm: clustering and region merging

In the previous sections we have proposed the feature extraction methods for color and texture. Once the features are well prepared, the next issue is which segmentation algorithm to adopt. It will largely determine the performance and complexity of the overall segmentation. Techniques available include region growing, split-merge, edge detection and clustering. Among them, unsupervised clustering [10,1,2] in feature space has certain advantages, in which it needs least human interaction and few pre-set thresholds. Moreover, it can represent the global distribution of the feature data in the image, which often guarantees the good segmentation result in a global view. A similar alternative to clustering is known as expectation-maximization (EM) algorithm that can be understood as a version of "soft" clustering. The EM algorithm can sometimes generate better results but its computational complexity is much higher. We focus on normal "hard decision" clustering method. The major drawback of clustering when used for image segmentation is that the local spatial information among image pixels is omitted. We try to add the Gaussian Markov Random Field/Gibbs Distribution(GMRF/GD) model [4,5,6,7] to the clustering algorithm to take into account the spatial interactivity. Furthermore, the spatial information can also be utilized by the proposed region merging strategy, which is executed after clustering and region labeling. Therefore, our segmentation method is a combination of clustering (with GMRF/GD model integrated) and the region merging process.

6.2.1 Clustering in the feature space

Clustering algorithms

Clustering the N dimensional feature space to K classes is very similar to the vector quantization (VQ) process. In VQ, a K-level N dimensional quantizer is a mapping that assigns each input vector a reproduction vector, drawn from a reproduction codebook with K codewords. The index of the codebook is used to represent the original vector thus compression coding can be achieved. In our application of segmentation while the mapping is the same, the result is further processed to group those pixels having the same index and spatially connected as regions. Although the aim is different, the main problem is the same, i.e., how to obtain the most representative K cluster centres, or codebook with K codewords, from a training set. In VQ it is known as a codebook design problem. The training set is partitioned into K non-overlapping clusters and their centres are chosen to be codewords. For unsupervised segmentation, the training set is the image feature data itself.

A well known VQ codebook training method is the *LBG* algorithm [10]. The objective is to get a codebook that minimizes the quantization error over all training data. In clustering terminology it means the average within-cluster distance is minimized among all possible clustering. When given a codebook, the partition of the training set can be decided by using the nearest neighbor measure and when given a partition, the codebook can be obtained by computing the center of each cluster. The *LBG* algorithm finds the best quantizer by iteratively adjusting the centers of clusters and the partition of the training set until the whole process converges.

Let $X = (X_0, X_1, \ldots, X_{M-1})$ be the training set of N dimensional vector samples, $Y = (Y_0, Y_1, \ldots, Y_{K-1})$ be the codebook and distance measure chosen is d, the *LBG* algorithm works as following:

(1) Initialization: Given an initial codebook Y(method of choice discussed later), set $n = 1$ and $D_0 = \infty$.

(2) Given the $Y = (Y_0, Y_1, \ldots, Y_{K-1})$, find the minimum distortion partition of the training set X, assigns sample X_i to index j if $d(X_i, Y_j) \leq d(X_i, Y_l)$ for all l. Computes the average distortion

$D_n = \frac{1}{m}\sum_{i=0}^{m-1} d(X_i, Y_j)$.

(3) If the iteration is converged, i.e., $D_n/D_{n-1} > 0.99+(15-n)*0.0006$, stop and output Y as the final codebook.

(4) Find the optimal codewords for the partition, $Y_j = \frac{1}{M_j}\sum_{i=0}^{M_j-1} X_i$, where X_i having the index j and M_j is the number of training data assigned to index j. Update $n = n+1$ and goto (1).

We modify the convergence criterion to avoid too many iterations: the iteration is stopped if $n \geq 15$ or the original criterion above is satisfied. The distance measure can be chosen as any form to meet different needs. A good measure for segmentation is Euclidean distance. For color features in $CIE - L^*u^*v^*$ space and texture features derived from the WFT, the Euclidean measure can be applied directly.

Initial condition of clustering

The aim of the algorithm is to generate a globally optimal codebook, i.e., a codebook that has the least reproduction error among all codebooks of the same size. A codebook is called locally optimal if slight changes in codebook cause an increase in distortion but the codebook is not globally the best. The initial selection of the codebook has substantial influence on the final convergence state, i.e., if the initial codebook is near some local optimal position, the *LBG* algorithm will converge to it instead of the global optimal point. Therefore the initial codebook is strongly preferred to be located near the global optimal state. The simplest selection method is to choose the first K training data as the initial codebook. Since the first K data may not be well separated, the global optimal codebook can not be guaranteed.

We use a simple and effective approach to solve this problem: the final K-entry codebook is designed by training codebooks of successively bigger sizes until size K is achieved. It is illustrated as following:

(1) Initialization: Given initial codebook containing only one codeword—the centre of all training data.

(2) Quantize the training data using current codebook of size k, find out the cluster i that has the largest clustering error, split the corresponding codeword Y_i into two codewords close to each other: $0.99Y_i + \epsilon$ and $1.01Y_i - \epsilon$. ϵ is a small perturbation vector equal to $0.01X_j$, where X_j is the training data in cluster i which is the farthest from cluster centre Y_i. Now the codebook has size $k+1$.

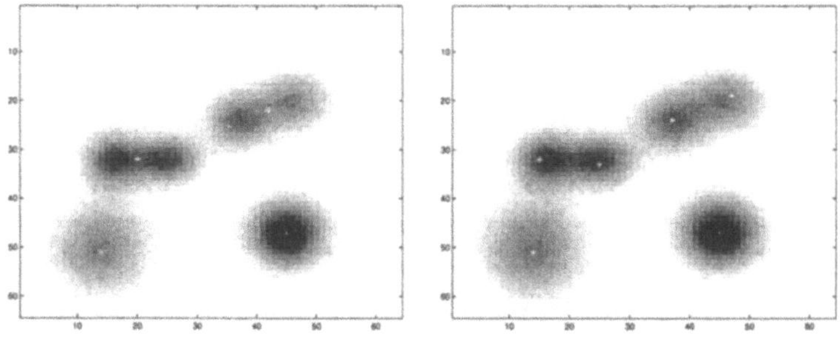

Figure 6.15: Clustering results for synthetic data

(3) Use *LBG* algorithm to train the enlarged codebook until it is converged.

(4) If $k < K$, goto (2).
If $k = K$, stop and output the codebook.

This approach produces the final codebook by gradually increasing the codebook size and optimizing the codewords. Every time the codebook size is increased, the new codewords added are designed along the direction to minimize the global reproduction error. Since the generation of codewords follows the direction of global optimization in each step, the final codebook can be expected to be located at those globally optimal points.

Experiment results have shown that this approach can spot the most salient cluster centres under various distributions. Figure 6.15 illustrates the distribution of a two-dimensional data set, which is generated by a mixture of 6 Gaussian distributions plus random noise. The 6 Gaussian distributions have various variance value and prior probability and two pairs of them are close to each other. The codebooks with 4 and 6 codewords are displayed, codewords marked by "+". It can be seen that under both circumstances the codewords correspond well to the best cluster centres that can be found.

Another advantage of the gradual training is that it can generate codebooks of various sizes at a time. When designing a K-entry codebook, we can also get codebooks of sizes 1 to $K - 1$ as by-product. It is useful in unsupervised clustering because it is generally not known *a priori* how many clusters are presented in the training set(image). When having codebooks of various sizes, we can choose one that best fits the training data according to some criterion. This is known as "cluster validation" problem, which is discussed in next section.

6.2.2 Cluster validation for unsupervised segmentation

The clustering method presented in the previous section has the ability to form representative feature vectors effectively and automatically. However, in order to use it in a fully automatic segmentation system, the number of clusters (or classes) actually existing in the image should be determined. For simplicity, we denote the number of clusters by K in the following. K is generally not known as *a priori* and has to be estimated directly from the image data itself. It is known as a *cluster validation* problem and is critical to the final segmentation result. If the K is chosen to be too big (i.e., more than that of the actual clusters in the image), the image will tend to be over-segmented so the result will be too fragmented than expected. On the other hand, if it is chosen to be fewer than the actual number, the image will be under-segmented in that some different regions will be mixed up.

The difficulty of the cluster validation lies largely in the inability to provide accurate sampling distributions for the various K classes and the lack of sufficient regularity conditions. Moreover, in some cases the best number of clusters itself is a vague concept because the data distribution is not well separated as several obvious clusters. Therefore, it is hard to determine the K even for a human observer. For example in Figure 6.15 it is not clear whether there are 4 or 6 clusters exist, and both answers seem reasonable. An answer can be only possible when there is a specific application or when some predefined criterion measure exists.

Due to its important role in many applications including unsupervised segmentation, a lot of research has been done on this topic [3,8,9,11,15,16] and many approaches have been proposed. We will briefly review these various solutions and then provide a simple criterion derived from the *maximum likelihood* estimate of the training data.

Review of relevant methods

Various cluster validation solutions have been proposed since 1970s. Generally they belong to a few main categories:

- The performance of some 30 heuristic methods of determining the K in cluster analysis is compared in [15]. They all use some stopping rules to find out the best number of clusters. These stopping rules are heuristic, ad hoc procedures which are mostly based on the between and within cluster distances. A threshold is heuristically established to indicate when a sufficiently good clustering representation is achieved. The testing of their performance is done with artificial multi-dimensional data sets consisting of externally isolated and internally cohesive clusters. A comparison given in [15] indicates some have better results than others.

- In some hierarchical clustering approaches such as ISODATA [20], some thresholds are set to decide whether a cluster is to be further split or two clusters are to be merged together. In this hierarchical way, it attempt to solve the cluster validation problem and the segmentation itself simultaneously. By setting parameters within some appropriate ranges, it can converge to a proper number of clusters. In [2], the color image segmentation using the ISODATA method is experimented on various color spaces. It is attractive due to its conceptual simplicity but it needs many pre-set parameter values which are decided by user experience and are not likely to work well for different kinds of images.

- In [9] a VQ strategy which jointly optimizes the distortion error and the codebook complexity is proposed. According to [9], the design of an optimal vector quantizer requires to find codebook with minimal representing errors and to specify the complexity of the codebook. Both design specifications are mutually dependent and cannot be optimized separately. In order to achieve the joint optimization, they adopt a VQ cost function which consists of quantizing error and the entropy of the codebook. The design of codebooks of different sizes is carried on and the codebook having best cost performance is selected. In this approach, the weight of codebook complexity in the cost function has decisive effect on the final codebook to be selected. For image compression coding task this weight is easier to set according to the trade-off between the bit rate and image quality, whereas in segmentation it is not intuitive how to set this value. Therefore we think this approach is more suitable for compression more than for segmentation.

- There is a group of similar approaches where the cluster validation is treated as a multiple decision problem. Criteria such as Akaike's information criterion (AIC)[11,16] and minimum description length (MDL)[8] have been proposed to determine the model order. Generally they are all based upon likelihood and the principal difference is the *penalty* term associated with the model order (K). However, it is pointed out in [3] that due to the fact that penalty terms in AIC and MDL are independent of the image size, they are dominated by the log likelihood term and therefore ineffective for assessing the proper number of classes.

A likelihood based model-fitting approach

In order to decide the number of clusters automatically for unsupervised segmentation, we propose a solution based on the likelihood estimation of the data under different K and select the best one according to this criterion. We first simplify the data model and show that under this simplification the log likelihood criterion turns out to be a simple combination of two terms, corresponding to the variance and the entropy of the classes respectively. The experiment result for synthetic data is given next. Finally the criterion is slightly modified to make it work for natural images.

Following the clustering approach described before, we can define the criterion of selecting K to be the negative of the log probability likelihood of the training data given the cluster result: $-\log\{P_K(X)\}$, where X is the sample data. The number of clusters is selected as:

$$K_{best} = \arg \min_{K_{min} \leq K \leq K_{max}} -\frac{1}{M}\log\{P_K(X)\} \tag{6.20}$$

where M is the number of data sample. The K_{min} and K_{max} are the lower and upper limit of cluster numbers existed.

For simplicity we assume that the sample data is independent of each other. Although the independence assumption may not hold for the segmentation application, it provides a good approximation and the estimation result is reasonably good. Therefore the overall probability likelihood can be expressed as:

$$-\frac{1}{M}\log\{P_K(X)\} = -\frac{1}{M}\log\prod_{i=1}^{M} p(x_i) = -\frac{1}{M}\sum_{i=1}^{N}\log p(x_i) \tag{6.21}$$

If a sample data x_i is classified to class k by the clustering procedure, it can be considered coming from the particular class k which have a probability ω_k of occurring(ω_k can be estimated as the ratio of the number of samples belonging to class k to the total number of samples). The probability of this data vector can be expressed as:

$$p(x_i) = \omega_k p_k(x_i) \tag{6.22}$$

It is also assumed that the data vectors x are N-dimensional, $x = \{x^1, x^2, \ldots, x^N\}$, and every component of the vector is conditionally independent of each other given the class k it belongs to.

$$p_k(x_i) = \prod_{j=1}^{N} p_k^j(x_i^j) \tag{6.23}$$

For simplicity, each of the components is modeled by a Gaussian pdf,

$$p_k^j(x_i^j) = \frac{1}{\sqrt{2\pi\delta_k^{j\,2}}} \exp\left(-\frac{(x_i^j - y_k^j)^2}{2\delta_k^{j\,2}}\right) \tag{6.24}$$

where y_k^j and δ_k^j are the mean and variance of the pdf of the class k, dimension j.

Combing Equation (6.22), (6.23) and (6.24) with 6.21 we have,

$$\begin{aligned}
&-\frac{1}{M}\log\{P_K(X)\} \\
&= -\frac{1}{M}\sum_{i=1}^{M}\log p(x_i) \\
&= -\frac{1}{M}\sum_{i=1}^{M}\log\left[\omega_{ik}\prod_{j=1}^{N}\frac{1}{\sqrt{2\pi\delta_{ik}^{j\,2}}}\exp\left(-\frac{(x_i^j - y_{ik}^j)^2}{2\delta_{ik}^{j\,2}}\right)\right] \\
&= -\frac{1}{M}\sum_{i=1}^{M}\log\omega_{ik} + \frac{1}{M}\sum_{i=1}^{M}\left(\sum_{j=1}^{N}\log\delta_{ik}^j\right) + \frac{1}{M}\sum_{i=1}^{M}\sum_{j=1}^{N}\frac{(x_i^j - y_{ik}^j)^2}{2\delta_{ik}^{j\,2}}
\end{aligned}$$

where by using notation ik we denote that sample x_i belongs to class k.

As the last term of the right side of the above equation is a constant, the log likelihood of the data can be expressed as a simple combination of the entropy and the log variance of the clusters,

$$-\frac{1}{M}\log\{P_K(X)\} = -\sum_{k=1}^{K}\omega_k\log\omega_k + \sum_{k=1}^{K}\omega_k\sum_{j=1}^{N}\log\delta_k^j \tag{6.25}$$

With this simplification, the best cluster number can be estimated easily using Equation (6.20). We demonstrate its effectiveness by using some synthetic data first. These data samples are two dimensional ($N = 2$), generated by using identical and independent Gaussian mixtures. Data distribution are displayed from Figure 6.16 to Figure 6.18 where there are 3,4 and 5 clusters existing. The corresponding negative of log likelihood computed by Equation (6.25) are listed from Table 6.1 to Table 6.3 respectively. For each case, we present three different distributions: in the

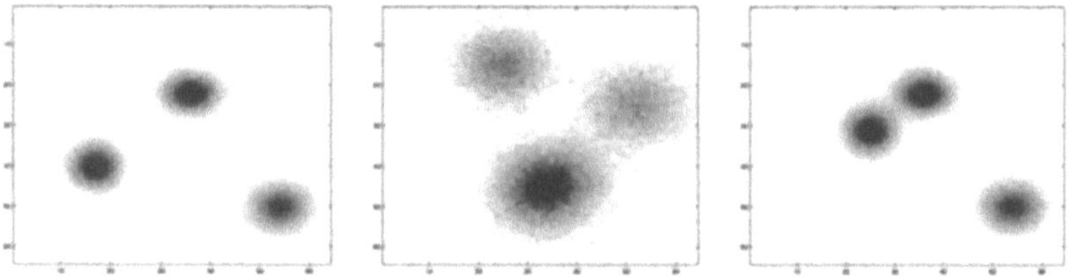

Figure 6.16: Distribution of synthetic data : 3 clusters

number of clusters	log likelihood		
K	left image	middle image	right image
2	4.806	5.269	4.269
3	4.112(min)	5.156(min)	4.133(min)
4	4.237	5.285	4.255
5	4.317	5.329	4.336
6	4.424	5.283	4.404

Table 6.1: Log likelihood computed with different K (3 clusters exists)

left graph the clusters are well separated, in the middle graph the clusters are separated but their variances are big, in the right graph some clusters are very close to each other(but still not mixed together). Data in Table 6.1 to Table 6.3 show that the number of clusters can be found out correctly under all these synthetic distributions. It seems that the log likelihood is a good criterion to detect the number of clusters in synthetic data which comply with the mixed Gaussian distribution.

When the experiments are extended to natural color images, we set K_{min} to 2 and K_{max} to 7. We find that the negative of log likelihood derived using Equation (6.25) tends to decrease monotonously as K increases from 2 to 7. Therefore the method of finding the minimum point suggested in Equation (6.20) can not be applied here otherwise the cluster number will always be set to 7 whether the image content is complicated or not. Several explanations can be found for this monotonous behavior of the log likelihood of real images. First, for natural images the assumption of independence among feature elements does not hold. The color channels are not independent of each other; for example, the three channels are highly correlated in RGB space. The situation will be better if

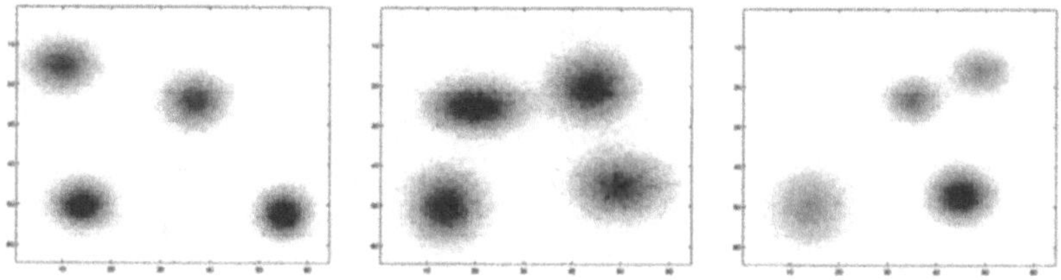

Figure 6.17: Distribution of synthetic data : 4 clusters

number of clusters	log likelihood		
K	left image	middle image	right image
2	5.492	5.528	5.041
3	4.887	5.146	4.624
4	4.506(min)	4.949 (min)	4.595(min)
5	4.584	4.989	4.664
6	4.684	5.027	4.782

Table 6.2: Log likelihood computed with different K (4 clusters exists)

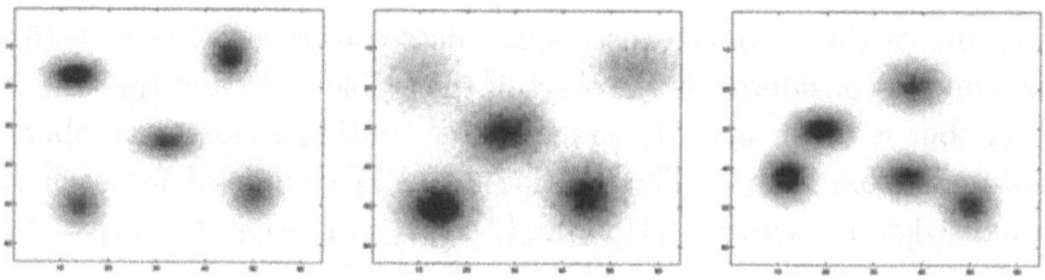

Figure 6.18: Distribution of synthetic data : 5 clusters

number of clusters	log likelihood		
K	left image	middle image	right image
2	5.369	5.465	4.991
3	5.194	5.319	4.766
4	4.815	5.193	4.720
5	4.433(min)	5.035(min)	4.615(min)
6	4.478	5.098	4.676

Table 6.3: Log likelihood computed with different K (5 clusters exists)

$CIE - L^*u^*v^*$ or HSV space is selected because the correlation between color channels in these spaces is smaller. Second and more important, the distribution of colors in real images is not so regular as mixed Gaussian distribution. Some clusters are very close to each other or maybe even mixed up. There are also many small irregular clusters existing and in some value range the distribution can be quite uniform or it may present a white noise alike appearance. All these possible situations make the real distribution highly irregular compared to the synthetic mixed Gaussian distribution where there are only several salient and smooth clusters. In Figure 6.19 the three dimensional histogram of $CIE - L^*u^*v^*$ data of the natural image in Figure 6.1 is displayed. It can be seen that the distribution is irregular and it is not obvious how many clusters actually exist.

Although it is difficult to determine the best cluster number or K for real world images, since it is critical to the final segmentation result we must get an estimate of it in order to achieve a reasonably good performance. For real world images, although the negative of log likelihood calculated using Equation (6.25) tends to decrease monotonously as K increases, we can find out a turning point where afterwards the further increasing of the K only causes small decrease of the Equation (6.25). This point is considered as the start of the stable state and the true cluster number is taken here. In practice the candidate cluster numbers we choose are from 2 to 7. The $-\frac{1}{M}\log\{P_K(X)\}$ computed for each K is normalized to be within $[0,1]$ ($-\log\{P'_2(X)\} = 1, -\log\{P'_7(X)\} = 0$).

$$-\log\{P'_K(X)\} = \frac{-\log\{P_K(X)\} + \log\{P_7(X)\}}{-\log\{P_2(X)\} + \log\{P_7(X)\}} \tag{6.26}$$

The smallest K which satisfies $-\log\{P'_K(Y)\} < \textit{threshold}$ is selected as the number of clusters, where *threshold* is set to 0.15 in our experiment.

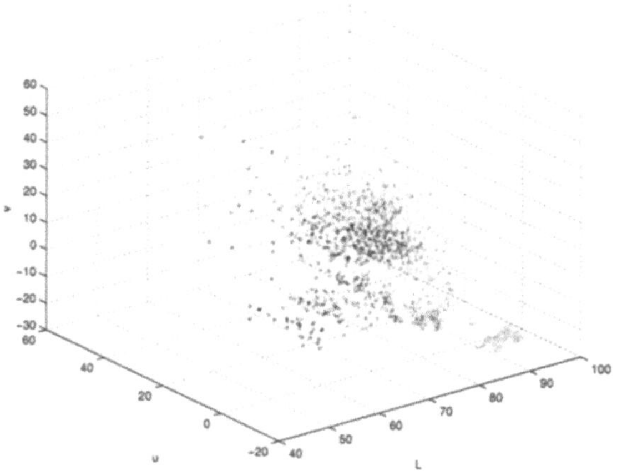

Figure 6.19: Histogram of a real world image

6.2.3 Markov random field model and Gibbs distribution

Need for spatial constraint

The clustering algorithm discussed in the previous sections only consider visual features. It does not take into account any spatial relationship among the image pixels. In fact, spatial information or the spatial constraint is very important in segmentation: the purpose of segmentation is to label out pixels spatially connected and having similar features as different regions. If segmentation is only based on features, the result will likely be more fragmented than expected. Although techniques like edge preserved smoothing will be helpful, the problem can not be totally solved. Our solution is trying to incorporate the spatial constraints by using the Markov Random Field and Gibbs Distribution model.

Basic concepts of Markov random field

A Markov Random Field (MRF) as a statistical approach to model and process image and other random signal has been extensively used since 1970s when the correspondence between MRF and Gibbs distributions (GD) was established. In our segmentation algorithm, we try to incorporate the spatial constraint of image data by using GD. The GD is used to characterize the spatial grouping of pixels into regions whereas the clustering of the previous section is used to group pixels of similar feature values into regions. The combination of the two is expected to generate better results.

The basic idea of applying MRF model in segmentation is as follows. If a pixel is of a certain region type, then neighboring pixels should also have a high probability of belonging to the same type. First, let us briefly introduce the basic concepts of MRF, i.e., neighborhood system, cliques, clique potential and GD.

Digital image is usually defined over a finite $N_1 \times N_2$ rectangular lattice of points: $L = \{(i,j)|1 \leq i \leq N_1, 1 \leq j \leq N_2\}$. The neighborhood system on the lattice L is defined as:

Definition 1: Subsets η of L described as

$$\eta = \{\eta_{ij}|(i,j) \in L, \eta_{ij} \subseteq L\} \tag{6.27}$$

is a neighborhood system of lattice L if and only if η_{ij} obeys:
1. (i,j) not belong to η_{ij} and
2. $if(k,l) \in \eta_{ij}, then(i,j) \in \eta_{kl}$

A hierarchically ordered sequence of neighborhood systems which is most commonly used in image modeling is shown in Figure 6.20. The neighborhood system η_{ij} is called *mth order neighborhood system.*

Markov Random Field is characterized by the Markov property, that is, the probability of a pixel taking a particular value is dependent only on its neighborhood pixels.

$$p(x_{ij}|x) = p(x_{ij}|x_{kl}, x_{kl} \in \eta_{ij}) \tag{6.28}$$

To concisely define the probability function of MRF, the definitions of cliques and GD are given below.

Definition 2: A clique C related to a neighborhood system η is a subset of neighborhood that,
1. C is a single pixel, or
2. if (i,j) and (k,l) both belong to C, then $(i,j) \in \eta_{kl}$.

The types of cliques associated with a 1st and 2nd neighborhood system are depicted in Figure 6.21. It can be seen that pixels in a clique are neighbors of each other.

Definition 3: A random field defined on a neighborhood system has Gibbs Distribution, if and only if its joint distribution is of the form:

$$p(x) = \frac{1}{Z} \exp\{-\sum_C V_C(x)\} \tag{6.29}$$

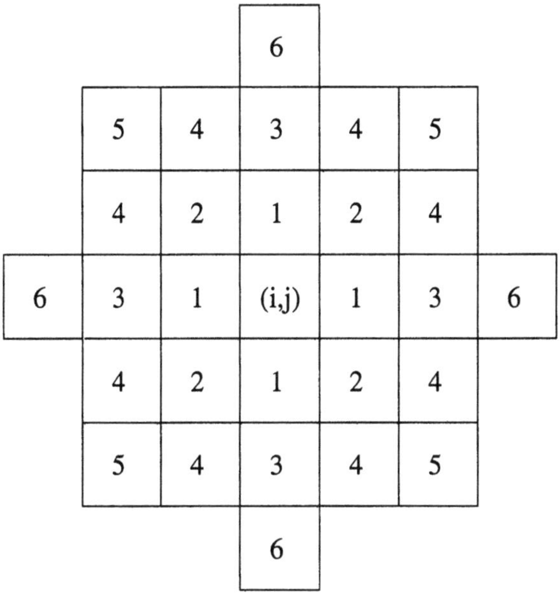

Figure 6.20: Hierarchically ordered neighborhood system

where $V_C(x)$ = potential associated with clique C, which depends only on pixels that belong to clique C.

Using the above probability formula, the MRF model allows us to model the joint probability distribution of the image pixels in terms of the local spatial interaction, which is expressed as GD. The usage of GD in segmentation and the related clique potential definition method are discussed in the following.

MAP segmentation algorithm

After the feature extraction step, every image pixel is characterized by a feature vector. We model the image as a collection of regions of uniform or slowly varying feature vectors. The only sharp transition of feature values occur at the region boundaries. Let the feature image be x. A segmentation of the image into regions is denoted by q, where $q_s = i$ means that the pixel at s belong to region type (cluster) i. Therefore, the segmentation problem is defined as an estimation of q given x. We try to maximize the *a posteriori* probability density function $p(q|x)$. By Bayes'

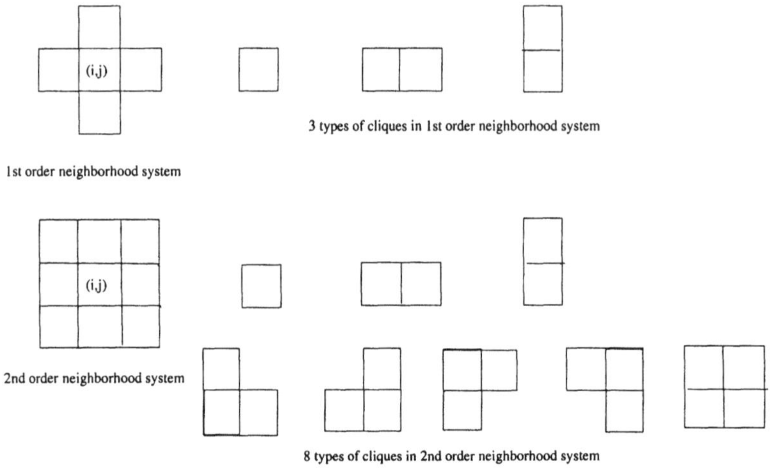

Figure 6.21: Clique types in 1st and 2nd order neighborhood system

theorem,

$$P(q|x) = \frac{P(x|q)P(q)}{P(x)} \tag{6.30}$$

where $P(q)$ is the *a priori* density of the region process and $P(x|q)$ is the conditional density of the observed image data given the distribution of regions. Since x does not effect the maximization process, we have,

$$P(q|x) \propto P(x|q)P(q) \tag{6.31}$$

Equivalently, we can maximize the logarithm of the right hand of the Equation (6.31): $\ln P(q) + \ln P(x|q)$.

In this maximum *a posteriori* (MAP) estimation, the two probability function $P(q)$ and $P(x|q)$ can be imagined as a two layer model. The high layer is the region process $P(q)$, which is modeled by a MRF, having the form of Equation (6.28) and Equation (6.29). It is used to characterize the spatial clustering of pixels into regions, that is, as we mentioned above, if a pixel is of a certain region type, then neighboring pixels should also have a high probability of belonging to the same type. Implicit in this distribution is the statistical information related to region size, shape, orientation and probability of various type of regions. The low layer $P(x|q)$ represents the feature distribution characteristic of the specific region type. In our implementation, we assume that inside a particular region, the features should have uniform intensities added with white noise. As we can see from above discussion, the two layers have different emphasis: the high layer deals with spatial continuity of the region and low layer constraints the feature uniformity inside the region. If the continuity in both spatial and feature domain can be well represented, the segmentation can be expected to have good performance. Now let us cover these two layers in more detail.

In the high layer, the region is modeled by MRF, using Equation (6.29). The probability is determined by the various clique potentials. The less the total energy, the more probable is the scene realization to happen. We apply a class of GD to model the region, considering only 2nd order neighborhood system and assuming that the random field is homogeneous.

In Figure 6.21 there are 10 types of cliques. For the single pixel clique, the clique potential is defined as:

$$V_C(q) = \alpha_k, if\ q_{ij} = k \tag{6.32}$$

α is the parameter representing the *a priori* probability of a certain region type or the percentage of pixels in various regions. The lower the value of α, the more likely the pixel belongs to that region type.

For cliques containing more than one pixels,

$$V_C(q) = \begin{cases} -\zeta, & if\ all\ q_{ij}\ in\ C\ are\ equal \\ \zeta, & otherwise \end{cases} \tag{6.33}$$

where each clique type has its corresponding ζ.
They are the parameters controling the size, shape and orientation of the regions. The parameter ζ is positive so the neighboring pixels are more likely to belong to same region than different regions. The bigger the value of ζ, the smaller the opportunity for small regions to appear.

It is assumed that the random field is homogeneous, that is, the clique potential parameters are not dependent on the location of the cliques, only dependent on the clique type and the pixels within the clique belonging to which region types.

In the low layer, the region features within the region are supposed to be uniform. The variation in intensity which is inevitable in reality is modeled as white noise. Assuming there are K region types in the image and the feature vectors are $y_q, q = 1..K$. Thus, given the region type k and the Gaussian noise n_{ij} with zero mean and variance δ, the feature vector of the pixel can be modeled as,

$$x_{ij} = y_q + n_{ij} \tag{6.34}$$

and $P(x|q)$ can be expressed as a Gaussian function ,

$$P(x|q) = \frac{1}{\sqrt{2\pi\delta^2}} \exp\left\{-\frac{1}{2\delta^2}(x_{ij} - y_q)^2\right\} \tag{6.35}$$

So $\ln P(q) + \ln P(x|q)$ can be expressed as:

$$\ln P(q) + \ln P(x|q) \propto -\sum_C V_C(q) - \sum_{ij} \frac{1}{2\delta^2}(x_{ij} - y_q)^2 \tag{6.36}$$

The global maximization of this log-likelihood corresponds to the best segmentation of the image under the MRF model.

Suboptimal greedy algorithm

Since there are $K^{N_1 * N_2}$ possible scene realizations altogether, the global maximization of the Equation (6.36) requires extensive computation. It can be done using Gibbs sampler or simulated annealing. Since the computational complexities of these algorithms are too high, we adopt a suboptimal implementation. Instead of maximization of the global probability function, we maximize the conditional probability density of every pixel $P(q_{ij}|x_{ij}, q_{kl}, (k,l) \in \eta_{ij})$, given its feature vector x_{ij} and the segmentation result of neighborhood pixels $q_{kl}, (k,l) \in \eta_{ij}$. Thus the objective function is :

$$\min\{\ln P(q_{ij}|x_{ij}, (k,l) \in \eta_{ij})\} \propto \min_k\{-\sum_C V_C(q_{ij} = k) - \frac{1}{2\delta^2}(x_{ij} - y_k)^2\} \tag{6.37}$$

The algorithm begins with an initial segment from the ordinary clustering procedure. Then it iterates between the maximization for every pixel using Equation (6.37) and estimating the vector codebook y. The circle is carried out until convergence. The convergence condition can be when the number of pixels with changing region type between cycles is under a threshold. In calculation of a pixel probability, the labels of neighboring pixels equal to their values of the previous circle. The pixels are updated within the iteration in raster scan order. The algorithm can be called a greedy algorithm. The result of this iterative algorithm is that small regions tend to be smoothed away and the segmentation becomes smoother and less fragmented than before.

Now we have the algorithm framework but still need to know the parameters used in Equation (6.37). The feature vector codebook (mean and variance of various classes) is easy to get in the estimation step, while the different clique potentials determining the region process are difficult to get *a priori*. Actually the main difficulty of using GD as a region model is how to estimate the parameters of the model. The parameter estimation issue is usually done off-line using some realization from the distribution as training data. Some approaches [7] require solutions to a set of non-linear equations or uses histogram and standard, linear, least square equations. In both implementations, training data of all region types should be given. However, in our home photo segmentation project, the objects are not restricted to a few kinds and the appearance of the same kind of object can be very different from picture to picture. We use MRF/GD model roughly as a spatial constraint and a supplement to the clustering algorithm carried out in feature space, rather than use different GD cliques potentials precisely to model the object, as done in some supervised segmentation applications. In fact, in our applications, the MRF/GD as a region model is only a supplement to the clustering algorithm. The Gibbs region model by itself is not very useful. It can be seen that, without the feature space knowledge derived from clustering, the optimal segmentation is just one region. However if combined with feature space clustering, it can impose some spatial constraint in the process of segmentation, so the spatial continuity can be emphasized.

Our model uses a second order neighborhood system and for simplicity omits the clique types containing 3 pixels or more. We assume all region types have the same prior possibility so that clique potentials associated with one pixel are not taken into account. Therefore after the simplification only four types of cliques are considered. The clique types whose pixels are four-connected are given potential value ζ_1 and whose pixels are eight-connected are given value ζ_2, where $\zeta_1 \geq \zeta 2$. In our implementations, the ζ_1 is set to be equal to half the average clustering error when the iteration begins and ζ_2 is set to be half of ζ_1. As the iteration evolves, we increase the ζ value to accelerate the smoothing process.

In Equation (6.37), the variance of each region type is considered in the maximization. In practice we find that adding this form will cause the region type with larger variance to become bigger and bigger during each iteration while the small regions disappear gradually. It seems that in this iterative procedure the variance of each region type should not be incorporated. So the Equation (6.37) is rewritten as:

$$\min\{\ln P(q_{ij}|x_{ij},(k,l)\in\eta_{ij})\} \propto \min_k\{-\sum_C V_C(q_{ij}=k)-(x_{ij}-y_k)^2\} \quad (6.38)$$

Summary

We adopt a MRF/GD model to include spatial constraints into the clustering algorithm. The image data is represented by a two layer model: at the high layer, the GD is used to characterize the clustering of image pixels into regions with similar features. At the low layer the feature uniformity within a region type is guaranteed. Given the feature vector codebook, the *a posteriori* probability function for the distribution of the regions is defined. It has two components, corresponding to the two layer constraints respectively. Since the global optimization is computationally prohibitive, a suboptimal estimation method is proposed. It alternates between maximizing the *a posteriori* probability density and estimating the vector codebook. This algorithm sub-optimally separates the image pixels into clusters based on both their feature vector proximity and spatial continuity. The advantage is that it keeps the significant regions while removing trivial details. It has advantage over both region growing algorithms that uses only local information, and clustering which uses only global feature distribution and neglects local spatial information. It is also superior than the edge detection method because it deals with regions directly. In edge detection it is often difficult to get regions from the detected boundaries because these boundaries are often not closed and discontinuous. In our implementation the regions are well defined and it is easy for subsequent processing such as object recognition.

6.2.4 Region analysis and region merging

As introduced in the previous sections, the segmentation algorithm adopted is clustering in the feature space, where the MRF model is applied to emphasize the spatial continuity. Whether MRF is applied or not, clustering can be viewed as a process in which each image pixel is assigned to one of a finite number of "region types" characterized by image properties (color, texture). It does not label out each object spatially. The definition of "object" applied here is a group of image pixels that are spatially connected (4-neighborhood) and belong to the same region type. Because the following cataloging and recognition procedure works on the objects, it is necessary to carry out a "region labeling" or "connected component analysis" process to give each spatially isolated object a unique label as its identification number.

When region labeling is finished, the whole segmentation routine can come to an end. However we would like to do some extra work which is region merging. The purpose is to remove those very small regions (which will be of trivial importance for the image interpretation) and to merge regions which share a very weak boundary. As said before, clustering takes place in feature space so its disadvantage is lack of spatial information. Although MRF model is incorporated, due to simplification only spatial information of a small local neighborhood is taken into account. Larger scale spatial interactivity is not used till now. Therefore it is preferable to combine the clustering with other segmentation techniques based on spatial operation, which include the "split and merge" algorithm [21] and edge detection approach. We will design a region merging method which works by examining and eliminating region boundaries based on their merit values. By region merging the spatial continuity in a larger scale can be used effectively.

In fact in the clustering stage the parameters have been deliberately set up so that an over segmented result will be obtained. Region merging is used to compensate for this over segmented result adaptively. The algorithm we design will only merge regions sharing weak boundaries and it uses different decisive rules for tiny, small and medium regions. The big regions will be left unchanged. This method will work particularly well for slow varying areas that are often likely to be separated into two or more parts by an over-segmenting clustering approach. Since there are no strong edges between them, our region merging procedure can effectively merge them together.

Region labeling algorithm

The region labeling procedure for binary image can be found in [21]. It works for images which contain objects (pixel value of 1) and background (pixel value of 0). Only a minor change is needed for images containing multiple kinds of objects as in our case. The algorithm is given in the following, where num_reg is used to denote the number of total regions, $T(i,j)$ represents the region type of the pixel (i,j) and $L(i,j)$ denotes the region label of the pixel.

(1) algorithm begins: let $num\_reg = 0$.

(2) Scan the image from left to right, top to bottom:

   (a) if $T(i,j) = T(i,j-1)$ and $T(i,j) \neq T(i-1,j)$, let $L(i,j) = L(i,j-1)$.

   (b) if $T(i,j) = T(i-1,j)$ and $T(i,j) \neq T(i,j-1)$, let $L(i,j) = L(i-1,j)$.

   (c) if $T(i,j) = T(i-1,j) = T(i,j-1)$ and $L(i-1,j) = L(i,j-1)$, let $L(i,j) = L(i-1,j)$.

   (d) if $T(i,j) \neq T(i,j-1)$ and $T(i,j) \neq T(i-1,j)$, then take the current pixel as the start of a new region: let $num\_reg = num\_reg + 1$, $L(i,j) = num\_reg$.

(e) if $T(i,j) = T(i-1,j) = T(i,j-1)$ but $L(i-1,j) \neq L(i,j-1)$, then the two regions are actually one region, let $L(i,j) = L(i-1,j)$,
previous region labels should be modified by executing subroutine **adjust**(i,j).

(3) calculate the information for each region: region area, the minimum rectangular box that contains the region.

The subroutine **adjust**(i,j) is given as:

(1) let $low = min(L(i,j-1), L(i-1,j))$
$high = max(L(i,j-1), L(i-1,j))$,
$num\_reg = num\_reg - 1$.

(2) scan image from left to right, from top row to current row, for each pixel (k,l),

(a) if $L(k,l) = high$, let $L(k,l) = low$.

(b) if $L(k,l) > high$, let $L(k,l) = L(k,l) - 1$.

Region merging based on edge merit

In the region merging process we decide whether or not to merge two regions based on the boundary merit, i.e., whether the boundary between them corresponds to a real edge or not. Edge is an image property related to both feature and spatial domain and it is very important for human visual perception. In digital images different objects are usually separated by salient edges therefore edge detection is a critical technique for many applications such as compression, segmentation, vision for industrial automation and stereo vision. By incorporating boundary verification the overall segmentation can be made more consistent with human perception. For region merging the merit of boundary is calculated from the color gradient around the boundary. Since color gradient is already obtained when performing adaptive smoothing, it can be directly used here.

There can be two different approaches to implement the region merging. One way is working directly on the boundaries: keeping record of all boundaries and their topological relationships, deciding whether to keep a boundary or eliminate it and adjust the topological relationship appropriately. The process begins with the weakest boundary and it repeats until all remaining boundaries can not be deleted anymore. The other approach is working on the regions: keeping record of all regions, deciding whether to merge a region with one of its neighbors by investigating its boundaries. In similar work reported in [22], the first approach was taken. A major problem with working on boundaries is that they can not be removed arbitrarily without considering topological constraints. Otherwise some unacceptable topologies will occur.

In our experiment we propose a method that works on regions. Different approaches are adopted for regions with tiny, small, medium or big area because of their different roles in the image. Area thresholds are set to decide which class the region belongs to. Regions smaller than 1/125 of the total image area are classified as "tiny". Those bigger than tiny but smaller than 1/25 of the image size is regarded as "small" and "medium" region can occupy up to 1/6 of the total area. Big regions which takes up more than 1/6 of the image area will be left unchanged because they are usually important for subsequent classification or recognition so we are very careful with them and do not merge them to prevent the possibility of any mixture of major objects. For a tiny region, the algorithm will merge it with its neighboring region sharing the longest border whatever the intensity of that border is. For a small or medium size region, the merit value of each of its boundaries is computed using the weighting factor $W(g(i,j))$ derived and used in color adaptive smoothing. The merit of a boundary is defined as the average of the $W(g(i,j))$ along the boundary, where $g(i,j)$ is the color gradient value. $W(g(i,j))$ takes value from 0 to 1 and it is a decreasing function with regard to $g(i,j)$. Therefore the larger the merit value of a boundary, the more likely it is to be eliminated. Among all boundaries which are not very short, the weakest one is selected as a candidate and it is compared with a merit threshold to decide whether to merge the two regions that it separates. If the merge is not suggested then the region under investigation will be left unchanged and will not be processed later. It is also guaranteed that other regions will not be merged with it in further processing. The only difference when processing small or medium size region is that for a medium size region a more strict threshold is applied to determine whether merging is permitted. The algorithm begins with the smallest regions and terminates when there are only big regions and those that can not be merged remaining. The overall algorithm is given below:

(1) algorithm begins, when there are tiny regions left in the image, do the following:

    (a) get the smallest region, calculate the length of its boundaries, find out the longest boundary.

    (b) merge the two regions separated by that boundary,

update the region labels and region information.

(2) when there are small and medium size regions not processed left in the image, do the following:

   (a) get the smallest region among them as the candidate region.
   (b) calculate the length and merit value of its boundaries. Among the boundaries not very short, select the weakest one as a candidate boundary.
   (c) compare the merit value of the candidate boundary with the appropriate threshold:
   if it can be removed, merge the two regions separated by this boundary, update the region labels and region information.
   if it can not be deleted, mark the candidate region as "cannot be merged" and it will not be processed again.

(3) merging terminates.

Compared with the approach that works directly on boundaries, the advantage of this method is that it is easy to implement and there are few topological constraints to consider. Every time the region is merged, the necessary adjustment on region labels and other region information can be easily achieved.

We have discussed various aspects of our segmentation algorithm in detail. Experiment results on synthetic data have been given to prove the effectiveness of the clustering algorithm and the cluster validation method. More experiment results on real home photos and some other test images will be provided to illustrate the performance of our solution of color and texture segmentation.

6.3 Experiment results

6.3.1 Experiment setup

We have discussed our feature extraction methods and segmentation algorithms. We will demonstrate the effectiveness of the algorithms on real home photos and some synthetic images.

The algorithms are implemented in C language on a SUN SPARC 20 workstation running UNIX system.

The collection of home photos used for testing contains over 2,000 images. The contents of the images vary greatly from each other. The majority of the photos are taken outdoor while there are also many indoor scenes. In most cases there are one or more persons present in the images while some photos are pure natural scenes, landmarks, or objects.

To test the performance of the wavelet texture features, the natural home photos can hardly meet our requirements because usually very few regular texture patterns are present in these images. To give a better evaluation of the texture features, we use some Brodatz texture patterns to make a few synthetic texture images to do the testing on texture segmentation. As to the segmentation involving a combination of color and texture, natural images are chosen as test data.

The experiments will be divided into 5 parts, emphasizing the MRF/GD constraint, color segmentation(color spaces comparison), region merging, texture segmentation, and the segmentation combining color and texture, respectively.

6.3.2 Experiment results

Color segmentation - performance of the MRF/GD model

First we will demonstrate the effect of the MRF/GD model in the segmentation of color images. The original image, clsutering results with and without MRF/GD model are presented in Figure 6.22 and Figure 6.23.

In these examples, the color features are the $CIE - L^*u^*v^*$ color components. The common parts of the two procedures include the transform from RGB to $CIE - L^*u^*v^*$ space, the edge-preserved smoothing step and the unsupervised clustering. The only difference lies with whether MRF/GD model, as spatial constraint, is applied or not after the clustering.

The results show that the clustering result with the MRF/GD constraint can be smoother than without it. Not only the region edges appear smoother, there are also less small regions which are noise look-alike existing in the results. It should be noted that there are no significant differences between the results because the MRF/GD model is applied in a limited way in this research and it will not greatly alter the clustering results.

Color segmentation - comparison of color spaces

Color is the most important clue for home photo segmentation because almost all digital home photos are stored in true color or indexed color format and the color feature itself is very reliable for segmentation. Color is a well defined feature and it is closely related to the surface property of the object material in the image. When lacking any other prior knowledge

(a) (b) (c)

(a) Original Image (b) Clustering result with MRF/GD model (c) Clustering result without MRF/GD model

Figure 6.22: Color segmentation—with or without MRF/GD model: example 1

(a) (b) (c)

(a) Original Image (b) Clustering result with MRF/GD model (c) Clustering result without MRF/GD model

Figure 6.23: Color segmentation—with or without MRF/GD model: example 2

of the object properties in the image, it is generally reasonable to assume that an object will present uniform color and different objects can be separated by their color appearances. Many color spaces have been proposed and studied for various color processing tasks [23,24,2]. In the experiment, we test the performance of two color spaces HSV and $CIE - L^*u^*v^*$ in segmentation.

The segmentation scheme is given as:

(1) Color space transformation from RGB to HSV or $CIE - L^*u^*v^*$.
For $CIE - L^*u^*v^*$ space, color features are L, u and v.
For HSV space, color features are v, $vs \cos h$, $vs \sin h$.
In both cases Euclidean distance is used to measure the color similarity.

(2) Edge-preserved smoothing for color feature.

(3) Clustering in the 3-dimensional color feature space:
Varying the number of clusters from 2 to 7 and select best K and the codebook.

(4) Segmentation using codebook size K derived above.
GMRF model incorporated by using Equation 6.38.

We try to use as few thresholds as possible in this algorithm. Only several parameters and thresholds must be set for the algorithm:
In the EPSM part, the iteration of smoothing is repeated for 3 times. In each iteration the parameter τ, which controls the degree of smoothing, is set to twice of the mean value of the color gradient of the whole image at the beginning of that iteration. As for the cluster validation part, as just discussed, only one threshold is necessary to find out the best number of clusters.

The segmentation results on various kinds of home photos(natural scene, city scene, portrait, objects...) are evaluated and compared. Some examples are displayed from Figure 6.24 to Figure 6.29. All the images are of 128×192 resolution.

In the first example, segmentation results from $CIE - L^*u^*v^*$ and HSV have only minor differences and it is difficult to judge the results. As both results are reasonable in these cases, it can be said that their performance is very close to each other. It is noteworthy to mention that for the same image the cluster number detected using $CIE-L^*u^*v^*$ or HSV are not exactly the same. Because of the different color representation by $CIE-L^*u^*v^*$ and HSV, the color histograms will present different shape, so the simple cluster validation criterion we adopt will probably not get

(a) (b) (c)

(a) Original Image (b) Segmentation results by *Luv* (c) Segmentation result by *HSV*

Figure 6.24: Color segmentation—comparison of color spaces: example 1

(a) (b) (c)

(a) Original Image (b) Segmentation results by *Luv* (c) Segmentation result by *HSV*

Figure 6.25: Color segmentation—comparison of color spaces: example 2

(a) (b) (c)

(a) Original Image (b) Segmentation results by *Luv* (c) Segmentation result by *HSV*

Figure 6.26: Color segmentation—comparison of color spaces: example 3

(a) (b) (c)

(a) Original Image (b) Segmentation results by *Luv* (c) Segmentation result by *HSV*

Figure 6.27: Color segmentation—comparison of color spaces: example 4

(a) (b) (c)

(a) Original Image (b) Segmentation results by *Luv* (c) Segmentation result by *HSV*

Figure 6.28: Color segmentation—comparison of color spaces: example 5

(a) (b) (c)

(a) Original Image (b) Segmentation results by *Luv* (c) Segmentation result by *HSV*

Figure 6.29: Color segmentation—comparison of color spaces: example 6

the same estimation. The difference, if existing, is usually small (+1 or -1).

In the next three examples, the $CIE - L^*u^*v^*$ model has a slightly better performance than HSV in that the major objects are less fragmented(grass in Example 2, trees in Example 3).

From Example 4 to 6, the experiment results strongly favour $CIE - L^*u^*v^*$ than HSV. In Example 5, flowers are not well segmented by HSV: the result is affected by small color variation, while $CIE - L^*u^*v^*$ gives encouraging result. In the Example 6 where a street scene is presented, both segmentation results are not very satisfactory due to the complexity of the image content. In this case, the ideal segmentation is very difficult to achieve by color alone. However, it can be observed that $CIE - L^*u^*v^*$ still out-performs HSV: the human face is kept as a whole object and the background(building, road, tree) is also treated better. The building, tree and road are labeled as different classes using $CIE - L^*u^*v^*$ while significant parts of them are all mixed together using HSV.

Generally speaking, the performance of HSV and $CIE - L^*u^*v^*$ for segmentation is comparable and similar in many situations. This is because both color spaces are perceptually uniform or sub-uniform. The difference is that the distance measure in HSV seems to emphasize more on the brightness variation, while proximity in $CIE - L^*u^*v^*$ is based more on the chromatic distance. HSV has good discriminating ability for different hues when the color intensity is high but the discrimination is poor when the color is dark. However for $CIE - L^*u^*v^*$ it seems that the discriminating ability for different hues does not decrease as the color becomes darker, and thus it is more perceptually uniform than HSV. So the distance derived from $CIE - L^*u^*v^*$ space reduces the effect of shading and highlights existing within objects. This results in different performance of these color spaces. $CIE - L^*u^*v^*$ is less sensitive to changes in lighting conditions than HSV, which means it is better when dealing with shadow and highlights. The results from $CIE - L^*u^*v^*$ is also more perceptually satisfactory than HSV and it will give a result closer to the manual segmentation, if there is one. In summary, the experiments show that the $CIE - L^*u^*v^*$ color space has similar or better performance than HSV in most cases. Therefore, it is favorable to use $CIE - L^*u^*v^*$ color space for segmentation.

Color segmentation - performance of region analysis and region merging

In this section, we will test our region labeling and region merging algorithm as described previously. After the region labeling and merging procedure, the final results of segmentation are given from Figure 6.30 to Figure 6.32. $CIE - L^*u^*v^*$ color features are used in these examples. The left images are the original photos while the middle ones are the intermediate results after clustering. The right images are segmentation results after region labeling and merging. In most cases visually acceptable results are derived: the important and large objects are segmented correctly, such as sky, tree, field, building, human face, road, etc. The over-segmented intermediate result by feature space clustering is compensated effectively by the region merging algorithm. In some cases the segmentation is not ideal as some mixture or over-segment exists. These kinds of error are very difficult to be corrected when only low-level features are considered. Usually, a more satisfactory segmentation is only possible when some high level prior knowledge or training is available.

The reason for the better performance for the combination of clustering and region merging can be summarized as: Two kinds of constraints can be applied to segmentation - one is the uniformity of feature within the region and the other is the discontinuity of the feature between regions. Clustering or region merging emphasize one side of these two aspects respectively. Moreover, clustering works on global feature distribution, while region merging works on local feature variation. By combining them, a better overall performance can be expected because both global and local information are applied. It is required that clustering obtain an over-segmented result because the information loss caused by under-segmentation can not be recovered or compensated by region merging. The requirement for region merging to work effectively is that the clustering procedure does not merge different types of regions.

Texture image segmentation

Texture is more difficult to process than color. In real world images, texture can often be perceived but most of them are not so regular and most often there are only few kinds of texture patterns in one image. Therefore natural images are not ideal for the experiments to test the texture features. To test the performance of the features extracted by the wavelet frame transform and edge-preserved smoothing, we use some synthetic texture images that contain a few different texture patches. The purpose

(a) (b) (c)

(a) Original Image (b) Intermediate segmentation result after clustering in *Luv* space (c) Final segmentation result after region merging

Figure 6.30: Performance of region merging: example 1

(a) (b) (c)

(a) Original Image (b) Intermediate segmentation result after clustering in *Luv* space (c) Final segmentation result after region merging

Figure 6.31: Performance of region merging: example 2

(a) (b) (c)

(a) Original Image (b) Intermediate segmentation result after clustering in *Luv* space (c) Final segmentation result after region merging

Figure 6.32: Performance of region merging: example 3

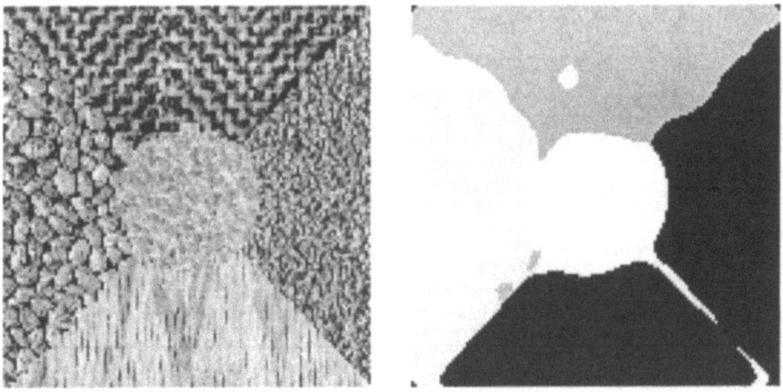

(a) Original image (b) Segmentation result

Figure 6.33: Texture segmentation: example 1

of this experiment is mainly for testing the performance of the features, i.e., their ability to describe and discriminate various kinds of textures. The cluster validation will not be a major concern here, so we manually set the cluster number in each case. Region merging step is not included in this experiment because we are more interested in the clustering result which reflects the performance of the features.

The segmentation scheme is given as:

(1) Wavelet frame transform to extract feature vectors:
9th order symmetric QMF filter
3-level decomposition, 9-dimensional feature vectors

(2) Edge-preserved smoothing for feature vectors.

(3) Clustering in the 9-dimensional texture feature space.

The four examples displayed in Figure 6.33 and Figure 6.36 are of 128×128 resolution. The image in Figure 6.35 is also used as an example to show the result of edge-preserved smoothing for texture vectors. In all the cases the segmentation results are encouraging. It proves the effectiveness of our feature vectors in describing and discriminating textures.

Segmentation combining color and texture

It may seem natural and easy for human beings to use different clues(color, texture...) effectively when they segment or interpret an image. In fact when a person is doing manual segmentation, he/she is very

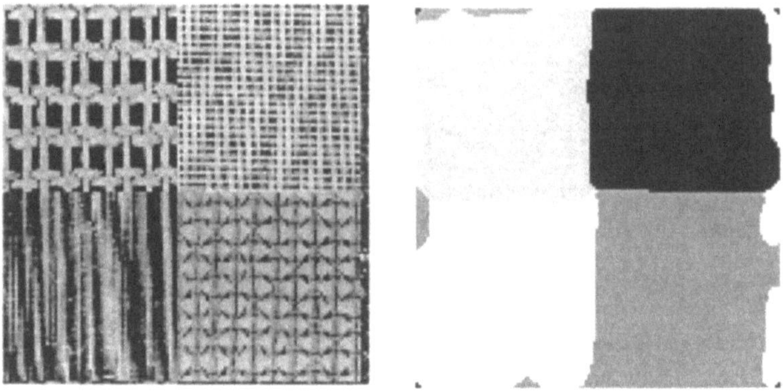

(a) Original image (b) Segmentation result

Figure 6.34: Texture segmentation: example 2

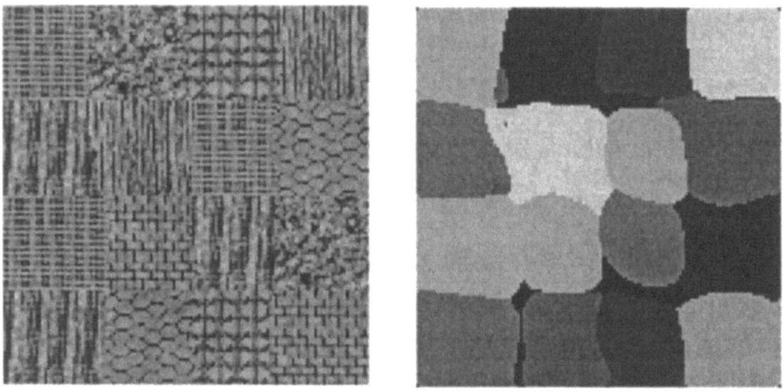

(a) Original image (b) Segmentation result

Figure 6.35: Texture segmentation: example 3

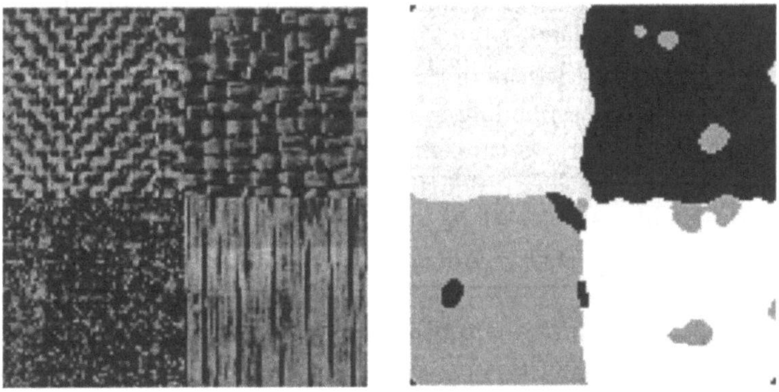

(a) Original image (b) Segmentation result

Figure 6.36: Texture segmentation: example 4

likely to incorporate some high level knowledge, whether consciously or not. The manual segmentation result may be based more on the high level human interpretation than on color or texture feature. So it is very hard for us to know how users combine color and texture in segmentation. When coming to the automatic segmentation, the combination of color and texture is a difficult and challenging issue because they belong to two different domains and have different physical meaning. In automatic segmentation algorithm, an appropriate distance measure is crucial to a good final result. For color or texture feature alone, a suitable distance measure is easy to select but it is not readily available for their combination. In some retrieval systems [18,19] based on low-level (color, texture, structure...) similarity, users can specify the importance of each feature by giving it an appropriate weight. The final score of a matching is based on the weighted distance of various features. The weights can be decided by the user according to their particular request, but for us the automatic selection of such weights are nearly impossible as they are really domain and application dependent and there is no general rule for deriving them.

The fixed weights are given to the color and texture features. This is done by setting the dynamic range of the texture feature to the same as that of the lightness feature. It is also preferable to decrease the dimension of the texture features, because in most natural scenes there are not so many subtle distinctions to discriminate as in the synthetic texture images (e.g., that shown in Figure 6.35). In most cases it is only necessary to discriminate between texture and non-texture area so we use a one-dimensional texture feature. It is calculated by using *Karhunen-Loeve* transform on the original texture vector. The transforming matrix is derived from the statistics of the whole image and the transformed feature component corresponding to the largest eigenvalue is selected as the one-dimension texture feature. Since the dynamic range of the texture feature is often quite small compared to that of the color features, if they are combined directly to form a feature vector, the texture difference will be overwhelmed by that of color. Therefore in our implementation the dynamic range of the texture feature is extended linearly to the same as the dynamic range of the lightness feature. After this the texture feature is added to the color feature as an extra fourth dimension. For gray images, the texture feature is combined with the lightness feature (L of the $CIE - L^*u^*v^*$) in the same way.

The segmentation scheme is given as:

(1) Color space transformation from RGB to $CIE - L^*u^*v^*$.

(2) Wavelet frame transform in the L channel to extract texture features:
5th order symmetric QMF filter
2-level decomposition, 6-dimensional feature vector

(3) Edge-preserved smoothing for color and texture feature vectors

(4) *Karhunen-Loeve* transform to extract the main texture feature

(5) Clustering in the 4-dimension (2-dimension for gray image) feature space

The experiment result is given from Figure 6.37 to Figure 6.38. The result using color alone is not satisfactory because the texture information which is very important for these images is not taken into account. The textured objects (building and clothes) are fragmented by the color segmentation. This kind of fragmentation can not be repaired by the region merging procedure because the color variation along the region boundary is high. By adding the texture feature, it can be observed that various objects are better segmented. The combination of the color and texture feature makes the segmentation closer to the ideal "object oriented" goal. A gray scale indoor scene is also given as example. It is not able to segment the sofa as an object by using lightness alone. By incorporating texture feature, the segmentation is satisfactory.

In the end it is noteworthy to point out that in our experiment with the home photos, we find that for the majority of the images, color features alone give satisfactory segmentation results. This is because in most

(a) (b) (c)

(a) Original Image (b) Segmentation using color only (c) Segmentation combining color and texture

Figure 6.37: Segmentation combining color and texture: example 1

home photos there does not exist any strong texture pattern. Sometimes there are objects with weak textured appearance but it can be smoothed away by the smoothing procedure. Therefore for most images the color segmentation results are acceptable. Only in a few cases the texture feature must be included to significantly improve the result. It is also found that the main challenge when trying to add texture as extra feature is that there are many irregular patterns existing in the image. They are not uniform in color, presenting many strong edges, but at the same time they can hardly be recognized as "texture" under any definition of texture. Therefore the traditional texture processing method can not be applied in these cases. Texture segmentation will give unreliable results in these circumstances. The existence of these regions makes the unsupervised segmentation very challenging and it is unlikely to be solved at the very low level. When lacking any prior information, the best way is to go for a color segmentation. If possible, it is highly preferable to apply some texture detection routine before deciding which feature to incorporate in the subsequent segmentation. If there is strong textured regions then it is better combine the color and texture segmentation. If there are only smooth regions and irregular regions then it is only necessary to do the color segmentation.

6.3.3 Summary

We have highlighted some experiment results on home photo segmentation. The MRF/GD model is proved to be useful in practice. Experiment results demonstrate that the $CIE - L^*u^*v^*$ color space performs better than HSV in the unsupervised clustering based segmentation on digi-

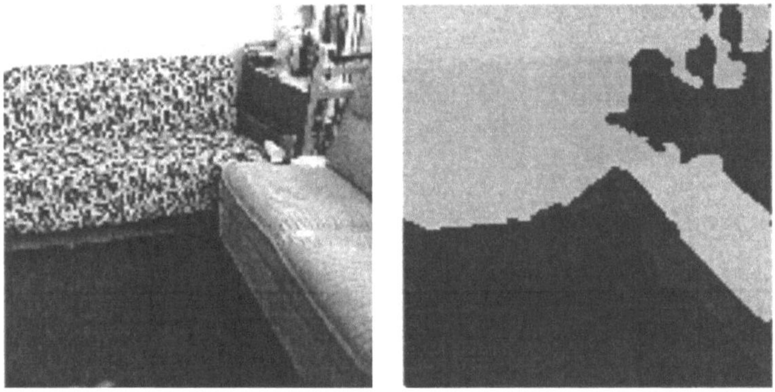

(a) (b)

(a) Original Image (b) Segmentation combining lightness and texture

Figure 6.38: Segmentation combining color and texture: example 2

tal home photos. The region merging algorithm can serve as an effective compensation step for the clustering based segmentation. Texture features extracted by the wavelet frame transform are found to be promising in discriminating different textures. The combination of color and texture for the segmentation of natural images is a challenging research area.

References

1. Y. Lu, T. Chen, "An Efficient Color CLustering Algorithm for Image Retrieving", IFMIP, 1998
2. K. Takahashi et al, "Color Image Segmentation Using ISODATA Clustering Method", Second Asian Conference on Computer Vision, Vol. 1, pp. 523-527, 1995
3. D. langan, J. Modestino, J. Zhang, "Cluster Validation for Unsupervised Stochastic Model-Based Image Segmentation", IEEE Trans on Image processing, Vol. 7, No. 2, pp. 180-194, 1998
4. S. Geman, D. Geman, "Stochastic Relaxation, Gibbs Distributions, and the Bayesian Restoration of Images", IEEE Trans on PAMI, Vol. 6, No. 6, pp. 721-741, 1984
5. D. langan, J. Modestino, J. Zhang, "Multiresolution Color Image Segmentation", IEEE Trans on PAMI, Vol. 16, No. 7, pp. 689-700, 1994
6. T. Pappas, "An Adaptive Clustering Algorithm for Image Segmentation", IEEE Trans on PAMI, 1992

7. H. Derin, H. Elliott, "Modeling and Segmentation of Noisy and Textured Images Using Gibbs Random Fields", IEEE Trans on PAMI, Vol. 9, No. 1, pp. 39-55, 1987
8. J. Rissanen, "Modeling by Shortest Data Description", Automatica, Vol. 14, pp. 465-471, 1978
9. J. Buhmann, H. Kuhnel, "Vector Quantization with Complexity Costs", IEEE Trans on IT, Vol. 39, pp. 1133-1145, 1993
10. Y. Linde, A. Buzo, R. Gray, "An Algorithm for Vector Quantizer Design", IEEE Trans on Comm, Vol. 28, No. 1, pp. 84-95, 1980
11. J. Zhang, J. Modestino, "A Model-Fitting Approach to Cluster Validation with Application to Stochastic Model-based Image Segmentation", IEEE Trans on PAMI, Vol. 12, pp. 1009-1017, 1990
12. P. Saint-Marc et al, "Adaptive Smoothing: A General Tool for Early Vision", IEEE Trans on PAMI, Vol. 13, No. 6, pp. 514-529, 1991
13. M. Levenson, "Adaptive Smoothing of Images with Local Weighted Regression", SPIE, Vol. 2823, pp. 85-99, 1996
14. R. Carmona and S. Zhong, "Adaptive Smoothing Respecting Feature Directions", IEEE Trans on Image Processing, Vol. 7, No. 3, pp. 353-358, 1998
15. G. Milligan, M. Cooper, "An Examination of Procedures for Determining the Number of Clusters in a Data Set", Psychometrika, Vol. 50, pp. 159-179, 1985
16. H. Akaike, "A New Look at the Statistical Model Identification", IEEE Trans. on Automatic Control, Vol. 19, pp. 716-722, 1974
17. J. Bigun et al, "N-folded Symmetries by Complex Moments in Gabor Space and Their Application to Unsupervised Image Segmentation", IEEE Trans on PAMI, Vol. 16, pp. 80-87, 1994
18. J. R. Bach et al, "The Virage Image Search Engine: An Open Framework for Imag e Management", Virage, Inc., San Diego
19. A. Gupta, "Visual Information Retrieval Technology: A Virage Perspective", Virage, Inc., San Diego
20. Sing-Tze Bow, "Pattern Recognition and Image Preprocessing", Marcel Dekker Inc., New York, 1992
21. Jiankang Wu, Digital Image Analysis, China Communication Press, Beijing, 1989
22. T. Pavlidos and Y. T. Liow, "Integrating Region Growing and Edge Detection, IEEE Trans on PAMI, Vol. 12, No. 3, pp. 225-233, 1990
23. H. Levkowitz, "Color Theory and Modeling for Computer Graphics, Visualization, and Multimedia Applications", Kluwer Academic Publishers, 1997
24. J. R. Smith, "Integrated Spatial and Feature Image Systems: retrieval, Analysis and Compression", Columbia University, 1997

Chapter 7

Human Face Detection

For image and video, it is very often that people are within the scene as its central content. For example, a home user hopes to find a sequence of photos containing his/her daughter. To identify people in an image or video frame or even recognize the person, the best and reliable way is to detect the human face as the first step. Human face perception has been a very appealing research topic in the computer vision community. Face detection, face tracking and face recognition have been studied for many years. Many face recognition algorithms have either assumed that the face has been cropped from the image [10] or they have imposed some constraints about the face or background such that face detection becomes easier [11] or for on-line system, motion and color are jointly used to trace the head and face [12,14]. But in general situation these assumptions are not true. Therefore, automatic human face detection still remains as an unsolved problem.

The basic face properties are skin color and facial structure. The methods of face detection can be categorized as model-based, feature-based, neural network-based and color-based. The model-based approach assumes a different face model in different coarse to fine scales. For efficiency, the image is searched at the coarsest scale first. Once a match is found the image is searched by next finer scale model until the finest scale is reached. The feature-based approach searches the image for a set of facial features and groups them into face candidates based on their geometrical relationship. The color-based approach labels each pixel according to its similarity to skin color. The neural network based approach searches face in the every image region by resizing the region into a fixed-size window and then feeding it as the trained network input. In [15] Sung and Poggio have developed an example-based trainable system and used it for locating vertical frontal views of human faces in complex scenes. The technique models the distribution of human face patterns by means of a few view-based "face" and "non-face" prototype clusters. At each image location, a difference feature vector is computed between the local image pattern and the distribution-based model. A trained multi-layer perception classifier determines, based on the difference feature vector, whether or not a human face exists at the current image location.

We found color-based approach can localize the face region fast but not reliable while Sung and Poggio's approach matches face very well but needs more time to scan the whole image with the variant scales. As matter of fact, we can use color and shape information to extract the face-like image objects as candidates (or we can call that hypothesis generation), and then verify those candidates based on the priory knowledge of face structure. In this chapter, color-based face detection method is discussed in Section 7.1. Face detection using shape, feature points and template will be discussed in Section 7.2, 7.3 and 7.4.

7.1 Color Segmentation of Faces

Our aim is to detect the human face in color images discounting the disturbing influences of surface orientation change, direction of the illumination and shadows. The result can then be combined with other information to segment the face from the background. We detect the face in two steps: First the image is segmented into homogeneously colored regions. Second, the segment corresponding to the face is detected. To this end, chromatic diagrams are examined, in theory, for the dichromatic reflection model and, in practice, for histogram based segmentation. The projection from 3-D to 2-D color space effects color distances and the 2-D chromaticities become unstable in the case of low lighting conditions. Ameliorating strategies are presented to overcome these difficulties. Experiments are conducted on color images taken from complex office environment. On the basis of theoretical and experimental results it is concluded that chromaticity diagrams allow face detection invariant to a change in surface orientation, viewpoint of the camera, and illumination intensity.

Computer programs that recognize faces could be applied to a wide variety of problems, including security systems, image and film processing, and human-computer interaction. Prior to the face recognition, the approximate location of the face needs to be detected in the image. The recognition task can then focus solely on the expected face location, thereby greatly reducing the required computation time. Our aim is to investigate the possibility of using color to obtain an initial estimate of the region in the image that contains the face. The images are taken in complex office environments. The result of the facial region detection using color could then be combined with other information, such as texture, symmetry, convexity etc. to segment the face from the background.

Face detection using color is complicated due to a number of factors: The observed color values are dependent on the color filters, dark current, gamma correction and the (automatic) white-balance settings of the camera. In an arbitrary office environment, the color and intensity of the illumination and thus the observed colors depend on whether the sun shines, or on which and how many lights are turned on. The color of the human face is further influenced by shading and highlights and depends on race, suntan, health etc. The demands for the face detection and recognition algorithm is that they operate in real time. Taking these factors into account, the task of face detection based on color is challenging.

Fleck, Forsyth and Bregler [1] present a system for detecting naked people in image databases. They use a human skin filter to identify images which contain large regions whose color and texture resembles the skin. Sun, Huang and Wu [8] detect potential face pixels in normalized color space. Segments are then merged to form elliptic shapes and the similarity with the face of the result is evaluated in L*a*b* space. The drawback of these color segmentation methods is that they do not account for the intrinsic problems of color space transformations, nor do they account for the image forming process. In contrast, Kender [5] explored the problems which arise when color image processing techniques based on saturation, hue and normalized color are applied . He points out that these color transformations are singular at some points and are unstable at many others. In addition, the transformations introduce anomalies into the frequency distribution of their generated values. Color segmentation methods that account for the process of image formation are studied more recently. One of the first methods based on physics considerations is by Klinker, Shafer and Kanade [6]. They developed a color segmentation algorithm based on the dichromatic reflection model proposed by Shafer [7]. This method is based on evaluating "dog-leg" clusters in sensor space. Based on a detailed analysis of the physics underlying color image formation, Gevers et al. [2] analyze the distribution of pixels belonging to homogeneously colored objects in sensor space. Region detection algorithms are developed which take these distributions into account, and as a result, are invariant to object geometry and highlights. The methods are based on the k-means clustering algorithm, and as such are computational expensive and depend on a good estimate of the initial clusters initialization. Furthermore, the number of clusters needs to be known in advance. This report extends the work of Gevers as we present a computational efficient face detection algorithm based on normalized color histograms where the result do not depend on proper initialization. We also analyze error propagation in normalized coordinates and the effect of normalization on color distances in chromaticity diagrams and propose ameliorating strategies.

To that end, we analyze in section 7.1.1, in theory, the distribution of pixels in various color spaces belonging to both matte and shiny objects when they are projected on various 3-D surfaces. The chromaticity diagrams that result from this projection are evaluated in section 7.1.2 for the frequency distribution of the chromaticity coordinates, for color distances and for the effect of error propagation. The method for face detection takes the two latter factors into account and is presented in section 7.1.3. The approach is verified by experiments in section 7.1.4.

7.1.1 Chromaticity diagrams

Dichromatic reflection model

Consider an image of an infinitesimal surface patch. Using red, green and blue color filters with spectral sensitivities given by $f_R(\lambda), f_G(\lambda), f_B(\lambda)$ to obtain an image of the surface patch illuminated by a spectral power distribution of the incident light denoted by $e(\lambda)$, the measured sensor values will be given by Shafer [7]:

$$C_n = m_b(\vec{n}, \vec{s}) \int_\lambda f_n(\lambda)e(\lambda)c_b(\lambda)d\lambda + m_s(\vec{n}, \vec{s}, \vec{v}) \int_\lambda f_n(\lambda)e(\lambda)c_s(\lambda)d\lambda \qquad (7.1)$$

for C_n giving the nth sensor response, $n \in \{R, G, B\}$. Further, $c_b(\lambda)$ and $c_s(\lambda)$ are the albedo and Fresnel reflectance respectively. λ denotes the wavelength, $\vec{n}$ is the surface patch normal, $\vec{s}$ is the direction of the illumination source, and $\vec{v}$ is the direction of the viewer. Geometric terms m_b and m_s denote the geometric dependencies on the body and surface reflection respectively.

At the moment an image is captured, the spectral sensitivities of the color filters, the spectral power distribution of the illuminant, and the spectral transmission of the object are constant. The term $\int_\lambda f_n(\lambda)e(\lambda)c_b(\lambda)d\lambda$ can therefore be abbreviated as the constant k_{f_n}, and the term $m_s(\vec{n}, \vec{s}, \vec{v}) \int_\lambda f_n(\lambda)e(\lambda)c_s(\lambda)d\lambda$ as constant l_{f_n}. This allows

Equation 7.1 to be written as

$$\begin{pmatrix} R \\ G \\ B \end{pmatrix} = m_b(\vec{n}, \vec{s}) \begin{pmatrix} k_R \\ k_G \\ k_B \end{pmatrix} + m_s(\vec{n}, \vec{s}, \vec{v}) \begin{pmatrix} l_R \\ l_G \\ l_B \end{pmatrix} \tag{7.2}$$

Linear color spaces are defined using the transformation:

$$\begin{pmatrix} P \\ Q \\ R \end{pmatrix} = \begin{pmatrix} a_1 & a_2 & a_3 \\ a_4 & a_5 & a_6 \\ a_7 & a_8 & a_9 \end{pmatrix} \begin{pmatrix} R \\ G \\ B \end{pmatrix} \tag{7.3}$$

where $a_1..a_9$ are constants and PQR are the transformed color coordinates. The actual values of $a_1..a_9$ in matrix A depend on the color space. Substitution of Equation 7.2 in Equation 7.3 gives:

$$\begin{aligned} \begin{pmatrix} P \\ Q \\ R \end{pmatrix} &= m_b(\vec{n}, \vec{s}) \begin{pmatrix} a_1 k_R + a_2 k_G + a_3 k_B \\ a_4 k_R + a_5 k_G + a_6 k_B \\ a_7 k_R + a_8 k_G + a_9 k_B \end{pmatrix} \\ &+ m_s(\vec{n}, \vec{s}, \vec{v}) \begin{pmatrix} a_1 l_R + a_2 l_G + a_3 l_B \\ a_4 l_R + a_5 l_G + a_6 l_B \\ a_7 l_R + a_8 l_G + a_9 l_B \end{pmatrix} \end{aligned} \tag{7.4}$$

A homogeneously colored matte object with constant k_R, k_G, k_B but with varying surface normal $\vec{n}$, and thus $0 \leq m_b(\vec{n} \leq 1, \vec{s}), m_s(\vec{n}, \vec{s}, \vec{v}) = 0$, will draw a half-ray, emanating from the origin, in linear color space. A homogeneously colored shiny object varying surface normal $\vec{n}$, and thus $0 \leq m_b(\vec{n}, \vec{s}) + m_s(\vec{n}, \vec{s}, \vec{v}) \leq 1$, will draw two half-rays in linear color space. All pixels that belong to the homogeneously colored shiny object are located in the triangle spanned by these two vectors. If the scene is illuminated by more than one differently colored light sources, a homogeneously colored object will exhibit more than two half-rays.

Distribution of pixels in 2-D and 3-D color spaces

Colors differ in saturation, hue and brightness. If we ignore the brightness component, we obtain a 2-D color space. The 2-D color space is obtained by the intersection of the 3-D half-ray with a surface. The requirements for this surface is that it does not contain the origin and that it cuts every half-ray exactly ones. The orientation of the surface can be arbitrary, the only requirement is that each color appears as an intersection. For example, the intersection surface can be described by a plane defined as:

$$b_1 x + b_2 y + b_3 z = 1 \tag{7.5}$$

or as an ellipse described as:

$$b_1 x^2 + b_2 y^2 + b_3 z^2 = 1 \tag{7.6}$$

The values b_1, b_2, b_3 determine the orientation of the intersecting surface. The representation of colors in such intersection surface will be called a chromaticity diagram, each point represents a chromaticity, that is a color modulo mere intensity changes. The chromaticity diagram can be transformed by a perspective transformation. The general form of the transformation is:

$$\begin{aligned} \overline{x'} &= \frac{c_{11}\overline{x} + c_{12}\overline{y} + c_{13}}{c_{31}\overline{x} + c_{32}\overline{y} + c_{33}} \\ \overline{y'} &= \frac{c_{21}\overline{x} + c_{22}\overline{y} + c_{23}}{c_{31}\overline{x} + c_{32}\overline{y} + c_{33}} \end{aligned} \tag{7.7}$$

where $\overline{xy}$ are the original chromaticity coordinates and $\overline{x'y'}$ the coordinates of the new chromaticity diagram.

The chromaticity coordinates are obtained by substitution of the transformed color coordinates of Equation 7.4 in, for instance, Equation 7.5:

$$m_b(\vec{n}, \vec{s})[b_1 p + b_2 q + b_3 r] = 1 \tag{7.8}$$

where p, q, r represent $(a_1 k_R + a_2 k_G + a_3 k_B)$, $(a_4 k_R + a_5 k_G + a_6 k_B)$, $(a_7 k_R + a_8 k_G + a_9 k_B)$, respectively. Equation 7.8 is solved for $m_b(\vec{n}, \vec{s})$:

$$m_b(\vec{n}, \vec{s}) = \frac{1}{b_1 p + b_2 q + b_3 r} \tag{7.9}$$

For matte objects without surface reflection, back substitution of Equation 7.9 into Equation 7.4 gives the chromaticity coordinates as:

$$\begin{aligned} \overline{x} &= \frac{p}{b_1 p + b_2 q + b_3 r} \\ \overline{y} &= \frac{q}{b_1 p + b_2 q + b_3 r} \end{aligned} \tag{7.10}$$

Note that the third row of Equation 7.4 is omitted as the dimensionality is reduced from three to two. The $\overline{xy}$ chromaticity coordinates are thus independent of the body reflection term $m_b(\vec{n}, \vec{s})$. As a result, the chromaticity coordinates are invariant to the surface normal $\vec{n}$ of the object and the direction of the illuminant $\vec{s}$. The invariance does not apply for the regions in shiny objects that contain specular components. For this case, the chromaticities are dependent on $\vec{n}, \vec{s}$ and camera viewpoint $\vec{v}$.

If a half-ray in 3-D color space (matte object) is intersected with a surface which intersects the half-ray exactly once, the half-ray maps onto

Transform	a_1	a_2	a_3	a_4	a_5	a_6	a_7	a_8	a_9
Opponent	1	-1	0	2	-1	-1	1	1	1
XYZ	.490	.310	.200	.177	.812	.011	.000	.010	.990
Perspective	c_{11}	c_{12}	c_{13}	c_{21}	c_{22}	c_{23}	c_{31}	c_{32}	c_{33}
$\overline{uv}$	4	0	0	0	9	0	-2	12	3

Table 7.1: *Listed are the specific* $a_1..a_9$ *values for the linear transform of Equation 7.3 from sensor color space to opponent and* XYZ *color space which are used in this report. The resulting color spaces are projected onto the* $\overline{opp}$ *and* $\overline{xy}$ *chromaticity diagrams. The* $\overline{uv}$ *diagram is obtained from the* $\overline{xy}$ *diagram by the perspective transformation of Equation 7.7 for which the values* $c_{11}..c_{33}$ *are listedf.*

a single point. If the object is shiny, the distribution of the pixels in 3-D space is confined within a triangle spanned by two vectors. Both vectors individually map onto two single points. The 3-D colors that are the result of a color mixture of these two vectors, will map onto the line between the two points. Thus, matte objects map on points in the chromaticity plane while shiny objects map on lines in the chromaticity plane.

Design of chromaticity diagrams for linear color spaces

We construct chromaticity diagrams for sensor color space, opponent color space [4] and XYZ color space. The latter two are transformed according to Equation 7.4. The specific values of matrix A are given in Table 7.1. The tristimulus values XYZ are related to CIE RGB tristimulus values [9]. We assume no a-priori knowledge of the spectral sensitivities of the color filters RGB of the color CCD camera and therefore adopt the values given in the table by default.

Conventionally, the chromaticity coordinates of a color are the ratios of each tristimulus value of the color to their sum. The instantiation of parameters of Equation 7.5 is therefore $b_1 = b_2 = b_3 = 1$ for the RGB and XYZ projections. Consider the opponent color transformation. Division of the first and second component by their sum results in a "color-blind" chromaticity diagram, as the condition that each half-ray intersects the plane only once is violated for this orientation of the intersection plane. For the opponent color space, we therefore orient the projection plane perpendicular to the first and second component, the orientation of the intersection plane is $z = 1$.

The $\overline{xy}$ chromaticity diagram of the XYZ space is transformed using Equation 7.7. The resulting chromaticity coordinates $\overline{uv}$ now corresponds to the CIE 1976 uniform color scale diagram, which is designed to give a perceptually more uniform space than that of the $\overline{xy}$ diagram. Opposed to chromaticity diagrams that might be obtained from the perceptual uniform 3-D color space L*u*v* and L*a*b*, this transformation has advantages: First, projection of these spaces on planes will result in two points instead of one. The cause is the discontinuity of the L* component:

$$L^* = \begin{cases} 116(\frac{Y}{Y_n})^{1/3} - 16 & \text{if } \frac{Y}{Y_n} > 0.008856 \\ 903.3(\frac{Y}{Y_n}) & \text{otherwise} \end{cases} \tag{7.11}$$

Second, due to the projection, perceptual uniform color distances no longer apply. Third, although the L* component encodes the intensity information, both the u*v* and a*b* are dependent on the Y term of Equation 7.11. Segmentation using only the u*v* and a*b* coordinates therefore remains dependent on the intensity.

The chromaticity diagram inherits structure from the original color space. The linear 3-D color space derived from sensory space is bounded by red, green, blue, white and black extremes. Likewise, 2-D chromaticity diagrams are bounded by red, green and blue extrema if linear color spaces are projected onto planes. This is shown in Fig. 7.1. Our aim is to detect the human face using 2-D color histograms obtained from chromaticity diagrams. The chromaticity coordinates therefore need to be digitized as

$$\overline{x'} = \text{Round}(S \cdot \overline{x}) \tag{7.12}$$

where $\overline{x}$ denotes an arbitrary chromaticity coordinate. The coordinates are scaled by a factor S, where S attains equal values for both coordinates.

7.1.2 Effects of the projection of 3-D color spaces on chromaticity diagrams

Error propagation

It is desirable that small tristimulus changes cause small transform changes. As can be seen from Equation 7.10, the transformation from 3-D colors pace to 2-D color space is unstable close to the black point. For instance, consider the effect of quantization errors in the RGB components. The maximum effect of quantization occurs for the $\overline{r}$ component if R changes from value 0 to 1 while the sum $R+G+B$ remains constant. The effect of this quantization is $\frac{S}{R+G+B}$. Thus a change of one

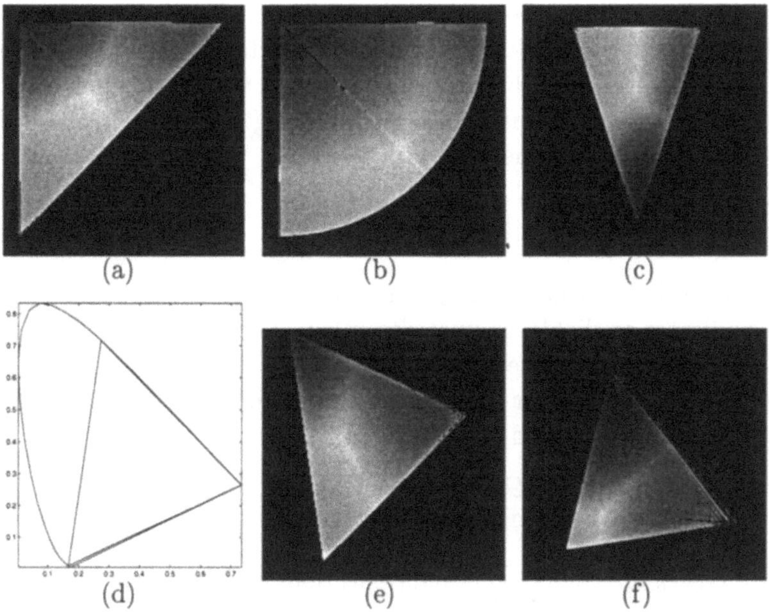

Figure 7.1: *Chromaticity diagrams, (a): RGB color space, projected on plane* $x + y + z = 1$*. (b): RGB color space, projected on plane* $x^2 + y^2 + z^2 = 1$*. (c): Opponent color space, projected on plane* $z = 1$*. (d): Projection of the columns of the* XYZ *color matching matrix on plane* $x+y+z = 1$ *yields the triangular shaped color gamut of the RGB camera. The "horseshoe" gamut corresponds to the 1931 average human observer. The camera has high sensitivity to red colors and a low sensitivity to blue colors. This is reflected in (e): The* XYZ *color space, projected on plane* $x+y+z = 1$*. (f): The* $\overline{uv}$ *diagram after perspective transformation of (e). Color distances in* $\overline{uv}$ *space are approximately perceptual uniform. Green colors are "compressed" by the transformation, spurious gaps occur at the purple line which connects the blue and red extrema.*

unit input will give a change of one unit output if $S \geq R+G+B$. Similarly, a change of one unit input will give a change of k units output if $S \geq \frac{R+G+B}{k}$. Thus, the probability of an error in the $\overline{r}$ component is linearly dependent on the sum of the RBG components: A twice as high value for $R+G+B$ results in a twice as low certainty of the correct value of $\overline{r}$. The exact error probability can be derived as follows: If an arbitrary normalized color coordinate $\overline{x}$ is derived using function$f(R,G,B)$ then the reliability of the value $\overline{x}$ is

$$P(\overline{x}) = |\frac{\delta f}{\delta R}| + |\frac{\delta f}{\delta G}| + |\frac{\delta f}{\delta B}| \tag{7.13}$$

A higher value of $P(\overline{x})$ indicates an unreliable $\overline{x}$ value, a value close to zero indicates a reliable chromaticity value.

For the case that linear color spaces are projected onto planes, the general form of the error propagation for chromaticity coordinate $\overline{x}$ can roughly be approximated as

$$P(\overline{x}) = \frac{c_1 B + c_2 G + c_3 R}{(c_4 B + c_5 G + c_6 R)^2} \tag{7.14}$$

where $c_1,..c_6$ are composed of multiplications and additions of the $a_1..a_9$ terms of Equation 7.4. The error propagation functions are expensive to compute. Due to the real time requirements of face detection, only projections on planes will be considered, where the error propagation is approximated by the function

$$P(\overline{x}) = \frac{1}{(B+G+R)} \tag{7.15}$$

As a result, this approximation is more accurate for the $\overline{rg}$ coordinates since the the terms $c_1,..c_6$ are approximately equal to one, than for the $\overline{uv}$ coordinates.

Frequency distribution due to the computation of chromaticity coordinates

There are other difficulties with the projection onto planes. Kender [5] analyzes the effect of the computation of $\overline{rg}$ with respect to spurious modes that occur in the distribution of the normalized coordinates. The essential problem is the use of the division in the computation of the projected coordinates. Because the input is digital, certain output quotients are "favored" over others, creating false modes in the digitized chromaticity diagrams. The cause is that fractions are equivalence classes of pairs of

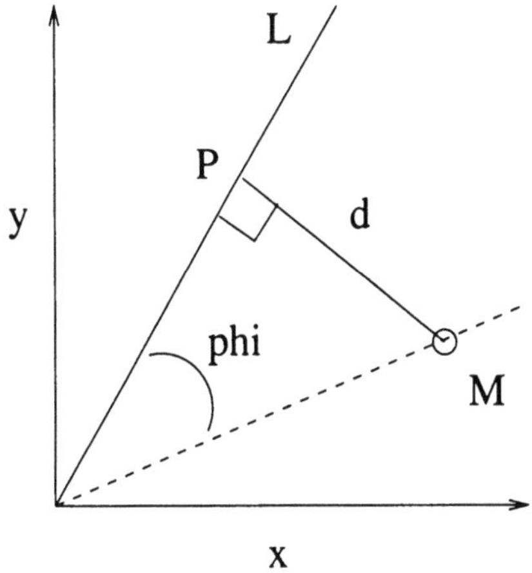

Figure 7.2: *For image segmentation using color histograms, we need to assign the pixels in the image to the closest local maxima occurring in the histogram. Therefore, we need to compute the distance between the color of the pixel and the color of the local maximum. The distance between the projection of the two lines on the chromaticity diagram depends on the orientation of the two lines in color space. If instead the 3-D color space coordinate of the pixel that is to be classified, and the 2-D color space coordinate of the local maximum is used, the distance is no longer dependent on the orientation of the two lines in color space.*

integers, and given the digital input, certain of these equivalence classes can have more representatives than others. For example, the $\overline{r}$ value of $1/2$ can be attained through various fractions, by many more input triples can can the value of $1/511$. Histograms are negatively affected by the spurious modes, as they may lead to spurious groupings of pixels. When discrete values RGB are transformed to the XYZ color space, the color space coordinates are transformed to real values. The transformation from RGB to XYZ effectively undigitizes the input XYZ values. However, the perspective transformation from $\overline{xy}$ to $\overline{uv}$, some indices in the $\overline{uv}$ diagram within the color triangle can not be attained, see Fig. 7.1. The occurrence of these spurious gaps might be prevented by adjusting the scale factor S of Equation 7.12 which, in turn, reduces the discriminative power of the $\overline{uv}$ diagram to distinguish small color differences.

Color distances in chromaticity diagrams

In image segmentation using color histograms, first the 2-D dominant colors are detected in the histogram. Next, individual pixels are assigned to a dominant color based on the minimal distance. Color distances are affected by the projection onto 2-D chromaticity diagrams. As pointed out by Healey [3], the distance between two 2-D chromaticity coordinates (which will be called "chromaticity distance"), where these coordinates correspond to two distinct half-rays in 3-D color space that are separated by a fixed angle, depends on the location of the lines in 3-D color space. Colors having equal distances in 3-D color space have different distances in 2-D space. Healey therefore computes the normalized $\overline{rg}$ coordinates by division of R and G by $\sqrt{R+G+B}$, which corresponds to the projection of RGB color space on the surface $x^2 + y^2 + z^2 = 1$, or alternatively, to the projection of $R^2G^2B^2$ on the surface $x + y + z = 1$.

However, for assigning pixels to 2-D dominant colors, the 2-D chromaticity representation of the pixels can be ignored, since the 3-D color information is still available. As an alternative to computing color distances in 2-D space, we therefore use the 3-D color of the pixel that is to be classified, and the 2-D color space coordinate of the dominant color. The dominant color represents a half ray in 3-D color space. The distance between the 3-D pixel and the 2-D local maximum is computed as the shortest distance from the 3-D pixel to this half ray. This distance will be referred to as "line distance".

To see this in two dimensions, consider the dominant color represented by line L and the 3-D coordinate of the pixel M as depicted in Fig. 7.2. Let ϕ denote the angle between L and the line M through the origin and pixel M. The shortest distance between the point M and the line L is the distance between the point M and the point P, where P is a point on the line L, The distance d between the dominant color and pixel M is

$$d = |M| \tan(\phi) \tag{7.16}$$

where $|M|$ denotes the length from the black point to M. Therefore, d depends only on ϕ and not on the orientation in color space of L or the line from the black point through M.

7.1.3 Method for face detection using chromaticity diagrams

Face detection is a two step process. First, the image is segmented into homogeneously colored regions using 2-D color histograms. Second, the region that most closely corresponds to the color of the face is detected.

The chromaticity coordinates are computed by the method described in section 7.1.1. The probability of errors in these coordinates is approximated, regardless of the color space transform, by Equation 7.15. Given a pixel, the histogram index corresponding to the chromaticity of the pixel is increased by the scaled intensity of the pixel. Thus, a probability value close to 1 corresponds to a high probability that the coordinate is correct. A value close to 0 corresponds to a high probability that the coordinate is erroneous. In effect, pixels with a high probability of error have small effects in the histogram.

The histogram is then iteratively smoothed with a Gaussian filter, with $.5 \leq \sigma \leq 10$. The local maxima detection algorithm automatically adjusts the value of σ until a specified number of local maxima are detected. Local maxima are found by evaluating, for every histogram index, the eight nearest neighbors. If the height at a histogram index exceeds that of its eight neighbors, the index is classified as a local maximum. The method is not able to detect local maxima which extend over more than one consecutive indices.

The face color is composed of melanin (yellow) and blood (red). To determine which local maximum corresponds to the face, the chromaticity distance is computed for each local maximum with the chromaticity value that corresponds to the RGB color value $(1, 1/2, 0)$. The local maximum with the minimal chromaticity distance is assigned to the face.

For $\overline{rg}$ and $\overline{opp}$ color space, individual pixels are assigned to the local maximum that corresponds to the face based on the minimal line distance between the 3-D pixel color and the 2-D local maxima colors. For $\overline{uv}$ space, individual pixels are assigned to the face local maximum based on the chromaticity distance, as this space is designed to yield approximate perceptual uniform color distances.

7.1.4 Experiments

In the experiments shown in Fig. 7.3 7.4 7.5, the region most likely to correspond to the face is depicted in color, the non-face regions are shown in white.

Segmentation of color images by 3-D histograms is dependent on the color and intensity. In section 7.1.1 it was shown that chromaticity diagrams, are invariant to shadows, the surface orientation of the face and to the direction of the light source. In Fig. 7.3 the results are shown for 3-D histogram segmentation in RGB space and for 2-D histogram segmentation in the $\overline{rg}$, $\overline{uv}$ and $\overline{opp}$ color space. The experiment shows that regions detected through the chromaticity diagrams are unaffected by shadows and varying illumination. In Fig. 7.3 the face is detected under varying direction of the illuminant. The experiment shows that the face region detection is unaffected by a change in the direction of the light source.

Matte objects cause peaks in the 2-D histogram, whereas highlights cause lines in the histogram, as was shown in section 7.1.1. The local maxima detection method, described in section 7.1.3, detects peaks in the histogram. As a result, the face detection method is negatively affected by highlights. Due to the instability of the color space transform, pixels of low intensity are likely to be misclassified. Both effects can be observed in the experiment of Fig. 7.3.

In section 7.1.2, the error propagation of the projection of linear color spaces on chromaticity diagrams was estimated as a function of the intensity: Color pixels with high intensity result in a low probability of error in the chromaticity coordinates. The histogram indices are therefore weighted with this probability function. In Fig. 7.4, a large part of the image is dark and as a result, the chromaticity coordinates are unstable. Weighting with intensity prevents that those pixels have a large effect on the histogram, and as a result negatively effect the detection of local maxima in the histogram.

Once the image is segmented into homogeneously colored regions, the dominant colors of the regions are inspected. The region with a color most closely corresponds to the face color is then assigned as the face region. The experiment shown in Fig. 7.5 show that this method seems robust to changes of the color of the illuminant and to changes of skin color. However, if two regions are detected which both approximately correspond to the skin color, it is not unlikely that the region not corresponding to the face will be selected.

The goal of this work is to detect the region belonging to the face discounting the disturbing influences of surface orientation change, direction of the illumination and shadows. The result can than be combined with other information as convexity and symmetry to segment the face from the background.

Using the dichromatic reflection model, we analyzed in theory the distribution of color pixels belonging to homogeneously colored objects in chromaticity diagrams. It was found that matte objects cause peaks in the 2-D chromaticity diagram. The method for detection of local maxima takes this information into account. As a result, the method presented detects the face invariant to a change in surface orientation, viewpoint of the camera, and illumination intensity but is sensitive to highlights. The transformation from 3-D to 2-D color space effects color distances and the

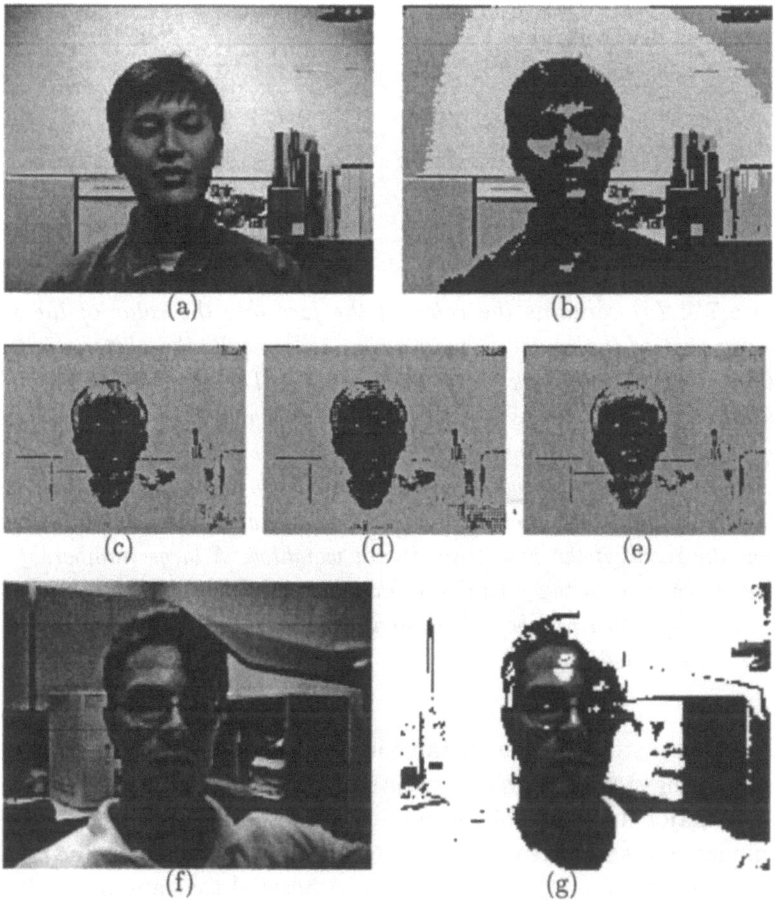

Figure 7.3: *Segmentation results for color image shown in (a). The face contains shadows and highlights, the illumination of the background changes gradually. (b): Segmentation based on the 3-D RGB histogram is negatively effected by shadows and illumination intensity. As a result, the face is split up in more than one segment. (c), (d) and (e): Segmentation based on chromaticity diagrams* $\overline{rg}$, $\overline{uv}$ *and* $\overline{opp}$, *respectively. The image is segmented in an achromatic and a face region. Segmentation based on chromaticity diagrams is invariant to shading and intensity changes. In section 7.1.1 it was shown that segmentation by 2-D histograms, obtained from chromaticity diagrams, is invariant to the direction of the light source. In (g) the direction of the illumination is altered. As is shown by the face detection results of (g), segmentation based on chromaticity diagrams is invariant to changes in the direction of the light source.*

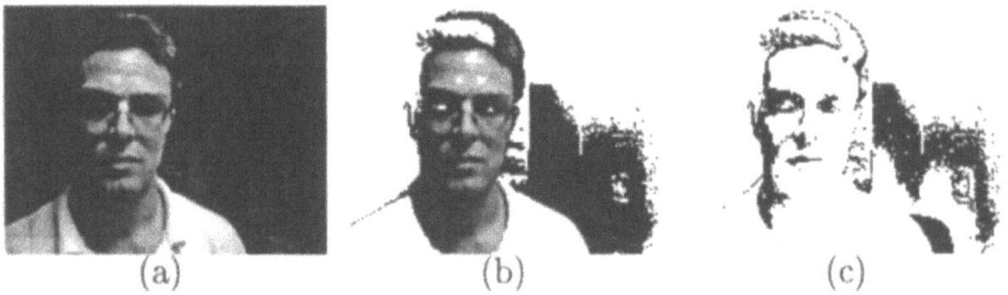

Figure 7.4: *(a) contains the color of the face and the color of the shirt. A large part of the image is very dark. As a result, the chromaticity coordinates due to the dark pixels are unstable. The weighting of the chromaticities with the intensity prevents that unstable chromaticities have a large effect on the chromaticity histogram. (b) shows the result of face detection based on the weighted histogram, two local maxima are found that correspond to the face color and to achromatic color. In contrast, (c) shows the result if the histogram is not weighted. A large number of local maxima, caused by the unstable dark pixels, are therefore detected. As a result, the specified number of segments can not be detected and the image is over segmented.*

2-D chromaticities become unstable in the case of low lighting conditions. Ameliorating strategies were presented to overcome these difficulties.

The major drawback of the presented method is that the number of dominant colors occurring in the image need to be specified. The method would benefit if a method would be incorporated that automatically detects the number of local maxima occurring in the histogram.

7.2 Shape Information As a Cue

7.2.1 Geometric characteristic of face

After the median filtering, there are still many small regions and the large regions with the holes in them and spurs and ditches on their boundaries. Morphological operations like *dilation, erosion, opening, closure* are applied to the binary images to remove isolated pixels, to eliminate the spurs and the ditches on the boundaries, to connect the small objects in the neighborhood, to fill the small interior holes. Then the large holes like eye holes are filled. After all these operations only a few large regions are retained. Women and people in tropical countries like Singapore or in

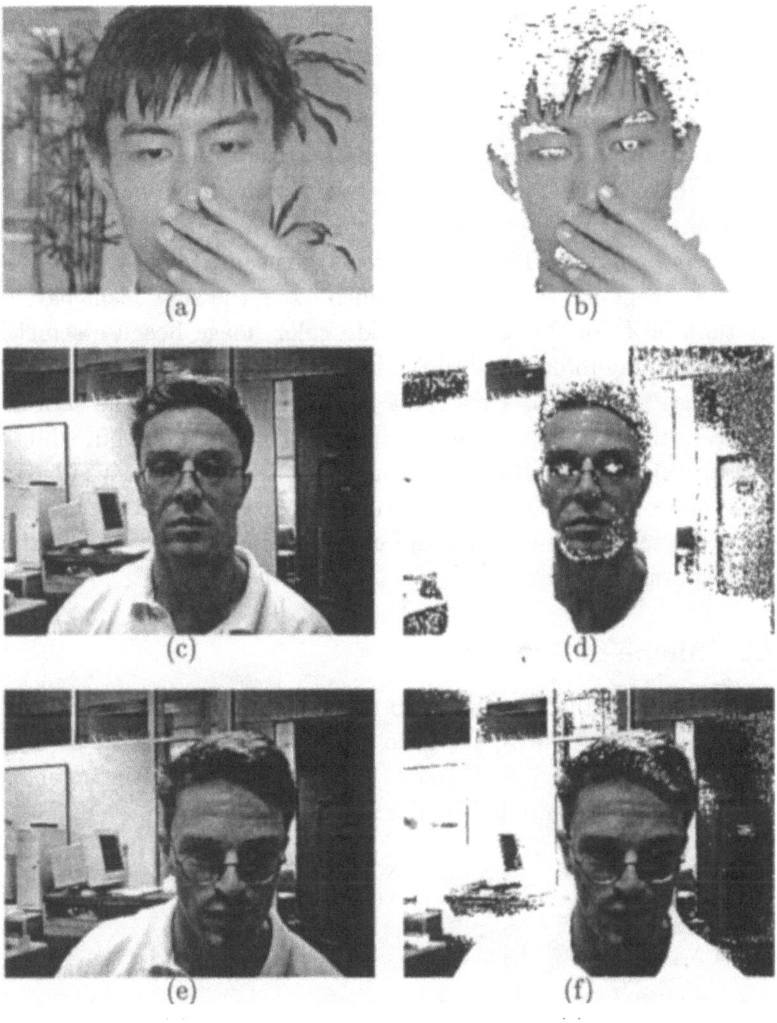

Figure 7.5: *The method for face detection is a two-step process: First, the image is segmented in homogeneously colored regions. Second, the region that most closely resembles the face color is detected. (b), (d) and (f) show that the second step of the face detection algorithm appears to be invariant to racial color. (f) and (h) show that the detection appears to be invariant to a change in illumination color. The detection method is negatively effected by background colors that resemble the color of the face. In (f), the region under the chin is illuminated by inter reflection of the chin. The face is therefore illuminated by two differently colored illuminants. As a result, the region under the chin is not assigned to the face.*

Summer often wear short-sleeved or sleeveless or low-cut shirts and skirts or shorts. So their exposed skin include not only face, neck, hand but also chest, arms and legs even trunk. After finishing all these preprocessing operations the objects in the image are mainly faces, arms, legs and other body parts plus some skin color like objects. From now on some priori knowledge is used to identify the face from other objects. For a good picture, it is unlikely that a face intersects with any image borders. Even if it is the case sometimes, this person must be taken in by accident and is the *persona non grata*. Therefore, objects connected to image borders are discarded except for those objects which cover the significant part (say, great than 30%) of the segmented skin color image because sometimes naked trunk may intersect with the image borders.

Although faces, legs, arms can't be discriminated by the skin color, they have different shapes. Limbs are generally long and thin while face is not. In [14] shape analysis involving ellipse fitting is employed based on the observation that the appearance of a face resembles an oval shape. To avoid the extensive computation of ellipse fitting, two shape descriptors are used in our research.

7.2.2 Shape descriptors

Eccentricity is defined as the ratio of major axis to the minor axis of the region, in other words, the ratio of the eigenvalues of the covariance matrix. Given the number of points in the region is N, the eccentricity of the region, e, is computed by the following formula,

$$x_0 = \frac{1}{N}\sum x, \qquad y_0 = \frac{1}{N}\sum y \tag{7.17}$$

$$M_{ij} = \sum (x - x_0)^i (y - y_0)^j \tag{7.18}$$

$$C = \begin{bmatrix} M_{20} & M_{11} \\ M_{11} & M_{02} \end{bmatrix} \tag{7.19}$$

$$e = \frac{M_{20} + M_{02} + \sqrt{(M_{20} - M_{02})^2 + 4M_{11}^2}}{M_{20} + M_{02} - \sqrt{(M_{20} - M_{02})^2 + 4M_{11}^2}} \tag{7.20}$$

where (x_0, y_0) is the centroid of the region and M_{ij} is the ij-th central moment C is covariance matrix. Eccentricity is a translation and rotation invariant measurement. For some symmetrical shapes, such as circle, some regular polygons, e equals 1. Of cause, for those hollow shapes like rings,

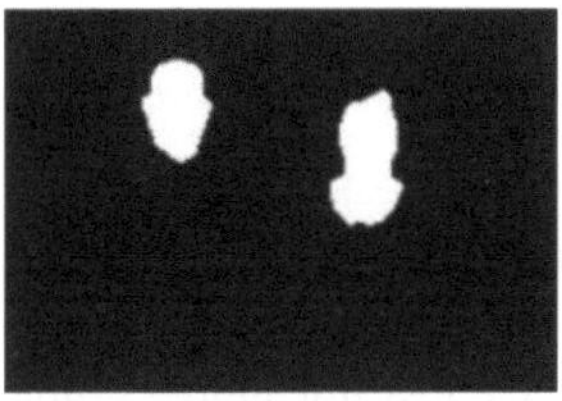

Figure 7.6: Small objects and long, thin objects have been discarded.

e still equals 1. Thus another measure, compactness, is needed to describe these shapes.

Compactness measures how closely-packed the shape is and is defined as the ratio of the squared perimeter (the number of pixels in the boundary of the shape) to the area (the number of pixels in the shape) of the region: $\textbf{perimeter}^2/\textbf{area}$. For the compact shape, disc, its compactness is 4π, for the other shapes, their compactness are greater than this value.

7.2.3 Experimental results

According to these measurements some long and thin objects like legs and arms can be discarded completely. After using these morphological operations and shape description measurements the result image in the Figur 7.11 is shown in Figure 7.6. But when these objects connect with the face and trunk, the problem is still there.

7.3 Face Feature Detection Using DOG Operators

To validate a candidate region as face, it needs to be checked if the facial features like eyes, nose, mouth are presented there. Before we describe the face structural information detection method we introduce a DOG (Difference of Gaussians)[19] operator which will be used later.

7.3.1 The DOG (Difference of Gaussians) operator

In the photo human eyes are always darker than surrounding area. How to detect such intensity changes? In image processing there are many edge detectors which are based on measuring the intensity gradient at a point in the image. The gradient operator ∇ is a first-derivative operator

$$\nabla = \begin{bmatrix} \frac{\partial}{\partial x} \\ \frac{\partial}{\partial y} \end{bmatrix} \tag{7.21}$$

The first-derivative operator gives a peak where intensity changes. Some examples of this kind are Roberts, Kirsch, Prewitt and Sobel operators. However most edges are not sharp steps. They are often gradual transitions from one intensity to another. In this case we will get a smooth hump instead of a steep peak. To find the accurate edge location is equivalent to find the local maximum (for a rising edge) or local minimum (for a falling edge). There are other methods to find these edges directly. One of them is the second-derivative operator which differences the first derivative. Then the problem has been changed into finding the places where the second-derivative is zero. When we apply second derivative operators to images, the zeros rarely fall exactly on a pixel. They may fall between pixels. We can find zeros by finding the *zero-crossing* in the second derivative as illustrated in Fig 7.7 for one dimensional signals. (A zero-crossing is a place where the value of a function passes from positive to negative.) For two dimensions the second derivative operator is denoted by ∇^2 and is called *Laplacian* operator:

$$\nabla^2 = \nabla \cdot \nabla = \begin{bmatrix} \frac{\partial}{\partial x} \\ \frac{\partial}{\partial y} \end{bmatrix} \cdot \begin{bmatrix} \frac{\partial}{\partial x} \\ \frac{\partial}{\partial y} \end{bmatrix} = \frac{\partial^2}{\partial x^2} + \frac{\partial^2}{\partial y^2} \tag{7.22}$$

In fact, the differencing operators are sensitive to the noise. One way to deal with the sensitivity of the Laplacian operator is to smooth the image first. If the Gaussian kernel

$$G(x,y) = \frac{1}{2\pi\sigma^2} e^{\frac{-r^2}{2\sigma^2}} \tag{7.23}$$

(where $r^2 = x^2 + y^2$) is applied the smoothed image

$$I = G(x,y) * f \tag{7.24}$$

Then the Laplacian operator is applied on the smoothed image

$$\nabla^2 I = \nabla^2 (G(x,y) * f) = (\nabla^2 G(x,y)) * f \tag{7.25}$$

where,

$$\nabla^2 G(x,y) = \frac{-1}{\pi\sigma^4}(1 - \frac{r^2}{2\sigma^2}) e^{\frac{-r^2}{2\sigma^2}} \tag{7.26}$$

It is to say there is no need to do these operations in two steps. Simply differencing the Gaussian to get a single Laplacian of Gaussian operator

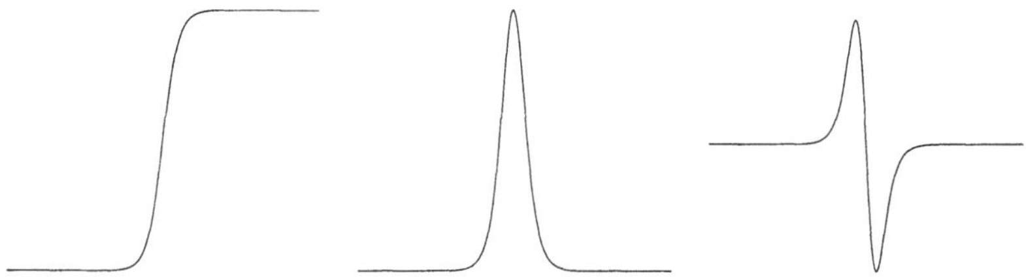

(a) (b) (c)

Figure 7.7: The notion of a zero-crossing. The intensity change (a) gives rise to a peak (b) in its first derivative and to a zero-crossing (c) in its second derivative.

(a) (b)

Figure 7.8: The one (a) and two (b) dimensional form of $\nabla^2 G$.

$\nabla_2 G$. $\nabla_2 G$ is a symmetric Mexican-hat-shaped operator and its one- and two-dimensional forms are shown in Fig 7.8. It can be interpreted that the Laplacian of a Gaussian is the derivative with respect to $2\sigma^2$ of a Gaussian. That is, it is the limit of one Gaussian minus a just every so smaller Gaussian. For this reason it can be approximated as the difference of two Gaussian. This is known as the *Difference-of-Gaussian* or DOG operator.

7.3.2 Face feature detection by DOG operator

$\nabla^2 G$ can be applied to edge detection. It is found that the elongated filter, a one-dimensional DOG operator in one direction and a one-dimensional Gaussian filter in the perpendicular direction, is more efficient than the round DOG operator for face feature detection.

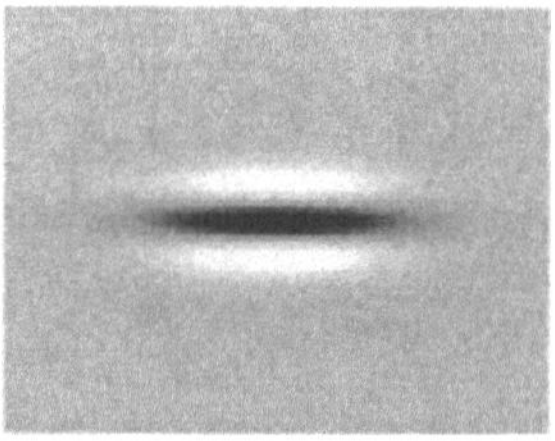

(a)

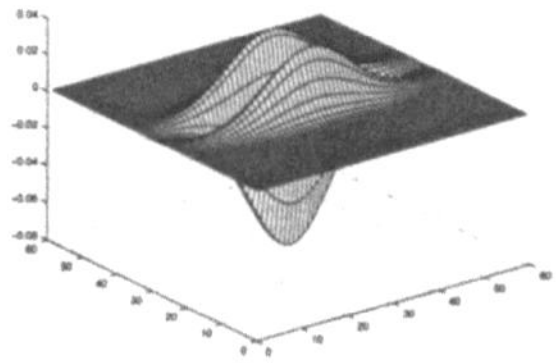

(b)

Figure 7.9: The elongated DOG operator.(a) Image form display. (b) Mesh surface plot.

The elongated DOG operator is separable and it can be represented by a product of two one-dimensional functions in perpendicular directions. For instance, operator illustrated in Fig 7.9 can be expressed as

$$G(x) \cdot \frac{d^2}{dy^2}G(y) \tag{7.27}$$

where $G(x) = \frac{1}{\sqrt{2\pi\sigma^2}} \exp^{-\frac{x^2}{2\sigma^2}}$ is a one-dimensional Gaussian distribution. This makes implementation relatively easy by convoluting the image with two one-dimensional vectors in two directions rather than a single two-dimensional matrix.

7.3.3 Experimental results

A thresholding operation is applied to suppress those small local maxima and limit the search range before the detection of local maxima. Fig 7.11 shows the output of convoluting original image with the elongated DOG operator and the feature points (marked with the crosses) detected by finding the local maxima. These results indicate that the elongated DOG operator is indeed able to detect the structural features in the face. Moreover, the operator is able to localize the eyes location accurately which are used in many face recognition application as the datum points to resize and normalize the face size and orientation [13]. A prototype face detection system is developed using skin color segmentation, shape verification and elongated DOG operator validation(shown in Fig 7.10).

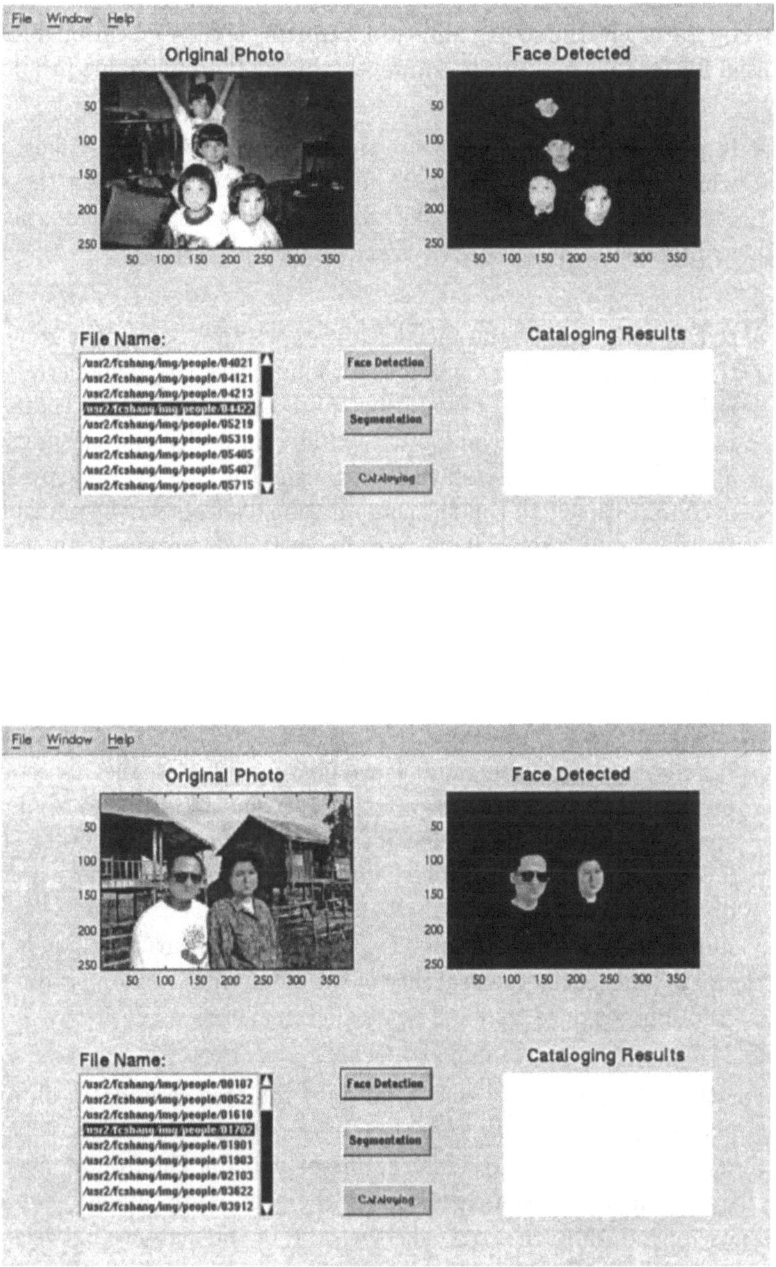

Figure 7.10: Human face detection results.

7.3.4 Discussion

DOG operator has the strong ability of localizing the eyes location and can be used for face normalization. However, this method has some problems:

- It produces too many feature points especially at the edges. But when we only examine those feature points falling into the face candidates obtained from skin color, the number of points is significantly reduced. The result is shown in Fig 7.12.

- It can only detect the facial features within the certain range of scale and orientation variations although Yow [20] demonstrated it is invariant to scale, orientation, pose and viewpoint over a wide range and the faces can be at the different scales and orientations. The problem may be resolved by using multi-scale steerable pyramid decomposition [21]. But the computational efforts will be multiplied. Fortunately for those large face (for instance,. greater than 40×40 pixels) image, it has the broad orientation variation tolerance which can cover all the non-intentional poses in the home photo album, even for the faces like in Fig 7.13 it can detect the feature points correctly. For the smaller faces such tolerance doesn't hold any more.

- It fails to detect the small facial features due to the uncertainty principle in spatial-frequency space. It cannot attain high resolution spatial-frequency discrimination while keeping the accurate space localization. This difficulty is fatal weakness because a large number of home photos contains small human portrait. For 256×384 image, human face is smaller than 35×35, thus facial feature region is very small. This curbs the usability of the elongated DOG operator. The solution is to use the high resolution image.

For those feature points which fall into the face candidates obtained from skin color, we use the geometry information between those points to verify if there is a true facial structure or not. For the frontal face, two eyes are symmetrical, the cheek under the eyes is textureless, two eyes and nose or mouth form a triangle, the ratio of the distance between two eyes to the distance between nose/mouth and the eye line. Using these prior knowledge the frontal face can be validated. But for the side view, due to the absence of one eye or even mouth, some feature points are lost. It is difficult to verify by the structural information.

(a) (b)

Figure 7.11: (a) Output of the elongated DOG operation. (b) Detected feature points (marked by cross).

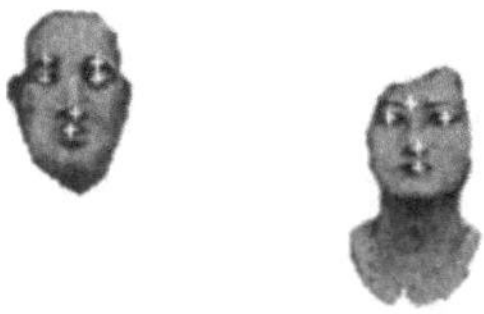

Figure 7.12: Feature points (marked by cross) falling into the face candidates obtained from skin color.

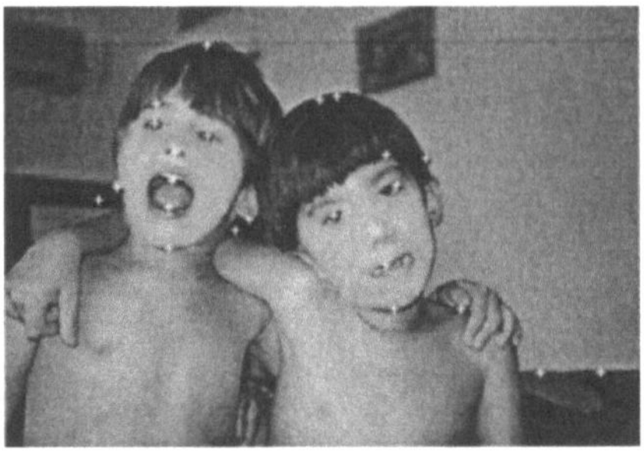

Figure 7.13: The elongated DOG operator can correctly detect the feature points in the faces although the heads tilt in a large angle.

7.4 Template-based Human Face Detection

7.4.1 Overview

Generally speaking most of human faces are all similar. They have roughly similar structures. They have the same facial components which are distributed over the face with the similar spatial relationship. However, human faces do have some variations for the different individuals. Precisely because of these variations, the world is getting varied, interesting. People takes advantages of these variations to recognize each other or if all the human faces were same, people would be confused and life would be in disorder. On the other hand, human face is a non-rigidity object, the same face will have different appearance in the different time with the change of the subject's mood, makeup and accessories. These variations come from the face itself. In fact for the faces in the image, a large number of variations results from imaging condition including illumination, taking viewpoint, subject's pose and etc. For the face recognition problem, which compares the input face image with a number of known faces and determines it matches the one of them, these variations are used to discriminate the one face from the other faces. On the contrary, for the face detection problem, which detects if there exists a human face in the input image, the key issue is to find out the similarity among the faces despite of those variations. There are many methods to deal with the variations. In essence most of them are templates-based methods. One of them is an example-based learning approach for locating vertical frontal views of faces in complex background [15]. We implemented this approach and combined it with our method. The procedure is divided into two steps:

first, a set of face templates is constructed through the example-based learning, then these templates are used to match the test image in every scale and every location to find out whether there exists a "matching" or not.

7.4.2 Normalized "face space"

Faces are structured objects in essence with the same key facial components geometrically arranged in roughly the same location. Thus, when we map these geometrical location related information into a high dimensional location space, it will form a unique distribution in this "face space".

To simplify the algorithms, the face is normalized first. A rectangle is drawn around the face with its upper edge just above the eyebrows, lower edge just under the mouth and left and right edge just outside the cheek as shown in Fig 7.14. To minimize the influence caused by noise this face window is *blurred* by a lowpass Gaussian kernel. Then the intensity of pixels is adjusted to reduce the illumination non-uniformity. The face window is resized to 19×19 using the bilinear interpolation method. Choosing a 19×19 normalized window size is somewhat arbitrary[15]. The main reason is that the 19×19 size is small enough to keep the "face space" tractable while large enough to preserve the facial details. The pixels near corners and boundaries are less relevant to the description of a face. In order to reduce the dimensionality of "face space" and eliminate the possible negative effect a 19×19 binary pixel mask shown in Fig 7.14(b) is used to zero out these pixels. Subtracting these pixels from $19 \times$ window, only 273 pixels are left. If each column of pixels is spread to form a long column of pixels, we get a 273 dimensional face vector. This face vector will span a 273 dimensional space which we call "face space".

7.4.3 Dimensionality reduction

When all sample faces are mapped into the high dimensional "face space", it will form a unique distribution. But all the faces will not be randomly distributed in this high-dimensional "face space", they will be compactly distributed in a small region. Thus, they can be characterized by a relatively low-dimensional subspace. This subspace can be approximated by the principal component analysis, which is often used to reduce the dimensionality while keeping the most of information. In our case, the "face space" is 273 dimension. If we perform a principal component anal-

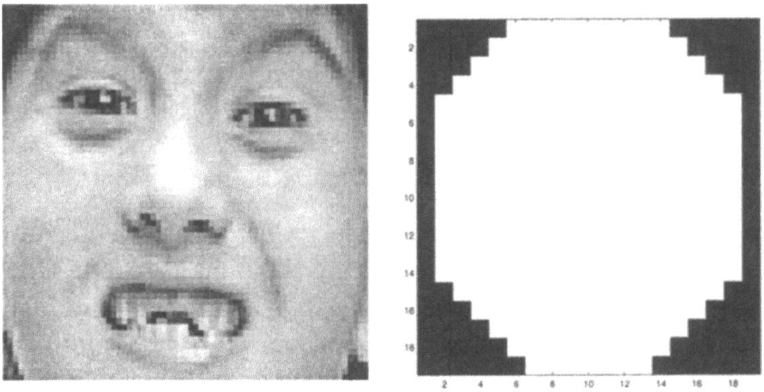

(a) (b)

Figure 7.14: (a) Part of face region concerned. (b) Mask

ysis and retain only those components which contribute more than 0.25 percent to the variance in the data set, the dimensionality of the subspace will reduce to 41 (shown in Fig 7.15). This proves performing principal component analysis is Significant, since it can reduce the complexity of the operations followed at the price of losing very little information.

7.4.4 Clustering and face template generation

We can imagine even in 41-dimensional subspace of "face space" the face distribution is still very complicated and not easy to be characterized by a few parameters. But it is reasonable to assume that this probability distribution is a mixture of Gaussian distributions with different means and deviations. That means we can split the subspace into a few clusters and for each cluster it can be characterized as a multi-dimensional Gaussian distribution. So we use the clustering algorithms to generate a few face templates.

Traditional k-means clustering algorithm is simple and easy to use, but it has a main drawback. In essence, k-means clustering is a local optimal algorithm but not a global optimal algorithm. Its performance is sensitive to the initial cluster centers. Good initial values will result in good performance. Many methods have been proposed to tackle this problem. Here a method called progressive increment of cluster numbers k-means clustering algorithm is proposed. This algorithm increases the number of clusters progressively from one to the preset value, so there is

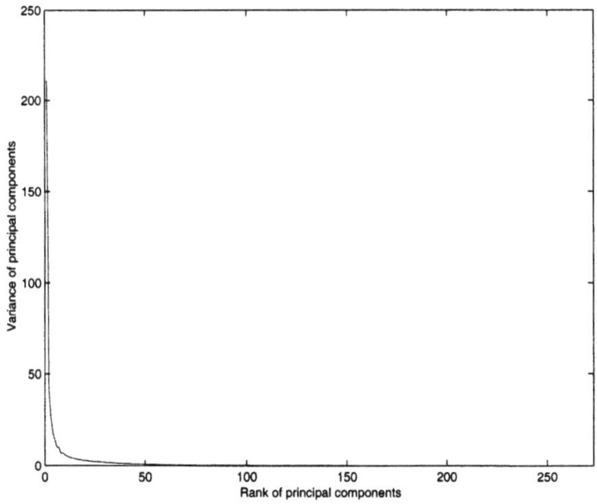

Figure 7.15: The variance of each principal component

little chance to trap into a local minimum due to the improper selection of initial values. This method works very well for the data with isolated clusters. For the partially isolated clusters, it also works reasonably well. The procedure of the algorithm is as following:

1. Compute the mean value of the sample data. Find the furthest point from the mean value;

2. Split the mean value into 2 cluster centers along the direction from the mean value to the furthest point.

3. Divide the sample data into the current clusters by assigning each sample into the nearest cluster center based on Euclidean distance.

4. Update the cluster centers to be the centroids of the current clusters.

5. Using the updated cluster centers, to reassign the data samples to the nearest cluster center. If the results remain unchanged proceed to the next step, otherwise, go to the last step.

6. If the number of current clusters is not less than preset number, go to the next step. Otherwise compute the deviation of the each cluster. Find the cluster which has the biggest deviation. In this cluster, find the furthest point from the its center. Increase the

number of clusters by 1. Split this cluster center into 2 along the direction from center to the furthest point. Assign one to it and another one to the new increased cluster. Go to the step 3.

About Mahalanobis distance

In Chapter 3 a distance measure named Mahalanobis distance is introduced. It is defined by:

$$D_M^2 = (\mathbf{x} - \bar{\mathbf{x}})^T \Sigma^{-1} (\mathbf{x} - \bar{\mathbf{x}}). \tag{7.28}$$

We said the Mahalanobis distance is better metric than Euclidean distance in measuring how far a point is from a set of points by considering its spatial distribution while the distribution of the set is not isotropy. When used in feature space to determine the decision boundary, Mahalanobis distance is superior to Euclidean distance. The initial point set is marked by '$*$'. The locus of the constant Mahalanobis distance (in the figure the distance is $\sqrt{2}$) from this set is drawn by the solid line. When some points (marked by '$\circ$') are added to enlarge the point set, the same Mahalanobis distance (drawn by dash-dot line) will cover a larger region. Because clustering algorithm is a iterative process, when Mahalanobis distance is used as the distance metric in the clustering algorithm, it tends to make a particular cluster bigger and bigger and make the algorithm unstable. This problem results from the fact that when more points fall into the set, the elements of covariance become larger, and the Mahalanobis distance becomes smaller. As we know the multivariate Gaussian probability density function is defined as

$$f(\mathbf{x}) = \frac{1}{(2\pi)^{\frac{d}{2}} |\Sigma|^{\frac{1}{2}}} exp[-\frac{1}{2}(\mathbf{x} - \bar{\mathbf{x}})^T \Sigma^{-1} (\mathbf{x} - \bar{\mathbf{x}})] \tag{7.29}$$

where $\mathbf{x}$ is a d-dimensional vector, $\bar{\mathbf{x}}$ is the d-dimensional mean vector, Σ is the d-by-d covariance matrix, $|\Sigma|$ is the determinant of Σ. Its log-likelihood is expressed as

$$\ln f(\mathbf{x}) = -\frac{d}{2} \ln 2\pi - \frac{1}{2} \ln |\Sigma| - \frac{1}{2}[(\mathbf{x} - \bar{\mathbf{x}})^T \Sigma^{-1} (\mathbf{x} - \bar{\mathbf{x}})] \tag{7.30}$$

or equivalently

$$\begin{aligned} -2 \ln f(\mathbf{x}) &= (\mathbf{x} - \bar{\mathbf{x}})^T \Sigma^{-1} (\mathbf{x} - \bar{\mathbf{x}}) + \ln |\Sigma| + d \ln 2\pi \\ &= D_M^2 + \ln |\Sigma| + C \end{aligned}$$

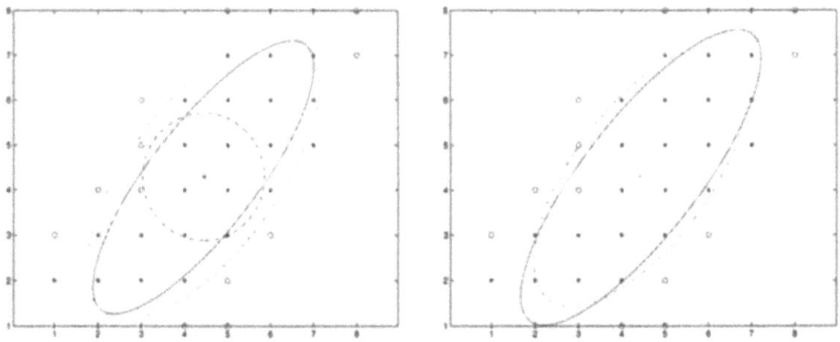

(a) (b)

Figure 7.16: (a)Loci of the same constant Mahalanobis distance (solid line and dash-dot line) for the different set sizes versus locus of the same constant Euclidean distance (dashed line). (b)Loci of the same constant modified Mahalanobis distance for the different set sizes.

where C is a constant. From this expression we find the cue. The modified Mahalanobis distance is shown in Fig 7.16(b). As in Fig 7.16(a) the initial point set is marked by '$*$'. The locus of the constant modified Mahalanobis distance from this set is drawn by the solid line. Additive points are marked by '$\circ$' and the locus of the same modified Mahalanobis distance for enlarged set is drawn by the dash-dot line. We can observe that for the enlarged point set the modified Mahalanobis distance pulls some points near while pushes some points far to keep the point set stable. Therefore, the modified Mahalanobis distance can be used as the distance metric in the clustering algorithm. Performing this clustering algorithm 6 face template are generated (see Fig 7.17).

7.4.5 Template matching

First, a minimum rectangle which embraces the largest region in the image is determined. Then a square window with the size equivalent to the longer side of the rectangle is shifted over the search region by the step of one pixel or several pixels to reduce the search locations. At the each location, subimage in the window is normalized to the 19×19 by bilinear interpolation and subsampling. Then the 6 modified Mahalanobis distances between the normalized region and 6 templates are computed respectively and only the minimum value among them is retained. Then the window size is shrunken by a factor of 0.9 and repeat the above op-

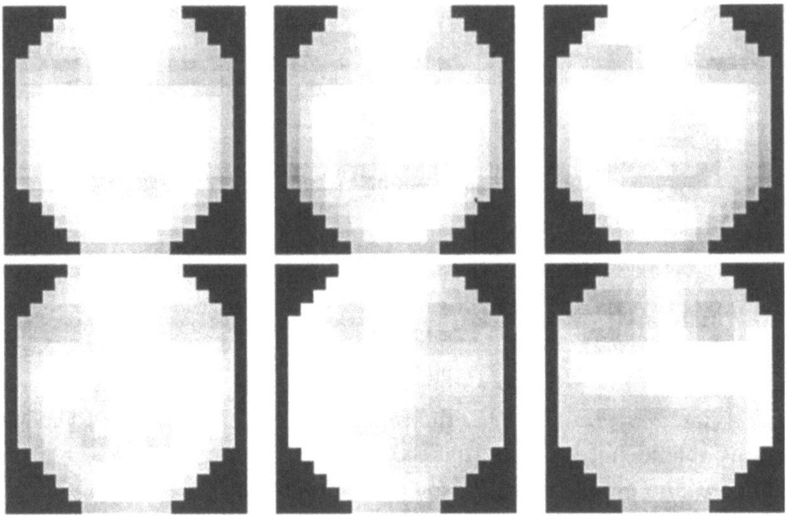

Figure 7.17: 6 face prototypes

erations until the window size is smaller than 19×19. So for each face candidate region, we get a two dimensional array of distance with the index representing the location and window size(scale) index respectively. Now the problem is converted to, the location, and the scale where the best match is found. From the experiments we observed that choosing the global minimum of the distance array as the best match is not reliable. It reaches its minimum when the window covers the target face exactly. Thereafter, it will rise up with the window shrinking further. Based on such hypothesis. In each scale the best location is determined first by finding the position where the distance is minimum. Thus two dimensional array is transformed into one dimensional array with the index indicating the scale(window size). If the distance is decreasing monotonously the minium window size is thought to be the best match scale. In these two cases the true face is thought to be detected. Otherwise, it is thought there does not exist a human face in the current candidate region.

Some detected faces are shown in Fig 7.18. For the more than 90% face candidate regions this method can successfully validate it is a face pattern. Some failed cases are caused by non-frontal views, some are caused by our non-global optimized minimum distance search method.

Figure 7.18: Faces detected by template matching

References

1. M. M. Fleck, D. A. Forsyth, C. Bregler, "Finding Naked People", European Conference on Computer Vision, Vol. II, pp. 592-602, 1996
2. T. Gevers, H. Stokman, A. Smeulders, "Photometric invariant region detection", British Machine Vision Conference, Vol. 2, pp. 659-669, 1998
3. G. Healey, "Segmenting Images Using Normalized Color", IEEE Transactions on Systems, Man, and Cybernetics, Vol. 22, No. 1, pp. 64-73, 1992
4. E. Hering, "Outlines of a Theory of the Light Sense", Harvard University Press, Cambridge MA, 1964
5. J. R. Kender, "Saturation, Hue and Normalized Color: Calculation, Digitation Effects, and Use", Technical report, Carnegie-Mellon University, November 1976
6. G. J. Klinker, S. A. Shafer, T. Kanade, "A Physical Approach to Color Image Understanding", International Journal Computer Vision, pp. 7-38, 1990
7. S. A. Shafer, "Using Color to Separate Reflection Components", Color Research Applications, Vol. 10, No. 4, pp. 210-218, 1985
8. Q. B. Sun, W. M. Huang, J. K. Wu, "Face Detection Based on Color and Local Symmetry Information", IEEE Third International Conference on Automatic Face and Gesture Recognition, pp. 14-16, 1998
9. G. Wyszecki, W. S. Stiles, "Color Science: Concepts and Methods, Quantitative Data and Formulae, John Wiley & Sons, 2nd edition, 1982
10. M. Turk, A. Pentland, "Eigenfaces for Recognition", Journal of Cognitive Neuroscience, Vol. 3, pp. 71-86, 1991
11. G. Chow and X. Li, "Towards a System for Automatic Facial Feature Detection", Pattern Recognition, Vol. 26, pp. 1739-1755, 1993
12. Q. B. Sun, C. P. Lam, J. K. Wu, "Real-time Human Face Location and Identification", Institute of Systems Science, 1996
13. Weimin Huang, Qibin Sun, Chian-Prong Lam, Jian-Kang WU, "A Robust Approach to Face and Eyes Detection From Image With Cluttered Background", Real World Computing, 1998
14. C. P. Lam, Q. B. Sun, J. K. Wu, "A Practical Automatic Face Recognition System", Proceedings of NATO Advanced Study Institute (ASI) Programme: Face Recognition, Scotland, UK, 1997
15. K. K. Sung, T. Poggio, "Example-based Learning for View-based Human Face Detection", Artificial Intelligence Laboratory and Center for Biological and Computational Learning, Massachusetts Institute of Technology, No. 1521, 1994
16. H. Li, R. Forchheimer, "Location of Face Using Color Cues", Picture coding symposium, Switzerland, Lausanne, 1993
17. S. Matsuhashi, O. Nakamura, T.Minami, "Human-Face Extraction Using Modified HSV Color System and Personal Identification Through Facial Iamge Based on Isodensity Maps", Conference of electrical and computer engineering, No. 2, pp. 909-912, Canada, 1995
18. J. Yang, A. Waibel, "Tracking Human Faces in Real-Time", School of computer science, Carnegie Mellon University, No. 210, 1995

19. D. Marr, Vision - "A Computational Investigation Into the Human Representation and Processing of Visual Information", W. H. Freeman and Company, New York, 1982

20. K. C. Yow, R. Cipolla, "Feature-Based Human Face Detection", Image and Vision Computing, Vol. 15, pp. 713-735, 1997

21. W. T. Freeman and E. H. Adelson, "The Design and Use of Steerable Filters", IEEE Transaction on Pattern Analysis and Machine Intelligence, Vol. 13, No. 9, pp. 891-906, 1991

Chapter 8

Visual Keywords

Despite the simplicity of keyword-based matching, text retrieval systems have achieved practical success in recent decades. Keywords, which exhibit meaningful semantics to users, can be extracted relatively easily from text documents. In the case of visual contents which are perceptual in nature, the definition of corresponding "keywords" and automatic extraction are unclear and non-trivial. Is there a similar metaphor or mechanism for visual data? In this chapter, we propose a new notion of visual keywords which are abstracted and extracted from exemplary visual tokens tokenized from visual documents in a visual content domain by soft computing techniques. A visual content is indexed by comparing its visual tokens against the learned visual keywords of which the soft presence of comparison are aggregated spatially via contextual domain knowledge. A coding scheme based on singular value decomposition, similar to latent semantic indexing for text retrieval, is also proposed to reduce dimensionality and noise. An empirical study on professional natural scene photograph retrieval and categorization will be described to show the effectiveness and efficiency of visual keywords.

8.1 Introduction

In the past few decades, successful text retrieval models (e.g. [26,24]) and systems (e.g. text search engines available on the world-wide-web) have been developed based on matching of keywords (or terms) between those specified in a query and those extracted from text documents in the database. Despite their conceptual simplicity, keywords are natural and yet powerful means for indexing and retrieval of text documents.

However, non-text materials are very different in content representation from text documents. Texts are conceptual and symbolic in nature. Keywords, which are relatively well-defined and well-segmented entities, convey meaningful semantics to human querists. Visual data are perceptual and pattern-based. Interpreting visual data is underconstrained in general. There are multiple interpretations of the world consistent with the visual data. Visual variations such as scale, translation, illumination etc. further complicate visual perception and understanding.

For instance, look at the photographs of natural scene shown in Fig. 8.1. Each column of photographs constitutes a semantics class of images perceived as similar by human users, although images in the same class could vary in significantly in color, texture, and spatial configuration. The classes are (from left to right), namely, coasts, fields, trees, snowy mountains, and streams/waterfalls respectively. How would a computer perform retrieval and classification based on the visual contents of these images? What would be the natural sets of features for indexing and retrieval of visual data? Can we describe and compare visual contents beyond primitive perceptual features such as color, texture, shapes etc specific to their contents? Are there corresponding "keywords" that are inherent and consistent in a visual domain?

Consider Figure 8.2. The left half (say I_0) shows a perceptually coherent view of a coast and the right half of the same figure is its scrambled version (say I_1). Based on distributions of color or other low level features solely, I_0 and I_1 will be considered very similar (if not identical) though they are perceptually dissimilar. Scrambling I_0 in different ways can easily produce perceptually incoherent images $I_2, I_3 \cdots$ etc. to fool a search engine that relies only on distribution of low level features and make its performance looks bad for comparison.

How would one describe visual content such as the coast image given in (left of) Figure 8.2? An intuitive and reasonable textual description could be: "there is cloudy blue sky at the top, dark blue sea on bottom left, brownish rocky highland (or mountain) on bottom right, and white bubbly waves along the bottom middle". The latter textual description utilizes visual features (color, texture) that characterize *types* of visual objects ('sky','sea' etc) as well as *spatial configuration* ('top','bottom right' etc).

This observation motivates the insight in our visual keyword approach. In essence, we argue that both local type information and spatial configuration information are useful in describing and comparing visual contents. Visual keywords are visual data types abstracted and extracted from visual documents in a content domain. They are inherent and con-

Figure 8.1: Some photographs from each class (column).

Figure 8.2: A coast image and its scrambled version

sistent features present in visual contents to alleviate the problems of ambiguity and variations in visual data. Although visual keywords are content-domain-dependent, our proposed framework allows them to be customized towards different visual content domains.

The rest of the chapter is organized as follows. Related works are discussed in the next section. In Section 8.3, the proposed visual keywords methodology is introduced. We describe how visual keywords are learned from visual data. We present a visual content description scheme based on spatial distribution of visual keywords and a coding scheme based on singular value decomposition for the resulting non-textual content descriptions. In Section 8.4 and 8.5, we describe evaluation experiments on professional nature scenery photograph retrieval and categorization respectively to demonstrate the effectiveness and efficiency of visual keywords. Last but not least, we conclude the chapter with an integrative view with outlook for future directions.

8.2 Related Works

Text retrieval based on keywords has been the main stream in the field of information retrieval [28]. Many existing visual retrieval systems (e.g. [25]) extract and annotate the data objects in the visual content manually, often with some assistance of user interfaces. It is assumed that once keywords are associated with the visual content, text retrieval techniques can be deployed easily. Although text descriptions are certainly important to reflect the (largely conceptual) semantics of multimedia data, they may result in combinatorial explosion of keywords in the attempt of annotation due to the ambiguous and variational nature of multimedia data. Also there is a limit to how much semantic information the textual attributes can provide [5].

On the other hand, in the past, visual content-based retrieval systems (e.g. [18,20,2]) have mainly relied on aggregate measure (e.g. histogram) of primitive features such as color, texture, shape etc for describing and comparing visual contents. These methods often produce results incongruent with human expectations [15]. For example, images sharing similar overall color distribution can differ greatly in semantic content. This has been argued in the previous section using Figure 8.2. This paradigm roughly corresponds to pre-attentive similarity matching which is a low-level function in human visual perception.

Nevertheless, a new low-level feature called banded color correlograms was proposed recently [8] to improve color histograms by exploiting local correlational structure of colors for hierarchical image classification. No attention is paid to global spatial configuration. Similar to our coding method presented in this chapter, singular value decomposition was used to reconfigure the feature space to reduce noise and dimensionality. However, our coding scheme applies to abstracted visual entities rather than low level features.

In contrast, recent region-based methods [6] [27] [30] pre-segment an image by color (or both color and texture) into regions and compute the similarity between two images in terms of the features (and spatial relationships [27]) of these regions. But image segmentation is generally unreliable. A poor segmentation can result in incongruent regions for further similarity matching.

The VisualSEEK system [27] and its descendents consider spatial relationships among regions extensively and combine them with primitive features of regions for image retrieval. The matching algorithm merges lists of image candidates, resulting from region-based matching between query and database images, with respect to some thresholds and tends to be rather complex and ad hoc in realization. Segmentation of regions is based on color only and no object or type information is obtained from the segmented regions.

In a different approach that advocates the use of configuration, the work reported in [15] hand-crafted relational model templates that encode the common global scene configuration structure for each category, based on qualitative measurements of color, luminance and spatial properties of examples from the categories. Classification is performed by deformable template matching which involves heavy computation. The manual construction of relational model templates is time consuming and incomprehensive. To avoid this problem, a learning scheme that automatically computes scene templates from a few examples [23] is proposed and tested on a smaller scene classification problem with promising results.

Going beyond primitive features, a new image representation called *blobs*, which are coherent clusters segmented in color and texture space, has been developed [6]. Similarity-based retrieval is performed using these segmented regions. For image classification, all the blobs from the categories in the training data are clustered into "canonical" blobs using Gaussian models with diagonal variance. A decision-tree classifier was trained on the distance vectors that measure the nearest distance of each canonical blob to the images. However, the classification result did not outperform that of color histograms. In general, image segmentation is not robust and may result in incoherent or fragmented regions. Although the construction of canonical blobs corresponds to the unsupervised option in our creation of visual keywords, we do not restrict ourselves to only clustering. Last but not least, in our work, the detection of visual keywords in an image preserves all probable occurrence scores instead of distance to nearest matching blob and an additional step summarizes the occurrence scores in spatial distribution based on contextual knowledge.

8.3 Methodology

In this chapter, we define a *visual document* as a complete unit of visual data. Examples include a digital image, a video shot represented by some key frame etc. A coherent unit in a visual document, such as a region of pixels in an image, is called a *visual token.* There are prototypical visual tokens present in a given distribution of visual documents. Using soft computing techniques, these visual keywords can be abstracted and extracted from a sufficiently large sample of visual tokens of a visual content domain.

Visual keywords could correspond to "things" like faces, pedestrians etc and "stuffs" like foliage, water etc in visual contents, represented by suitable visual characteristics. They are called "keywords" as in text documents for the following reasons. First, they represent unique *types* (or classes) of visual tokens occurring in a visual content domain. Next, a visual content is described by the presence or absence of these typed visual entities at a spatial abstraction, rather than directly by the visual entities or primitive features. Last but not least, the higher-order semantic structure implicit in the association of these typed visual entities with the visual documents are exploited to develop a coding scheme.

Figure 8.3 summarizes our proposed framework in a flow diagram. The top row depicts the extraction of visual keywords. A systematic and automatic component called *tokenization* extracts visual tokens from visual documents. A *typification* component creates visual keywords from the set of visual tokens. The visual keywords are visual representation resulting from supervised or/and unsupervised learning.

The middle row of Figure 8.3 shows the steps to produce visual content signature based on extracted visual keywords. During indexing (or retrieval), a visual document (or a query sample), is subjected to tokenization to produce visual tokens. The location-specific visual tokens are evaluated against the visual keywords and their soft occurrences aggregated spatially (*type evaluation* + *spatial aggregation*) to form a *Spatial Aggregation Map* (SAM) as visual content signature for the visual document.

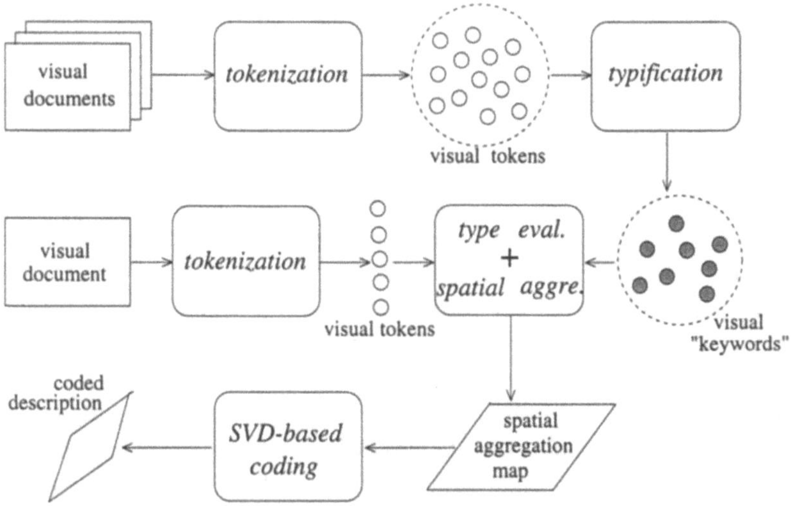

Figure 8.3: The methodology of visual keywords

With appropriate similarity measure, the SAMs of visual documents can be used in similarity matching for image retrieval and categorization applications.

Last but not least, the bottom row illustrates a coding process based on singular value decomposition to reduce the dimensionality and noise in SAMs.

8.3.1 Typification

The typification component in Figure 8.3 aims to induce the types (or classes) of visual tokens from sufficiently large number of examples in a visual content domain. Both supervised and unsupervised learning methods can be employed. Thus, while visual keywords are visual content domain-dependent, our framework allows them to be customized for the domain via learning.

Unsupervised learning

Alternatively unsupervised learning methods such as Self-Organizing Maps (SOM) neural networks [9], Fuzzy C-Means (FCM) algorithm [3], and the Expectation-Maximization (EM) algorithm [17] can be used to discover regularities in the visual tokens in visual documents. Soft clusters (visual keywords) that represent prototypical visual tokens are formed from a training set of visual tokens sampled from visual documents of a given visual content domain.

The term *soft clustering* is opposed to hard (or crisp) clustering whereby each input pattern is assigned to one and only one cluster (i.e. winner-take-all) during the clustering process. In the case of soft clustering, an input pattern can belong to multiple clusters with different uncertainty degrees. This has advantage over the crisp version (e.g. K-Means clustering) because a visual token, based on its feature vector, may resemble multiple visual keywords and a crisp assignment may result in incorrect clustering. With soft memberships, it can still contribute to the computation of the relevant visual keywords.

We first look at the probabilistic memberships computed using the EM algorithm and then point out its similarity with the fuzzy memberships computed by the FCM algorithm . Note that the cluster centers are the visual keywords.

Suppose we have N input patterns $X_j = (X_j^1, X_j^2, \cdots, X_j^D), j = 1, 2, \cdots, N$ to be clustered into M Gaussian clusters $E_i = g_i(X; \mu_i, \Sigma_i), i = 1, 2, \cdots, M$ where μ_i and Σ_i are means and covariance matrices respectively. Typically the E-step of the EM algorithm computes

$$P_{ij} = \frac{P(X_j|E_i) \cdot P(E_i)}{\sum_{k=1}^{M} P(X_j|E_k) \cdot P(E_k)} \quad i = 1, 2, \cdots, M \tag{8.1}$$

$$\overline{X}_i = \frac{\sum_{j=1}^{N} P_{ij} \cdot X_j}{\sum_{j=1}^{N} P_{ij}} \quad i = 1, 2, \cdots, M \tag{8.2}$$

$$SS_i^{pq} = \frac{\sum_{j=1}^{N} P_{ij} \cdot X_j^p X_j^q}{\sum_{j=1}^{N} P_{ij}} \quad i = 1, 2, \cdots, M; \; p, q = 1, 2, \cdots, D, \tag{8.3}$$

and the M-step computes new values of the parameters of the Gaussian model as

$$P_i = \frac{\sum_{j=1}^{N} P_{ij}}{N}, \tag{8.4}$$

$$\mu_i = \overline{X}_i, \tag{8.5}$$

$$\Sigma_i^{pq} = SS_i^{pq} - \overline{X}_i^p \overline{X}_i^q, \tag{8.6}$$

where $i = 1, 2, \cdots, M$.

The posterior probability $P_{ij} = P(E_i|X_j)$ in (8.1) indicates the degree of X_j being assigned to cluster E_i and thus acts as the weight of each input in computing the weighted sum in (8.2) and (8.3). They sum up to 1 ($\sum_i P_{ij} = 1$ for each X_j) and their counterparts in the FCM is the fuzzy membership degree $\mathcal{G}_{ij}$ which is computed [3] as

$$\mathcal{G}_{ij} = \frac{(\frac{1}{d^2(X_j,V_i)})^{\frac{1}{(\kappa-1)}}}{\sum_{i=1}^{M}(\frac{1}{d^2(X_j,V_i)})^{\frac{1}{(\kappa-1)}}}, \tag{8.7}$$

where $d^2(X_j, V_i) = (X_j - V_i)^T A(X_j - V_i)$, A is some positive definite matrix, $\kappa > 1$ is the fuzziness index, and V_i are the cluster centers (i.e. counterparts of $\overline{X}_i$), updated as

$$V_i = \frac{\sum_{j=1}^{N}(\mathcal{G}_{ij})^{\kappa} \cdot X_j}{\sum_{j=1}^{N}(\mathcal{G}_{ij})^{\kappa}}. \tag{8.8}$$

To sum up, we see that both the EM and FCM make use of soft membership degrees to weigh *every* input in updating the new centroid positions iteratively though they are derived from different objective functions (maximum likelihood and sum of distance respectively). This is in contrast to the hard clustering like K-Means where P_{ij} (or $\mathcal{G}_{ij}$) is either 1 or 0.

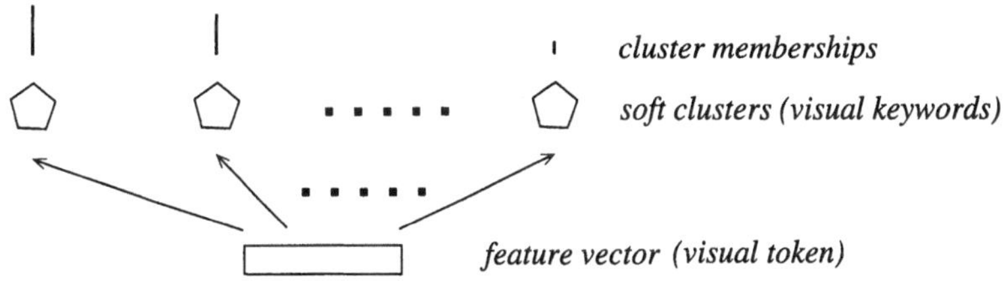

Figure 8.4: Visual keywords as soft cluster centers

Likewise upon completion of clustering, the cluster centers can be used to detect visual keywords in a visual content. The feature vector X_j associated with a tokenized visual token will be determined and the soft presence of the visual keywords will be computed as the memberships $\mathcal{G}_{ij}$ ($\in [0, 1]$, $\sum_i \mathcal{G}_{ij} = 1$) (Figure 8.4). These soft presences will undergo a spatial aggregation step to serve as an index for the visual content (Section 8.3.2).

Supervised learning

For supervised learning, view-based detectors such as neural network recognizers for salient objects such as human faces, pedestrians, foliage, clouds etc can be induced from a training set of positive and negative examples of visual tokens collected from visual documents of a given visual content domain (e.g.[19]). Suppose the domain is natural scene images and we employ neural networks as object detectors. Then we need to design neural network object detectors for foliage, skies, sea waves, snowy mountains etc and train them using positive and negative examples of these objects represented in suitable feature vectors (e.g. color, texture). Detectors may be further specialized for different views (e.g. different types of foliage, skies of cloudy and clear days etc) to improve the accuracies of the view-based neural network object detectors. In this supervised paradigm, a visual keyword is a neural network trained on a class of visual objects (Figure 8.5).

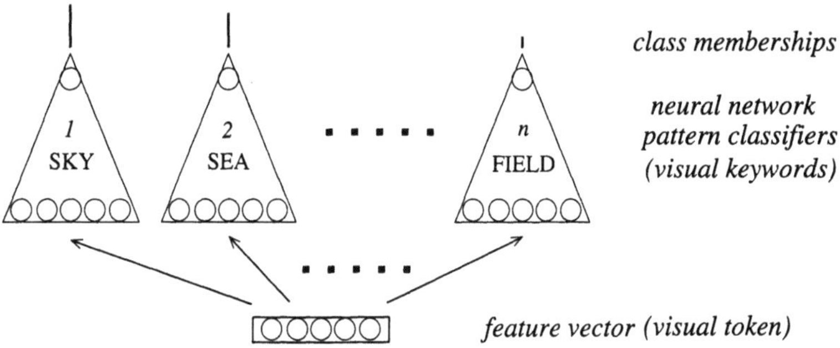

Figure 8.5: Visual keywords as neural network pattern classifiers

In Figure 8.5, each triangle represents a feedforward neural network pattern classifier $f_i(X_j)$ [4] trained to recognize a visual keyword of type i based on the feature vector X_j that characterizes a visual token j,

$$\mathcal{G}_{ij} = f_i(X_j). \tag{8.9}$$

The pattern classifier can be trained using the backpropagation learning algorithm or constructed as a Radial Basis Functions (RBF) network [4]. Though it is possible to train a large multi-class network for all the visual keywords simultaneously, it is recommended to have multiple smaller networks, each for a visual keyword, to reduce the complexity of the training task. That is, pattern classifier 1 in Figure 8.5 will be presented with positive and negative examples of sky visual tokens to modify the connection weights, pattern classifier 2 trained with positive and negative examples of sea visual tokens, and so on.

After the training, the pattern classifiers can be used to detect visual keywords in a visual content. The feature vector X_j associated with a tokenized visual token will be computed and fed into each pattern classifier i as an unknown input. Each pattern classifier $f_i(.)$ will output a class membership $\mathcal{G}_{ij}$ of X_j to visual keyword i. To ensure each network's contribution falls within $[0, 1]$ and sums up to unity, we can apply the softmax function [4] as normalization. The class memberships for each visual token in the visual content will be aggregated spatially to form a signature for the visual content. The details of tokenization, type evaluation, and spatial aggregation will be given in Section 8.3.2.

Learning by instruction

While the unsupervised learning approach may produce visual keywords without clear semantics, the supervised learning approach generally requires many examples for training neural network classifiers. Yet another alternative approach is to explicitly teach the visual keywords to the system by a user.

That is, visual keywords are visual prototypes specified by a user. Using an appropriate visual tool, the user crops domain-relevant regions from sample images and assigns sub-labels and labels to form vocabulary and thesaurus respectively. Suitable visual features (e.g. color, texture) are computed for each cropped region into a feature vector. i.e.

$$c_i : (s_{i1}, v_{i1}), (s_{i2}, v_{i2}), \cdots, (s_{ij}, v_{ij}) \cdots \tag{8.10}$$

where c_i are concept labels, s_{ij} are sub-labels for specific instances of concept i, and v_{ij} are feature vectors for regions ij. For instance, the sub-labels for the **sky** (label) visual keywords shown in Fig. 8.15 are cloudy, blue, bright, yellow, dark-cloudy, purple, gray, and orange respectively.

Then an image to be indexed is compared against the visual vocabulary to detect visual keywords automatically. The fuzzy detection results are registered in a *Type Evaluation Map* (TEM) and further aggregated spatially into a *Spatial Aggregation Map* (SAM). With visual thesaurus, the SAM can be further abstracted and reduced to a simpler representation, *Concept Aggregation Map* (CAM). This workflow is summarized in Figure 8.6.

8.3.2 Description scheme

Based on visual keywords, we have developed a description scheme (DS) for visual contents. In essence, the proposed non-textual DS combines both local type information and spatial configuration information. Below we describe a 3-layer visual information processing architecture (Figure

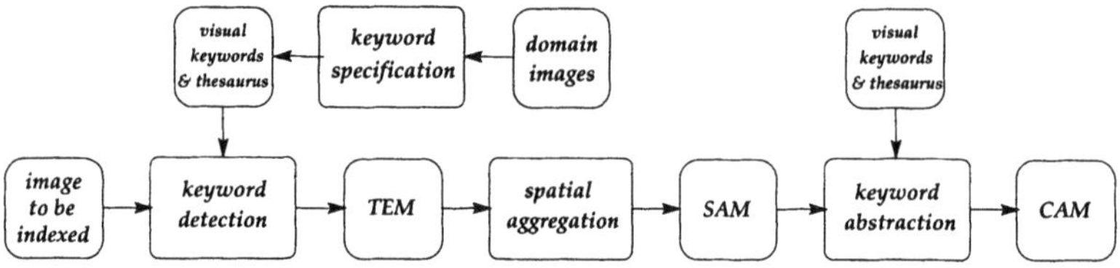

Figure 8.6: Indexing by spatial aggregation of visual keywords

8.7) that computes a description for a visual content as a spatial distribution of visual keywords. This architecture can be easily realized as a neural network.

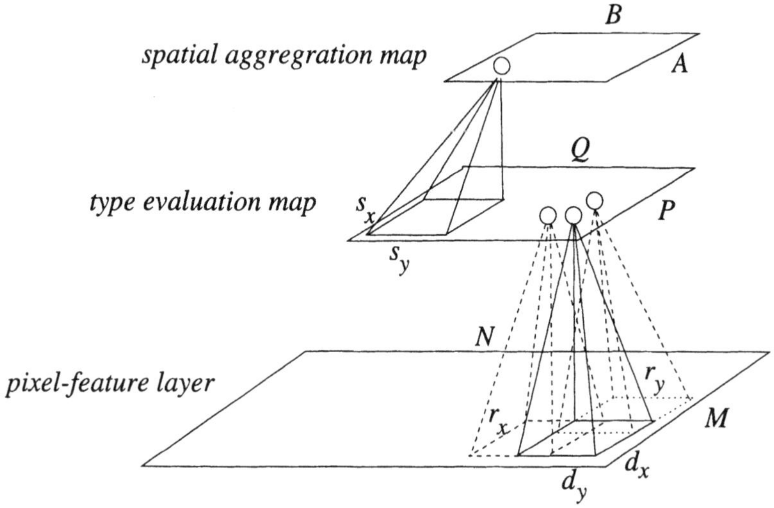

Figure 8.7: Visual keyword detection and spatial summary

The lowest layer is a collection of low-level feature planes at pixel level called *Pixel-Feature Layer*. For example, the color feature of an image can have three R, G, B planes of the same resolution.

The middle layer, *Type Evaluation Layer* or *Type Evaluation Map* (TEM), is an abstraction of the lowest layer. More precisely, given an image I with resolution $M \times N$, its TEM $\mathcal{G}$ has a lower resolution of $P \times Q, P \leq M, Q \leq N$. Each pixel or node (p, q) of TEM $\mathcal{G}$ has a receptive field [1] $\mathcal{R}$ that specifies a two-dimensional region of size $r_x \times r_y$ in I which can influence the node's value. That is, $\mathcal{R} = \{(x, y) \in I | x_p \leq x \leq x'_p, y_q \leq y \leq y'_q\}$ where $r_x = x'_p - x_p + 1, r_y = y'_q - y_q + 1$, and (x_p, y_q) and (x'_p, y'_q) are the starting and ending pixels of the receptive field in I respectively. We further allow tessellation displacements $d_x, d_y > 0$ in X, Y directions respectively such that adjacent pixels in $\mathcal{G}$ along X direction (along Y direction) have receptive fields in I which are displaced by d_x pixels along X direction (d_y pixels along Y direction) in I. That is, two adjacent $\mathcal{G}$ pixels share pixels in their receptive fields unless $d_x \geq r_x$ (or similarly $d_y \geq r_y$).

For simplicity, we fix the size of receptive field (r_x, r_y) and the displacements (d_x, d_y) for all pixels in $\mathcal{G}$ and assume that $(M - r_x)$ is divisible by d_x ($(N - r_y)$ is divisible by d_y). That is, the spatial dimensions of TEM $\mathcal{G}$ is determined by (r_x, r_y) and (d_x, d_y): $P = \frac{M-r_x}{d_x} + 1$, $Q = \frac{N-r_y}{d_y} + 1$. If this is not the case (i.e. indivisible), we can always center the collective receptive fields at the center of I and ignore the residues at the boundaries.

A visual token corresponds to a receptive field in I. It can be characterized by different perceptual features such as color, texture, shape, etc deemed appropriate for the visual content domain. It is represented as a feature vector in type evaluation process, to feed as an input vector to neural network object detectors (supervised visual keywords) or to compute its soft memberships to fuzzy/probabilistic clusters (unsupervised visual keywords).

The number of visual tokens in a visual document can be quantified by the spatial dimensions of its TEM $\mathcal{G}$. Every pixel or node (p, q) in a TEM $\mathcal{G}$ registers the set/class membership of a visual token governed by its receptive field against T supervised/unsupervised visual keywords which have been extracted a priori. In short, a TEM is a 3-dimensional map, $\mathcal{G} = P \times Q \times T$, that captures local type information. More than one TEM can be designed to tessellate I with different configurations of receptive fields and displacements (e.g. multi-resolution).

Likewise, the highest level, *Spatial Aggregation Layer* or *Spatial Aggregation Map* (SAM), is a summary of TEM. A receptive field S of size $(s_x \times s_y)$ and a displacement size (c_x, c_y) are used to tessellate the spatial extent (P, Q) of TEM with $A \times B, A \leq P, B \leq Q$ receptive fields. The memberships $\mathcal{G}(p, q, t)$ ($\in [0, 1]$) of visual keywords t at TEM pixel (p, q) that falls within the receptive field of SAM pixel (a, b) are aggregated as,

$$\mathcal{H}(a, b, t) = \sum_{(p,q) \in \mathcal{S}(a,b)} \mathcal{G}(p, q, t). \tag{8.11}$$

where $\mathcal{S}(a, b)$ denotes the receptive field of (a, b). In short, SAM is a 3-dimensional map, $\mathcal{H} = A \times B \times T$. In a linear form, SAM is a vector of $A \times B \times T$ dimensions. More than one SAM can be used to tessellate TEM with different configurations of receptive fields and displacements, thus encoding contextual knowledge as different spatial layout templates for relevant categories of visual contents (more details below).

8.3.3 Selection

Intuitively, when one searches for relevant text documents, supplying specific keywords tends to be more effective in retrieving relevant documents than using common terms which appear in many documents. For example, the word 'disease' will return a lot more documents than using the word 'cancer' or 'lung cancer'.

The same intuition can be applied to the case of visual keywords. In this chapter, we propose a simple visual keyword selection scheme as follows. The frequencies of visual keywords detected in the set of visual documents from which they are created are tabulated or histogrammed. Next we systematically eliminate visual keywords starting with those of highest frequencies of occurrences and test the effectiveness of the remaining number of visual keywords on a classification task (could be a retrieval task as well). We repeat this elimination process of visual keywords selection until the performance starts to degrade and keep those visual keywords that give the optimal performance. The method can reduce the number of visual keywords significantly (as will be shown in the experimental results in Section 8.4) and simplify the computation of coding (to be described next).

8.3.4 Coding scheme

In text retrieval, *Latent Semantic Analysis* (LSA) [7] exploits higher-order semantic structure implicit in the association of terms with documents. Using singular value decomposition (SVD) with truncation, LSA captures most of the essential underlying structure in the association of terms and documents, yet at the same time removes the noise or variability in word usage that plagues word-based retrieval methods. The derived coded description achieves a reduction in dimensionality while preserving structural similarity in term-document association for good discriminating power in similarity matching.

Similarly, in this chapter, we form a frequency matrix X that associates location-dependent visual keywords and visual documents as follows. Each column denotes a visual document in its linearized SAM representation. Each row is about the frequency of a visual keyword appearing in a particular spatial region of the visual documents. That is, $X(i, j) = \mathcal{H}_j(i)$ where j indexes a visual document and i is a linear index in $A \times B \times T$, before subject to cell transformation as given in [10] to obtain a measure of the first order association of a visual keyword and its context.

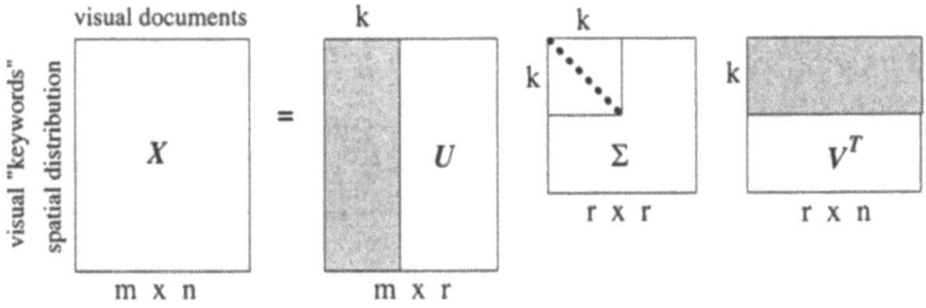

Figure 8.8: Singular value decomposition

Next we apply SVD to X as shown in Figure 8.8 [7]. In this figure, m is the number of SAMs ($= A \times B \times T$), n is the number of visual documents, r is the rank of X, k is the number of factors to be selected, U, V are the matrices of left and right singular vectors, and Σ is the diagonal matrix of singular values. i.e.

$$X = U \Sigma V^T \tag{8.12}$$

A coded description Λ_D of a visual document D (a query example or a database document) is computed as

$$\Lambda_D = \mathcal{H}_D^T U_k \Sigma_k^{-1} \tag{8.13}$$

where U_k, Σ_k are approximated (truncated) versions of U, Σ respectively.

Using this coded description, a query example q can be compared to all existing visual documents D in the database by evaluating the similarity between vectors Λ_q and Λ_D, and the documents ranked by their similarities to the query. In practice, the z top ranked documents or all documents with similarity exceeding some predefined threshold are returned as query results. Possible similarity measures include, but not limited to: cosine, $1 - \frac{d}{d_{max}}$, $e^{-d/2}$ [6] where d is some distance measure such as Euclidean distance and d_{max} is some large distance value for normalization purpose.

8.4 Image Retrieval

In this section, we report experimental results of using visual keywords for image retrieval. A total of 500 natural scene professional photographs from prepackaged Corel PhotoCD collections [15,23,8] and "The Natural Wonders of Europe" VideoCDs are collected as test data in our experiments. The images are preclassified into the following non-overlapping classes (with sizes in brackets): `coasts` (112), `fields` (111), `trees` (101), `snowy mountains` (108), and `streams/waterfalls` (68). Figure 8.1 shows a variety of images from each class (column) in the same left-to-right order given in previous sentence.

8.4.1 Unsupervised learning

The images are size-normalized to resolution of 256×256 and preprocessed into 6 pixel-feature planes of same resolution: 3 RGB color planes and 3 wavelet-based texture planes. The texture features are based on one level of orientation (horizontal, vertical, diagonal) wavelet details [29].

Each image is scanned with a 32×32 receptive field and a 16×16 displacement size for TEM on each of the pixel-feature planes simultaneously. In this case, TEM has 15×15 pixels. The means are computed for each pixel-feature region covered by a receptive field and taken as a feature vector for the visual token. In short, a visual token is represented by a 6-dimension feature vector summarizing its average color and orientation components.

With 500 images, there are $112,500$ visual tokens available for visual keyword creation. In our experiment, fuzzy c-means clustering is adopted to create visual keywords. The resulting T fuzzy cluster centers are the visual keywords. Different number of visual keywords ($T = 200$ to 1600 step 200) were attempted and the one which gave best result is $T = 1000$. Visual keyword detection is carried out by computing a visual token's fuzzy memberships to the fuzzy clusters.

There are two spatial configurations (SAMs) used to summarize detected visual keywords. The first one ($sc25$) has 5×5 receptive fields of size 3×3 each. The second one ($sc3h$) consists of 3 horizontal rectangular receptive fields of sizes $4 \times 15, 7 \times 15$, and 4×15 respectively. Intuitively, $sc25$ is designed for `fields` and `trees` images where the layout are relatively uniform. On the other hand, $sc3h$ is intended to capture the spatial layouts for majority of the `coasts`, `snowy mountains`, and `streams/waterfalls` images. The spatial configurations are depicted in Figure 8.9.

Visual keyword selection based on their frequencies was carried out on the 1000 visual keywords. The distribution of frequencies of visual keywords occurring in the 500 images is shown in Figure 8.10. Eventually, visual keywords selection by eliminating the high frequency candidates

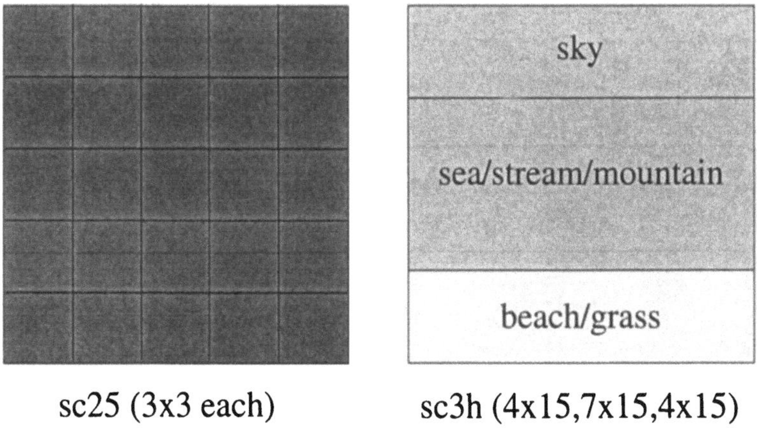

Figure 8.9: Context-based spatial configurations

reduces the number of visual keywords from 1000 to 167 before SVD-based coding. The similarity measure adopted is $s(x, y) = 1 - \frac{d(x,y)}{d_{max}}$ where $d(x, y)$ is the Euclidean distance between vectors x and y, and d_{max} is the maximum Euclidean distance for normalization purpose.

The standard *precision* P and *recall* R performance criteria are adopted

$$P = \frac{|Relv \cap Retr|}{|Retr|}, \tag{8.14}$$

$$R = \frac{|Relv \cap Retr|}{|Relv|} \tag{8.15}$$

where $Relv$ is the set of relevant visual documents for a query q and $Retr$ is the set of visual documents returned for q.

While $Retr$ is determined by some parameter in a retrieval system, $Relv$ concerns subjective judgement about all visual documents in a database for a given query q issued by a user. To minimize subjectivity, we approximate relevance with crisp class membership. That is, given a query $q \in C_i$, the relevant visual documents are all $d_j \in C_i$. P and R are reformulated as

$$P = \frac{|C_i \cap Retr|}{|Retr|}, \tag{8.16}$$

$$R = \frac{|C_i \cap Retr|}{|C_i|}. \tag{8.17}$$

The experiments are conducted by treating each of the 500 images in turn as a query image to retrieve relevant (i.e. same class) images from

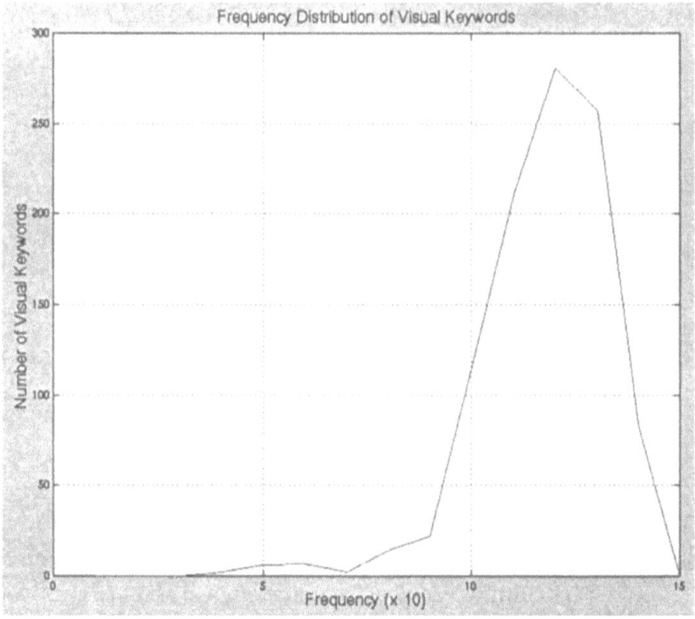

Figure 8.10: Frequency distribution of visual keywords

all the 500 images. Precision and recall are computed for each query and averaged over all the queries. Figure 8.11 summarizes the *precision-to-recall* curves of different methods compared.

The C-Hist and T-Hist curves are produced by using histograms of RGB color and wavelet-based texture features respectively. The curve labelled CT-Hist is obtained by combining the similarities of C-Hist and T-Hist with ratio $\frac{1}{4}$: $\frac{3}{4}$ respectively tuned for best performance. The curves with legend VK(sc3h) and VK(sc25) correspond to the results of using SAMs as signatures with spatial configurations sc3h and sc25 respectively. The number of visual keywords is 1000, after experimenting with 200 to 1600 (step 200). These curves clearly show that the visual keyword approach outperforms methods that rely on aggregate measures of color (C-Hist), texture (T-Hist), or both (CT-Hist). We will see a more detailed comparison later.

Figures 8.12 and 8.13 illustrate the effect of coding. The curves with labels VK(sc3h)-180 and VK(sc25)-180 are based on the coded descriptions with 180 SVD factors for VK(sc3h) and VK(sc25) respectively. The number of SVD factors are selected from 80 to 220 (step 20). For VK(sc3h), the improvement as shown by the gap bewteen the relevant curves is more

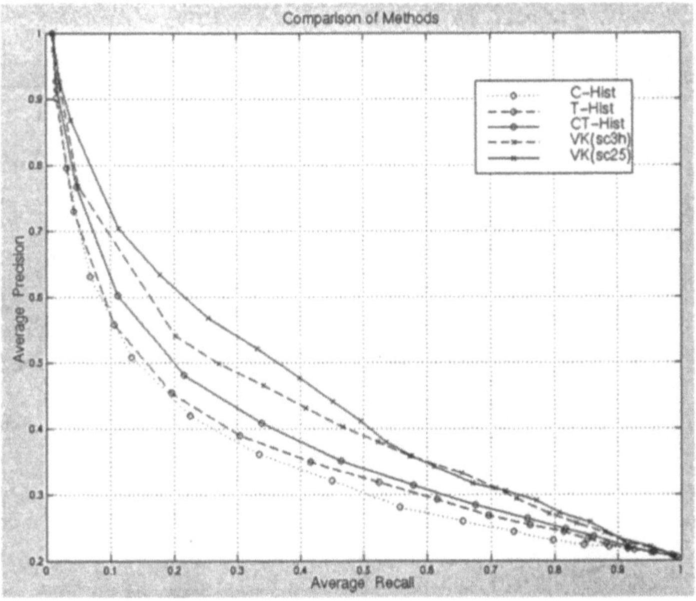

Figure 8.11: Comparison of Different Methods

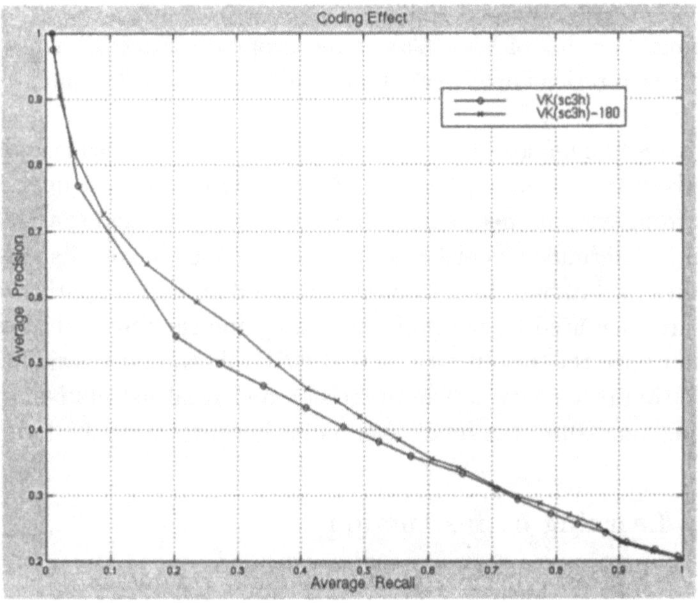

Figure 8.12: Effect of coding for VK(sc3h)

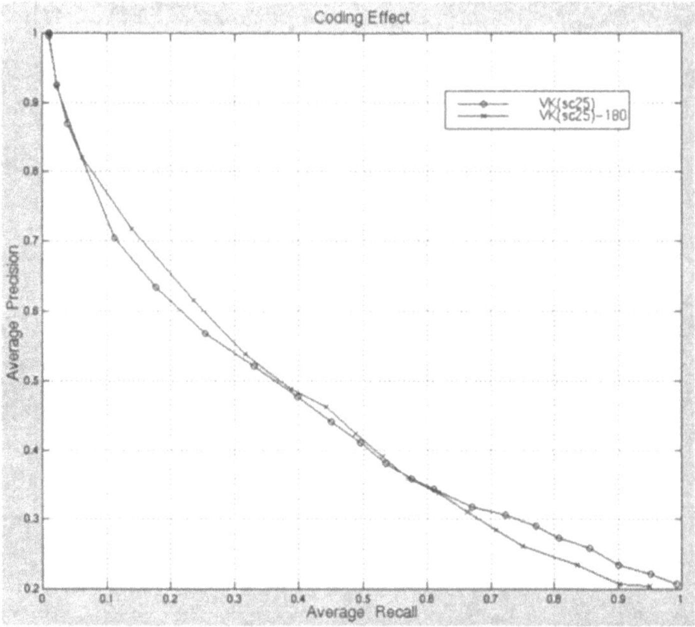

Figure 8.13: Effect of coding for VK(sc25)

significant than that of VK(sc25). In terms of reduction of dimensionality, the reduction ratios for VK(sc3h) and VK(sc25) are 16.7 : 1 and 138.9 : 1 respectively.

Figure 8.14 compares CT-Hist and VK(sc3h+25)-180 which combines both VK(sc3h)-180 and VK(sc25)-180 as follows. Given a query image chosen from existing images in the database, the preferred spatial configuration is determined as either sc3h or sc25, depending on its class. The signatures of database images based on the determined spatial configuration are then used for similarity matching and ranking. Tables 8.1 and 8.2 summarize the absolute (in actual P/R values) and relative (in percentage) improvements at fixed precision and recall points respectively. As a single measure, the break even point improves from 3.8 to 4.7.

8.4.2 Learning by instruction

In this set of experiments, seven semantical categories of 111 visual keywords are cropped from samples of 500 professional photographs (Fig. 8.1). The categories (and quantitites) are: `sky` (10), `water` (20), `mountain/beach` (12), `snowy mountain` (10), `field` (26), `tree` (24), and

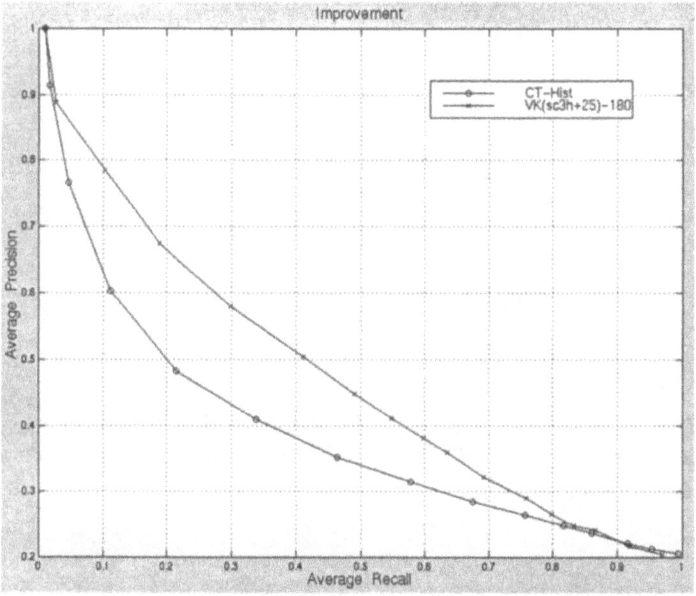

Figure 8.14: Improvement over CT-Hist

R	in abs. value	in rel.%
0.1	0.17	26.2
0.2	0.17	32.7
0.3	0.15	33.3
0.4	0.13	33.8
0.5	0.11	30.9

Table 8.1: Improvements in Precision

P	in abs. value	in rel.%
0.4	0.21	58.2
0.5	0.22	109.1
0.6	0.16	144.0
0.7	0.10	131.3
0.8	0.06	133.3

Table 8.2: Improvements in Recall

`shadow/dont-care` (9). Fig. 8.15 to 8.19 show the appearances of some visual keywords for selected categories. Each visual keyword has a semantical label and sub-label.

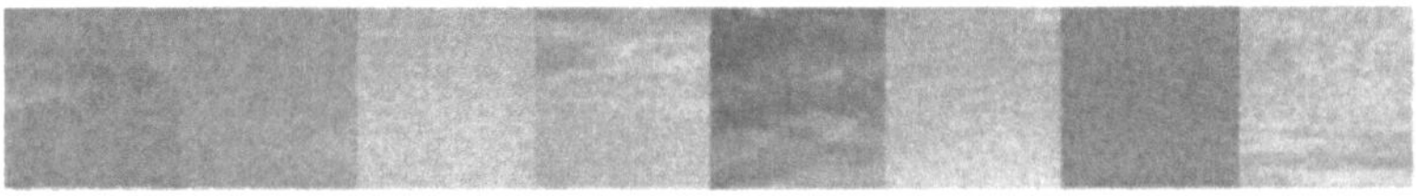

Figure 8.15: Selected visual keywords for `sky`

Figure 8.16: Selected visual keywords for `water`

The images are size-normalized to 256×256. Three scales ($31 \times 31, 41 \times 41, 51 \times 51$) are adopted for visual token scanning. The features used to characterize a visual keyword and token are based on color and texture. For color, each $w_x \times w_y$ region are down-sampled into 4×4 YIQ channels, which work better than simple means and local color histogram. For texture, we adopted similar Gabor filters-based features [16] with 5 scales and 6 orientations. Both TEM and SAM have 6×6 resolutions.

In this case, visual tokens corresponding to scales ($31 \times 31, 41 \times 41, 51 \times 51$) are extracted into feature vectors t_k and compared against the visual keywords v_{ij} (as in Equation (8.10)) to compute the fuzzy membership vectors $\mu_k(t_k, v_{ij})$. The most confident scale is taken as the final candidate

Figure 8.17: Selected visual keywords for **snowy mountain**

Figure 8.18: Selected visual keywords for **field**

for detection.

$$\mathcal{T}(p,q,i,j) = \mu_z(t_z, v_{ij}). \tag{8.18}$$

Each SAM pixel (a,b) aggregates the fuzzy memberships for visual keyword ij over those TEM pixels (p,q) covered by (a,b),

$$\mathcal{S}(a,b,i,j) = \sum_{(p,q)\in(a,b)} \mathcal{T}(p,q,i,j). \tag{8.19}$$

As a sub-label s_{ij} for visual keyword v_{ij} describes a specific appearance of the concept labelled by c_i, they are visual synonyms that allow abstraction by further aggregation over visual keywords sharing identical concept labels,

$$\mathcal{C}(a,b,i) = \sum_j \mathcal{S}(a,b,i,j). \tag{8.20}$$

This is useful when more general semantical concepts take precedence over specificity captured in different visual keywords. This concept-oriented visual thesaurus is different from the visual relations proposed by R.W.Picard [21], which are founded on similarities between low-level visual features.

The similarity matching adopted in our experiments for two images x, y is the city block distance, which performs better than other measures

Figure 8.19: Selected visual keywords for **trees**

(e.g. Euclidean distance, cosine) experimented,

$$s(x,y) = \sum_{(a,b)} \sum_{i,j} |\mathcal{S}^x(a,b,i,j) - \mathcal{S}^y(a,b,i,j)|, \tag{8.21}$$

or

$$s(x,y) = \sum_{(a,b)} \sum_{i} |\mathcal{C}^x(a,b,i) - \mathcal{C}^y(a,b,i)|. \tag{8.22}$$

In our experiments, retrieval based on visual keywords and thesaurus outperforms methods that rely on global histograms of color and texture significantly. In this chapter, we show some sample retrieval results to illustrate our point. In Fig. 8.20 to 8.23, the top-left image is the query image and the top 15 retrieved images are ranked in descending similarities from top down, left to right.

Figure 8.20: Retrieving *Snowy Mountains* by global colors and textures

As the global measures of color and texture do not care about semantics at spatial locations, the retrieved images could be far from expectation. For example, in Fig. 8.20, the query image is a snowy mountain and only retrieved images 3, 5, 6, 9, 13 are of the same class. For the same query, the visual keyword approach has returned all except 14 (stream below mountains) relevant (i.e. snowy mountain) images. In the same token, only retrieved images 5, 10, 11 are trees (query) in Fig. 8.22. In fact, the query contains coconut trees which are rare in our test data. Nevertheless, using visual thesaurus which only considers the abstract concept

Figure 8.21: Retrieving *Snowy Mountains* by visual keywords

Figure 8.22: Retrieving *Trees* by global colors and textures

Figure 8.23: Retrieving *Trees* by visual thesaurus

of trees, images (2-6,10-11, 13-14) which exhibit different types (color, texture, shape) of trees are returned.

In short, visual keywords and thesaurus allows visual content description and similarity matching in terms of location-sensitive semantics with both specificity and abstraction as necessary.

8.5 Image Categorization

In this section, we report experimental results of using visual keywords for image categorization. Classification of documents is a critical function in conventional libraries. It organizes vast amount of documents into hierarchy of categories and thus facilitates efficient searching of documents by the users. The same need is valid for digital libraries. Moreover, new functionalities such as information filtering agents that alert users of relevant classes of information based on his/her profile have to make similar classification judgements. With rapidly increasing amounts of multimedia material becoming available, manual annotation and classification of these documents become a forbidden task. While text categorization has received much attention in the information retrieval and filtering community (e.g. [11,12]), the case of visual data is relatively less explored.

The leave-one-out method and K-nearest-neighbor (K-NN) classifier are adopted. Each of the 500 images is used as an unknown input to the K-NN classifier using the rest of the 499 images as training set. The classification rate is averaged over all 500 images. For K-NN, the number of nearest neighbors was ranged over $K = 1$ to 30 and the best result is chosen. Voting is done by summing up the similarity values of the votes (up to K) for each class and the class with maximum sum of similarity values is output as decision of classification. Table 8.5 summarizes the classification rates (all classes and individual classes) for different methods compared. The classification rate is adopted as the performance measure here as it gives a single effectiveness measure of classification systems [13] (i.e. error rate = 1 - classification rate).

In Table 8.5, the labels C-Hist and T-Hist denote the methods that use histograms of RGB and wavelet-based texture values respectively for comparing natural scene images. The label CT-Hist is the result of combining the similarities of C-Hist and T-Hist in $\frac{1}{4}$ and $\frac{3}{4}$ proportions respectively tuned for best performance. The labels VK and VT refer to the visual keywords and visual thesaurus approaches respectively.

method	overall	(A)	(B)	(C)	(D)	(E)
C-Hist	52.6	57.1	39.6	66.3	41.7	63.2
T-Hist	47.4	62.5	20.7	72.3	54.6	17.6
CT-Hist	53.0	67.0	26.1	62.4	58.3	51.5
VK	78.8	83.9	77.5	74.3	79.6	77.9
VT	79.0	79.5	85.6	74.3	78.7	75.0

Table 8.3: Classification results for all classes (overall) and each class (A) coasts (B) fields (C) trees (D) snowy mountains (E) streams/waterfalls

Clearly, the visual keywords approach is more effective than global measures for the classification task. The classification rate based on 7 visual semantical categories ($\mathcal{C}(a,b,i)$) is similar to that based on 111 specific visual keywords ($\mathcal{S}(a,b,i,j)$). In classes (coasts, snowy mountains, and streams/waterfalls) where sky and mountains (and in a lesser extent, water) are common, specificity is crucial in discrimination. On the other hand, the field class manifested itself in many variations (color, texture) of visual keyword `field`. In this case, abstracting them into one single concept field pays off.

8.6 Conclusions and Future Directions

Visual keywords are adaptable high-level features that can be statistically induced from example-based learning. They are canonical visual entities abstracted from visual contents to serve as reference model for location-specific registration of visual keyword occurrences as TEM. On the other hand, domain-specific contextual knowledge can be realized by different spatial configural templates that describe a (sub-)class of images most appropriately. This will be implemented as multiple SAMs that aggregate visual keyword occurrences in different tessellations, resulting in favoritism in similarity matching for their respective (sub-)classes of images.

In a nutshell, the visual keyword approach integrates both statistical and domain knowledge by supporting multi-feature, multi-context representation for multimedia content-based retrieval and categorization.

The future directions for visual keywords is rich. We mention three possibilities here. First, other feature transformation methods besides SVD are worth looking into. For example, the holographic reduced representation from subsymbolic paradigm to code symbolic predicates as numerical patterns via circular convolution [22] is an interesting option.

Second, better means to select or weigh the visual keywords or/and spatial configurations by minimizing some cost function are available. For instance, we can train a neural network to weigh the SVD factors based on relevance feedback from a user to fine-tune the precision and recal performance towards user's preference. A similar attempt was described in [14].

Last but not least, the visual keywords framework is readily extensible to other media (i.e. audio "keywords", video "keywords"). For example, in the case of audio domains, audio "keywords" refer to prototypical audio patterns such as dog barking, baby crying, cheering roar during a football goal shot etc. Tokenization involves placing time windows across audio signal and typification abstracts audio keywords from appropriate audio features. Spoken word detection or recogition is a special case just as object detection or recognition in the case of visual keywords. With a uniform "keywords" metaphor or mechanism in place for different media, we can provide an elegant and adaptable framework to unify the feature representations and similarity matching functions in multi-modal applications.

References

1. M. A. Arbib, "The Handbook of Brain Theory and Neural Networks", The MIT Press, 1995
2. J. R. Bach, et al, "Virage Image Search Engine: An Open Framework for Image Management", Storage and Retrieval for Image and Video Databases IV, Proc. SPIE 2670, pp. 76-87, 1996
3. J. C. Bezdek, "Pattern Recognition with Fuzzy Objective Function Algorithms", Plenum, New York, 1981
4. C. M. Bishop, "Neural Networks for Pattern Recognition", Clarendon Press, Oxford, 1995
5. R. M. Bolle, B. L. Yeo, M. M. Yeung, "Video Query: Research Directions", IBM Journal of Research and Development, Vol. 42, No. 2, pp. 233-252, 1998.
6. C. Carson, et al, "Color- and Texture-Based Image Segmentation Using Em and Its Application to Image Query and Classification", Submitted to IEEE Trans. PAMI, 1999
7. S. Deerwester, et al, "Indexing by Latent Semantic Analysis", J. of the Am. Soc. for Information Science, Vol. 41, pp. 391-407, 1990
8. J.Huang, S. R Kumar, R. Zabih, "An Automatic Hierarchical Image Classification Scheme", Proc. of ACM Multimedia'98, pp. 219-228, 1998
9. T. Kohonen, "Self-Organizing Maps", Springer,1997
10. T. K Landauer, D. Laham, P. Foltz, "Learning Human-Like Knowledge By Singular Value Decomposition: A Progress Report", Advances in Neural Information Processing Systems 10, Cambridge: MIT Press, pp. 45-51, 1998
11. L. S. Larkey, W. B. Croft, "Combining Classifiers In Text Categorization", Proc. of SIGIR'96, pp. 289-297, 1996
12. D. D. Lewis, M. Ringuette, "A comparison of Two Learning Algorithms for Text Categorization", Proc. of SIGIR'94, pp. 81-93, 1994
13. D. D. Lewis, "Evaluating and optimizing autonomous text classification systems", Proc. of SIGIR'95, pp. 246-254, 1995
14. J. H. Lim, J. K. Wu, A. D. Narasimhalu, "Learning for Content-Based Multimedia Retrieval", Proc. of Intern. Forum of Multimedia and Image Processing, Anchorage, Alaska, USA, pp. 074.1-074.8, 1998
15. P. Lipson, E. Grimson, P. Sinha, "Configuration Based Scene Classification and Image Indexing", Proc. of CVPR'97, pp. 1007-1013, 1997
16. B. S. Manjunath, W. Y. Ma, "Texture Features For Browsing And Retrieval Of Image Data", IEEE Trans. PAMI, Vol. 18, No. 8, pp. 837-842, 1996
17. T. M. Mitchell, "Machine Learning", McGraw-Hill, 1997
18. W. Niblack, et al, "The QBIC Project: Querying Images by Content Using Color, Textures and Shapes", Storage and Retrieval for Image and Video Databases, Proc. SPIE 1908, pp. 13-25,1993
19. P. C. Papageorgiou, M. Oren, T. Poggio, "A General Framework for Object Detection", Proc. ICCV, pp. 555-562, 1996

20. A. Pentland, R. Picard, S. Sclaroff, "Photobook: Content-Based Manipulation of Image Databases", Intl. J. of Computer Vision, Vol. 18, No. 3, pp. 233-254, 1995

21. R. Picard, "Toward a Visual Thesaurus", Proc. of Springer-Verlag Workshops in Computing, MIRO'95, Glasgow, 1995

22. T. Plate, "Holographic Reduced Representations", IEEE Trans. on Neural Networks, Vol. 6, No. 3, pp. 623-641, 1995

23. A. L. Ratan, W. E. L. Grimson, "Training Templates for Scene Classification Using a Few Examples", Proc. IEEE Workshop on Content-Based Analysis of Images and Video Libraries, pp. 90-97, 1997

24. S. E. Robertson, K. Sparck Jones, "Relevance Weighting of Search Terms", J. of the Am. Soc. for Info. Sc., Vol. 27, pp. 129-146, 1976

25. L. A. Rowe, J. S. Boreczky, C. A. Eads, "Indices for User Access to Large Video Database", Storage and Retrieval for Image and Video Databases II, Proc. SPIE 2185, pp. 150-161, 1994

26. G. Salton, "The SMART System - Experiments in Automatic Document Processing", Englewood Cliffs, NJ: Prentice Hall, 1971

27. J. R. Smith, S. F. Chang, "VisualSEEk: A Fully Automated Content-Based Image Query System", Proc. ACM Multimedia 96, Boston, MA, November Vol 20, 1996,

28. K. Sparck Jones, P. Willett, "Readings in Information Retrieval", Morgan Kaufmann Publishers, Inc, 1997

29. M. Unser, "Texture Classification and Segmentation Using Wavelet Frames", IEEE Trans. on Image Processing, Vol. 4, No. 11, pp. 1549-1560, 1995

30. M. E. J.Wood, N. W. Campbell, B.T. Thomas, "Employing Region Features for Searching an Image Database", Proc. 1997 British Machine Vision Conference, pp. 620-629, 1997

Chapter 9

Fuzzy Retrieval

Our world has always been called the "information society", and a major portion of our economy is devoted to the handling, storing, selecting, processing and analyzing of information. We also realize that our world is full of uncertainty, with problems that are often not clearly defined, and with imprecise and vague descriptions that may not be quantifiable. These two elements: immense amounts of information coupled with massive uncertainty, together constitute the most challenging research issue.

It is also well known that large portion of information we perceive is in visual form such as images. Description of image contents are inexact and subjective: After seeing a person's face, five people would have five different descriptions. To describe the facial outline of a face, one might say "it is rounded, but seems little bit oval, too". Problems arise when we have thousands of facial images and want to pick up some faces with rounded chin, big eyes, and thick hair. No one can give clear and exact definition to the descriptions such as "rounded chin". As for eye size, different people would have different criteria.

Because of the diversity of image contents and the subjective descriptions of images, it is not wise to archive images using manual descriptions. On the other hand, computer feature extraction can produce relatively objective measures of visual characteristics of images. When images are archived along with their feature measures, the archival is referred to as a feature-based image database. In feature-based image databases, feature measures are objective representation of image content. Different types of users / applications may have different interpretations of the same images with the same feature measures. That is to say that there must be a context-dependent mapping between feature measures and users interpretations (or content to the users). Fuzzy logic offers a possible mapping which is most acceptable to human.

Fuzzy recall of images is a natural phenomena of human memories. In our conversation, one might say "Oh I recall the person you are talking about. Yes, she has an oval face and big eyes.". Fuzzy retrieval from an image database has application potential. An immediate application is criminal identification. According to witnesses' descriptions, the database should be able to search and identify the criminal if his/her photo is in the database. Other applications include textile pattern retrieval, medical image analysis and archival based on contents of medical records, etc. For discussion convenience in this chapter, we will use face image database as an example in the following sections.

In retrieving a computerized database using fuzzy queries, there are several important issues. First, images must be properly archived according to their feature measures. Before an image is inserted into the database, computer feature extraction must be performed to generate feature measures which can represent the visual characteristics of the image. Second, feature measures must be correctly mapped to fuzzy subsets which conceptually categorize the images. Third, fuzzy query interface and query processing should be formulated so that searching for the most relevant images from a large database is possible. All three issues, *feature extraction, fuzzy membership learning, and fuzzy query processing*, are open research topics. In this chapter, we will first define various problems that arise in content-based fuzzy retrieval of image databases (Section 9.2). Section 9.3 is dedicated to fuzzy database model. Section 9.4 is devoted to fuzzy query processing, while section 4 is for the learning of fuzzy membership function. The last section contains some experimental results.

9.1 Problem Definition

9.1.1 Content-based fuzzy retrieval

If we classify queries according to their conditions and results, there are four types as listed in Table 9.1. In the traditional information retrieval field, the most popular queries are Boolean: the query definition is exact, and the query result obtained exactly satisfies the query conditions. Nowadays, similarity retrieval has been accepted in many application areas. People realize that quite often we can only find the best match to the query condition - an exact match does not exist. In this case, the query is exactly defined, but the result is presented as a ranked list of items which approximately match the query conditions.

query type	query condition	query result
conventional	Boolean, exact	exact match
similarity retrieval	exact	best match
fuzzy logic query	complete, boolean	best match
content-based fuzzy retrieval	incomplete, fuzzy	best match

Table 9.1: Query types

As a result of rapid progress in multimedia database research, there is an unavoidable trend of including fuzzy concepts in query definition. That leads to a brand new research topic: fuzzy retrieval of multimedia information. In fuzzy retrieval, the query conditions are inexact, the query results are approximate.

A similarity query is processed in the feature space, and efforts have been made to develop efficient methods to process similarity queries of multimedia data, see [19, 28]. Unfortunately, there is little work done in fuzzy query processing. In this section, we will first give reasons for fuzzy queries not being processed in the feature space, like ordinary similarity queries are, and then address new concepts and technologies that must be developed to process fuzzy queries required by many multimedia applications such as image database systems.

For the sake of problem definition, let us look at a scenario: for a given set of facial images, we want to find a facial image with a long chin, big eyes, and thin hair. Here, the retrieval process is in terms of images, or objects in a more generic terminology. Images are described by a set of natural concepts (long, big, thin) with respect to several visual features (chin, eyes, hair). Fuzzy sets provide us means to capture the vagueness and imprecision of the natural concepts. This scenario suggests the following representation framework as defined in Chapter 2:

- Fuzzy retrieval of multimedia information is in terms of multimedia objects O, each characterized by a set of features $F^1, F^2, ..., F^m$. A multimedia object "facial image", for example, can be characterized by facial features such as chin, eyes, nose, mouth.

- A feature F^i can be either numerically characterized by feature measures in the feature spaces $F^i_1 \times F^i_2 \times ... \times F^i_n$, or conceptually described by fuzzy subsets $\{A^i_1, A^i_2, ..., A^I_p\}$, which defined *fuzzy space* $A^i_1 \times A^i_2 \times ... \times A^i_p$.

- According to the definition of "*fuzzy* π*−granule*" by Zadeh (1979), the multi-dimensional feature space is referred to as a universe of discourse U, where a fuzzy subset of U is defined by its membership function. Therefore, fuzzy membership functions relate the fuzzy space of a feature to its corresponding feature space.

  If we choose to use width and height to measure the eye size, width and height are two feature measures for the facial feature eyes. Eye size can also be described by concepts "small, medium, large", which are referred to as fuzzy subsets. Fuzzy membership function $m_{small}(width = 1.5cm, height = .5cm) = 0.9$ say that for an eye with width of 1.5cm and height of .5cm is small with a grade of membership 0.9. In this case, the membership function is a mapping from (width, height) to $[0, 1]$. Conceptually, this mapping is from feature space to fuzzy space, and referred to as *fuzzification.*

- Hence, an object can be represented as a triple $O = [F, A, I]$, where F represents the feature measures in the feature space, A stands for the fuzzy space representation, and I is the image.

- For a given object (such as facial image), feature measures can be derived from the object data (image data in facial image case) by specific feature extraction methods. When fuzzy membership functions are defined, conceptual descriptions of the object in terms of fuzzy sets can be derived from its feature measures.

- A fuzzy query provide only a conceptual description of an object to be searched (referred to as *query object*). The conceptual description usually is in terms of fuzzy sets and possible confidence values. In other words, the query object is described in the fuzzy space, and most often it is not completely described. For example, a facial image is described with respect to six features: chin, eyes, hair, eyebrow, mouth, nose. In most cases, a witness can only provide descriptions on about three features. This incomplete description is denoted by A^*. *The fuzzy query object* is then denoted by $O_q^f = [, A^*,]$.

9.1.2 Fuzzy sets over multi-dimensional universes

Extracting shape and texture features to reflect the visual characteristics of images is a research topic which has attracted interest since 1970s [11]. In face database in [28], image features are extracted over six sub-regions, and are referred to as six facial features: chin, hair, eye, eyebrow, nose, and mouth. All extracted feature measures are in vector form and written as $\mathbf{x}^i = (x_1^i, x_2^i, ..., x_{M_i}^i)^T$, where i stands for i-th facial feature, M_i is the dimension of the i-th feature vector. A typical value of M_i is sixteen.

As a result of imprecision and vagueness of descriptions of facial features, we have designed a number of fuzzy sets for each facial feature using fuzzy descriptions. For example, we have nine fuzzy subsets conceptually representing chin types: *tapered, oblong, short oval, rounded, long tapered, long oblong, short oblong, short rounded, long rounded.* These fuzzy sets are defined over the multi-dimensional (M_0) universe $\mathbf{x}^0 = (x_1^0, x_2^0, ..., x_{M_0}^0)$. The membership function for fuzzy set B_j^i, where i denotes the facial feature and j denotes the fuzzy subset for a facial feature, takes the following form:

$$m_{B_j^i}(\mathbf{x}) = e^{-(\mathbf{x}-\mathbf{u}_j^i)^T \Sigma_j^i (\mathbf{x}-\mathbf{u}_j^i)} \tag{9.1}$$

where $\mathbf{u}$ is the central point of the membership function in the multi-dimensional feature space. It is actually the Gaussian shape function as shown in Figure 9.3(a). There is a linguistic meaning for the fuzzy subset "approximately $\mathbf{u}$". Σ is the covariance matrix of all data points falling into the fuzzy subset.

9.1.3 Fuzzy queries cannot be processed in the feature space

One may ask "why fuzzy retrieval? why process fuzzy query in fuzzy space?" The answer to the first question is obvious: fuzzy retrieval of images is required by system users. It is a natural way in which human beings think and communicate. The second question can be interpreted as "although initial queries are fuzzy, can we process them in the feature vector space (here in this chapter, we use the term *feature space*) as we usually do for documentation retrieval?". To explain why we process a fuzzy query in the fuzzy space, not in the feature space, let us now look at Figure 9.1.

Figure 9.1 clearly shows that there are two possible flows for fuzzy query processing. One is to defuzzify a fuzzy query definition in order to map from the fuzzy space into the feature space, and then process the query in the feature space. In this case, we could make use of already existing information retrieval techniques such as those for document retrieval in a vector space described by Salton [19]. The other is to fuzzify feature measures of images to get their fuzzy vector representation and then process the query in the fuzzy space. Unfortunately, fuzzy queries are very often incompletely defined, it is nearly impossible to defuzzify

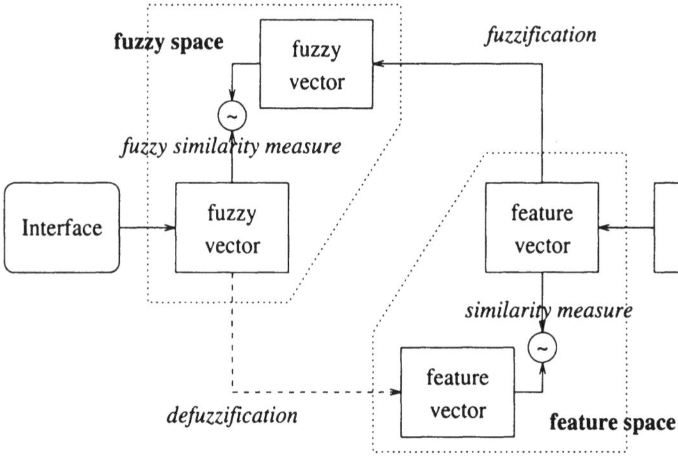

Figure 9.1: There are two possible fuzzy query processing flows. Because of incompleteness of fuzzy query condition definition, defuzzification of fuzzy query into the feature space is not possible, subsequently, fuzzy query processing cannot be processed in the feature space.

them into the feature space. This means that we have to adopt the second process flow and process fuzzy query in the fuzzy space. It should be also mentioned that mapping from the fuzzy space to the feature space by defuzzification may be not unique. This increases the difficulty of fuzzy query processing in feature space. It will be further explained in the section dealing with query processing.

9.1.4 Fuzzy querying of multimedia information calls for new technology for its processing

Based on our representation framework, fuzzy retrieval of images from an image database can be formally defined as

For a fuzzy query object $O_q = [\emptyset, A^*, \emptyset]$, find an ordered set of objects $O_1, O_2, \ldots$ from the database DB such that

$$\begin{aligned} sim(O_q, O_1) &= \max_{O \in DB} sim(O_q, O) \\ sim(O_q, O_2) &= \max_{O \in (DB - O_1)} sim(O_q, O) \\ \ldots &= \ldots \end{aligned} \tag{9.2}$$

where $sim(O_q, O)$ is a similarity measure between a query object and an object from the database. It can be evaluated either in the image space, the feature space, or the fuzzy space. In most cases, direct evaluation of similarity in the image space is impossible because of the complication of image data. As discussed in the previous subsection, since fuzzy query object O_q^f has null feature and null image in its triple representation, so similarity evaluation in the feature space is impossible. Therefore, the equation for fuzzy query processing becomes

$$\begin{aligned} sim(A_q^*, A_1) &= \max_{A \in DB} sim(A_q^*, A) \\ sim(A_q^*, A_2) &= \max_{A \in (DB - A_1)} sim(A_q^*, A) \\ \ldots &= \ldots \end{aligned} \tag{9.3}$$

where the similarity between the query object and an object from the database is reduced to the similarity between their fuzzy space representation. Now our main concern becomes: is there any available technique which can be used to evaluate $sim(A_q^*, A)$? If the answer is no, what is the solution to this problem?

There is no technique available which can be readily used to evaluate this similarity measure. The rest of this section will explain the reason. A new solution to this problem will be explained in more detail in the following sections.

As the evaluation of similarity $sim(A_q^*, A)$ is in the fuzzy space, let us now have a look at some relevant research topics in the field of fuzzy information processing.

Fuzzy reasoning tries to reach a conclusion by moving from one feature space to another via fuzzy reasoning rules, which are coded in terms of fuzzy subsets, for example, a fuzzy reasoning technique by Peng [17]. Fuzzification and defuzzification processes are used to convert between the feature space and the fuzzy space. The main effort in this area is to define and control the reasoning flow. A typical reasoning rule can be: "if $p(o)$ then $q(o)$", where o represents an object. For example, consider a tomato; p and q are two fuzzy subsets conceptually characterizing the two properties of the object o. For example, a rule for the tomato can be "if a tomato is red then it is ripe". It seems that our retrieval problem does not fall into the category of the problems fuzzy reasoning tries to solve because we are looking for ways to evaluate the similarity among object instances of the same class and the evaluation is with respect to the same fuzzy subsets.

Fuzzy reasoning can be considered as a tool which can readily solve problems in *fuzzy control* and *fuzzy recognition*. For example, if we want to classify tomatoes into "ripe" and "unripe" categories, or want to control the temperature of the tomato store, we would expect fuzzy reasoning rule to play an important role.

Fuzzy reasoning has been used to deal with certain image similarity retrieval problem [4]. They consider images containing patterns, such as colors and geometric shapes. Instead of a feature space, they use a delta feature space to capture feature differences between a pair of patterns. Fuzzy subsets "low", "medium" and "high" are used to represent the degree of feature difference. The final result is derived by evaluating all fuzzy subset values of pairs of patterns contained in a pair of images. Clearly, they calculate similarity query using a fuzzy classification method. The query is exactly defined, image data of the query object are given, its feature measures and fuzzy descriptions can all be derived. It does belong to the second type of query in the Table 9.1 - similarity retrieval, not the fourth type - content-based fuzzy retrieval. The only difference between this technique and ordinary similarity retrieval is that it uses fuzzy concept for similarity evaluation when processing a query.

Li & Liu [14] developed a fuzzy PROLOG database. A fuzzy relation is characterized by an n-variate membership function $\mu_R : D_1 \times D_2 \times ... \times D_n \rightarrow [0, 1]$. A domain D_i can take real value such as 33 or fuzzy set values such as "middle-aged" for the domain "age". This scheme belongs to the third type of query in Table 9.1 - fuzzy logic query. It cannot be applied to our case because image data is characterized in multi-dimensional space and a single fuzzy subset value is not adequate for its description.

Other relevant work, such as feature-based image database systems by Bach et al [2] and fuzzy recognition of face expressions by Ralescu and Iwamoto [18] can give us insight into ideas, but not solutions.

9.2 Fuzzy Database Model

In this section, we will describe a fuzzy database model using a face database as an example. In the face database, each face is described by facial features. Facial features are further described by feature vectors extracted from the face images and commonly used concepts.

There are several fuzzy relational models [14]. Unfortunately, they cannot support large images and their fuzzy schema does not provide a solution to content-based fuzzy image retrieval. We extend the relational database model to accommodate facial images and their fuzzy descriptions by allowing ADT's (Abstract Data Types) in the relation tables.

For convenience of discussion, let us quote the definition of conventional relational model as follows:

Given a set of domains $D_1, D_2, ..., D_k$, written $D_1 \times D_2 \times ... \times D_k$, R is a relation on those k domains if there is a set of ordered k-ary tuples

$(d_1, d_2, ..., d_k)$ such that d_1 is in D_1, d_2 is in D_2, and so on.

We can see, from the above definition, that a relation R is a two dimensional table. Tuples of R are rows of that two dimensional table, while columns of the table are referred to as attributes, and written as $A_1, A_2, ..., A_k$. Each attribute A_i is associated with a domain D_i.

In a conventional relational database, attribute values are atomic and precise. Li & Liu [14] extends the relation model to accommodate fuzziness, while Stonebraker [22, 21] extends the relational model to support large object storage and typing, and Kim [12] considers the object-oriented model one type of extended relational model of data. Wu extended relational model to accommodate images [34] and geographic data [6]. The extension here mainly involves three aspects: data type extension, procedure attachment, and class hierarchy and inheritance. Here in image database systems, images are large objects with variable size. They require special processing procedures for their input, output, display, storage and manipulation. To accommodate images and related information we need to extend the domain to include abstract data types, and to define procedures for image manipulation. After proper formalization, fuzzy description of images can be well captured by ADTs.

Abstract data type is composed of atomic data types and/or ADTs in either flat or hierarchical way. That is to say that ADT can represent object classes and can be defined recursively. Following six ADTs are used for the facial image database system.

```
ADT facial_feature_measure {
  ADT FacialFeature chin;
  ADT FacialFeature hair;
  ADT FacialFeature eye;
  ADT FacialFeature eyebrow;
  ADT FacialFeature nose;
  ADT FacialFeature mouth;
  }

ADT FacialFeature {
  float FeatureVector[16];
  }

ADT image_data {
  unsigned char *image;
  }

ADT fuzzy_age {
  FuzzyMembership young;
  FuzzyMembership middle;
  FuzzyMembership old;
  }

ADT fuzzy_feature_description {
```

```
  ADT fuzzy_chin;
  ADT fuzzy_hair;
  ADT fuzzy_eyes;
  ADT fuzzy_eyebrow;
  ADT fuzzy_nose;
  ADT fuzzy_mouth;
  }

ADT fuzzy_chin {
  FuzzyMembership tapered;
  FuzzyMembership oblong;
  FuzzyMembership short_oval;
  FuzzyMembership rounded;
  FuzzyMembership long_tapered;
  FuzzyMembership long_oblong;
  FuzzyMembership short_oblong;
  FuzzyMembership short_rounded;
  FuzzyMembership long_rounded;
  }
```

Here we list only fuzzy ADTs for chin. Using ADTs we can have an extended relation table for facial image as follows

```
Table Facial_image {
  char person_id[10];
  char person_name[40];
  ADT fuzzy_age;
  ADT fuzzy_feature_description;
  ADT facial_feature_measure;
  ADT image_data;
  }
```

Existing models [14] impose a degree of certainty on the tuple of a relation by defining an k-variate membership function

$$\mu_R : D_1 \times D_2 \times ... \times D_k \rightarrow [0,1] \tag{9.4}$$

The degree of data certainty is embedded in ADTs in our extended data model by a data type definition:

$$\mu_r : FuzzyMembership \rightarrow [0,1] \tag{9.5}$$

For example, the facial image of a person aged 15 years old has the "fuzzy_age" slot values (1, 0, 0). From these values we are pretty sure that he is young. Our model can well model reality. With this model, the fuzzy query processing will be carried out in the fuzzy space by searching for the best matches.

To define an ADT, the registration process is similar to that by Stonebraker (1986):

```
define ADT_name {
   input = input_procedure_name;
   output = output_procedure_name;
   storage = storage_type;
   display = display_procedure_name;
   match = match_procedure_name;
   }
```

where *input_procedure_name* refers to the procedures which converts the ADT before storage. It can be the compression routine, for example, for the image data. There are two storage types: small and fixed size objects are stored inside the tuple, large and/or variable size objects are stored elsewhere using multiple fixed length data chunks. In this case, a pointer will be created at the position of the ADT in the tuple to indicate the address of its actual storage.

When an image is accessed, either the image data or its descriptions will be displayed. This is achieved by calling the display procedures. The matching procedure is acting as an operator, which calculates the fuzzy similarity measure between a pair of images. Fuzzy similarity measure will be discussed further later. The registration of the fuzzy similarity operator is done by:

```
define operator fuzzy_similarity {
    token = ~;
    left_operand = fuzzy_ADT_name;
    right_operand = fuzzy_ADT_name;
    result = float;
    precedence like *;
    }
```

9.2.1 Extended tuple relation calculus for image retrieval

After extension of relation model for fuzzy image database, we now extend a tuple relation calculus on the extended model for content-based fuzzy query processing. The definition of the extended tuple calculus is as follows:

1. Every atomic formula is an extended tuple calculus formula. An atomic formula is of three forms.

   (a) $\mu_R(t)$

   Where R is an extended relation name, t is a tuple variable. $\mu_R(t)$ denotes the degree to which t satisfies the relation.

   (b) $t[i]\vartheta C$ or $C\vartheta t[i]$

Where $t[i]$ denotes the i-th component of t. C is a constant. ϑ can be any of the conventional arithmetic comparison operators: $=, \neq, <, \leq, >, \geq$ and special comparison operators for ADTs: $>>, <<, \simeq$. $\simeq$ here denotes the similarity measures on ADTs, which can be either fuzzy or nonfuzzy. This atomic operation returns the degree to which $t[i]$ and C satisfies the ϑ operation.

(c) $t[i]\vartheta u[j]$
This atomic formula is the same as previous one except that it performs a comparison between two tuple variables t and u.

2. If φ is an extended tuple calculus formula, then so is (φ) and $\neg(\varphi)$.

3. If φ_1 and φ_2 are extended tuple calculus formula, then so are $(\varphi_1 \wedge \varphi_2)$ and $(\varphi_1 \vee \varphi_2)$.

4. Nothing else is an extended tuple calculus formula.

As defined in last subsection, the extended relational table *Facial_image* has six attributes: person_id, person_name, fuzzy_age, fuzzy_feature_description, facial_feature_measure, and image_data. If we denote a tuple of the relational table *Facial_image* by u, $u[3]$ represents the attribute value of fuzzy_age. Using above extended tuple calculus, similarity queries is to find a similar tuple from the database so that:

$$R = R_{1_{above\ \theta}} = \{t | \mu_{R_1}(t) \geq \theta\} \tag{9.6}$$

where θ is a threshold and

$$\begin{aligned} \mu_{R_1}(t) \quad = \quad & \mu_{facial-image}(u) \ \wedge \ u[3] \simeq w[3] \ \wedge \ u[4] \simeq w[4] \ \wedge \\ & u[1] = w[1] \ \wedge \ u[2] = w[2] \ \wedge \ u[5] \simeq w[5] \ \wedge \ u[6] \simeq w[6] \end{aligned} \tag{9.7}$$

where w represents the query condition, and u represents tuple in the database. The above equation says that u satisfies the retrieval conditions provided u is a tuple in the table *Facial_image*, and it six attributes are equal or similar to the query condition. In case of content-based fuzzy queries, w is a fuzzy query object. Its fifth (feature measure) and sixth (image) attributes are not defined. In most cases, we do not know name ($u[2]$) and identification number ($u[1]$) of a person, hence, above equation is reduced to

$$\mu_{R_1}(t) \quad = \quad \mu_{facial-image}(u) \ \wedge \ u[3] \simeq w[3] \ \wedge \ u[4] \simeq w[4] \tag{9.8}$$

It is the same as equation 9.4 except that here we have a threshold and the result should be ordered according to the similarity measure.

9.3 Fuzzy Query Processing

Fuzzy query processing consists of two parts: preprocessing and processing. The preprocessing tries to recover fuzzy membership functions from user defined fuzzy queries. The processing is then to search the database to find the best matches based on the fuzzy similarity measures. The fuzzy similarity measures are between *fuzzy vectors*, whose elements are fuzzy membership values in the *fuzzy space* defined by the fuzzy subsets of the same facial feature. As a preparation for fuzzy query processing discussion, we will look at the feature space and the fuzzy space in the first subsection.

Fuzzy query processing is effected by a fuzzy query interface through which query conditions are obtained. Fuzzy query interface should be friendly to users and provide the ability to get as much information as possible about the query. By the nature of a fuzzy query, the information obtained from the user through fuzzy query interface is fuzzy and incomplete. The query processing then consists of approximate reasoning to find the most relevant images from the database.

9.3.1 Feature space and fuzzy space

Recall that, after feature extraction, a feature vector $\mathbf{x}^i = (x_1^i, x_2^i, ..., x_{M^i}^i)^T$ is obtained for each image with respect to the i-th facial feature. It is a vector in the M^i dimensional feature space. Recall also that fuzzy subsets $B_j^i, j = 1, ..., q_i$ for facial feature i can be considered as a fuzzy vector in the q_i dimensional fuzzy space. The mapping from the feature space to the fuzzy space is referred to as *fuzzification*. Defuzzification refers to the mapping from the fuzzy space to the feature space.

Both fuzzification and defuzzification are non-linear mappings. Figure 9.2 and Figure 9.3 show two examples of membership functions and their corresponding fuzzy spaces. We see from Figure 9.2 that the fuzzy membership functions defined in the feature space is mapped to two straight lines in the fuzzy space. Obviously, defuzzification, mapping from fuzzy space to feature space is not unique. It is one-to many mapping in the case shown in Figure 9.2, and may be many-to-many mapping in some other cases.

Figure 9.3(a) shows Gaussian membership functions of three fuzzy subsets in a two-dimensional feature space. The three subsets define the fuzzy space shown in Figure 9.3(b). The trace of all possible combinations of fuzzy membership values are inside the shaded area, which we call

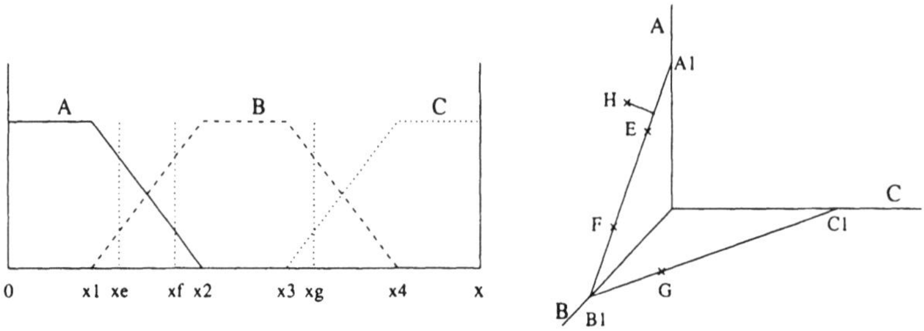

Figure 9.2: (a) Fuzzy subsets A, B, C defined on universe x and (b) their fuzzy vector trace in the fuzzy space $A - B - C$ shown as thick lines. The fuzzy subsets defined in the interval $[0, x_1]$ are mapped to a point A_1 in the fuzzy space since within this interval, $A = 1, B = 0, C = 0$. It is a many to one mapping. Similarly, fuzzy subsets defined in intervals $[x_1, x_2], [x_2, x_3], [x_3, x_4]$ are mapped to straight line A_1B_1, point B_1, and straight line B_1C_1 in the fuzzy space, respectively.

domain of fuzzy set definition. Again, the defuzzification for this set of membership functions is not unique.

We have observed, from these two examples, that for a set of defined fuzzy set membership functions, the domain of their definition occupies only a portion of the fuzzy space. Any point outside the definition domain would violate the original fuzzy set membership definition.

9.3.2 Fuzzy query interface

When the user selects to activate the fuzzy query module, the prompt panels for all six facial features will appear in sequence. In the prompt panel for a facial feature, there are slots for all fuzzy subsets for a user to fill in certainty values, see Figure 9.8). The certainty values are in terms of percentages. The user can choose to either fill in a value or leave it blank. Quite often, one may have no idea about certain facial features. For example, when you see a person, the only impression left may be her large and bright eyes. With this interface, the query condition obtained from the user is represented as a vector array $(Q^i_j, j = 1, ..., M_i, i = 1, ..., q)$, where most of the elements will be blank due to the limited knowledge of the user. We refer to this vector as the *certainty vector.* The certainty vector is in the fuzzy space.

The difficulty of query processing in due to the following three problems:

- Query conditions are user-dependent, in other words, subjective;

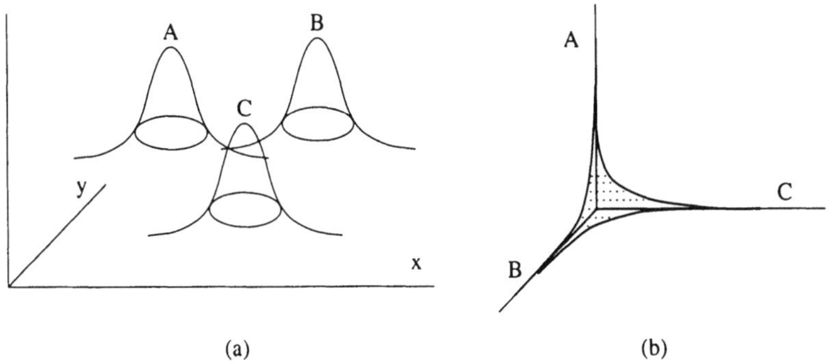

Figure 9.3: (a) Fuzzy subsets A, B, C defined in a two dimensional feature space (x,y). (b) They form a fuzzy space. The fuzzy vector trace in the fuzzy space is shown as the area enclosed by bodied lines.

- The certainty vectors may not comply with the constraints imposed by fuzzy membership functions. In the fuzzy space, they may not fall into the domain of fuzzy set definition, and consequently cannot be directly used to search for the best matches;
- Mapping from the fuzzy space to the feature space is not unique and usually impossible due to incompleteness of the query conditions.

Having taken account of these problems, we develop a fuzzy query processing procedure as shown in Figure 9.4. The first step of query processing is to process the certainty vector with the context model to make it user-independent. The second step is to consider the certainty vector as a product of a confidence value and a fuzzy vector. The confidence value is then separated from the certainty vector to produce a valid fuzzy vector. Because of the incompleteness of the query definition, after these two preprocessing steps, we still may not be able to locate the fuzzy vector in the fuzzy space - very often, there are too many blank elements in the fuzzy vector. The fuzzy vector with blank elements cannot be mapped into the feature space. Therefore, searching for the most relevant images should be carried out in the fuzzy space.

9.3.3 Context model

The fuzzy query conditions defined by the user with the fuzzy query interface are subjective. This is mainly because different people have different views for the same object. For example, two boys see a girl whose weight

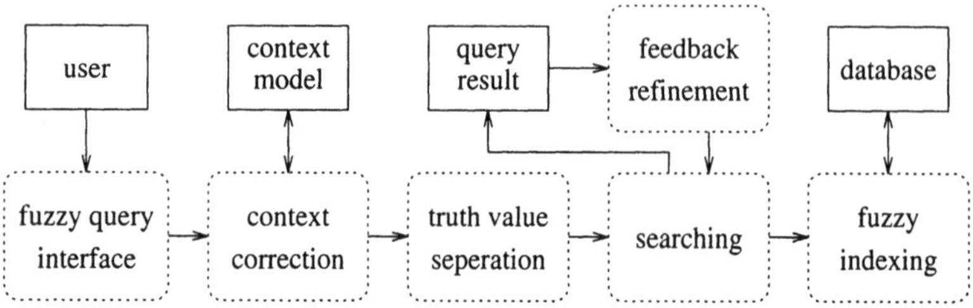

Figure 9.4: Diagram of fuzzy retrieval

is 120kg, a boy weighting 200kg would think of her being slim, while a boy weighting only 60kg would certainly consider her very big. For the facial image retrieval, when a witness is a small child, from his eyes, the object's facial features would be scaled up by a factor greater than 1. To deal with this context-sensitive query definition, a special context model has been developed. When a user is logged in, a default context model for him or her is loaded. An alternative context model can be also selected by the user in case the fuzzy query is formed by someone who is not the end user. After this processing step, fuzzy queries are considered to be user independent.

To learn a context model for a person, a set of standard images are presented to the person and he/she is asked to describe facial features using given fuzzy subsets. The learning module then records his/her description and derives the model, and saves it into a user dictionary.

9.3.4 Extraction of the confidence value

In the fuzzy space, coordinates represent fuzzy subsets. For a set of defined fuzzy subsets, all valid fuzzy vectors will fall into the domain of a fuzzy set definition as illustrated by Figure 9.2 and Figure 9.3. When users define their fuzzy queries, it is difficult to impose some constraints to users to let the resultant certainty vector fall into the domain of fuzzy set definition. Usually, the certainty vector can be considered as the product of a confidence value and a valid fuzzy vector:

$$Q^i = t^i \, B^i \tag{9.9}$$

where t^i is a confidence value, and B^i is a valid fuzzy vector for the i-th facial feature. Therefore, fuzzy query preprocessing should include a process to extract the confidence value from the certainty vector. We know, from Figure 9.2 and Figure 9.3, that the confidence value extraction process must move the certainty vector into the domain of fuzzy set definition in the fuzzy space. Certainly, this process very much depends on the fuzzy membership function. The confidence value extraction process consists of two steps. The first step is to derive the boundaries of the domain by examining the intersection part between fuzzy membership functions. The second step is to extract the confidence value so that the resultant fuzzy vector falls into the domain. Following is an example of this process. For the fuzzy membership function illustrated in Figure 9.2(a), in the fuzzy space, we have

$$\sum_j B_j(x) = 1 \tag{9.10}$$

where B_1, B_2, B_3 are A, B, C, respectively. That is, for any x, summation of the membership value of the three fuzzy subsets is always 1. For example, at x_1, $A = 1, B = 0, C = 0$, and at x_2, $A = 0.75, B = 0.25, C = 0$. In this case, separation of confidence value is straightforward: we scale the certainty vector to meet the constraints by above equation, and the confidence value will be the scale factor. The confidence value is then used to weight the facial feature when computing the overall fuzzy similarity measure.

Suppose the fuzzy subsets A, B, C shown in Figure 9.2 represent the concepts "small", "medium", and "large" for eye size. When a user is asked to put certainty values for these three concepts of a person he saw, it is very rare that the results can follow the constraints.

What will happen if the certainties he input are (0.9, 0.3, 0)? After separation, the confidence value is 1.2 and the valid fuzzy vector is (0.75, 0.25, 0), the point E in Figure 9.2(b). The matching will not have any problem because all fuzzy vectors in the database are valid ones. If the certainties input by the user, (0.9, 0.3, 0), is straightforward used in searching, it will not match (0.75, 0.25, 0), instead, (0.8, 0.2, 0) is the nearest one to (0.9, 0.3, 0), the point H in Figure 9.2(b).

For the fuzzy membership functions in Figure 9.3(a), the domain of fuzzy sets is an area rather than a set of lines. In this case, there can be several valid pairs of fuzzy vectors and confidence values which fit into equation 9.9, and any of them can be considered as a valid solution.

After these two steps of preprocessing, we get fuzzy vectors for all facial features. We call them *fuzzy query vectors* in our discussion.

9.3.5 Incomplete query condition

Now we are ready to deal with the incompleteness of fuzzy query conditions. When user defines the query, he/she just specifies what he/she knows, and leaves unknown terms blank. For example, when a witness describes a criminal, all he can recall is that the chin of this criminal is long, and eyes are large, but not quite certain. He cannot provide any other information since he was very frightened. That is, in fuzzy query definition, chin can be defined with high certainty for long and zero certainty for the rest. In case of eyes, the certainty for large cannot be high since he is not sure. The rest for eyes (medium, small) should be left blank for the same reason. The certainty for other facial features are all blank because he does not have any idea.

Blank elements in the certainty vector, and then in the fuzzy vector do not mean the same as zero. Blank means "not known", or "not sure", while zero simply means "no". To deal with this incompleteness we can only make use of already defined elements, and ignore blank elements. That is: do not process anything which is not known.

We know that fuzzy queries are defined in fuzzy space, while feature measures of images are in feature space. The incompleteness of the fuzzy query definition forces us to process a fuzzy query in the fuzzy space. If we could convert the fuzzy query vector in the fuzzy space to a feature vector in the feature space, we can directly invoke similarity retrieval technique and content-based index ContIndex described in [29] to process the fuzzy query. Unfortunately, it is not possible. Both fuzzy space and feature space are multi-dimensional. Mapping from the fuzzy space to the feature space is usually very difficult and not unique. Mapping the incompletely defined fuzzy query vector in the fuzzy space to the feature space is even more difficult, and usually is impossible. If we cannot even locate the incompletely defined fuzzy query vector in the fuzzy space, how can we map it to the feature space?

Now the only choice left to us is to map image feature vectors of images in the database from the feature space to the fuzzy space. This can be easily done by fuzzification. After fuzzification, images in the database are described as points in fuzzy space, which we call *fuzzy image vectors.* We can then evaluate the similarity between fuzzy query vector and fuzzy image vector.

9.3.6 Similarity measure

After preprocessing the user defined fuzzy queries, we are ready to find the similarity between fuzzy query vector and fuzzy image vector. For the sake of discussion, let us now consider the similarity measure of fuzzy age as an example, to define the similarity measures between the fuzzy query vector $Q_j, j = 1, 2, ..., q$ and the fuzzy image vector $B_j, j = 1, 2, ..., q$.

Note here we have omitted the superscript, Q_j, B_j are fuzzy subsets in the same fuzzy space.

The fuzzy space is not orthogonal. The coordinates represent the fuzzy subsets. Fuzzy subset membership functions overlap each other as defined by fuzzy set theory. Therefore, ordinary correlation and distance measures cannot be used as similarity measures. Previous work on fuzzy similarity measures [3] mainly discuss the similarity measures between fuzzy sets, and processes fuzzy queries using fuzzy logic [14]. They do not provide us with a solution for retrieval of multimedia data which are characterized by multidimensional features.

Similarity plays a fundamental role in theories of knowledge and behavior. Tversky [23] studied features of similarity from cognitive point of view. We now study similarity measures in multidimensional fuzzy space as metric distance functions. A metric distance function, *dis*, is a scale that assigns to every pair of points a nonnegative number, called their distance, in accordance with the following three axioms:

Minimality: $dis(a,b) \geq dis(a,a) = 0.$

Symmetry: $dis(a,b) = dis(b,a);$

Triangle inequality: $dis(a,b) + dis(b,c) \geq dis(a,c).$

The distance between Q and B, defined as follows, satisfies these three axioms and can be used as a similarity measure between fuzzy vectors in the fuzzy space:

$$dis(Q,B) = \sqrt{\sum_{j,k} |Q_j - B_j| cor(A_j, A_k) |Q_k - B_k|} \quad \text{if } Q_j \text{ not blank} \qquad (9.11)$$

$cor(A_j, A_k)$ is the correlation between fuzzy subsets A_j and A_k which define the j-th and k-th coordinates of the fuzzy space, and is defined as

$$cor(A_j, A_k) = -card(A_j \cap A_k)/card(A_j \cup A_k) \qquad (9.12)$$

The cardinality of a fuzzy set $card(A)$ is define as

$$card(A) = \int m_A(x)dx \qquad or \qquad card(A) = \sum_x m_A(x) \qquad (9.13)$$

Note here the distance is evaluated against non-blank components of the query object. “Blank” means “not known”. It is meaningless to evaluate a “not known” item. To demonstrate the basic idea behind this distance measure, let us again have a look at Figure 9.2(b).

$cor(A, B), cor(B, C)$ are not equal to zero (it is $-frac19$). This is equivalent to the case that the angles between coordinates A and B, and between B and C are less than 90°. A simple triangular derivation will show that the negative sign of $cor()$ will partially take account of the correlation between coordinates.

The distance measure defined by Equation 9.11 well coincides with the above three axioms by its definition. Let us have a look at three fuzzy vectors E(0.75, 0.25, 0), F(0.25, 0.75, 0) and G(0, 0.75, 0.25) shown in Figure 9.2(b). The distance among them computed using equation 9.11 are: $dis(E, F) = 0.67, dis(F, G) = 0.5, dis(E, G) = 0.87$. Here, $dis(E, F) + dis(F, G) = 1.17 > dis(E, G) = 0.87$.

9.3.7 Relevance feedback for query refinement

By a feedback function, the user can select from the current query result one or several images he/she thinks are closest to the desired one. The feedback function can then extract the information from the selected images to refine the query. Our feedback method assumes that feedback images are selected in a sequence that the most desirable one is selected first, and that the selection will be based on the most similar features among those selected images. Suppose N images have been selected, the feature vectors for feedback is computed using following procedures:

1. With a predefined threshold, find facial features with respect to which those N selected images are similar,

2. For the rest of the facial features, find facial features with respect to which $N-1, N-2, ...$ selected images are similar.

3. For those facial features, with respect to which no images among N selected images are similar, the first image is taken as a representative for the facial features.

4. Find the center of the facial feature vectors by averaging over the images which are similar with respect to the facial features.

5. Perform a similarity search using the computed center of the facial feature vectors.

9.4 Learning Fuzzy Membership Functions

One of the bottlenecks for fuzzy system applications is that there is no effective method for deriving fuzzy membership functions for applications.

Currently, application developers empirically design fuzzy membership functions. Empirical design is only effective for single dimension of feature measures, such as age. It cannot deal with multiple dimensional feature measures such as those extracted from face images by image processing methods. It would be ideal to have a system which can automatically learn the association between multi-dimensional numerical feature measures and fuzzy subsets from a sample set of data items sufficiently representing the whole domain.

Neural and fuzzy systems estimate sampled functions and behave as associative memories. They can estimate functions without a mathematical description of how the output should correspond to the multi-dimensional numerical inputs. It is because of this ability, they are known as *model-free* estimators [13]. Fuzzy neural networks can learn to function as a transformation function based on a sample set of *feature measure* and *fuzzy subset* pairs. Wang used feedforward neural network with backpropagation learning method to learn these associations [24].

We feel that model free learning require very large sample set. In many applications, the size of available sample data sets are limited. In this case, opposing model constraints can reduce the sample data set size requirement, and embed the desired concepts and shapes into the membership functions. Therefore, we propose to use feedforward networks with Gaussian units.

9.4.1 Need for learning fuzzy membership functions

As mentioned in the previous sections, every image in the database has its fuzzy membership values stored along with it. These values cannot be manually set for all images in a large database. Therefore a procedure which computes the fuzzy membership is essential. The procedure which assigns the various fuzzy membership function values based on the *multi-dimensional* feature vectors is an important component in fuzzy retrieval. The contour of a fuzzy membership function represents the semantic properties of the underlying feature it estimates [7]. A number of contours such as lines, S-curves, bell shapes are employed to function as a fuzzy membership function. The calculation of the fuzzy membership values is a multi-dimensional mapping, which maps the n dimensional numerical feature measures of a feature to the m dimensional fuzzy space for that particular feature, as shown in Figure 9.5.

For example, in the case of face image retrieval, let us assume that we have computed a 16 element feature vector F^{eye} from images, which has to be mapped to 3 fuzzy subsets, *small, medium and big.* Then the

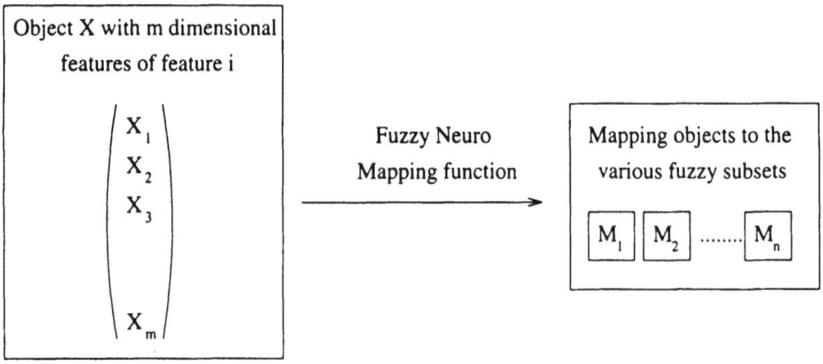

Figure 9.5: Mapping feature measures to fuzzy subsets

fuzzy membership function, m has to map a 16 dimensional feature vector representing eye size to the 3 fuzzy subsets of eye size, i.e

$$\begin{aligned} \text{eyesize}_{small} &= m_{small}(F) \\ \text{eyesize}_{medium} &= m_{medium}(F) \\ \text{eyesize}_{big} &= m_{big}(F) \end{aligned}$$

This function, m should be reconfigurable and work for different domains and applications. Moreover *interpretation* of these images varies among people. Therefore when images are being classified to the various fuzzy sets, the confidence values set for each fuzzy subset will be different among different people. The truth membership values are usually computed as a mean of the membership values as classified by different people. This method of computing the truth membership values accounts for the *subjective* interpretations of features by different people. Once this association is obtained, a procedure has to be devised which can *learn* this *association* and behave as a fuzzy membership function. The solution must be able to provide a domain to truth membership mapping function by analyzing sufficient equidistantly spaced truth membership values. In addition to this it would be ideal to have a system which can *automatically* correlate the truth membership values with the domain and create fuzzy regions. This will be the first step in developing a generic fuzzy retrieval system.

Artificial Neural Networks have the remarkable ability to cluster the feature measures to classes, in our case fuzzy subsets [16]. Neural networks can find natural membership functions for the data and directly create fuzzy regions [24].

In an image retrieval environment, typically we are confronted with problem of finding a fuzzy membership function for the multi-dimensional numerical feature measures. Therefore the neural networks which can take real number inputs and map them to their corresponding fuzzy subsets yielding the membership function values, is appropriate to the problem of fuzzy image retrieval [10,9]. The structure of the network is shown in Figure 9.6. $x_1, ..., x_n$ represent the real number inputs to the neural network. The w_{ij} are real number weights for the link between input x_i

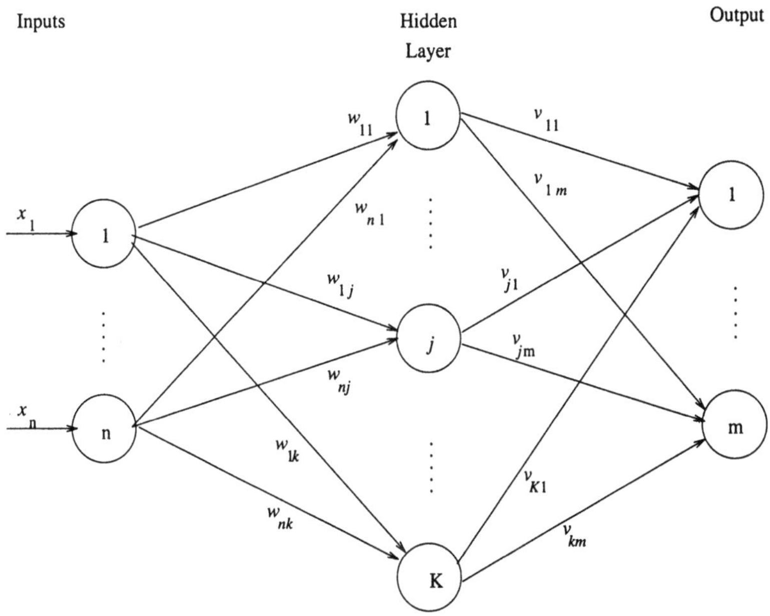

Figure 9.6: A neural net with real number inputs and outputs considered as fuzzy membership values

and hidden unit j. The input to the hidden neuron is computed as,

$$I_j = x_1 w_{1j} + x_2 w_{2j} + ... + x_n w_{nj},\ 1 \leq j \leq K$$

where standard fuzzy arithmetic is used to compute I_j. The output from the jth hidden neuron will be

$$Z_j = f_1(I_j),\ 1 \leq j \leq K$$

where f_1 is an activation function which can be a sigmoidal or Gaussian function. The v_{jm} represent weights for the link between hidden unit j and output unit m. It then follows that the input to the output neuron will be computed as

$$I_o = z_1 v_{1o} + z_2 v_{2o} + ... + z_K v_{Ko},\ 1 \leq o \leq m$$

for the m output units. The fuzzy membership value is then obtained from the final output as,

$$Y = f_2(I_o)$$

where f_2 is a sigmoidal activation function. Most of these network systems have a function μ_{ij} between each x_i and w_{ij} as some form of an interpretation for the input x_i. These μ_{ij} are usually triangular fuzzy numbers.

Training this kind of feedforward network can be done using a modified version of the backpropagation algorithm. The membership function can be trained from the membership values at finite data points along the membership curve.

9.4.2 A Fuzzy neuro membership function

For a network to function effectively as a fuzzy membership function, it has to be reconfigurable and it should be easy to train new feature measures. In other words, this network should be able to automatically cluster the feature measures to fuzzy subsets.

A three layered neural network with one hidden layer of Gaussian units is used for learning and representing the membership functions for a fuzzy set. The hidden layer of Gaussian units works as a membership function and helps to speed up the training process [25]. The learning of membership functions is through the learning algorithm of these three layer feedforward neural networks.

Let us denote the pth data point of the input by $X_p = (x_{p1}, x_{p2}, ..., x_{pn})$ and the membership value at that point by t_p. When the n-dimensional input is presented to the network, ideally the network output, y_p, should correspond to the desired output, t_p. The output of the feedforward network for the input X_p is computed according to the following procedure.

The activation function of the hidden units is a Gaussian function expressed as

$$z\_in_j = \sum_i \frac{(x_i - c_{ij})^2}{2\sigma_{ij}^2}$$

$$z_j^h = f_1(z\_in_j) = exp(-\sum_i \frac{(x_i - c_{ij})^2}{2\sigma_{ij}^2}) \tag{9.14}$$

where c_{ij} and σ_{ij} are weights from input unit i to hidden unit j, representing the center of gravity and standard deviation of each cluster. A detailed discussion on the clustering algorithm used can be found in [25]. The Gaussian activation function defines quadratic decision surfaces in the feature space and approximates fuzzy membership functions very well.

The activation of output neuron m is then computed as

$$y\_in = \sum_{j=1}^{k} v_{jp}\, z_j$$
$$y_m = f_2(y\_in) = f_2(\sum_{j=1}^{k} v_{jm}\, z_j)$$

where f_2 is a sigmoidal activation function. If the network is trained with sufficient sample data points from the n-dimensional input space, then the output y_p should be the same as t_p.

The gradients of the activation function for the hidden units with respect to c_{ij} and σ_{ij} are computed as

$$\frac{\partial z_j^h}{\partial c_{ij}} = \frac{z_j^h (x_i - c_{ij})}{\sigma_{ij}^2}$$

$$\frac{\partial z_j^h}{\partial \sigma_{ij}} = \frac{z_j^h (x_i - c_{ij})^2}{\sigma_{ij}^3} \qquad (9.15)$$

Because the Gaussian activation function defined by equation 9.14 and the standard sigmoid function are differentiable, this kind of neural network can be trained using the back-propagation learning algorithm.

9.4.3 Training the neural network

The neural network, which is a feedforward network, has to be trained with sample input and output pairs before it can simulate a fuzzy membership function. The standard backpropagation technique can be used to train the network [8,15]. As mentioned earlier, the desired target value of the network for an input is the membership value for that data in fuzzy space.

A set of input-output pattern is first prepared for the system to learn the association. It is generally assumed that the domain of the input chosen is sufficient to represent the input pattern. While training the network, the activation of an output neuron may not be our desired fuzzy membership function value. In this case, the error in membership function value for the pth input-output pattern is $t_p - y_m$, when t_p corresponds to output y_m. Each such output unit computes an *error information term*,

$$\delta_m = (t_p - y_m) f_2'(y\_in_m)$$

This δ_m propagates to all hidden units j from output unit m. The *weight correction term* for links between hidden unit j and output unit m is calculated as

$$\Delta v_{jm} = \alpha \delta_m z_j$$

Each hidden unit sums the δ inputs from units in the layer above and multiplies it by the derivative of its activation function to calculative its error information term,

$$\delta\_in_j = \sum_m \delta_m v_{jm}$$
$$\delta_j = \delta\_in_j f_1'(z\_in_j)$$

and its weight correction term as

$$\Delta w_{ij} = \alpha \delta_j x_i$$

After the error information terms have propagated and the weight correction terms computed, the weights for the links between the input and hidden layer units and the weights for the link between the hidden layer units and output units are updated as,

$$v_{jm} = v_{jm}(old) + \Delta v_{jm}$$
$$w_{ij} = w_{ij}(old) + \Delta w_{ij}$$

9.5 Experimental Results of Fuzzy Retrieval

The implementation and testing of the content-based fuzzy retrieval of images was carried out on a facial image database system, CAFIIR [28].

9.5.1 Face database indexing and retrieval

The face database contains 132 images, together with their facial feature measures, personnel particulars, and linked criminal records. All these data are artificially created only for experimental purpose, and do not refer to any real people. The experiments include determination of fuzzy subsets and membership functions, implementation and testing of the retrieval method.

In the face database system, each of the six facial features, namely, chin, hair, eyes, eyebrow, nose and mouth, is characterized by three feature measures: 1) landmark coordinates, from which certain feature dimensions, such as the length of the eyes, can be derived; 2) The first 12 principal coefficients of the Principal Component Analysis (PCA) of the feature region (ROI) with the region positioned by landmarks and contains one feature only. For example, the chin region has a banana shape and contains chin image only. No part of the mouth is included. Therefore, the 12 principal coefficients reflect the major gray scale changes (chin shape, texture) of the chin. 3) Fitting parameters of deformed template [32]. This is only available for a few facial features.

chin	PCA of ROI	pointed, rounded, tapered, squared, bony cheek, short-chin, long-chin, jowls
hair	thickness	thin, normal, thick
eyes	height	small, medium, large
eyebrow	thickness	sparse, medium, thick
nose	legnth	short, medium, long
mouth	width	narrow, medium, wide

Table 9.2: Feature measures and fuzzy subsets for facial description

The experiment has been designed to test the validation of the content-based fuzzy retrieval method described in this chapter. To avoid complications, we choose the feature measures and their corresponding fuzzy subsets for facial description as listed in Table 9.2.

Among six facial features, we choose 12-dimensional feature measure vector (PCA) for chin, and one dimension measure for all others. Consequently, fuzzy subsets are chosen as in Table 9.2. The membership function of fuzzy subsets for chin has Gaussian shape as illustrated in Figure 9.3. The fuzzy membership function for other facial features has trapezoid shape, see Figure 9.2.

Fuzzy membership function

More attention has been paid to fuzzy membership functions for the chin feature. There are two possible ways: one is to partition images into certain number of clusters using clustering algorithm. A group of people is then asked to view these clusters and to check facial feature consistency within clusters and to assign facial feature description to each cluster. When clusters have been formed, parameters of the membership functions can be derived from the images in these clusters.

The other way is to have a set of facial sample images and to have a group of people. Each of them is asked to describe facial features of sample images using a given set of concepts together with certainty values. For example, if we want to describe eyes as either "large", "medium" and "small", a viewer should put valid description such as "large 0.8", "medium 0.4" and "small 0.0" for each given sample facial image. Having gathered these descriptive data, fuzzy membership functions will be derived to best fit the data. In this method, we do not expect viewers to give consistent descriptions over all sample images. In other words, the descriptions obtained are subjective, and there is an inherently embedded context model in the descriptions. To overcome this difficulty, we give a confidence measure to each viewer based on how objectively he/she can produce descriptions. These confidence measures are then used as weights in the algorithm for membership function derivation.

The first method is easier to implement than the second. It organizes facial image features into categories based on feature measures. For example, we use PCA for chin, the first 12 coefficients represent the most salient gray scale changes on the chin image. The clusters generated will also reflect the major appearance variations on the chin images. The second method is preferred by many domain experts because there is greater human involvement in the fuzzy subset definition and fuzzy membership learning.

In the experiment here, we adopt the first method because of its simplicity, and because we are testing our fuzzy retrieval method, not the fuzzy membership learning methods.

Q	query object →	70	40	
No.	Similarity measure	B_1	B_2	B_3
1	0.88	64	35	0
2	4.24	57	42	0
3	8.00	50	50	0
4	12.55	92	7	0
5	16.00	100	0	0
6	19.33	42	57	0

Table 9.3: The best match to the query object $(0.7, 0.4, \emptyset)$ (membership function values have been scaled by 100)

Fuzzy query processing

In the fuzzy query preprocessing, separation of the confidence values and the membership functions is very important. For the facial features other

query object →				80			40		
Similarity measure	B_1	B_2	B_3	B_4	B_5	B_6	B_7	B_8	B_9
21.33	40	14	20	80	24	10	52	36	2
26.13	38	12	18	76	22	10	52	38	2
40.00	26	8	14	60	20	8	44	42	2
87.19	67	22	25	99	27	17	41	18	3
87.19	60	18	20	99	25	15	36	18	3
95.19	42	16	14	99	51	24	25	16	5
95.19	73	24	23	99	28	19	33	16	5
99.19	40	14	12	99	40	19	22	15	3

Table 9.4: The best match to the query object $(\emptyset, \emptyset, \emptyset, 0.8, \emptyset, \emptyset, 0.4, \emptyset, \emptyset)$ (membership function values have been scaled by 100)

than the chin, the fuzzy membership functions have the form as shown in Figure 9.2(a). We can apply the constraint in equation 9.10 to separate the confidence from the membership function. Table 9.3 shows the best matches for the query object $(0.7, 0.4, \emptyset)$. After confidence value separation, it becomes $(0.636, 0.364, \emptyset)$. It matches the database object $(0.64, 0.35, 0)$ the best. The query object and the six best matches are also plotted in Figure 9.7, which gives us an intuitive view of the similarity between the query object and database object retrieved as the best matches. From the figure we can see that the algorithm selected those database objects which are the most similar ones, and that ordering of retrieved database objects is conceptually correct. The database object 6 is considered to be less similar to the query object than object 5 because in database object 6 fuzzy subset B_2 (rather than B_1) is dominant. This evidence shows that the similarity measure defined in equation 9.11 coincides well with fuzzy subset definition, and is conceptually correct.

Table 9.4 lists the retrieval results for "chin" query object. From the table we can see that the ordered query result reflects the similarity between the query object and the best matches well. Some retrieved objects have large values for fuzzy subsets other than those having specified values in the query object. For example, the fourth retrieved object has a large membership value for the first fuzzy subset. However, this will not effect the validity of the query result because the null value in the query object means "not known" - his chin may be pointed, but the user did not notice. It is retrieved as long as its feature matches the query object

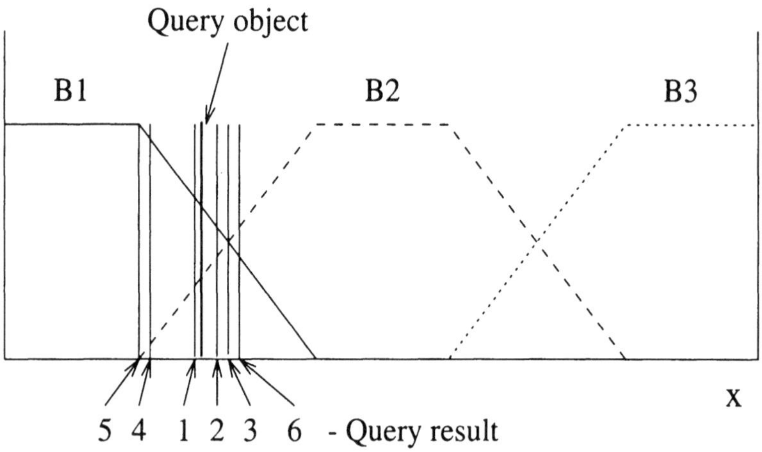

Figure 9.7: The best match to the query object in terms of fuzzy vector.

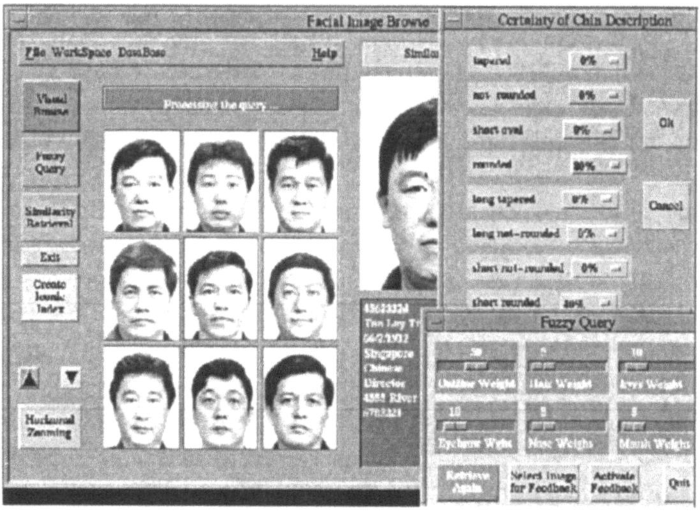

Figure 9.8: Fuzzy retrieval of images. The query was defined as to retrieve facial images with round chin (0.8), short round chin (0.4), normal hair (0.8), thin hair (0.4). The value inside the brackets are certainty values.

Query object				80			40			40	80	
Similarity measure	B_1	B_2	B_3	B_4	B_5	B_6	B_7	B_8	B_9	C_1	C_2	C_3
27.17	40	14	20	80	24	10	52	36	2	21	78	0
42.13	38	12	18	76	22	10	52	38	2	0	100	0
54.66	26	8	14	60	20	8	44	42	2	0	50	50
100.07	40	14	12	99	40	19	22	15	3	35	64	0
101.04	42	16	14	99	51	24	25	16	5	21	78	0
102.00	67	22	25	99	27	17	41	18	3	0	85	14
103.19	60	18	20	99	25	15	36	18	3	0	100	0
111.19	73	24	23	99	28	19	33	16	5	0	100	0
142.13	54	18	40	64	20	12	78	34	2	0	28	71

Table 9.5: The best match to the query objects $(\emptyset, \emptyset, \emptyset, 0.8, \emptyset, \emptyset, 0.4, \emptyset, \emptyset)$ and (0.4, 0.8, $\emptyset$) (membership function values have been enlarged by 100)

well with respect to those fuzzy subsets whose membership values are specified in the query object.

Table 9.5 is a retrieval example using both chin and hair. The chin query object is $(\emptyset, \emptyset, \emptyset, 0.8, \emptyset, \emptyset, 0.4, \emptyset, \emptyset)$ and the hair query object is (0.4, 0.8, $\emptyset$). It means that we want to retrieve facial images having "rounded (80% sure) and short rounded (40% sure) chin" and "thin (40% sure) and normal (80% sure) hair". The weights for chin and hair are 0.5 and 0.1, respectively, which implies emphasis on the chin feature.

The interface and the query result is shown in Figure 9.8. Within the interface panel, there are six push down menus for the six facial features. The user is asked to fill in certainty values for these fuzzy subsets used to describe the facial features, and to skip those about which he/she has no idea. Retrieved images are displayed on nine small display buttons. Clicking on any display button will lead to the corresponding image to be displayed in a large display area on the top-right of the screen (half covered by the push-down menu titled "certainty of chin description"). Particulars of the person are also displayed in a message area right beneath the image display area. This message area is also half covered by the push down menu titled "fuzzy query" and used to control weights among facial features and to activate query feedback.

Since there is no objective criteria for fuzzy retrieval methods, content-based fuzzy retrieval methods can be only evaluated subjectively by viewers. The fuzzy retrieval results such as one in Figure 9.8 shows conceptual consistency with our perception. We are planning to conduct a subjective evaluation by a group of users.

Conceptual acceptance by users of the fuzzy retrieval results needs valid fuzzy membership functions and good fuzzy retrieval method. Here we have proposed and tested a novel fuzzy retrieval method which offers an unique fuzzy query processing technique. It processes fuzzy queries in the fuzzy space and query results are in terms of a best match technique.

9.6 Conclusion and Remarks

Fuzzy retrieval is a natural means to access image data. In this chapter we have described extended image data model, tuple calculus, fuzzy query processing, a fuzzy content-based indexing method, and learning fuzzy membership functions using neural networks. The experimental results have shown its effectiveness.

References

1. Y. H. Ang, "Enhanced Primal Sketch Face Recognition", The Workshop on Looking at People: Recognition and Interpretation of Human Action, 13th IJ-CAI, France, August 1993
2. J. Bach, S. Paul, R. Jain, "A Visual Information Management System for Interactive Retrieval of Faces", IEEE Trans. on Knowledge and Data Engineering, Vol. 5, pp. 619-628, 1993
3. H. Bandemer, W. Nather, "Fuzzy Data Analysis", Dordrecht: Kluwer Academic Publishers, 1992
4. E. Binaghi, A. D. Ventura, A. Rampini, R. Schettini, "Fuzzy Reasoning Approach to Similarity Evaluation in Image Analysis", International Journal of Intelligent Systems, Vol. 8, pp. 749-769, 1993
5. J. J. Buckley, Y. Hayashi, "Fuzzy Neural Networks: A Survey", Fuzzy sets and systems, Vol. 66, pp.1-13, 1994
6. T. Chen, J. K. Wu, "Data Model for Knowldge-based Pictorial Database Systems", Acta Automatica Sinica, Vol. 16, No. 2, pp. 128-133, 1990
7. E. Cox, "The Fuzzy Systems Hand Book, A Practitioner's Guide to Building, Using and Maintaining Fuzzy Systems", AP PROFESSIONAL, Cambridge, MA, 1994
8. L. Fausett, "Fundamentals of Neural Networks: Architectures, Algorithms and Applications", Prentice Hall, Englewood Cliffs, New Jersey, 1994
9. S. Horikawa, T. Furuhashi, Y. Uchikawa, S. Okuma, "A fuzzy Controller Using A Neural Network and Its Capability to Learn Expert's Control Rules", Proceedings of the International Conference On Fuzzy Logic And Neural Networks, pp. 103-106, Iizuka, Japan, 1990

10. H. Ishibuchi, H. Tanaka, "Identification of Real-Valued and Interval-Valued Membership Functions by Neural Networks", Proc. Intern. Conf. on Fuzzy Logic and Neural Networks, pp. 179-182, Iizuka, Japan, 1990
11. A. Jain, "Fundamentals of Digital Image Processing", Englewood: Prentice-Hall International, Inc., 1989
12. W. Kim, "On object-oriented database technology", UniSQL, Inc. Technical Report, 9390 Research Blvd., Austin, Texas 78759, 1993
13. B. Kosko, Neural Networks and Fuzzy Systems - A Dynamical Systems Approach to Machine Intelligence", Prentice Hall, Englewood cliffs, NJ, 1992
14. D. Li, D. Liu, "A Fuzzy PROLOG Database System", Taunton, Somerset, England: Research Studies Press Ltd, 1990
15. J. L. McClelland, D. E. Rumelhart, "Explorations in Parallel Distributed Processing", The MIT Press, Massachusetts, 1988
16. W. Meier, R. Weber, H. J. Zimmerman, "Fuzzy Data Analysis - Methods and Industrial Applications", Fuzzy sets and systems, Vol. 61, pp. 19-28, 1994
17. X. T. Peng, A. Kandel, P. Z. Wang, "Concepts, Rules, and Fuzzy Reasoning: A Factor Space Approach", IEEE trans System, Man, and Cybernetics, Vol. 21, No. 1, pp. 194-205, 1991
18. A. Ralescu, H. Iwamoto, "Reading Faces: A Fuzzy Logic Approach to Representation, Recognition and Description of Facial Expression", 13th Int. Joint Conf. on AI, Chambery, Savoie, France, 1993
19. G. Salton, M. J. McGill, "Introduction to Modern Information Retrieval", Auckland: McGraw-Hill Advanced Computer Science Series, 1983
20. G. SenthilKumar, J. K. Wu, "Content-Based Retrieval Using Fuzzy Interactive and Competitive Neural Network", First International Symposium on Photonics Technologies and systems for Voice, Video and Data Communications, pp. 2-12, Philadelphia, Pennsylvania, USA, 1995
21. M. Stonebraker, M. Olson, "Large Object Support in POSTGRES", IEEE Data Engineering Conference, Vienna, pp. 355-362, 1993
22. M. Stonebraker, "Inclusion of New Types in Relational Data Base Systems", IEEE Data Engineering Conference, Los Angles, 1986
23. A. Tversky, "Features of Similarity", Psychological Review, Vol. 84, pp. 327-352, 1977
24. S. Wang, "Generating Fuzzy Membership Functions: A Monotonic Neural Network Model", Fuzzy Sets and Systems, Vol. 61, pp. 71-81, 1994
25. N. Weymaere, J. Martens, "A Fast and Robust Learning Algorithm for Feedforward Neural Networks", Neural Networks, Vol. 4, pp. 361-369, 1991
26. J. K. Wu, "Neural Networks and Simulation", New York: Marcel Dekker, Inc., 1994
27. J. K. Wu, A. D. Narasimhalu, B. Mehtre, C. P. Lam, Y. J. Gao, "CORE: A Content-Based Retrieval Engine for Multimedia Information Systems", ACM Multimedia Journal, Vol. 3, No. 1, pp. 25-41, 1995
28. J. K. Wu, Y. H. Ang, C. P. Lam, H. H. Loh, A. D. Narasimhalu, "Inference and Retrieval of Facial Image Retrieval", ACM Multimedia Journal, Vol. 2, No. 2, pp. 1-14, 1994

29. J. K. Wu, "Content-based Indexing of Multimedia Databases", IEEE Trans. Knowledge and Data Engineering, Vol. 9, No.6, pp. 978-989l, 1997

30. J. K. Wu, A. Desai Narasimhalu, "Fuzzy Content-based Image Database", Information Processing and Management, June, 1998.

31. J. K. Wu, F. Gao, P. Yang, "Model-based 3-D Object Recognition", Second International Conference on Automation, Robotics and Computer Vision, Singapore, 1992

32. A. L. Yuile, "Deformable Templates for Face Recognition", Journal of Cognitive Neuroscience, Vol. 3, pp. 59-70, 1990

33. L. A. Zadeth, "Fuzzy Set and Information Granularity", Advances in Fuzzy Sets Theory and Applications, Amsterdam: North-Holand, pp.3-18, 1979

34. X. Zhang, J. K. Wu, W. T. Wang, "A Versatile Image Database Management System IMDAT", Acta Electronica Sinica, Vol. 16, No. 4, pp. 15-20, 1988

Chapter 10

Face Retrieval

We would like to demonstrate some core techniques for content-based multimedia systems using the CAFIIR system: Firstly, CAFIIR is an integrated system. Besides database management, there are image analysis, image composition, image aging, and report generation subsystems, providing means for problem solving. Secondly, the richness of multimedia data requires feature-based database for their management. Therefore, CAFIIR is feature-based. An indexing mechanism, *iconic index*, has been proposed for indexing facial images using hierarchical self-organization neural network. The indexing method operates on complex feature measures and provides means for visual navigation. Thirdly, special retrieval methods for facial images have been developed, including visual browsing, similarity retrieval, free text retrieval and fuzzy retrieval.

Multimedia database systems are integrated systems. Except data management and retrieval, they can offer data manipulation, analysis, recognition, and even planing and decision making. Some complicated problems can be solved by case-based reasoning in multimedia database environment.

As an example of multimedia database systems, CAFIIR stores and manages a large number of facial images together with criminal records [16]. It provides users with a flexible means to manipulate, archive, retrieve, and make use of facial images and text data. The facial images are visual than descriptive. Each digital image is a large array of pixels, of an arbitrary size, and a facial image database contains thousands or even hundred thousands of images. Therefore, this huge visual database needs special techniques for its management, namely, embedded functions for image preprocessing, feature extraction, presentation (screen display and report formatter); visual access to image data via special indexing techniques; application-specific image inference to derive new images based on images and other available information.

Feature-based indexing, and special query processing are difficult research issues for multimedia database systems. Here, we present a content-based indexing method ContIndex, which provides a mechanism to create index on composite feature measures, and facilitates visual browsing and similarity retrieval. Other than visual browsing, similarity retrieval, and free text retrieval, fuzzy retrieval is desirable for image databases. A novel fuzzy query processing method is presented.

As a feature-based multimedia database system, CAFIIR offers an iconic indexing method and four special data retrieval methods. A fuzzy query processing method in fuzzy space is also used in the system, which is described in Chapter 9.

In the following sections we will first give an overall description of CAFIIR and the data model of the facial image data in Section 10.2. Section 10.3 deals with iconic indexing mechanism using neural networks. Sections 10.4 and 10.5 is devoted to data retrieval. Visual browsing, similarity retrieval are visual queries and included in Section 10.4, while descriptive queries, fuzzy retrieval, free text retrieval are in Section 10.5. Further improvement of queries, query feedback and combined query are in Section 10.6.

10.1 CAFIIR system

As shown in Figure 10.1, the CAFIIR system consists of five functional subsystems: facial image preprocessing and feature extraction subsystem provides functions for creating, processing, editing images and text; facial image and criminal record database subsystem provides functions for creation, processing, editing, storage and management of facial image and criminal record data; facial composition works interactively to compose facial images by choosing the desired facial components; based on growth model and available image of a person, facial aging subsystem derives facial image of the same person at different age; image output formatting produces formatted output.

The image database retrieval engine is shown in Figure 10.2. Retrieval by attributes is a conventional data access method which is useful for system administration. It is constructed using functions provided by a database, management system, dbVista, on top of which the object-oriented image database is built.

Four retrieval methods, namely, similarity retrieval, visual browsing,

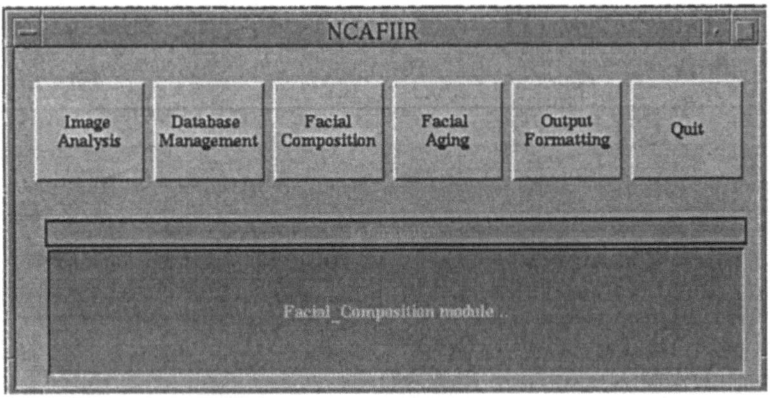

Figure 10.1: Subsystems within CAFIIR.

fuzzy retrieval, and free text retrieval are special to the image database. Visual browsing and similarity retrieval are visual. They are supported by iconic indexing. Both fuzzy retrieval and free text retrieval are descriptive. The fuzzy index used for fuzzy retrieval is created by the mechanism of iconic indexing. The difference between the iconic index and the fuzzy index is: iconic index is created using composite feature measure, while fuzzy index is created using composite fuzzy membership function. Both composite feature measure and composite fuzzy membership function are vector arrays. Therefore, the same indexing mechanism can be applied to both case. However, the similarity measures are different. The fuzzy similarity measure will be discussed later in this section. Free text retrieval provides access to criminal records via their text description and to facial images via their special feature description. By "free text" we mean little constraint is imposed on the query specification. It is, therefore, a lot more user friendly.

Let us now look at the information retrieval problem from a point of view of inference. Information systems such as databases and knowledge-based systems, are aimed at solving problems. Inference is referred to as the act of drawing a conclusion from premises. Traditional expert system performs logical inference. The difficulties of expert systems which seem to be impossible to overcome are learning and knowledge acquisition. On the other hand, case-based reasoning performs inference by analogy. In case-based reasoning, one uses memory of relevant "past" cases to interpret or to solve a problem case. Reasoning by analogy has several advantages. First, the performance is enhanced by its shortcuts in reasoning, and the capability of avoiding past errors. Second, learning has

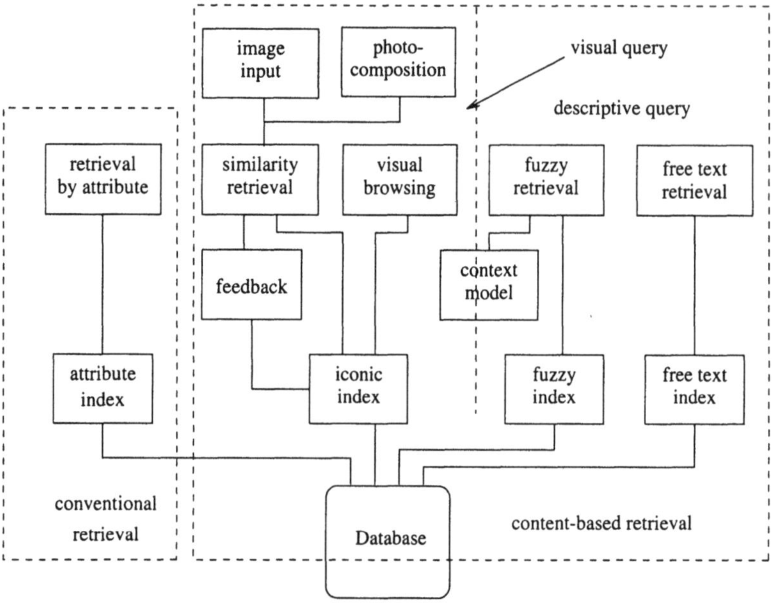

Figure 10.2: Block diagram of retrieval engine of CAFIIR

been much simplified, and the knowledge acquisition bottleneck is much easier than all other methods. Third, recalled cases can serve as explanations of the problem, which are more satisfactory than those generated by either expert systems or connectionist systems.

Two fundamental problems of case-based reasoning are: indexing method used to organize cases in the memory, and methods for finding the most relevant cases at reasoning time. Multimedia database systems provide ideal environment for representation of complicated cases. These two fundamental problems, the case organization and searching for the best match, correspond to modeling, feature-based indexing, and query processing in multimedia database systems. In CAFIIR, the past crime and criminal cases are organized by an extended object-oriented data model, which will be explained later. To speed up searching for the most relevant cases, iconic indexing mechanism provides an efficient way for navigation.

As shown in Figure 10.2, a criminal identification problem can be solved by similarity retrieval. According to the witness' description, a sample image is composed using image composition subsystem, and submitted to similarity query processing module. The module then derives feature measures from the sample image. With the derived similarity measure, the module traverses the iconic index tree down to the leaf level, finds a few most similar images, and displays them on the panel. After viewing the results, the user can revise the query either by adjusting the weights of similarity measure, or by activating feedback function with one or more the most relevant images selected from the results. The whole inference flow is a closed loop of information derivation, within which the user plays an active role.

The fuzzy query processing is another inference flow of case-based reasoning, where fuzzy membership functions and fuzzy similarity measure play an important role. With fuzzy membership functions and fuzzy index, the criminal and crime cases are organized into a *fuzzy case space.* The fuzzy similarity measure provides a criterion to find the best match.

10.1.1 Data model

The data hierarchy in CAFIIR is shown in Figure 10.3. As we can see from Figure 10.3, there are two major object types: *face record* and *crime record.* A face record is created for each person whose facial image is to be stored in the system. A face record consists of three types of records: 1. *Person record,* which stores the identification number, name, date of birth, address, etc. 2. *Feature record,* consisting of two structured feature descriptions. One is the feature measure obtained by image feature extraction method. Feature measures are usually numerical and internal to the system. The other is description of visual features of facial images generated either by automatic mapping from feature measures or by manual text input. 3. *Image record,* consisting *image header* and *image data.* Image header keeps record of the parameters and history of the image data. The items of the image header include: date of acquisition, perspective view, size, etc. Usually, image data are of different size and therefore, are split into several physical fixed length records for their storage. There may be several image records in a face record.

A *crime record* consists of routine description of a crime, such as time, type, weapon used, etc., and a more detailed text description of the crime. The length of text description can vary from one paragraph to several pages. Again, we split the text description into fixed length records for the storage. Text index will be created to gain access to this text description. One crime record may have several *witness records* and several *victim records*, which consist of items to describe witnesses and victims.

The correspondence between face record and crime record is many-to-many. A person may commit several crimes, and one crime may involve several criminals. We use $HAVE-A$ to indicate this relationship. These

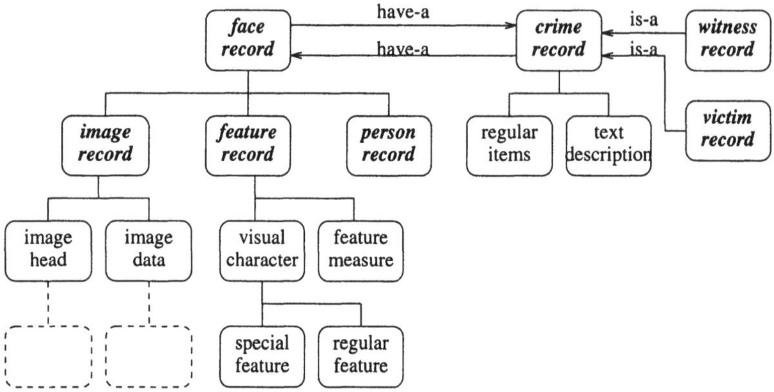

Figure 10.3: Data hierarchy in CAFIIR

links will facilitate either access of face record from crime record, or access of crime record from face record. Once a face record is retrieved, a list of crimes which this person has committed will be gathered on request.

Object-oriented model is the most preferred data model for multimedia database systems. We extended the object-oriented model to describe the data hierarchy in CAFIIR. There are two major extensions: extension of elementary data types and extension of procedure definition.

We first extend the elementary data types to include vector, array, and text paragraph. In CAFIIR, vector represents internal feature measure, unsigned character array represents digital image, and paragraphs of text are used to describe a crime or special features of a face. Vector, image array, and text paragraph can be constructed by elementary data type, char, integer, real, and string. We consider them as elementary data type because they show strong integrity. An image can be mapped to another image by image processing functions or mapped to feature measures by feature extraction functions. An indexing process can be performed on text paragraphs. These mapping and processing are carried out in terms of whole image, feature vector, or text. At the database level, they are treated entirely as a whole entity.

In object-oriented model, a set of procedures should be defined on each object class. Here we extend the model to include procedure types which perform mapping across object classes. It consists of: the feature extraction procedure which generates a set of internal feature measures from a facial image; and feature mapping procedure that maps these internal feature measures to facial feature description.

10.1.2 Indexing of facial images

Visual query of image database is advantageous for several reasons: First, it provides views of facial image database at every position, so as to enable visual navigation. Second, visual query is sometimes absolutely necessary when one cannot form a definitive opinion without actually seeing the image.

Retrieval based on similarity measures should be the basic access method to the facial image database. The user interactively composes a sample facial image according to the witness' description using the image composition module of CAFIIR, and then presents it to the query language to find facial images which are most similar to the sample. The results are ranked according to similarities.

Query by fuzzy descriptions of facial features is also desirable. Quite often, a witness comes and says that he cannot clearly remember the criminals face but he knows that his face is somewhat square, and eyes a little bit small. These fuzzy descriptions should be used to direct the user to certain position of visual navigation.

These three type of queries, namely, visual, fuzzy and similarity queries can be realized by using iconic index based on composite feature measures. They cannot be realized by conventional indexing techniques such as B-trees and inverted file. Conventional indexing techniques are based on individual keys, which are definite and too simple to represent visual features of facial images.

We have proposed an *iconic indexing* method by extending the concept of indexing with abstraction and classification, and by proposing a spatial self-organization neural network. The proposed spatial self-organization neural network is used to generate spatially self-organized index tree. In the following subsections we will discuss issues on iconic indexing.

10.1.3 Feature extraction

The features of similarity serve as an organizing principle by which people classify objects, form concepts, and make generalization. Facial feature extraction and mapping feature measures to facial feature categories are essential to the system performance . The difficulties of these two issues lie in the facts that

- It is not clear so far how humans recognize faces, and what features are used by human to distinguish between faces. Therefore it is not yet possible for cognitive science to provide practical hints to computer recognition of facial images.

- There is no an image processing method which can readily solve our problem. For example, it is nearly impossible to automatically extract accurate face outline for some facial images.

- Subjective descriptions of facial features are fuzzy. There is no clear definition of facial feature categories. This makes mapping from feature measures to facial feature categories very difficult.

Having considered these difficulties, we have designed our feature extraction procedure by working together with domain experts. First, a facial feature category table is defined. It contains six *facial aspects*: chin, hair, eyes, eyebrows, nose, and mouth. Each facial aspect contains several items and possible descriptive values (such as large, middle, small, etc.) for those items. To be consistent with this facial feature category table, image feature extraction is carried out on whole images as well as facial components to generate features on these six aspects to form a composite feature measures. Each aspect of the composite feature measure is a feature vector of dimension M^i, and denoted by $\mathbf{x}^i = (x_1^i, x_2^i, ..., x_M^i)^T$. The composite feature measure is then represented by $X = (\mathbf{x}^1, \mathbf{x}^2, ..., \mathbf{x}^6)$.

According to user requirements the facial images stored in the system are all frontal images. After investigation of various methods [9, 20], we choose to use facial landmarks together with selected principal component analysis coefficients of face images as feature measures. To reduce the effects of image variations, a normalization process is performed before feature extraction. Feature enhancement of facial features prior to principle component analysis is found to be effective in improving visual similarities of image feature measures. Fitting spline model to facial chin by optimization is very efficient, a few fitting parameters very well reflect the chin shape.

10.1.4 Content-based indexing

Content-based retrieval systems do not necessarily have content-based indexing. *Content-based indexing* is aimed at creating indexes in order to facilitate fast content-based retrieval of multimedia objects in large databases. Generally speaking, an index consists of a collection of entries, one for each data item, containing the key for that item, and a reference pointer which allows immediate access to that item. To accelerate searching of specific data items, most database systems use a tree indexing mechanism. In an index tree the intermediate nodes are abstractions of their child nodes.

The index in traditional databases is quite simple. It operates on attributes, which are of primitive data types such as integer, float and string. For example, to build a binary index tree on the age of people in a database, the first two branches can be created for "age $\geq$ 35" and "age $<$ 35". Here the operation is simple and the meaning is definite and obvious. The situation becomes very complex in content-based indexing, which operates on complex feature measures. Let us take chin of faces as an example. In the face image system in [17], the chin is characterized by the first 16 coefficients of principal component analysis and 5 landmark coordinates. To create index tree, the boundaries among branches are very complex and the meaning of the index tree become vague. We cannot imagine how traditional indexing methods can be applied here.

The three issues of similarity, namely, objects are represented as collections of features, similarity depends on context and frame of reference, and features are characterized by multiple multi-modal feature measures, have posed special requirements on content-based indexing algorithm. The challenges for content-based indexing are:

- The index must be created using all features of an object class, so that visual browsing of the object class is facilitated, and similarity retrieval using similarity measure can be easily implemented.

- The context and frame of reference in similarity evaluation suggest that nodes in index tree show consistency with respect to the context and frame of reference. For example, if, in a level of an index tree, the similarity is evaluated with respect to eye size, the nodes in this level will represent object categories with various eye sizes. This implies that the index tree has similar property as classification tree.

- Multiple multi-modal feature measures should be fused properly to generate index tree so that a valid categorization can be possible. Two issues must be addressed here: first, one measure alone is usually not adequate because of the complexity of objects. Second, to ensure the specified context and frame of reference, care must be taken in feature selection process.

ContIndex method is designed to meet these challenges. The indexing tree is defined by adapting tree classifier concept. A special neural network model has been developed to create nodes using multiple multi-modal feature measures. Algorithms have been developed to support multimedia object archival and retrieval using ContIndex.

10.2 Content-Based Indexing of Multimedia Object

We can see, from the challenges and special requirements discussed in the previous section, that ContIndex share some characteristics with classification tree. Therefore, we adapted classification tree definition for ContIndex. To handle multiple features of object, we introduced horizontal links in ContIndex. Iconic images are also necessary for intermediate nodes. Those iconic images will visually represent the categories of the corresponding nodes and facilitate visual browsing. The final topic of this section is the retrieval algorithm based on ContIndex.

10.2.1 Definition

Let us now give a formal definition to ContIndex.

Assume Σ *is a set of multimedia objects,* $\Omega = \{\omega_1, \omega_2, ..., \omega_m\}$ *represents a set of* m *classes to which* Σ *is to be classified. Assume also that* Ω *satisfies that*

1. $\omega_i \neq \Sigma$ *for all* $i = 1, 2, ..., m$;

2. $\bigcup_{1 \leq i \leq m} \omega_i = \Sigma$;

3. $\omega_i \neq \omega_j$ *for* $i \neq j$;

The indexing process consists of recursive application of mapping $\Sigma \rightarrow \Omega$ *denoted by* $\Gamma = \eta(D, \Omega)$, *where* D *is a set of parameters to define the mapping, and classes in* Ω *represent the categories of multimedia object set* Σ, *and are associated with nodes of the index tree* $\{N_1, N_2, ..., N_m\}$.

In ContIndex tree, number of classes m is kept the same for all intermediate node for manipulation efficiency. In this case, the index tree is a m-tree. The mapping Γ is defined by D and Ω. According to the definition, Ω is a set of classes representing the goal of the mapping. D is related to a set of feature measures used for the mapping. When the mapping is defined, D is represented by a set of *reference feature vectors.* For simplicity, only one feature is used to create a level of the index tree.

Figure 10.4 shows the first three levels of a ContIndex tree. Features selected for creation of these three levels are: $F_{l0} = F^i, F_{l1} = F^j$ and $F_{l2} = F^k$. Nodes are labeled with number of digits which is equal to their level number (the root is at level 0). For example, N_{21} is a node in second level, and is the first child of node N_2. $N_{21}, N_{22}, ...$ are children of node N_2. They are similar with respect to feature $F_{l0} = F^i$, inherit the reference feature vectors of feature F^i, and represent categories $(\omega_{21}, \omega_{22}, ...)$ with respect to feature $F_{l1} = F^j$. New reference feature vectors will be created for them upon the creation of these nodes.

A top-down algorithm for the creation of m-tree ContIndex is summarized as follows:

1. Attach all objects to root and start the indexing process from the root and down to leaf node level.

2. For each node at a level: Select a feature, partition the multimedia objects into m classes by using a set of feature measures, create a node for each class, and generate a reference feature vector(s) of the selected feature and an iconic image for each node.

3. Repeat the second step until each node has at most m descendants.

4. Start from second level, build horizontal links with respect to features which have been already used at the levels above.

10.2.2 Horizontal links

When a user starts browsing the database using this index, he/she sees categories of the objects with respect to feature $F_{l0} = F^i$. The user then selects one node (assume N_2) and down one level. Now he/she arrive at the second level and gets a set of nodes $N_{21}, N_{22}, ..., N_{2m}$. These nodes are associated with object categories with respect to feature $F_{l1} = F^j$. These categories are numerically represented by reference feature vectors and visually represented by icon images. Since these nodes have the same reference feature vectors for feature F_{l0} and different reference feature vectors for feature F_{l1}. Their icon images should appear different with respect to feature F_{l1} and similar with respect to feature F_{l0}. We create another index tree with $F_{l0} = F_j, F_{l1} = F_i$, and switch among index trees whenever necessary. But, this would require too many index trees with every possible selection of features. It would be also very inconvenient to switch among index trees.

The horizontal zooming in ContIndex offers a satisfactory solution to this problem. Horizontal zooming is facilitated by horizontal links between nodes in the same level. Let us have a look at nodes in the second level. Nodes at this level under the same parent N_p, $N_{p1}, N_{p2}, ..., N_{pm}$, represent categories with respect to feature F_{l1} and under the same category with respect to feature F_{l0}. Now suppose user finds N_{pq} is preferable with respect to feature F_{l1} and wants to have a look at categories of feature

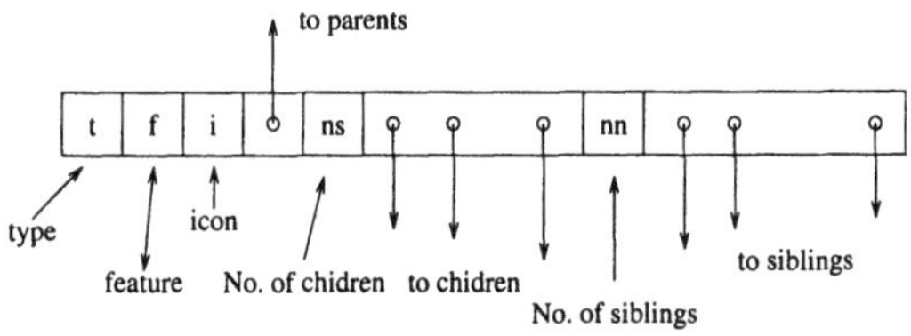

(a) node structure of ContIndex tree

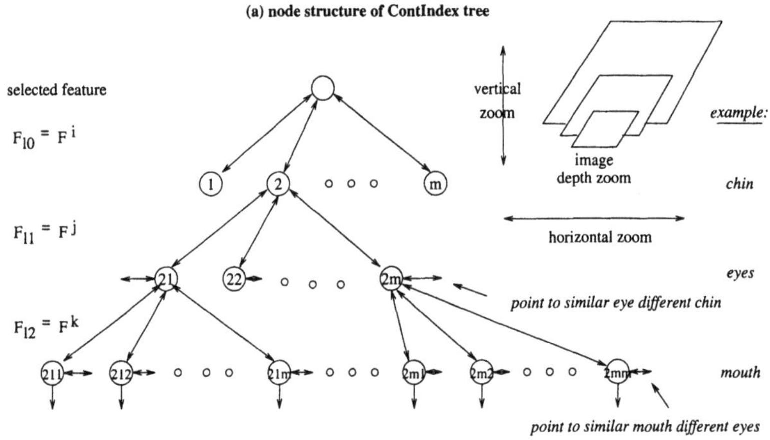

(b) ContIndex facilitates content-based retrieval and visual browsing. It is created by self-organized neural networks on multi-modal feature measures.

Figure 10.4: The structure of content-based index ContIndex. As indicated in the figure, features selected for creation of these three levels of the index tree are: $F_{l0} = F^i, F_{l1} = F^j$ and $F_{l2} = F^k$. Nodes are labeled with the number of digits which is equal to their level number. For example, N_{21} is a node in second level (the root is at level 0). It is the first child of node N_2.

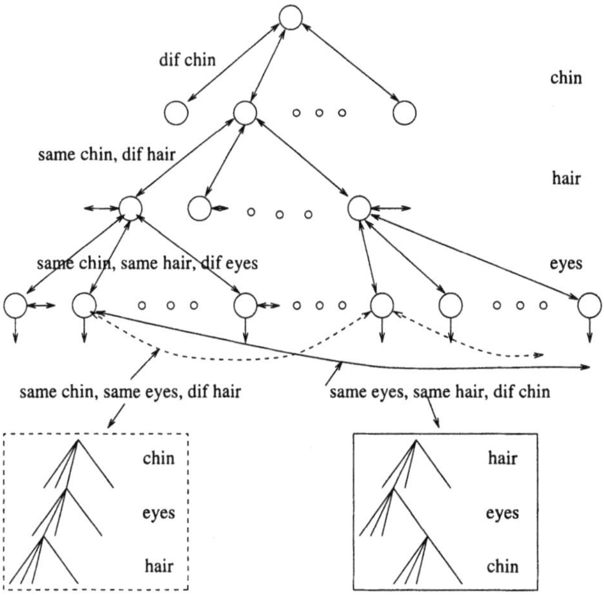

Figure 10.5: ContIndex indexing tree and its horizontal links.

F_{l0}, which are represented by nodes $N_{1q}, N_{2q}, ..., N_{mq}$. To achieve that, we can simply create horizontal links among these nodes. The algorithm is as follows:

Horizontal link creation

- At level l:
  Node labeling convention: $N_{p_1 p_2 ... p_l}$.
  for$(p_l = 1, p_l < m + 1; p_l + +)$
  - for feature F_{l0}, find nodes $N_{1p_2...p_l}, N_{2p_2...p_l}, ...N_{mp_2...p_l}$, which represent categories with respect to feature F_{l0} and are similar with respect to all other features. Make bi-directional horizontal links among them.
  - perform same operation for features $F_{l1}, ...F_{l_{l-1}}$.
- Repeat the above labeling process for all levels.

10.2.3 A practical example

Figure 10.5 is a practical example of ContIndex indexing tree created for a face image database system CAFIIR. In the face image database, each image is described by 6 facial features, namely, hair, eyebrows, eyes, nose, mouth and chin. Feature measures (16 principal components and landmarks) are extracted from the image regions which cover these facial features. The index was created by using one facial feature at each level. Three levels are shown in the figure. At the level three, there are two types of horizontal links. These two types of horizontal links create two virtual indexing trees as shown in boxes.

10.2.4 Iconic images construction

According to the definition, an intermediate node of ContIndex tree is an abstract representation of all its child nodes. ContIndex is content-based, the content of this intermediate node should be a representative of the contents of its child nodes. That is to say that an image (referred to as icon image), a set of feature measure vectors, and interpretation of the content must be created upon creation of an intermediate node. As far as feature measures are concerned, feature measure vectors are computed as centroid of its child nodes. The interpretation is then the name of the category this intermediate node represents.

There are several ways to generate icon image for an intermediate node. One possibility is to average icon images of its child nodes. The icon image obtained this way may be blurred due to averaging. To avoid icon image blurring, we can choose one of its child node which is the nearest to the centroid, and use the icon image of this child node as the icon image of this intermediate node.

Principally, icon image of an intermediate node must show certain characteristics of the category this intermediate node represents. For this reason, in some applications line drawings are used as icon image to illustrate the categories.

10.2.5 Content-based retrieval using ContIndex

One major type of content-based retrieval is that for a given query object find the best matches from a database. The query object can be given by using a sample object, or by descriptive or numerical specification. Suppose now that from a given query object, feature measures can be derived. The retrieval process is then to find the best matches using ContIndex.

Since the criterion used to search the best matches is the similarity measure. This similarity is the weighted summation of similarities on features of the objects. The weights are usually adjustable by users. Therefore, these weights cannot be built into index. ContIndex offers flexibility for the content-based retrieval. The retrieval process is a top-down classification process starting from the root of the tree. At each node, the process chooses from the child nodes one or more nodes which are the nearest to the query object with respect to the feature used for creation of this node in the index creation process. The number of child nodes to be chosen depends on the weight for the feature. A higher weight implies that the feature is more critical, and therefore, less child nodes should be chosen. The retrieval algorithm is as follows:

$$\begin{aligned} sim_l(O^q, O) &= w_{l0} sim_{l0}(F^q_{l0}, F_{l0}) + w_{l1} sim_{l1}(F^q_{l1}, F_{l1}) + ... \quad (10.1) \\ & w_{l0}, w_{l1}, ... = 0 \text{ for all } l0, l1, ... > l \end{aligned}$$

where subscripts $l0, l1, ...$ denote the levels of the tree. For example, F_{l1} denotes the feature used in level $l1$ for index creation, w_{l1} is the weight for the feature F_{l1} in the query. Weights are normalized so that the summation of them equals to 1. Since the retrieval process is top-down. The similarity measure $sim_l()$ stands for similarity at level l. It counts features that have been used at levels above l and level l. Therefore, w_{lx} is set to zero if lx is below l. The procedure for content-based retrieval by ContIndex tree traversal is given as follows:

- Start the search from the root and examine all chosen nodes level by level.
- For all chosen nodes in a level, compute the similarity between the query object and child nodes with respect to the features used at that level and all levels above in index creation process.
- Examine the total weights in the similarity computation. If it is small, more nodes will be chosen. Less nodes will be chosen otherwise.
- Repeat the second and third steps until leaf nodes are reached. The selected leaf nodes will be ranked according to the similarity and presented as the final retrieval result.

Insert and delete operation on ContIndex tree are much simpler than the retrieval operation described above.

10.3 ContIndex Creation by Self-organization Neural Networks

Having discussed the procedure for index tree construction, we need to explain the mapping $\Gamma = \eta(D, \Omega)$ which is used to perform clustering in a self-organization manner based on multi-modal feature measures. As discussed in previous sections, the mapping must be able to generate valid categories using multi-modal feature measures, and nodes created must be spatially self-organized to facilitate visual browsing.

The first issue is crucial because multimedia objects, for example, images, have their visual features according which domain experts categorize them. To be consistent with domain expert, firstly, extracted feature measures should well capture the characteristics of these visual features, and secondly, the clustering algorithm should be able to generate desired categories based on these feature measures.

Visual features are usually complex, and cannot be represented by one simple feature measure. That is to say that multi-modal feature measures are needed for most cases. For example, to classify hand-written characters, one needs to combine several feature measures (Fourier descriptor, critical points, grey image, etc.) to obtain high recognition accuracy [15, 22].

Notice also that feature measures may contain diverse visual information while the similarity used for index creation must have certain context and frame of reference. When we cluster images into categories using these feature measures, the result may not be as anticipated. It is because these feature measures may contain information on other aspects of the image than defined context and frame of references only. For example, Principal Component Analysis (PCA) has been widely used for feature extraction. PCA is defined on a set of images, say eye images, and represents the principal variations of this set of images. These principal variations do not necessarily fully coincide with a context and frame of reference in the index, say, the size of the eyes. Usually, the information of the context and frame of reference is contained in PCA, but is mixed with other information. Therefore, proper "feature selection" (here we use pattern recognition terminology) should be performed before using these feature measures to create index. To accomplish that, we use LEP (Learning based-on Experiences and Perspectives) neural network model to fuse multi-modal feature measures and to self-organize index nodes.

In the following subsections, we will first brief the structure of LEP neural network which perform the mapping, discuss multi-modal feature measure fusion using LEP neural network, and then explain spatial self-organization using Kohonen's self-organization map. The bi-directional learning will be discussed in the last subsection.

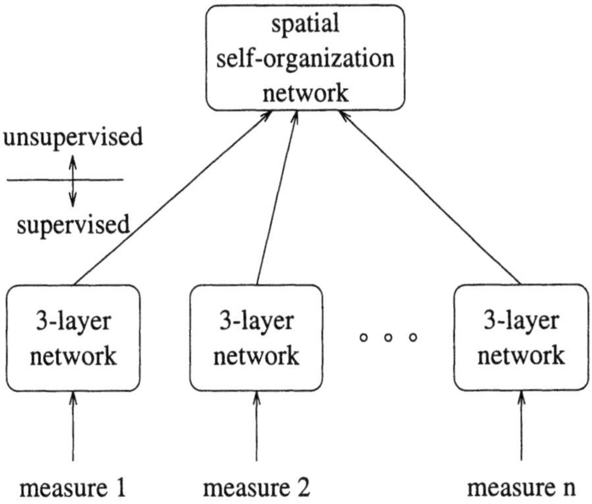

Figure 10.6: LEP (Learning based on Experiences and Perspectives) neural network model for ContIndex index creation.

10.3.1 LEP neural network architecture

The structure of the LEP network model for ContIndex index creation is shown in Figure 10.6. It consists of two macro-layers: feature selection layer (supervised learning) and self-organization layer (unsupervised learning). Feature measures ($F_j^i, j = 1, 2, ...$) are fed into their respective feedforward networks. These networks have the same number of input units as the dimension values of the feature measures. The number of output units of these three networks are the same, which is the number of categories of the training data set. The outputs of the feature selection units of these networks contain information with respect to the desired categories contributed by these measures.

The self-organization macro-layer generates node parameters using the output from feature selection macro-layer. For $m - tree$ ContIndex, the number of output nodes is m. When the application requires certain categories appear in one level of the index tree, the user needs to prepare a training data set, and uses it to train the feature selection macro-layer for the initial set up. The number of classes in the training data set equals to the number of output units of the feature selection network. It can be different from m provided the training data set reflects the desired categories.

10.3.2 Fusion of multi-modal feature measures

Conceptually, properties of an object appear as perspectives. Perspectives of an object depends on viewers, view points, and means of observations. We call that as the first type of perspective. For example, weight, height, photos of a person are first type perspectives of this person; to examine the heart of a patient, images and signals can be obtained by means of microwave resonance imaging, computer tomography, angiography, electrocardiograpy, etc. These images and signals are measures of the heart, and represent first type perspectives of the heart properties. The second type of perspective refers to the way to evaluate the data of the first type perspectives. For example, when measuring the similarity between heart problems based on these images and signals, similarity measures such as distances and correlations should be developed according to the domain experts' knowledge. Each of these similarity measures evaluates the data in a particular way and has a particular interpretation.

On other words, the first type perspectives of objects correspond to multimedia data and multi-modal feature measures, and the second type perspectives address the importance of similarity measures when evaluating the feature measures.

Multiple perspective data are multi-modal. To fuse multi-modal feature measures, feature selection is the first step. We use three layer feedforward networks for feature selection. From the viewpoint of pattern recognition, feature selection is aimed to reduce the feature dimensionality to save the implementation cost and to avoid so-called peaking phenomenon. In the case of data fusion, it is aimed to focus to certain information which is most relevant to specified categories. Let us see PCA for eye images again. What PCA does is just to capture the principal variations in terms of gray scale changes of images. When it is applied to images of eyes, it does not necessarily just contain information used to generate specified eye categories such as eye size. Therefore, to filter out all irrelevant information, we need to perform feature selection on PCA coefficients of eye images. It can be considered as a type of "focus attention".

To demonstrate that three layer feedforward network is suitable to the feature selection for data fusion, let us formally define feature selection [23]. Assume that the feature measure is a n dimensional vector and is written as

$$\mathbf{x} = [x_1, x_2, ..., x_n]^T \tag{10.2}$$

As defined in Section 10.3.1, each $\mathbf{x}$ may belong to one of m possible classes $\omega_1, ..., \omega_m$. It is further assumed that these data are generated by a random process and that the model of the process can be characterized by class-conditional density function $p(\mathbf{x}|\omega_i)$ and a priori class probabilities $p(\omega_i)$. In the case of supervised feature selection here, the optimization is performed over all admissible mappings Θ, which "selectively" map the feature measure onto a new space $(y_1, y_2, ..., y_n)$.

$$J(\Theta_{optimal}) = \max_{\Theta} J\{\Theta(\mathbf{x})\} \tag{10.3}$$

Once Θ is determined, the selected feature vector $\mathbf{y} = [y_1, ..., y_n]^T$ is then given by

$$\mathbf{y} = \Theta(\mathbf{x}) \tag{10.4}$$

The criterion function J for optimization here is defined as probability of mis-recognition and given as

$$e = \int [1 - \max_{i} p(\omega_i|\mathbf{y})]^2 p(\mathbf{y}) d\mathbf{y} \tag{10.5}$$

Fortunately, the error criterion function coincides with the one defined in backpropagation learning for multi-layer feedforward networks [24]. With backpropagation learning algorithm we can find the optimal mapping which is defined by the learned weights of the network.

It has been proven [25] that multi-layered feedforward networks with as few as one hidden layer using arbitrary squashing functions (e.g., logistic, hyperbolic tangent) are capable of approximating any Borel measurable function from one finite dimensional space to another, to any desired degree of accuracy, provided sufficient hidden units are available. Generally speaking, the input-output mapping of such a network is analytic and can represent all continuous mappings. Therefore, we choose to use three layer networks in the feature selection layer.

10.3.3 Spatial self-organization

For visual browsing of databases, spatial organization of nodes are preferable. For example, to view types of eyes with respect to eye size, we prefer all icon images are displayed with the size from largest to smallest on the screen. For this purpose, Self-Organizing Map (SOM) by Kohonen [7] is an effective neural network paradigm for our ContIndex creation. On the other hand, we have to incorporate multiple perspective concept into SOM to guarantee reliable learning.

The second type perspective concepts is implemented here by combining several similarity measures. for example, in the competition among output units for self-organization, the winning unit c is selected based on both a correlation and minimum distance basis [15, 17].

$$\begin{aligned} a_c &= \min_i a_i \\ a_i &= dis(\mathbf{x}, \mathbf{p}_i)/cr^k(\mathbf{x}, \mathbf{w}_i) \\ dis(\mathbf{x}, \mathbf{p}_i) &= [\sum_j (x_j r_{ij} - p_{ij})]^{1/2} \\ cr(\mathbf{x}, \mathbf{w}_i) &= abs(\sum_j x_j w_{ij})/[\sum_j x_j^2 \sum_j w_{ij}^2]^{1/2} \end{aligned} \tag{10.6}$$

where a stands for activation of the output units in the self-organization network. $\mathbf{w}, \mathbf{p}$ are weight vector and template vector, respectively. r_{ij} defines the relative importance of the elements in a feature vector, and $dis(), cr()$ are distance and correlation functions, respectively. k is a parameter to adjust the effect of normalized correlation to the whole similarity measure.

The output units are arranged as a two-dimensional array in the spatial self-organization network in Figure 10.6. The number of output units is m for m-tree index. Suppose there are K input units and L output units in the network. Each input unit is connected to every output unit with a certain synaptic weight $\{w_{kl}, k = 1, 2, ..., K; l = 1, 2, ..., L\}$. For l-th output unit, a template vector $\{p_{kl}, i = 1, 2, ..., K\}$ and a weighting vector for input feature vector to define relative importance of their elements $\{r_{kl}, k = 1, 2, ..., K\}$ are stored. They will be matched against input vectors during learning. Both link weights and template vectors are long-term memory items and are stored as two link weights from input units to output units.

Let $\mathbf{x} = (x_1, x_2, ..., x_K)^T$ be the K-dimensional real input feature vector presented to the input array at time $t = 1, 2, 3, ...$ Then the output units begin to compete with each other. The winning unit c is selected based on both correlation and minimum distance basis defined in equation 10.6.

After a winning unit is selected, all the units within its neighborhood are updated. Let $N_c(t)$ be the neighborhood around unit c at time t. N_c is usually set very wide in the beginning to acquire a rough global order, and then shrink monotonically with time in order to improve the spatial resolution of the map. This procedure is crucial for the topological ordering. The weight vector updating formula is

$$\mathbf{p}_i(t+1) = \begin{cases} \mathbf{p}_i(t) + \alpha(t, d_i)[\mathbf{x} \cdot \mathbf{r}_i - \mathbf{p}_i(t)]a_c\beta(e_c) & \text{if unit } i \text{ is in } N_c(t) \\ \mathbf{p}_i(t) & \text{otherwise} \end{cases} \tag{10.7}$$

where $\alpha(t, d_i)$ is an *adaptation gain* and decreases with time. It is a function of both time t and distance d_i, and usually has the shape of Gaussian function. As d_i becomes large the update becomes smaller.

a_c represent the confidence measure of the winning unit. If a_c is approximately equal to 1 the unit wins with high confidence therefore the template update can be large. $\beta(e_c)$ is a function of experience record e_c, which counts the number of times the unit has won. $\beta(e_c)$ is inversely proportional to the experience record e_c. If a unit has experienced a lot of learning the templates should not vary too much. On the other hand, experience records are attenuated by the so-called forgetting function, which is a simulation of human forgetting phenomena. Forgetting enhances the adaptability of the neural network. The forgetting function takes the form of exponential form $e_c e^{-\gamma t}$.

Similarly, the update of correlation weights is defined as

$$\mathbf{w}_i(t+1) = \begin{cases} \frac{\mathbf{w}_i(t)+\alpha(t,d_i)a_i\beta(e_c)\mathbf{x}(t)}{\|\mathbf{w}_i(t)+\alpha(t)\mathbf{x}(t)\|} & if \;\; i \in N_c(t) \\ \mathbf{w}_i(t) & otherwise \end{cases} \tag{10.8}$$

As a result of competitive learning with a dynamic neighborhood window, the weight vectors (templates) tend to approximate the probability density function of the input vectors in a spatially ordered fashion.

10.3.4 Bi-directional learning on experiences

Multimedia objects in the database represent event/object cases. ContIndex performs abstraction/generalization of these events/objects cases and produces content-based index. Intermediate nodes in the index tree represent categories of cases. They are generalization of cases, and cases are instances of these categories. If, for example, under a category there are similar patients a doctor has been cured, this category represents the experience of this doctor regarding this type of patients. In general, an intermediate node represents a certain concept, which is an abstraction of cases under it. To capture the validity of the concept, for each intermediate node, a record of confidence is maintained. The confidence record of a concept is high if the number of cases supporting it is large. The validity of these concepts is also subject to updating and changes of cases, and consequently must undergo feedforward learning (learning from instances).

On the other hand, concepts must be verified by domain experts. When a domain expert makes use of a concept represented by an intermediate node or a particular event/object case at leaf node level of the index, this concept/case is meant to be successfully verified. Its confidence level should be raised. It is referred to as feedback learning (learning by commitment).

Real world data is spatially and temporally varying. High confidence records for today does not mean much for tomorrow. Therefore, we introduced *forgetting process* to update the confidence record. It also controls the degree of adaptability of the content-based index. The forgetting process can be adjusted by an attenuation factor $\gamma\ (T)$

$$\gamma\ (T)\ =\ e^{-\ \kappa\ T} \tag{10.9}$$

where T is a temporal parameter. It can be the total number of input cases the network has processed since last forgetting process. κ is a small constant used to adjust the degree of forgetting. The forgetting processes are performed periodically.

After a forgetting process, the confidence records of some nodes in the index may become very small. This suggests rare use of those concepts, and they can be discarded from the index tree. The forgetting process further expands adaptability of the index: in the long term, as the environment changes, outdated concepts are erased, and new concepts are developed.

10.4 Experimental Results

The experimental results are given in this section and discussed using face images. A Computer-Aided Facial Image Inference and Retrieval (CAFIIR) system was developed primarily for criminal identification. Each face image was characterized using six features: chin, eyes, hair, eyebrow, nose, and mouth. Retrieval of similar face images is based on the similarity measure of all six features. For visual browsing purpose, we created $9-tree$ ContIndex so that icon images can be displayed with 3×3 array.

The first prototype of CAFIIR was completed on July 1993, when there are only about 150 face images, that are donated by police officers and our colleagues and students. Now the system has been tested against 1000 face images.

When creating an index, features used at levels are interactively selected, as in Figure 10.7. Several indexes can be created for one database. As an example, Figure 10.5 shows an index created using chin, hair, eyes, etc. The horizontal links in this index brings much flexibility to the index. As shown in figure 10.5, at third level, with the help of these two horizontal links, the index can provide virtual views of other two indexes

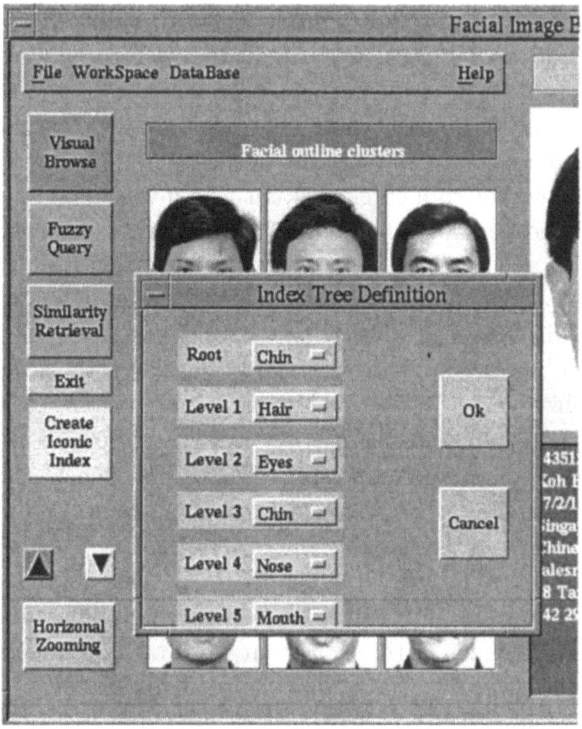

Figure 10.7: Interface for creating indexes interactively. When the button "Create Index" is clicked, a push-down window "Index tree definition" appears. User can then select features for each level of the index. The creation process is activated by clicking at the button "ok".

each of them has different order of these three features for these three levels.

Let us have a look at the creation process of the first level of the index in Figure 10.5 by using LEP neural networks.

By system configuration, we mean to set system parameters so that the system can work properly for an application site. In the case of face retrieval system, assume that the system is installed in a city's police headquarters for criminal identification. There, the police has their own collection of face images, and their own way of categorizing face features. To obtain proper system parameters for face image categories, a set of sample images must be collected and used to train the LEP networks in the system. This is the *configuration phase* of the system. After setting of system parameters, the system is in its *operating phase* and ready to operate.

In CAFIIR, face images are categorized according to six features. Therefore, six sets of parameters must be learned for the LEP network in the configuration phase. These parameter sets will be used to create levels of the index tree. To create the first level of the index tree in Figure 10.5, parameters for chin categories must be invoked.

In our experimental study, the collection of face images are donated by our colleagues and students. Nine chin types were identified in the training data set. They are: pointed, rounded, tapered, squared, bony cheek, short-chin, long-chin, jowls [1]. For computer categorization of face images, landmark points are simi-automatically identified, the face images are then normalized, a "U" shape chin image is extracted for each face image. Principal component analysis (PCA) is then performed on these chin images, and the first 16 components are used as chin feature measures. In the experimental study, landmark coordinates around chin are also considered as one measure.

According to the concepts explained in Section 10.3.2, we have two feature vectors, PCA and landmarks, which are of different models, and are results by looking at the chin from two first type perspectives. The detailed architecture of the LEP network is illustrated in Figure 10.8. The top most layer is a self-organization layer and the other four layers are supervised learning network used to fuse these two feature vectors. There are two separate three-layer feedforward networks for PCA and landmarks, respectively. The fourth layer is used to combine these two feature measures. The network units in these four layers are: (16, 10); (9, 9); (9, 9); and 9. That is: the PCA network has 16 units in the first layer and 9 units in the second and third layer; landmark network has 10 units (5 landmark points) in the first layer and 9 units in the second and third layer. The fourth layer acts as both the output layer for supervised learning network and the input layer for self-organization network. The configuration process is aimed to learn all weights in this four layer network, which will be used to calculate the input to the self-organization network. On other hand, parameters of self-organization network, such as sample vectors of output units, will be learned during indexing process, and stored as node parameters of index tree.

To learn the parameters of supervised learning network, the first three layers are trained independently using PCA and landmark training data sets. In this training process, the weights from the first layer to the second layer, and from the second layer to the third layer are learned. Then, both PCA and landmark data sets are applied simultaneously to train

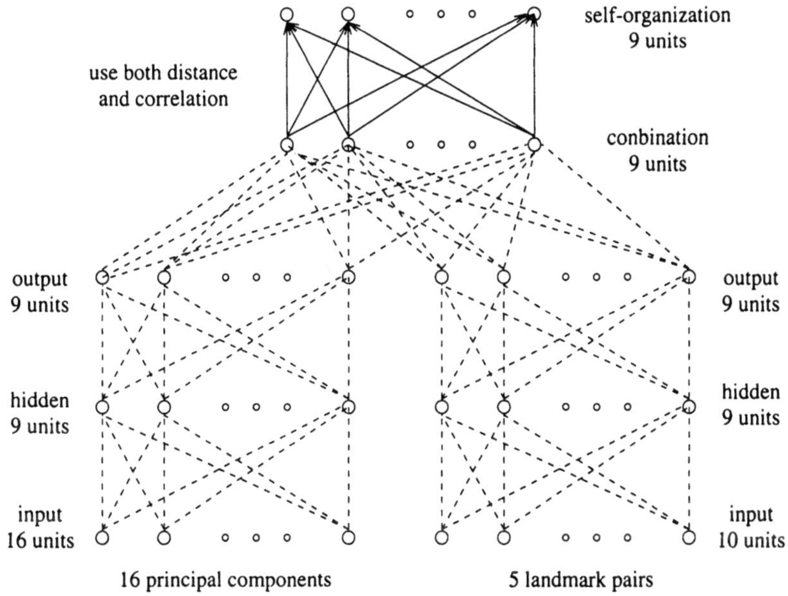

Figure 10.8: Network architecture to create ContIndex in CAFIIR. All weights indicated by dashed lines must be learned in the configuration phase.

the weights from the third layer to the fourth layer. When the training is completed, the weights are saved into a file. These weights will be loaded into the network when an index creation process is stimulated.

Figure 10.9 is a screen dump of a visual browsing. It is at the second level of the index. It can be seen from the panel for "index hierarchy" that the second level is highlighted and that "hair" was used at this level. At the first level, icon image with long chin was selected. This can be also seen from the connection of the first level and the second level in the index tree graph. 9 icon images on the left side display panel represent categories of facial images with respect to hair thickness are shown. The facial hair thickness is arranged in a descending order from bottom-left to top-right. Note also that all these 9 icon images have long chin. This property is inherited from their parent node.

At the second level, if we select an icon image and then click "horizontal zooming" button, images with similar hair and different chin will appear on the display buttons. The horizontal links enable the flexibility of the indexes. The user can browse through the database freely without the limitation of the initial order of features selected to create the index.

The efficiency of ContIndex is similar to conventional index trees since they have the same tree structure. That is, for a L level of $m - tree$, it reduces the number of search operations from m^L to mL. On the other hand, ContIndex support similarity retrieval, to avoid missing of possible similar candidates when the given sample is at the boundaries among tree branches, more than one (k) candidates will be selected for further examination. The total number of search operations in a retrieval will be $m + mk(L - 1)$. For a face image database of 6×10^5, a $9 - tree$ ContIndex has 6 levels. Assuming that, at each level, 4 candidates are selected, then one retrieval needs 189 matching operations. The searching time is reduced by a factor of 3175. Since the number of candidates to be selected at each level depends on the total weights at that level, the searching time will slightly depend on the weight assignment. In practice, one can choose to create several indexes with different sequences of features. To reduce the searching time, the searching algorithm can choose the index with the feature at the first level which has the maximum weight assigned.

ContIndex will not show much improvement for small databases, for example, database of 100 images. In this case, searching the two level tree needs about 45 operations, which is the same order as 100.

Principally, ContIndex has similar dynamic property to conventional index trees. At the time the ContIndex tree is created, the tree is well balanced because of the neural network's self-organization property. Af-

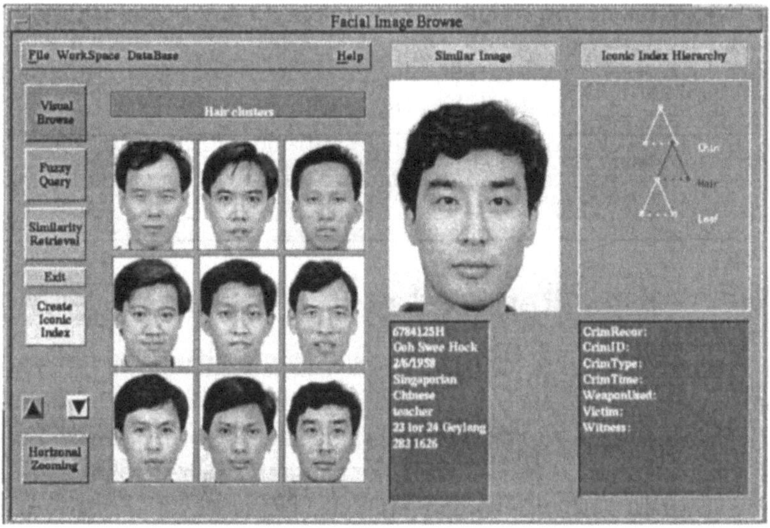

Figure 10.9: Browsing the facial image database. It is now at the second level of ContIndex tree. As shown by the icon image in the display window, face image categories are spatially arranged according to the hair feature with respect to thickness: from bottom-left to top-right the hair thickness is in a descending order. The user can select any category by clicking at the icon image and then down-wards arrow to go down one level. Horizontal zooming is carried out by selection of icon image and clicking at the horizontal zooming button.

ter many insertions and deletions, the tree may tend to be un-balanced. Therefore, after certain period, the indexes need to be re-built.

Thinking about the number of B-tree indexes we must create for the six facial features, each of them are characterized by 16-dimension feature vectors in our experiment. With so many indexes, the retrieval cannot be efficient and balancing among indexes with respect to given weights are also very tedious.

As far as retrieval accuracy concerned, it is solely dependent on the feature measures extracted, and similarity function used in the retrieval. The indexing method presented here does not affect the retrieval accuracy. Evaluation of content-based retrieval is a critical issue in developing a good content-based retrieval engine.

10.5 Conclusion and Remarks

The content-based indexing ContIndex presented in this chapter has some salient features. It can handle multiple features of multimedia objects while offering retrieval flexibility. Using self-organization neural networks, ContIndex can create index by fusing multi-modal feature measures with desired context and frame of references. More work is needed to improve its dynamic property.

10.6 Visual Retrieval of Facial Images

There are two types of visual retrieval. One is visual browsing. By using iconic index tree the user can browse through the entire collection of the image data in three (vertical, horizontal, and depth) directions. The other is similarity retrieval, with which one submits either a composed image or a digitized photo as a sample, and then searches for the most similar facial images. The results are facial images, personal data, and crime list of the suspects.

10.6.1 Facial composition

Facial composition subsystem is aimed at deriving a desired facial image by changing some facial components, and warping related parts of the underlying face image. The subsystem basically comprises of the facial component template generation module and the photo-fitting module. A facial component database is maintained by the facial component template generation module to provide categorized images of eyes, eyebrows, noses, and mouths. Each facial component is bounded by a contour. When capturing a component from a facial image, a contour template is moved to the right position, scaled and adjusted to fit the component. The captured component is then stored in the facial component database.

For the photo-fitting module, various facial components are selected from the facial component database to fit into a facial image. When a facial template image is first selected, it is modeled by a 2-D wireframe. As compared to the selected facial components the original facial components of the template face are of different sizes, shapes and orientations. Hence, when fitting a new facial component onto the template, the nodes of the wireframe will be moved to accommodate the facial components. Corresponding to the movement of the wireframe, the underlying image will be warped to fit the new positions of the wireframe nodes. Finally, the edges where the new facial components meet the template image are blended

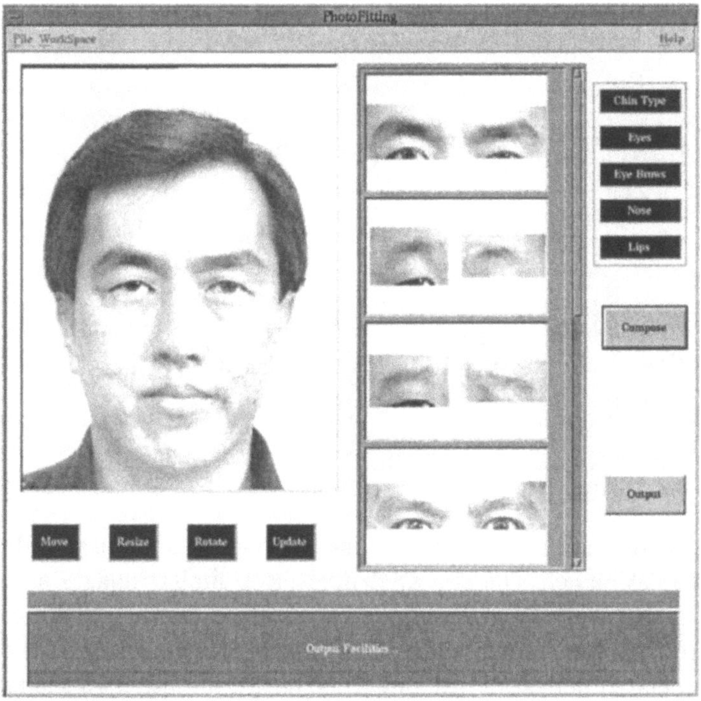

Figure 10.10: Facial image composition by selecting desired facial components

together. Two images with different eyes, nose, and month generated by the facial composition subsystem are shown in Figure 10.10.

10.6.2 Browsing and similarity retrieval

As we have already seen in the index tree construction process, the similarity measure is extensively used on various feature aspects. Therefore the index tree traversal is based on similarity measures, and similarity retrieval is implemented using index tree traversal. The index tree can be regarded as a decision tree. When a sample facial image is presented, the similarity retrieval behaves in the same way as pattern classification via a decision tree. It follows the tree down to the leave nodes. At each level the decision is made by similarity measure. Suppose we use distance as the similarity measure, the node in the next level is selected if $d(\mathbf{x}, \mathbf{t}^i) = \min_j d(\mathbf{x}, \mathbf{t}^j)$, where $\mathbf{x}$ is sample image, and $\mathbf{t}^j$ is the template

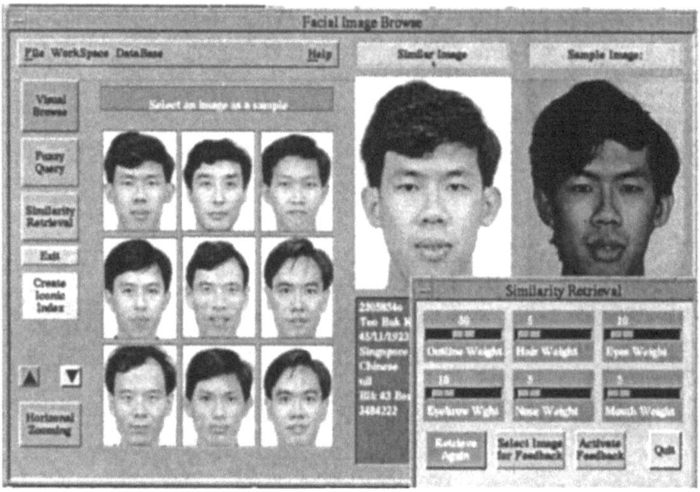

Figure 10.11: Similarity retrieval. The sample image is displayed on the right display panel. The retrieved nine most similar images are in left display panel. Anyone of them can be displayed on the middle panel to compare with the sample image after placing the cursor on it and click. The associated person record and crime record are listed on the two text panels beneath the image. Parameter panel for weight adjustment and feedback is put on the bottom right part, covering part of the text panel.

of the j-th node. At the leaf node level, all leave nodes similar to the sample image will be selected. A typical similarity retrieval example is shown in Figure 10.11. The similarity retrieval was able to find the image of the same person even if the sample image was taken three months later, with noticeable differences, such as in hair, appearing in these two images. Other eight retrieved images shown in the left side display panel are ordered are ordered in descending degree of similarity.

To gain flexibility, we created a parameter panel shown at the right bottom of the figure. The parameter panel provides two functions: The first one is to adjust relative weights of six feature aspects and activate the query again. For example, if you expect hair changes of a person to be frequent, you can put small weight to hair feature aspect. The other function is query feedback. The user can choose from the current query result one or more images which he/she regards as having the most resemblance to the desired image and activate the feedback process. This feedback mechanism can be used to refine the query results until a satisfactory set of images is returned. This will be discussed in greater detail in Section 10.5.

Visual query of a facial image database can also be achieved by visually browsing through the database via the interactive index tree traversal. The system presents the user with the root of the index tree by displaying the icons of its descendants. At a node of the index tree the user chooses browsing directions: up, down, left, and right. Going up is implemented via a pointer to its parent node, while moving down is accomplished by interactively selecting a specific descendant icon. The selected icon is then considered a current node, and its children are displayed. Horizontal browsing should be done by selecting a feature aspect of interests. Hence, a facial image is first selected before selecting the eye aspect link. *(First, the image is selected, then the eye aspect link from that image is selected.)* It will show you the images with different eyes but with all other features remain the same. Zooming in and out can be done to select images with different resolution. This can only be done at leaf node level. All non-leaf nodes do not have multi-resolution icon images.

10.7 Descriptive Queries

Quite often, descriptive queries are preferable. With CAFIIR one can retrieve images by fuzzy descriptions or free text descriptions.

10.7.1 Fuzzy retrieval of facial images

Fuzzy retrieval of CAFIIR consists of two parts: fuzzy query preprocessing and fuzzy query processing. The preprocessing tries to recover fuzzy membership functions from user defined fuzzy queries. The query processing is then applied to search the database to find the best matches based on the fuzzy similarity measures. A diagram of fuzzy query processing is shown in Figure 10.12.

Fuzzy query definitions are subjective. That is to say that different persons could have different views for the same object. For example, a big eye from a small person's point of view can be just of normal size to a large person. To deal with this context-sensitive query definition, a special context model is formed. When a user is logged in, a context model for him/her is automatically loaded. The context model can be also selected by a user. In the case, a fuzzy query is formed by someone who is not the user. After mapping by context model, fuzzy queries are considered to be uniform.

In the fuzzy space, coordinates represent fuzzy subsets. The coordinate value represents the membership value. When fuzzy queries are defined by the user, the truth value of the definition and the membership function value for fuzzy subsets are mixed together. Before going to similarity calculation, a process to extract truth value from fuzzy definition is performed.

We know that the difficulty of fuzzy query processing is not only due to its fuzziness, but also due to the incompleteness of the fuzzy query. When user defines the query, he just specifies what he/she knows, and leaves unknown terms unspecified. Therefore, unspecified terms are not of zero value although sometimes zero values are used to fill those blanks. To deal with this incompleteness, let us consider the problem of fuzzy query processing in fuzzy space.

After feature extraction, we have feature vectors written as $\mathbf{x}^i = (x_1^i, x_2^i, ..., x_{M_i}^i)^T$, where i stands for i-th feature aspect, M_i is the dimension of i-th feature vector.

As a result of imprecision and vagueness of feature descriptions in facial images, we have designed a number of fuzzy sets for each feature aspect as fuzzy descriptions. For example, we have nine fuzzy subsets conceptually representing chin types: *tapered, oblong, short oval, rounded, long tapered, long oblong, short oblong, short rounded, long rounded.* These fuzzy sets are defined over the multi-dimensional (M_0) universe $\mathbf{x}^0 = (x_1^0, x_2^0, ..., x_{M_0}^0)$. The membership function for fuzzy set B_j^i, where i denotes feature aspect (here the number of feature aspect is 6) and j denotes the fuzzy subset for a feature aspect, takes following form:

$$m_{B_j^i}(\mathbf{x}) = e^{-(\mathbf{x}-\mathbf{u}_j^i)^T \Sigma_j^i (\mathbf{x}-\mathbf{u}_j^i)} \tag{10.10}$$

where $\mathbf{u}$ is the central point of the membership function in the multi-dimensional feature space. There is a linguistic meaning for the fuzzy subset "approximately $\mathbf{u}$". Σ is the covariance matrix of all data points falling into the fuzzy subset.

We know that the fuzzy membership function $B_j^i, j = 1, ..., M_i, i = 1, ..., 6$ is a multidimensional (M_i) vector array. Each fuzzy membership function vector $B_j^i, j = 1, ..., M_i$ defines a *fuzzy space* for i-th feature aspect. Here, the fuzzy space corresponds to the *feature space* which is defined by the feature vector $\mathbf{x}^i$. Fuzzification maps points from feature space to fuzzy space, while defuzzification maps points from fuzzy space to feature space.

We know that fuzzy queries are defined in fuzzy space, while feature measures of images are in feature space. When processing fuzzy query, if we can convert fuzzy queries from fuzzy space to feature space, we

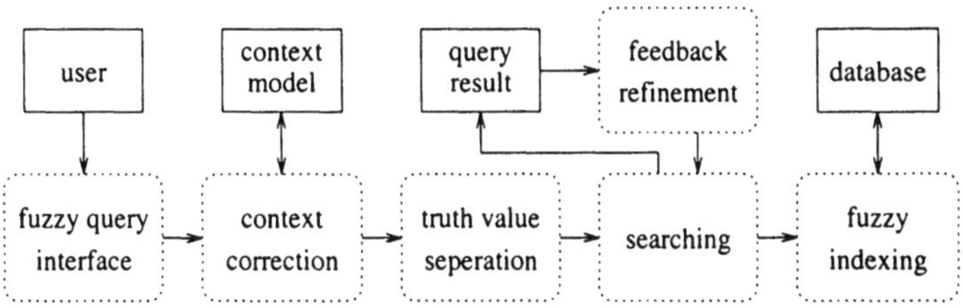

Figure 10.12: A flowchart of fuzzy query processing

can then directly invoke the similarity retrieval technique for query processing. Unfortunately, this is not possible. Fuzzy queries are fuzzy and incomplete. Usually, a user-defined fuzzy query does not provide enough information to locate a point in fuzzy space, and for some feature aspects, no information is provided at all. Both fuzzy space and feature space are multi-dimensional. Defuzzification can map points in fuzzy space to point in feature space when those points in fuzzy space are completely specified. It is obvious here that defuzzification cannot help. When a fuzzy query is incompletely defined, it can be represented by a hypercube in fuzzy space. Let us consider, for example, a fuzzy space of hair, where there are three fuzzy subsets: thin, normal and thick. When the user says a person's hair is thin with a certainty of 0.5, this fuzzy query can be represented as a plane in this 3-dimensional fuzzy space.

An alternative way for fuzzy query processing is to map image feature measures from feature space to fuzzy space. This can be easily done by fuzzification. After fuzzification, images in the database are represented as points. Now we can find the possible solution by evaluating the distance between the points representing images in the database and the hypercube representing the fuzzy query. To simplify the fuzzy processing, let us now use *fuzzy vector* to represent a point in fuzzy space. The fuzzy query is also represented as the fuzzy vector by leaving out those undefined fuzzy subsets. By doing so the similarity between a fuzzy query and an image data can be computed so that images close to the query definition can be retrieved.

Unfortunately, fuzzy space is not orthogonal, ordinary correlation and distance measures cannot be used as similarity measures. Previous work on fuzzy similarity measures and fuzzy retrieval do not provide us with any solution. We have proposed a fuzzy similarity measure, which is the so-called *fuzzy space distance* between fuzzy query vector

$Q_j, j = 1, 2, ..., M_i$ and fuzzy image vector $B_j, j = 1, 2, ..., M_i$, where Q_j, B_j are fuzzy subsets, and are in the same fuzzy space.

$$dis(Q, B) = \sum_j |m_{Q_j}(x) - m_{B_j}(x)| \sum_{k \geq j} sim(Q_j, B_k) |m_{Q_k}(x) - m_{B_k}(x)| \quad (10.11)$$

where $sim(Q_j, B_k)$ is defined as

$$sim(Q_j, B_k) = card(Q_j \cap B_k) / card(Q_j \cup B_k) \quad (10.12)$$

The cardinality of a fuzzy set $card(Q)$ is define as

$$card(Q) = \int m_Q(x) dx \qquad or \qquad card(Q) = \sum_x m_Q(x) \quad (10.13)$$

The fuzzy query processing produces a set of images which best fit the query definition, and arranged in a descending order with respect to their fuzzy similarity measures. The fuzzy processing is performed based on the fuzzy iconic index, which is created by the iconic indexing algorithm discussed in previous section. When the collection of images is very large, and the fuzzy query is incomplete, the query processing can only bring the user to an intermediate node of the index tree. The user can browse down the tree to find the right image. Feedback is also possible here to refine the query. Figure 10.13shows the fuzzy retrieval of images with *round, maybe short round chin* and *normal, maybe thin hair.*

10.7.2 Free text retrieval

Quite often, people are identified by their special features, such as moles, scars. Special facial features are very difficult to be easily described in a structured way, and users are usually not familiar with the terminologies or codes used to describe the special features. We let the user describe the special features of faces using one or more sentences in (relatively) free format.

To index the special features and the crime record based on the text description, we adopted the *free text retrieval* technique developed in. Every word in the text is checked against a stop word list. The word is eliminated if it is in the stop word list. The stop word list consists of the common used words, such as *the, a,* which bare little semantic significance within the context. Notice here, words such as on, in, near are essential to represent the location of special features, and therefore, cannot be included in the stop word list. The remaining words are then stemmed using Porter's stemming algorithm to remove the word variants.

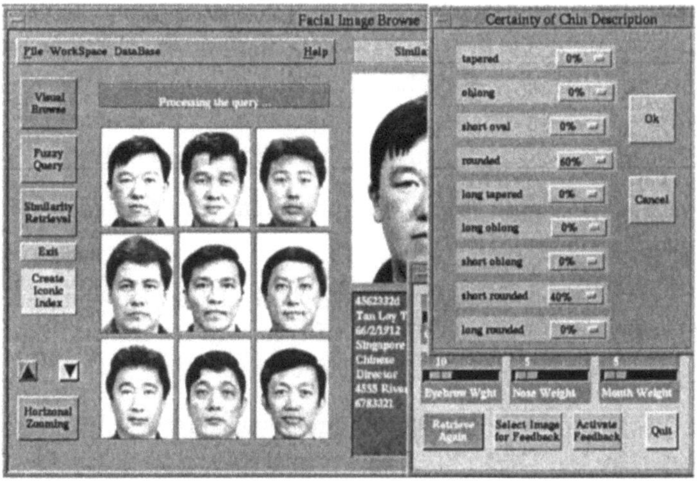

Figure 10.13: Fuzzy retrieval of images: round chin (0.8), short round chin (0.4), normal hair (0.8), thin hair (0.6). The value inside the brackets are truth values.

Under this algorithm, words *face, facial, facing* would be reduced to the word *fac*. This will reduce the total number of distinct terms in the index, and increase the effectiveness of the retrieval because these similar words generally have similar meanings and can be identified by a single stemmed word. Stemmed words are indexed using an inverted file.

In the retrieval phase, the user is asked to submit a query in a free format. This means the query can be a sentence, a short paragraph, or a list of keywords and/or phrases. The defined query is then subjected to the same processing used for indexing. After initial search, few face records or crime records which are among the best matches are presented to the user. At this stage, the user can modify his query and submit again, or just select a few facial image or crime records, the system will perform feedback process until the user is satisfied with the results.

10.8 Further Improvement of Queries

10.8.1 Feedback for query refinement

By feedback function, the user can select from current query result, one or several images he/she thinks are most closest to the desired one. Feedback function then finds the information from the selected images, and refines the query. Our feedback method assumes that feedback images are selected in a sequence that the most desirable one is selected first, and that the selection will be based on the most similar features among those selected images. Suppose N images have been selected, the feature vectors for feedback are computed using following procedures:

1. With a predefined threshold, find similar feature aspects among N images,
2. For the rest of feature aspects, check if they are similar among $N-1, N-2$, selected images. If it is not, use the first image as a representative for the feature aspect.
3. Find the center of the selected images with respect to those similar aspects,
4. Perform similarity search using the computed feature vectors.

10.8.2 Combined query

The combined query is accomplished using the following equation:

$$S(\mathbf{t}, \mathbf{p}) = \prod_i s_{exact}(\mathbf{t}_i, \mathbf{p}_i) \sum_j s_{sim}(\mathbf{t}_j, \mathbf{p}_i) w_j \tag{10.14}$$

where $s_{exact}()$ is the exact match between template $\mathbf{t}$ and the stored pattern $\mathbf{p}$. It takes the value of either 0 or 1. Any mismatch between these feature aspects will reject the hypothesis. $s_{sim}()$ is the similarity measure between feature aspects which does not require an exact match. The overall similarity measure is the weighted summation of similarity measures of those individual feature aspects. The work to combine a selected number of retrieval methods to form a combined query is now in progress.

10.9 Implementation and Concluding Remarks

The system has been implemented using C programming language in an X Window environment with Motif widget set. It can run on workstations with X Window environment and Motif libraries. dbVista, a network database, was used for the prototype development owing to the availability of source code. Due to legal constraints, no photographs of actual criminals were included in the prototype system. Instead, the system has been tested using about 200 facial images donated by police officers and KRDL staff. Further testing is being conducted using 2000 images.

Multimedia database is a new and challenging research area. We have presented here a computer-aided facial image inference and retrieval system CAFIIR. As an example of multimedia database, we have shown a complex feature-based index mechanism, iconic index, and 4 special retrieval methods for image data. We believe that these techniques are general enough to be applied to other image databases. However, we also note that it is important that images are of sufficient quality in order to achieve consistent results in image content-based retrieval.

References

1. Y. H. Ang, "Enhanced Primal Sketch Face Recognition", Workshop on Looking At People: Recognition and Interpretation of Human Action, 13th International Joint Conference on Artificial Intelligent, Chambery, France, 1993
2. J. Bach, S. Paul, R. Jain, "An Interactive Image Management System for Face Information Retrieval", IEEE Trans. on Knowledge and Data Engineering, Special Section on Multimedia Information Systems, 1993
3. V. Bruce, M. Burton, "Processing Images of Faces", Ablex Publishing, Norwood, New Jersey, 1992
4. I. Craw, P. Cameron, "Coding Faces for Recognition", 13th International Conference on Artificial Intelligence, Chambery Savoie France, 1993
5. W. I. Grosky, R. Mehrota, "Index-based Object Recognition In Pictorial Data Management", CVGIP, Vol. 52, pp. 416-436, 1990
6. A. Gupta, T. E. Weymouth, R. Jain, "An Extended Object-Oriented Data Model for Large Image Bases", Proc. Second Symposium on Large Spatial Databases, Zurich, Switzerland, 1991
7. T. Kohonen, "The Self-Organizing Map", Proc. IEEE, Vol. 78, pp. 1464-1480, 1990
8. J. J. Lim, "Free Text Databases", Technical Report, Institute of Systems Science, National University of Singapore, 1992
9. A. Pentland, "Eigenface for Recognition", J. of Cognitive Neuroscience, Vol. 3, pp. 59-70, 1991
10. M. F. Porter, "An Algorithm for Suffix Stripping", Program, Vol. 14, pp. 130-137, 1980
11. A. Ralescu, H. Iwamoto, "Reading Faces: A Fuzzy Logic Approach to Representation, Recognition and Description of Facial Expressions", 13th International Conference on Artificial Intelligence, Chambery Savoie France, 1993
12. A. Tversky, "Features of Similarity", Psychological Review, Vol. 84, pp. 327-352, 1977
13. G. Wolberg, "Digital Image Warping", IEEE Computer Society Press, Los Alamitos, 1990

14. J. K. Wu, "Knowledge-based Pictorial Systems", Journal of China Institute of Communications, Vol. 9, No. 4, pp. 74-80, 1988

15. J. K. Wu, "Neural Networks and Simulation", Marcel Dekker, New York, 1994

16. J. K. Wu, Y. H. Ang, C. P. Lam, Moorthy K, A. D. Narasimhalu, "Facial Image Retrieval, Identification, and Inference System", Proceedings of ACM Multimedia, Anaheim, USA, 1993

17. J. K. Wu, Y. H. Ang, C. P. Lam, H. H. Loh, A. D. Narasimhalu, "Inference and Retrieval of Facial Images", ACM Multimedia Journal, Vol. 2, No. 1, pp. 1-14, 1994

18. J. K. Wu, T. Chen, L. Yang, "A Knowledge-based Image Database System (ISDBS)", Science in China, Vol. 34, No. 1, pp. 87-93, 1990

19. J. K. Wu, F. Gao, P. Yang, "Model-based 3-D Object Recognition", Proc. Second International Conference on Automation, Robotics and Computer Vision, Singapore, 1992

20. A. L. Yuile, "Deformable Templates for Face Recognition", J. of Cognitive Neuroscience, Vol. 3, pp. 59-70, 1991

21. L. Zadeh, "Similarity Relation and Fuzzy Ordering", Information Science, Vol. 3, pp. 177-206, 1970

22. C. Y. Suen, C. Nadal, R. Legault, T. A. Mai, L. Lam, "Computer Recognition of Unconstrained Handwritten Numerals", Proc. IEEE, Vol. 80, pp. 1162-1180, 1992

23. P. A. Devijver, J. Kittler, "Pattern Recognition: A Statistical Approach", Prentice Hall, Englewood Cliffs, NJ, 1982

24. J. L. McClelland, D. E. Rumelhart, "Explorations in Parallel Distributed Processing", MIT press, Cambridge, Massachusetts, 1986

25. K. Hornk, M. Stinchocombe and H. White, "Multi-Layer Feedforward Networks Are Universal Approximators", Neural Networks, Vol. 2, pp. 359-366, 1989

Chapter 11

System for Trademark Archival and Retrieval

With the ever increasing number of registered trademarks, the task of trademark office is becoming increasingly difficult to ensure the uniqueness of all trademarks registered. Trademarks are complex patterns consisting of various image and text patterns, called *device mark* and *word-in-mark* respectively. Due to the diversity and complexity of image patterns occurring in trademarks and multi-lingual word-in-mark, there is no successful computerized operational trademark registration system. In this chapter, we will discuss key technical issues: multiple feature extraction methods to capture the shape, similarity of multi-lingual word-in-mark, matching device mark interpretation using fuzzy thesaurus, and fusion of multiple feature measures for conflict trademark retrieval. A prototype System for Trademark Archival and Registration (STAR) will be briefly presented.

Trademarks can be as simple as consisting of a few characters and as complex as having both text and image of certain complexity. Some trademark image design is influenced by modern art and hence the images are near impossible for description. Retrieval of trademarks using associated text description would not work. Due to diversity and complexity of trademark images, it is very difficult to capture its visual properties such as shape, structure and complexity. Multiple and sophisticated feature extraction methods should be developed. Trademark protection is world wide and the words in the trademarks are multi-lingual. This increases the difficulty of searching conflicting trademarks in a large database.

Due to technical difficulties, there is little work done on trademark registration system. Because of the uniqueness of trademark retrieval, the

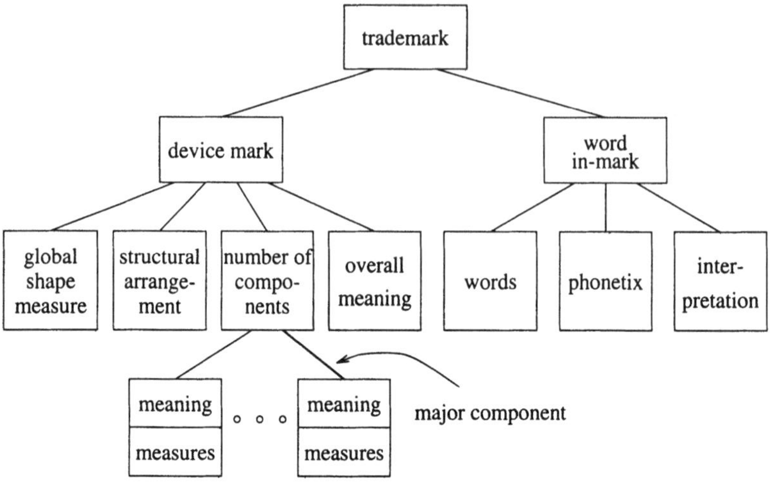

Figure 11.1: Structural Representation of Trademarks

above mentioned image database techniques cannot apply. Here we will discuss the trademark retrieval problem by using a set of real trademarks. These include: a special similarity measures for multi-lingual word-in-mark, multiple feature extraction methods, fuzzy thesaurus for matching concepts, and a combined retrieval strategy. The details of some of these techniques can be found in [5].

11.1 Representation of Trademarks

The technical difficulties in implementing automated search of trademarks are the following: an unlimited variety of symbolic patterns, multi-lingual words, unlimited abbreviations, styled characters, importance of meaning of the words (rather than appearance), abstract graphics. All these variations can occur singly or in any combination of the above. We use structural classification of trademarks as shown in Figure 11.1.

Trademarks are represented as structural patterns consisting of word-in-mark and device mark. The word-in-mark is text, and the device mark is graphic or image. The structural classification can be illustrated by 12 trademark images of airline companies shown in Figure 11.2. Trademark image "INTERFLUG" (3,2) has word-in-mark only. Trademark images (1,1), (1,2), (1,3), (3,3), and (4,1) have device mark only. Image (4,2) can be considered as device mark, as character "M" is not just a character but has graphics. It looks like a crown with a potential for conflict with

Figure 11.2: Trademarks of some Airline Companies. We use row and column number to label these trademark images. For example, Finnair will be labeled as (1,3) image.

trademark (1,2). Trademark images (2,1), (3,1) have both word-in-mark and device mark.

According to trademark registration rules, word-in-mark similarity will be considered in three aspects: word-in-mark text, phonetics, and interpretation. The device mark is either a graphic or an image object. Styled characters are also considered as graphics, such as "M" in image (4,2) in Figure 11.2. Most device marks consist of several components. To describe their shape or texture, we need to separate them by segmentation process.

The description of a graphic or image device involves the shape/texture description of components and the spatial relationship between components. For example, trademark image (3,3) in Figure 11.2 has two components. The component "circle" contains the component "leaf". Or in the other words, the components "leaf" is within the component "circle". In the device mark of trademark image (3,1) in Figure 11.2, there are four components. The spatial relationships among these four components can be described in many ways. To avoid the complexity of spatial relationship description in the retrieval, we choose to describe device mark structures by *outline/background shape* and *component grouping*. This will be discussed further in the next section.

Most device marks of trademarks carry particular meaning. For example, image (4,1) is an eagle. When searching for similar trademarks, the meaning of device marks is weighted quite high. For example, both image (1,2) and (4,2) in Figure 11.2 have the meaning "crown". They are similar in meaning even though they are totally different as far as structure and shape are concerned. Of course, structure and shape are also important when computing the similarity. In case the device mark does not have a particular meaning, then structure, shape, and texture measures are the only factors used to evaluate the similarity value. This is true, for example, for the trademark shown in (3,1) of Figure 11.2.

11.2 Segmentation of Trademarks

Segmentation of trademark is the first step for trademark archival. At this step, the user needs to enter the trademark particulars (owner, date of application, etc.), enter word-in-mark and identify major graphic component. Since the nature of trademark images is very complex and lacks any commonality, fully automatic segmentation is almost impossible. Hence, we have adopted a semi-automatic and interactive segmentation.

A partial automatic segmentation is performed by labeling the components using color segmentation technique [8], and the result is presented to the user, through an interactive user interface. The results of such a segmentation are presented in different colors for different components for easy identification (or grouping) by the user. The user-interface facilitates grouping of one or more components together. Once a component or a group of components is selected by the user, they are extracted and highlighted. The image feature measures are then computed.

Figure 11.3 shows the interface panel of segmentation module. On the left side of the window there are function buttons for loading trademark image, filling in trademark particulars, etc. User can choose to activate button "Word-In-Mark", "Device Mark", or "Composite Mark" depending on the type of the trademark loaded. A trademark image loaded will be displayed in the center (on the right side of the function buttons). If the word-in-mark is in English, its phonetics will be derived automatically, otherwise user needs to type in phonetics. The device mark panel appears when either "Device Mark" or "Composite Mark" button is activated. The buttons on the first row are used to specify certain aspects of the device mark: Component grouping captures the structural information of the device mark. This indicates spatial arrangement of the components of trademark (e.g.,triangular, rectangular, circular, star, concentric, parallel, symmetric). The meaning of a component is contained in a small dictionary, on which a fuzzy thesaurus is built. Optionally, a component can be designated as major (important) component, when there are more than one components. Buttons in the second row provide functions to select components and compute feature measures. In case of composite trademarks like the one shown in figure 11.3, the device mark is too small for feature extraction. In such cases full sized (or an enlarged version) image will be loaded by activating the "Aux-Image" button.

11.2.1 Color segmentation

In color trademark images, the components of device mark are in different colors. Color segmentation is the only way to segment components of device mark. Color segmentation partitions 3-D color space. It is referred to as color coding [8] and extensively used in printing industry. A block diagram of color segmentation is shown in Figure 11.4. The input color trademark images are represented as RGB primary colors images. The statistics of the image data in 3-D color space are then calculated. A sophisticated clustering algorithm in color space has been designed to find right color classes. Distance measures in classification are computed in the uniform color space to guarantee visual quality of segmented images. During pixel-wise classification we designed an algorithm which takes into account both cluster population and image data spatial correlation, so as to reduce noises in segmented images. Compensation of illuminating non-uniformity is also in consideration.

Clustering in 3-D color space

Color image pixels can be regarded as points in a 3-D color space. As the number of components of a device mark is small and each component is represented by one color, and the optical reflection characteristics of each component tends to be consistent. Thus, the color of each component appears as one cluster in the color space. Color segmentation is used to first find out these clusters and then to assign a code to each of these

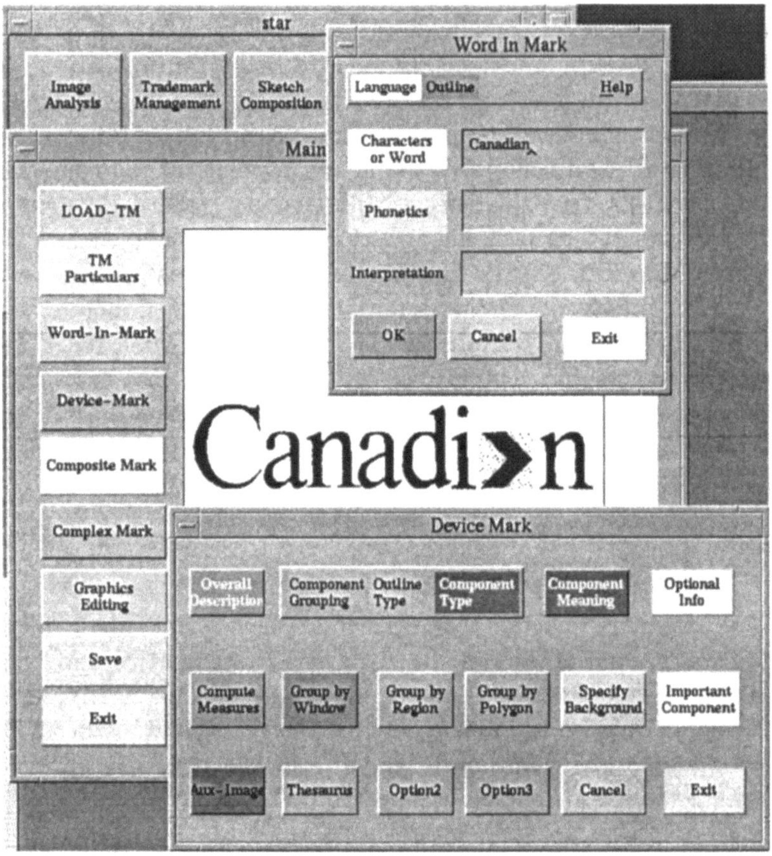

Figure 11.3: Segmentation of Trademark Images.

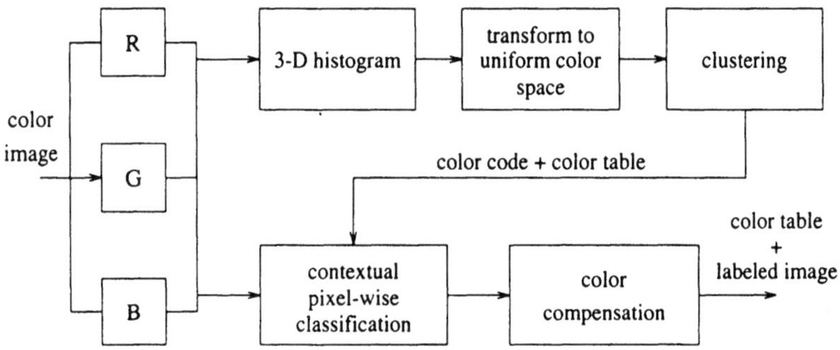

Figure 11.4: Block Schematic of Color Segmentation.

clusters.

Unfortunately, for a given set of color images, there is not enough information about the number and population of clusters and , training data is usually not available. Therefore, we make the assumption that each color cluster has normal distribution with one peak value and there is a sufficient distance between every two color clusters. In this case, clustering can be simplified as a method for finding peaks and estimating distribution parameters.

The distance measure is of importance in clustering. The measure should be consistent with the visual resolution and should also be uniform in all directions in the entire color space. We used CIE 1976 uniform color system (L^*, u^*, v^*). The distance (color difference) can be calculated by an Euclidian distance:

$$d(L^*, u^*, v^*) = [\Delta L^* + \Delta u^* + \Delta v^*]^2 \tag{11.1}$$

Color code assignment of image data

To assign each pixel of image with color code is to classify the pixels one by one. We will describe in detail two major problems in reducing the classification error: design of classification method, and utilization of spatial information.

Design of classification method

We have obtained the number of classes, the coordinates of center of each class, and corresponding amplitude value through cluster analysis in color space. Bayes classifier is not applicable because covariance matrices are not available. We can use minimum distance classifier. Minimum distance classifier makes implicit assumption that all classes have the same population. It is very often that within an image difference of number of pixels for colors is quite large. In this case, minimum distance classifier will result in large classification errors. Hence, we use a classifier which takes account of population differences in the color space. Suppose we have N samples to classify into M clusters: $\omega_1, \omega_2, ...,$ each cluster is Gaussian distributed $N(m_i, \sigma_i)$, contains N_i samples. All clusters have the same covariance matrix. With the assumption $N_i >> 1$, we have the optimal decision rule:

$$d(\mathbf{x}, \mathbf{m}_j) - 2log[p(\omega_j)] = \min_i \{d(\mathbf{x}, \mathbf{m}_i) - 2log[p(\omega_i)]\} \tag{11.2}$$

where $d()$ is the Euclidian distance from the sample to the center of class ω_i calculated in the uniform color space. The ratio of the population of class ω_i to the total samples, N_i/N can be calculated by the ratio of corresponding amplitude value to the total values obtained by clustering in 3-D color space.

Use of spatial correlation information

There has been some research attempt to improve the image classification accuracy through the use of spatial information. These methods fall into three main categories: (1) relaxation method, which represents spatial correlation information by consistency coefficients, (2) contextual classifier, which directly makes use of spatial information, (3) use of image texture measure, together with spectrum data. The first two methods are very complicated and computationally expensive. The third method does not seem to be applicable in our case. We proposed to use a so-called predictive classifier based on the Markov field model of image data. In the first order Markov field, a pixel is closely related to its two neighbors (top and left) or four neighbors (top, down, left and right). It means the probability that a pixel and its four direct neighbors belong to the same class is relatively high. The following decision procedure is then applicable:

Perform classification using equation 11.2 in a raster scanning manner. For the current pixel

- Record the class label of top and left neighbor pixels ω_u and ω_l and corresponding distance measures $d_u()$ and $d_l()$.
- Calculate the decision function $d_c()$ which measures the similarity between the present pixel and class ω_u, if $|d_u - d_c| < \theta$ then the pixel is assigned class ω_u, otherwise, class ω_l is given the same consideration. If the pixel can not be classified to either class ω_u or class ω_l, it will be classified using equation 11.2.

This method makes use of spatial correlation property of image data. It reduces noise in color coded images and saves considerable computation time.

11.3 Capturing Visual Features of Trademark Images

There are some work on shape description of trademark images. For example, Cortelazzo used hierarchical contour coding [6]. The problem with this technique is the complexity in the retrieval of very large amount of trademarks.

Some trademark images are structured patterns. There are two issues in describing these visual patterns. One is the structural feature - how the trademark image is composed by components. The other is shape/complexity measure of individual components.

11.3.1 Structural description

Traditionally, structural features are represented by semantic networks or other tree/network data structures such as the one in [6]. To simplify the searching effort, we designed a flat representation by specifying the outline and component grouping types. By studying visual characteristics of trademark images, we have observed:

- Overall shape is more important than detailed structures. We choose to describe overall shape, individual components, and how components constitute the whole image.

- Many trademark images have outline/background, but the outline/background are not as important as the inside contents. Less importance is assigned to it.

- Components grouping has limited number of types. The type assignment is interactively done by the user.

Figure 11.5 shows a few types of outline/background (in the first row) and a few types of component grouping (in the second row) of trademark images.

11.3.2 Feature measures

To characterize the visual features of the overall shape and individual component of trademark images, we have studied several feature extraction methods. We found that each feature extraction method, either for shape, structure or texture, only captures one aspect of the visual pattern. Therefore, we have extracted three feature measures of the trademark images and fuse them together to characterize diverse and complex trademark images. These three feature measures are: Fourier descriptor of the shape, moment invariants, and projections. Fourier descriptor captures the outline shape, moment invariants represent the symmetry property, and projections describe the internal structure of the trademark images. Combination of these three feature measures will give a good description of visual features of trademark images.

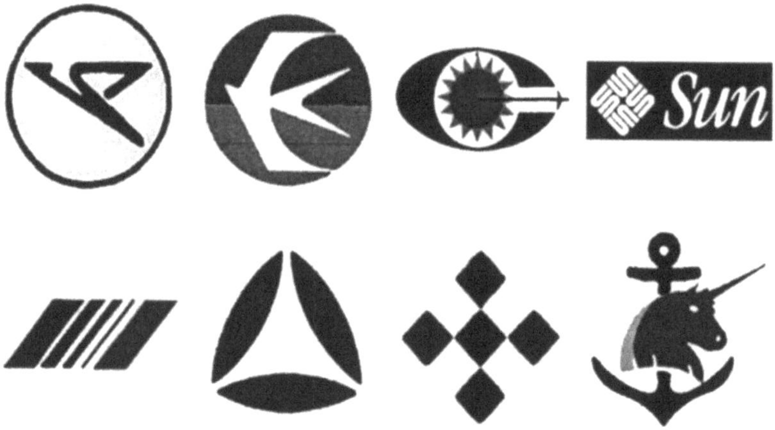

Figure 11.5: Illustration of Trademark Structures. Trademarks in the first row have different types of outline/background. In the second row, the four trademarks show different types of component grouping: parallel, triangular, star, and intersection respectively.

Fourier descriptor

Fourier descriptor for shape description was first proposed by Ali [10], and more sophisticated method is reported in [11]. A brief description of the algorithms is as follows.

First, the contour of the trademark image is found after morphological filtering, then accumulated angular function of the contour is computed. Assume that the curve under consideration occupies m pixels $V_0 ... V_{m-1}$. The starting point V_0 is selected and we define the change in angular direction at pixel V_k as $\Delta\phi_k$. As contours are represented as 2-dimensional arrays in a square grid coordinate system, the direction of the line segment between any two neighboring pixels, $\Delta\phi_k$, is in multiples of $\pi/4$. The cumulative amount of angular bend between the starting point V_0 and point V_k is defined as

$$\phi_k = \sum_{i=0}^{k} \Delta\phi_i \qquad 0 \leq k \leq m-1 \tag{11.3}$$

The Fourier coefficients c_k is computed by the following Discrete Fourier transform equation:

$$c_k = \frac{1}{N} \sum_{j} \phi_j e^{-2\pi ijk/N} \tag{11.4}$$

In the Fourier transform domain, only the amplitudes are used as the feature measure. Since Fourier descriptors are derived by using the cumulative angular change in the contour, it is clear that these values only represent the topology of the contour and they contain no information relating to the absolute position or notational orientation of the trademark image. Therefore, the Fourier descriptors generated are invariant under translation and rotation. It is not sensitive to the starting point because of periodicity of Fourier transform.

Moment invariants

Consider an image as a 2-D object in the space with gray level function as density function, $f(x, y)$, we define the $pq'th$ moments as

$$m^{pq} = \sum_x \sum_y x^p y^q f(x, y) \tag{11.5}$$

The *Normalized Central Moments* to measure symmetry property of the objects can be derived accordingly:.

$$\eta_{pq} = \sum_x \sum_y (x - \bar{x})^p (y - \bar{y})^q f(x, y) \tag{11.6}$$

where $\bar{x} = \frac{m_{10}}{m_{00}}, \bar{y} = \frac{m_{01}}{m_{00}}$. From the second and third moments, a set of seven *invariant moments* are computed as follows:

$$\begin{aligned}
\phi_1 &= \eta_{20} + \eta_{02} \\
\phi_2 &= (\eta_{20} - \eta_{02})^2 + 4\eta_{11}^2 \\
\phi_3 &= (\eta_{30} - \eta_{02})^2 + (3\eta_{21} - \eta_{03})^2 \\
\phi_4 &= (\eta_{30} + \eta_{12})^2 + (3\eta_{21} + \eta_{03})^2 \\
\phi_5 &= (\eta_{30} - 3\eta_{12})(\eta_{30} + \eta_{12})[(\eta_{30} + \eta_{12})^2 - 3(\eta_{21} + \eta_{03})^2] \\
&+ (3\eta_{21} - \eta_{03})(\eta_{21} + \eta_{03})[3(\eta_{30} + \eta_{12})^2 - (\eta_{21} + \eta_{03})^2] \\
\phi_6 &= (\eta_{20} - \eta_{02})[(\eta_{30} + \eta_{12})^2 - (\eta_{21} + \eta_{03})^2] \\
&+ 4\eta_{11}(\eta_{30} + \eta_{12})(\eta_{21} + \eta_{03}) \\
\phi_7 &= (3\eta_{21} - \eta_{03})(\eta_{30} + \eta_{12})[(\eta_{30} + \eta_{12})^2 - 3(\eta_{21} - \eta_{30})^2] \\
&+ [(3\eta_{12} - \eta_{30})(\eta_{21} + \eta_{03})[3(\eta_{30} + \eta_{12})^2 - (\eta_{21} + \eta_{03})^2]
\end{aligned} \tag{11.7}$$

This set of moments has been shown to be invariant to translation, rotation, and scale change.

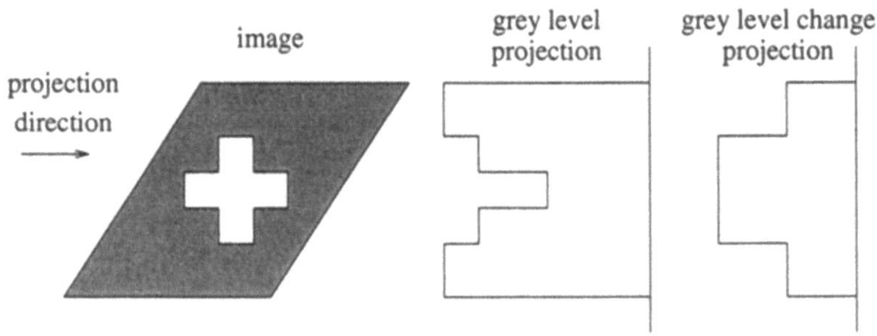

Figure 11.6: X-Projection of gray level and gray level changes of images.

Projections

There are two types of projections: gray level projection and gray level change projection. The gray level projection is illustrated in Figure 11.6. In the 2-D grid coordinate system, the X-projection of gray level is defined as the number of black pixels alone horizontal projection lines while the X-projection of gray level change projection is defined as the number of gray level changes alone horizontal projection lines. Projections capture certain internal structural properties of the images which Fourier descriptor and moment invariants do not.

11.3.3 Match shape interpretation using fuzzy thesaurus

Device mark meaning are conceptually defined words or phrases. To reduce description diversity, we adopted Vienna classification [1] which describes trademarks into a hierarchy of category, division and section. A fuzzy thesaurus was built to evaluate the similarity between sections of Vienna classifications, using a fuzzy multi-linkage thesaurus builder developed by Gao [2].

In a thesaurus, a term represents a concept, which may be related to other concepts with many-to-many relationships. It is designed to include three types of thesaural relationships; they are equivalence, hierarchical, and associative. The equivalence relationship indicates that the terms are considered synonymous or quasi synonymous. The hierarchical relationship indicates the generic relationship between terms that are broader and narrower in concept. The associative relationship is found between terms which are closely related conceptually but are neither hierarchical nor equivalence relations. We implement these three types of relationships into six classes of detailed relationships: synonymous, related, subclass, super-class, part-of and user-defined relationship. The

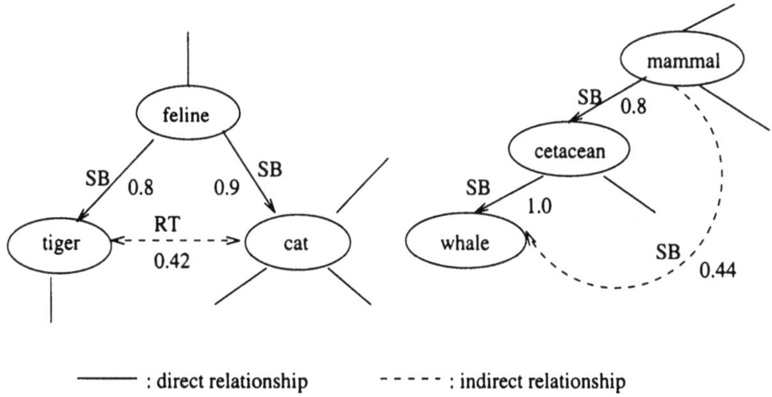

Figure 11.7: Examples of querying indirect relationship terms

user-defined relationship extends the flexibility of the thesaurus builder, by allowing users to define any desired type of relationship. The relationships among concepts are usually imprecise. We assign each thesaural relationship with a fuzzy factor to describe the degree of (strength of) relationship. Semantics-wise, the fuzzy factor represents the concepts of "very","fairly","slightly" and "rarely", etc.

The thesaurus builder's structure is like a semantic network. Each term is multi-linked with other terms. Term relationships are reciprocal, when one side of a relationship has been supplied the system should automatically provide the other side. It is the same when a relationship between two terms is deleted. In query processing, the fuzzy factor is used to rank the candidates.

Users can also use fuzzy reasoning to expand the searching range and retrieve more terms which have no direct relationship with the query term as shown in Figure 11.7.

11.4 Composite Similarity Measures

Images usually have structured contents. Each of the components in the contents may have different features and can be measured using different features. This has been very well demonstrated by trademarks. The similarity among trademarks should take account of all aspects of word-in-mark and device mark. The contribution of individual aspects to the overall similarity is balanced by weights. The composite similarity measure for trademarks can be defined in terms of weighted distance and written as follows:

$$d_{cj} = w^w d^w_{ci} + w^d d^d_{cj} \qquad (11.8)$$

where d_{cj} is the overall or composite similarity measure for the "current sample" trademark and j-th trademark image in the archive, w^w, w^d and d^w, d^d are weights for word-in-mark and device mark, respectively, and d^w, d^d are distances for word-in-mark and device mark, respectively.

$$d^w_{cj} = \begin{cases} 0 & \text{if } wim_c = wim_j = false \\ \theta_w & \text{if } wim_c \mid wim_j = false \\ w^w_w d^w_{wcj} + w^w_p d^w_{pcj} + w^w_i d^w_{icj} & \text{if } wim_c = wim_j = true \end{cases}$$

where wim_c, and wim_j are boolean functions to represent the presence or absence of word-in-mark in the current or j-th trademark respectively, w^w_w, w^w_p, w^w_i and $d^w_{wcj}, d^w_{pcj}, d^w_{icj}$ are weights and distances of words, phonetics, and interpretation for the current trademark and the j-th trademark, respectively. θ_w is the penalty when one trademark has a word-in-mark but the other does not.

Similarly, the similarity for device mark is defined as

$$d^d_{cj} = \begin{cases} 0 & \text{if } dev_c = dev_j = false \\ \theta_d & \text{if } dev_c \mid dev_j = false \\ \frac{1}{N_{comp}} \sum_k (w^d_m d^d_{mkcj} + w^d_p d^d_{pkcj} + w^d_g d^d_{gkcj}) & \text{if } dev_c = dev_j = true \end{cases}$$

where dev_c and dev_j are boolean functions to represent the presence or absence of device mark in the current or j-th trademark respectively, θ_d is the penalty when one trademark has a device mark but the other does not. w^d_m, w^d_p, w^d_g are weights for the meaning, structure, and shape/texture aspects for the device mark and $d^d_{mkcj}, d^d_{pkcj}, d^d_{gkcj}$ are distances of the meaning, structure, and shape/texture aspects of k-th component of the device mark of the sample trademark and a component of the device mark of the j-th trademark. Notice that the graphics components of device mark do not have any particular ordering when they are segmented. Any graphics component in the sample trademark can match any graphics component in the j-th trademark. The distance of the device mark is then defined as the minimum distance between these two device marks.

Notice also that graphics components are not necessarily treated equally. For example, in the trademark image (3, 3), the leaf graphic part is more important than the circle. Therefore, we distinguish such component as *major component*. If the major component of the device

$Word_1$	$Word_2$	Sim_w	Sim_p
asi	asea	0.750000	0.333333
foral	feral	0.975000	0.975000
cosmic	coshmick	0.937500	0.979167
armor	amor	0.975000	0.800000
creeza	kreeza	0.916667	1.000000
heart	hart	0.975000	0.968750
Chikngrillas	Chickutay	0.854167	0.825000
aero	aeron	0.975000	0.750000
gaynor	caynore	0.857143	0.833333
communication	com*tion	0.942308	0.932692
3M	Three M	0.142857	1.000000
Fujitsu	Kodar	0.000000	0.000000

Table 11.1: Similarity Values for a Set of Word-Pairs.

mark of the current trademark matches the major component of the device mark of the j-th trademark, more weight should be put to such a distance than the distances of the other components.

$$d_{cj}^{d} = (1 - w_{imp})(d_{cj}^{d} - \frac{1}{N_{comp}} d_{imp-cj}^{d}) + w_{imp} d_{imp-cj}^{d} \tag{11.9}$$

where w_{imp} and d_{imp-cj}^{d} are the weight factor and the distance for the major component.

We can adapt distance measure (in a broad sense) between device marks because the shape/texture measures are represented as vectors after feature extraction. Similarity measure for word-in-mark is measured by the number of the same ordered characters in the two words. The formula is:

$$d_{w}^{w} = 1 - sim_{w} = 1 - \sum_{k} w_{k} l_{k} / l_{word} \tag{11.10}$$

where s_w is the word similarity measure, l_k, l_{word} are length of the k-th common factor between two words and the length of the whole word. Several cases will be checked when actually computing the length of common factors. The word length is taken to be the average length of two words. Table 1 lists similarity measures between sets of two words, where Sim_w, Sim_p are similarities for word and phonetics.

11.5 Evaluation and Learning of Similarity Measures

Retrieval of conflicting trademarks of similar shape is referred to as content-based retrieval or feature-based retrieval. The evaluation was performed by the following formalism in Chapter 2 with application to the shape retrieval engine to tune the similarity functions.

11.5.1 Selection of training and test data sets

There were two categories of training/test shapes: geometric shapes and trademark shapes. The variation of geometric shapes can be designed objectively. For example, one series of geometric shapes are regular polygens consisting of triangular, square, ..., until their extreme - circle. Geometric shapes are also designed to have variations on outline shape, interial structure, and symmetry.

11.5.2 Learning of similarity functions

Figure 11.8 shows a network architecture for learning of similarity functions with fusion of these three shape feature measures, namely, fourier descriptors, moments, and projections. This network is a variation of multilayer feedforward network with back-propagation learning algorithm. Since our goal is to learn similarity functions between pairs of input patterns, we replace the input layer of an ordinary feedforward network by comparison layer.

The network consists of four layers: a data layer, a comparison layer, a hidden layer, and an output layer. The data layer has two arrays of network units: one sample data array and one data array. For a training data set $d_i^s, d_{i1}, d_{i2}, \ldots$, data pairs $(d_i^s, d_{i1}), (d_i^s, d_{i2}), \ldots$ are fed to the data layer sequentially, and in the output layer, unit number 1, 2, ... are expected to be active. That is to say that the activation of output units code the similarity of the input data pair.

In the comparison layer, there can be several arrays of units each representing one comparison method. Currently, we use two comparison methods: delta and normalized correlation. Comparison is made for every component of feature vectors.

The layers above the comparison layer constitute a feedforward network, which is designed to learn similarity function. The number of layers here determines the complexity of the similarity function. If we want the similarity function to be linear, two layers are adequate. Three or more

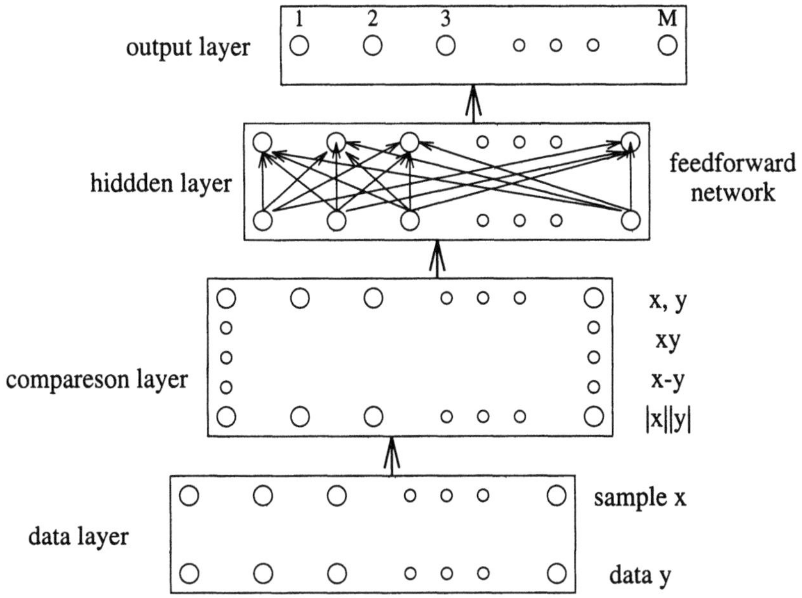

Figure 11.8: Neural networks for learning similarity functions and fusion of multiple feature measures.

layer network will be able to simulate any non-linear functions [4].

We must note that the distances/similarity between pairs of objects in the ranked lists are usually not equal, as illustrated in Figure 11.9. In this case, it may not be true that the j-th output unit becomes active when the sample data and the data item d_{ij} is presented to the network. For example, the first output unit will be active when the first and the second data item are presented because both of them are very close to the sample data. To accommodate that, we can perform learning after all data items in a training data set have been presented. The training procedure is as follows:

1. Construct the network by letting the number of nodes of one array in the data layer equal feature measure size, and the number of output node equal number of elements in the ranked list. Choose the hidden layer according to the complexity you want the similarity function to have.

2. For one training data set, the sample data will remain attached to the sample data array, while other data items d_{ij} in the training data set is fed to the data array one by one. Run the network for

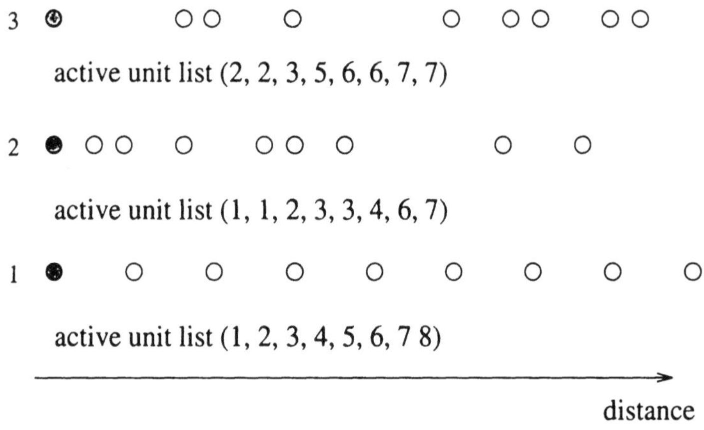

Figure 11.9: In the ranked lists of retrieval, the pair-wise distance may not be uniform. Here, filled circles represent sample data, and non-filled circles are data items in the ranked lists according to their similarity (here in the figure, the similarity is defined as distance) to the sample data. The first line is an ideal case where all pair-wise distances are the same. The second and third lines show the differences.

each data item, and record the activation of output units in a list.

3. The list of activation of output units is a queue containing the coding of similarities of the input pairs $(d_i^s, d_{ij}), j = 1, 2, ...$ If the network is already properly trained, the similarity coding in the list should be in an incremental order. Calculate the error by finding the wrong order of those similarity codings. Back-propagate the error and modify the weights of the feedforward network.

4. Randomly apply training data sets to the network until all data sets have been applied.

5. Repeat this learning process until the network reaches certain stable state. If it converges, take these weights to formulate the similarity function. Otherwise, check the consistency of the training data.

11.5.3 Evaluating the shape retrieval

After learning of similarity function for shape retrieval, an evaluation was conducted to test the effectiveness of the shape retrieval engine. The evaluation was carried out using the selected trademark shape test data set.

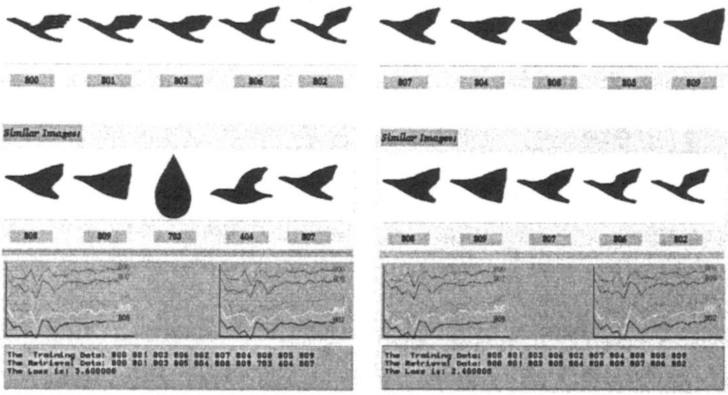

Figure 11.10: Above: a set of training data set - a sample trademark image followed by a set of similar trademark images arranged from the most similar to less similar. Below show the last 5 images of the two retrieval results. Curves are plot of shape feature measures of these images. On the left, without learning, there are unexpected images appear in the retrieval result, and image 806 and 802 never appear. On the right, after learning, the retrieval result is much more meaningful. The loss here (3.6 and 2.4) is scaled up by factor 10.

Figure 11.10 shows an example of the testing, which consists of several parts of screen dumps. The training data set contains several variations: first is the variation of detailed structure on the wing, and then followed by the angle between wing and body. The bird is finally transformed into a triangular like shape. Since the three shape measures are sensitive to angles, birds with large angle between wing and body (806, 802) were not retrieved for the retrieval engine using the composite similarity measure in equation 11.9(refer to the low-left part of Figure 11.10, which shows the last five retrieved trademark images). Although image 703 and 404 are similar to the sample with respect to overall shape, they should not be ranked so high in the retrieval result from the point of view of trademark officers.

After learning, the retrieval engine has taken into account the factors of human interpretation which are represented in the training data set. Hence, the retrieval result on the low-right part of Figure 11.10 is conceptually acceptable to trademark officers. This is well reflected by the loss of the retrieval: after learning, the loss is reduced to 0.24 from 0.36 (without learning).

11.6 Experimental Results

Searching for the conflicting trademarks is carried out after presenting a completely segmented sample trademark. Indices are created for each graphic feature measures using the indexing method ContIndex described in [7]. It is used to narrow down candidate search space and reduce the searching time. This becomes effective and necessary when the database size is large. All possible candidates will be verified using the composite similarity measure discussed above.

Figure 11.11 shows a experimental result of searching using a sample trademark with device mark only as shown in the right display panel. The retrieved trademarks are ranked from the most similar to the least similar. The first 9 trademarks are displayed on the 9 display areas in the order from top-left to bottom-right. By clicking on a display areas a corresponding trademark particulars and image will be displayed on the left. Activating button "more" to the left of 9 display areas will enable you to view more retrieved trademarks.

Figure 11.12 shows searching results using word-in-mark. In (a), "ia" is the most similar one to "Canadian" because it is completely included in "Canadian". When phonetics is added to similarity measure, "ia" is no longer the most similar one - they do not have phonetics similarity since "ia" takes phonetics of two characters "i" and "a". (b) was obtained by using both words and phonetics.

The prototype STAR is implemented in Unix workstation using C programming language programming in an object-oriented manner. The first version of the prototype is tested against 3000 real trademarks collected from advertisements. Images are scanned in using color scanner and then normalized to a standard size of 400 $\times$ 400. Images are stored in the database using JPEG compression. After compression, each image is about 10-20 KB. A system of 10,000 trademarks will take 100-200 MB disk space.

The system was tested against 500 trademarks given by a trademark office. The time taken to archive those given trademarks (3 days) and the retrieval results are all to their satisfactory: semi-automatic segmentation does take time in trademark archival phase, but it takes less time than manual filing of trademarks. STAR offers similarity retrieval capability which is very useful to guarantee the uniqueness of trademarks, but it is impossible with manual filing. The average time for one retrieval of this trial system was around 5 seconds, including query processing, decoding and displaying trademark images.

Scaling up of the system is not a problem. There are three major com-

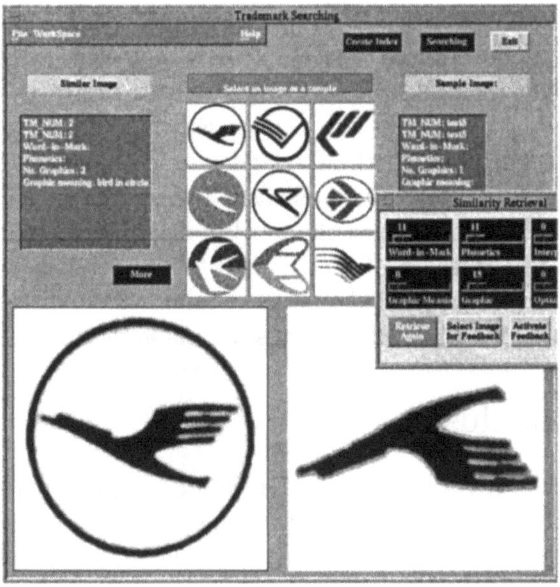

Figure 11.11: Sample search output for a device mark as query trademark.

(a) (b)

Figure 11.12: Trademark Search Output: (a) Retrieval using words only. Among trademarks retrieved, "ia" is considered as the most similar because "ia" is wholly included in "Canadian". The words of all others partially match "Canadian", and therefore, ranked behind "ia". (b) Retrieval using words and phonetics. The words and phonetics have the same weights in the similarity measure. Among retrieved trademarks, "Canadian" and "Aerocancun" are considered the most similar because the common part "can" of both trademark words has the same pronunciation.

ponents in query processing: matching word-in-mark, matching graphic meaning by fuzzy thesaurus based on Vienna classification, and similarity searching of device marks. Vienna classfication has limited vocabulary, increase of database size does not increase searching time. According to [7], the time needed to search the ContIndex of feature measures is proportional to the logirithm of the amount of trademarks in the database. We also use inverted file to index the word-in-mark, therefore, the searching time will not increase significantly when the database size increases. On the other hand, the retrieval time is nothing when it is compared with manual search. The time of manual search is in terms of hours.

11.7 Conclusions

We have presented a trademark archival and registration system STAR in this chapter. It was developed using our content-based retrieval engine CORE. We have tackled difficult issues for conflicting trademark retrieval, namely, searching multi-lingual word-in-mark and diverse trademark images. We have developed special similarity measures for word-in-mark, fuzzy thesarus to search trademark image by meaning match, and three feature extraction methods and learning method to fuse these feature measures for searching trademark images by shape. Our experimental results have shown the effectiveness of these techniques.

References

1. International Classification of the Fifurative Elements of Marks, Vienna Agreement of June 12, 1973, World Intellectual Property Organization (WIPO), WIPO Publication No. 502(E), Geneva, 1993
2. Y. J. Gao, J. J. Lim, A. D. Narasimhalu, F"uzzy Multilinkage Thesaurus Builder in Multimedia Information Systems", The 3rd International Conference on Document Analysis and Recognition, Montreal, Canada, 1995
3. K. Hornk, M. Stinchocombe, H. White, "Multi-layer Feedforward Networks Are Universal Approximators", Neural Networks, Vol. 2, pp. 359-366, 1989
4. J. K. Wu, "Neural Networks and Simulation", Marcel Dekker, Inc., New York, 1994
5. J. K. Wu, B. M. Mehtre, Y. J. Gao, P. C. Lam, A. D. Narasimhalu, "STAR - A Multimedia Database System For Trademark Registration", Applications of Databases, Lecture Notes in Computer Science, Vol. 819, Proc. First International Conference, Vadstena, Sweden, pp. 109-122, 1994
6. G. Cortelazzo, G. A. Mian, G. Vezzi, P. Zamperoni, "Trademark Shape Description by String-Matching Techniques", Pattern Recognition, Vol. 27, No. 8, pp. 1005-1018, 1994

7. J. K. Wu, "Content-based Indexing of Multimedia Databases", IEEE Trans. on Knowledge and Data Engineering, Vol. 9, No. 6, pp. 978-989, 1997

8. J. K. Wu, "Color Coding of Images", Journal of Signal Processing of China, Vol.5, pp. 1-6, 1986

9. J. K. Wu, A. D. Narasimhalu, "Fuzzy Content-based Image Databases", Information Processing and Management, to appear

10. F. Ali, T. Pavlidis, "Syntactic Recognition of Handwritten Numerals", IEEE Trans. Syst. Man. Cybern., Vol. 7, pp.537-541, 1977

11. K. Arbter, W. E. Snyber, H. Burkhardt, G. Hirzinger, "Application of Af fine-Invariant Fourier Descriptors Recognition of 3-D objects", IEEE Trans. Pattern Anal. Machine Intell., Vol. 12, No.7, 1990

Chapter 12

Digital Home Photo Album

12.1 Digital photo is becoming popular

In the current digital era, there have already been plenty of digital photos converted from the prints or generated directly from the digital cameras. The general trends today are:

- Now many people have a PC at home.
- Digitizing traditional paper prints into digital forms has become easy and convenient. Color scanners can be found in many places. Color development centers begin to provide service of digitizing photographs and storing them in the Photo CD and the resolution can be high enough to satisfy the most of possible uses.
- With the technology advancement, a digital camera is affordable. With the built-in CCD (charged-coupled device) chip, digital camera converts and digitizes the intensity of light received into the digital image. Images can be transferred from the camera to the computer memory.
- What is even more important is that there is hundreds of giga bytes of images in the World-Wide Web. World-Wide Web has become the part of everyday life.
- Digital photos have many advantages: easy to transfer and exchange in the Internet, convenient to publish on line, free to process, never fading, saving storage space, etc.
- In essence the digital photo is a kind of image and almost all the image processing techniques can be applied to the digital photo,

so it is possible to process them with special effects that can't be imposed on paper prints.

Obviously in the next a few years digital photos will become more and more popular and even substitute the paper prints in the main family photo collection.

There have been efforts made in developing photo album:

- Kodak's Shoebox[1] is an application from Kodak's Photo CD software family. It provides versatile solution for various kinds of task related to Photo CD management. Some features of Shoebox are, easy textual annotation, search by text, various display modes (slide show, zoom, crop ...). In general, there is nothing novel except for flexible indexing.

- Club Photo's Living Album[2] has an attractive display interface that is really like an album. It deals with 36 images in a catalog and can record/playback sound attached to a photo. Its indexing function is weaker compared to that of Shoebox.

- Ricoh's PhotoStudio[3] is a software attached to Ricoh's digital camera. With PhotoStudio, the user can load pictures from the camera. The catalog can also include images from other cameras. PhotoStudio provides an ordinary textual cataloging and thumbnail browsing utility but its image processing tools are powerful. With these tools, the user can create special effect on the photo. One feature that is worth mentioning is a tool called "Magic Wand". It can extract a homogeneous region with respect to color and the tolerance of the homogeneity preset. The digital camera and PhotoStudio also support sound recording and software controlled online photo-taking.

- Apple's PhotoFlash[4] can support Apple's online QuickTake digital camera. It supports image search by sketch drawing in a catalog but it is only suitable for simple structure image and not very robust.

  Generally speaking, these image database system are helpful in the cataloging, indexing, annotation and search by textual descriptive keywords.

12.1.1 What do the home users want?

Home photos are used by family members. It means users are not experts. Some of them may only be interested in their photos and have little knowledge or interest about computer and technical issues. It means that the design should be user centered and the user interface should be friendly. A photo image archival and retrieval system must support high-level cognitive work. Evaluation of its effectiveness has to be in terms of its impact on the users' work. For it to be truly useful, we need to first understand the large context that determines their information needs and purposes for using such system. Hence we conducted two user studies.

12.1.2 User study 1

The purpose of the first user study was to get an overview of users' habits, preference, convention around photos at home, to support the conceptual framework of our projects and was not intended to produce a shrink-wrapped product for the user. We wanted to know

- Who is involved in home photos? What extent are they involved in?
  - adults
  - kids
  - guests
  - casual or serious photographer
  - special objectives behind photography (flower collection...)
- What are they doing with the image?
  - sort
  - view
  - annotate/index
  - present to others
  - manipulate
- What kind of images?
  - people
  - nature
  - sights
  - events
- Why do people do all that?
  - recall events
  - enjoy memories

  - show things/share experience with others
  - be entertained

- How do they accomplish their tasks?
  - put photos in a big album by topics
  - write a catalog or index for a image collection
  - write annotation on the back of the photo
  - display images on the wall or in a frame

In order to answer all these questions, we conducted exploratory interviews, learning about people's present work processes and tools and their perceived needs for a photo image retrieval system.

From home user interviews including families, couples, singles with the photographic skills of holiday snapshot and serious hobby, we gained some impressions presented below:

- When the users want to find an image, they retrieve their memories for information related to the image, then locate the image.
- They try to mirror their memory in the chronological order of their photos. Memories around an event are the user's search engine.
- They do not retrieve images directly at the beginning. Memories are connected with a series of images. The computer home photos management system should also make use of memory while retrieving images.
- A strong consistent mental model is reflected in the user's activities around home photos. They regard their photo collection as their family history. Therefore, history or a tree of events may serve as central interface metaphor.
- Things we should not count on are indexing, annotating, cataloging. People do not do these often since they are of little fun and time-consuming. The exception is that they sometimes use annotation for communication.
- To look at the problem as a social activity is crucial. A typical situation might be: I do the shots, my wife archives them into the albums, guests view them and our kids mess around with the photos...
- Users like photo compilations of specific topics (our son, my nicest shots ...), but there are problems unless users make reprints compilations by topic which collide with the order by memory or history.

12.1.3 User study 2

To understand how users describe the content of the photo image and what is the most perceived part in the image the second user study was conducted. The interviewees were asked to accomplish the following 4 assignments:

- Describe the photo content by recalling a personal picture which is not presented.
- Describe an unknown family photo after a quick look.
- Instruct others locating a personal photo at home by describing the photo contents.
- Describe an unknown landscape/scenery picture after a quick look.

From their descriptions we found people always divided the image content into foreground and background if such division is possible. If the foreground are objects they pointed out what they are (e.g. car, house etc.), relative location (e.g. behind, in the right side, in the front of etc.) and described their properties like color, material, texture, style, size, shape etc. When they referred the people as the foreground, they often gave the human heads, the relationship between them, arrangements, dress style, gender, age etc. For the background they often pointed out the geographical location where the picture taken (e.g. my house, Australia, Sentosa etc.) and generally described the environment type (e.g. beach resort, city etc.). They sometimes mentioned the abstract impression (e.g. beautiful scene), whether (e.g. cloudy, raining, nice etc.) and time (not the exact dates, e.g. winter 95, my birthday 93, Chinese New Year etc.)

12.1.4 The gap between ideal and realistic

From the user study we learn that people generally organize their home photos based on the event, people, time etc., and do not categorize photos based on color or texture information. It indicates that users want to find instances of high-level concepts rather than images with specific low-level properties. Many current image retrieval systems are based on appearance matching, in which, for example, the computer presents several images, and the user picks one and requests other image with similar color, color layout and texture. For this type of queries, at first glance the results may show certain similar appearance. But after a careful observation, their contents are less relevant.

This sort of query is useful for some domain-specific application such as medical images database, in which, doctor often want to refer the similar cases treated before, but may be unsatisfactory in home photo archive for several reasons:

- Features are too low level to be understood by the home users. It is difficult for them to match the low level features with the high level concepts.
- It is difficult to get a sample query image in most cases.
- Such a query does not address the high-level content of the image at all, only its low-level appearance. Users often find it hard to understand why particular images were returned and have difficulty controlling the retrieval behavior in desired ways.
- There is usually no way to tell the system which features of the "target" image are important and which are irrelevant to the query.

Without image understanding, the computer can not provide the high level organization that is natural and convenient for people. With current technology it is not possible to capture high level objects immediately. We observe that high level objects are made of regions of coherent color and texture arranged in a meaningful ways. Thus we begin with low level color and texture processing to find coherent regions and then use the properties of these regions and their relationship with one another to group them at progressively higher levels. We expect to use low level feature information (color, texture, shape) to automatically identify high level concepts in the image such as trees, buildings and people and other kind of things that users might request.

Object-oriented content based retrieval is much more useful and desirable. In this connection we must develop a utility which can retrieve images in high level. To achieve this goal, we divide our research into two steps: First, we map image regions into object category. Second we interpret these object categories into semantic expression. Cataloging is the bridge which connects the low level image properties with the high level semantic expression. The proposed home photo album system diagram is illustrated in Fig 12.1. In the system many user interactive operations are involved since the system need relevant feedback from the user to refine the retrieval results gradually. We assume here that the input image is already segmented into homogeneous regions. Image object cataloging is the topic of this research. The basic idea of cataloging is that a set of features is extracted from the interested regions of raw images, then in the feature space the features of regions with same contents are classified into the same category. We can not directly catalog image objects in raw images, because there is too much information in the raw image and these information is not salient enough to be used to catalog. We must extract a little information to represent the region contents. This information is what we call as features. Obviously the performance of cataloging depends on whether the features are effective enough to distinguish different categories or not. Although the classifier also plays an important role in cataloging, extracting the good feature is a more important and fundamental issue. For the poor discriminative feature even the best classifier can't achieve the good performance. But for the strong discriminative feature, even a less powerful classifier may also achieve good performance.

12.2 Object-based Indexing and Retrieval

In the community of content-based image retrieval, most of the available techniques provide functionalities to search for images based on visual features, such as color, texture, shape, etc.[5, 7] One of the kernel problems for image categorization and retrieval is to let computers to learn to understand what users really see in an image, so as to establish the links between semantic descriptions of objects and image features. The following issues are addressed in this section:

- Image feature extraction: To extract effective features for distinguishing among various objects.
- Object modeling: There are three object models, namely, textured object model, face model and appearance model.
- A novel learning algorithm for acquiring human knowledge of visual objects in particular application domains.
- An interactive interface for on-line knowledge acquisition and query refinements.

The system provides functions for object-based image retrieval. The algorithms proposed in this work have been tested on a database with 2400 digital home photos. Preliminary experimental results are presented. In the rest of the section, detailed discussion is given to object categories, object modeling, object clustering, image categorization, and object-based image retrieval.

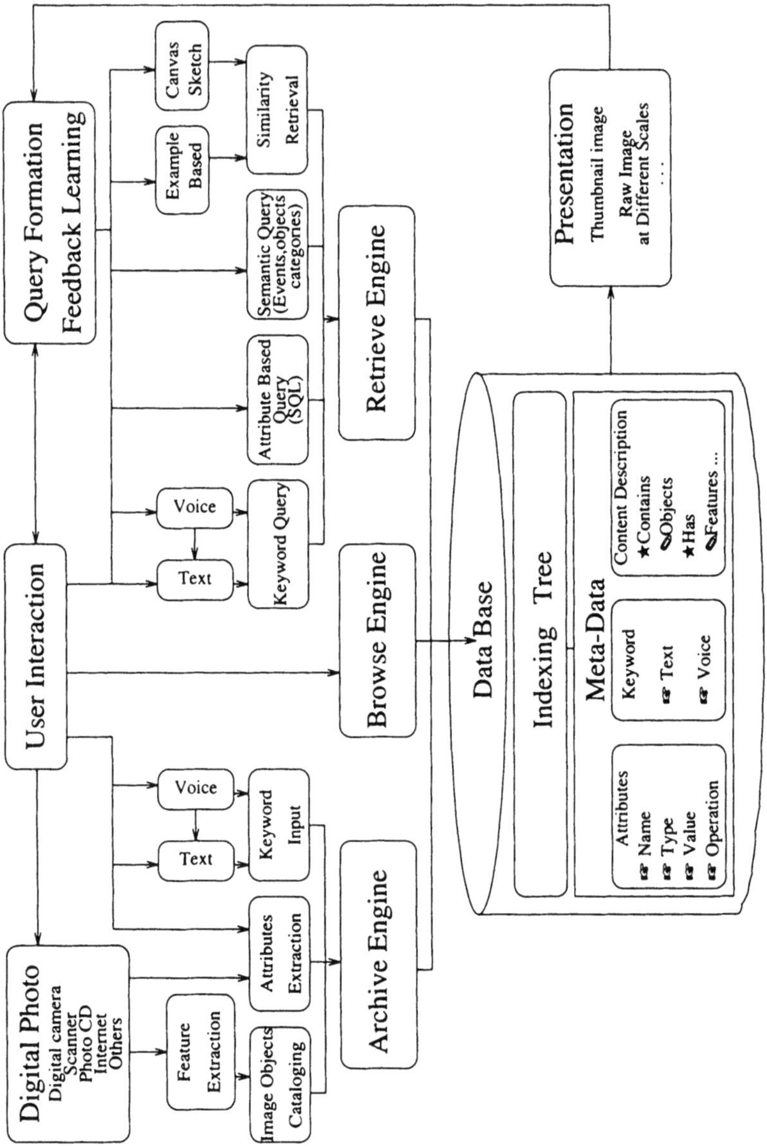

Figure 12.1: Home photo archival and retrieval system structural model.

12.2.1 Object categories

It is true that different people may tell different stories about the same image. For instance, a green region with particular texture in an image can be "*trees*" in some cases, and "*forest*" in another. Similar green stuff may also be called "*meadow*", "*plants*", "*grass*", or "*mountain*". The interpretation of image content is subjective and it is related to the context of the images. We also noticed that one object, (e.g. sky) may have multiple appearances (e.g. clear sky, cloudy sky, sunset sky, etc.). Therefore, the system should be designed to accommodate a large number of object categories that can be customized by the users to their particular application needs. Interface and algorithms should be built to assist the users in learning and creating customized object categories.

A diagram of object categories is illustrated in Figure 12.2. An object category is defined as a collection of the objects that possess similar properties and are described by the same object models. The object model [14] assigned to each object category is employed to compute the features for each member object and separate them from each other.

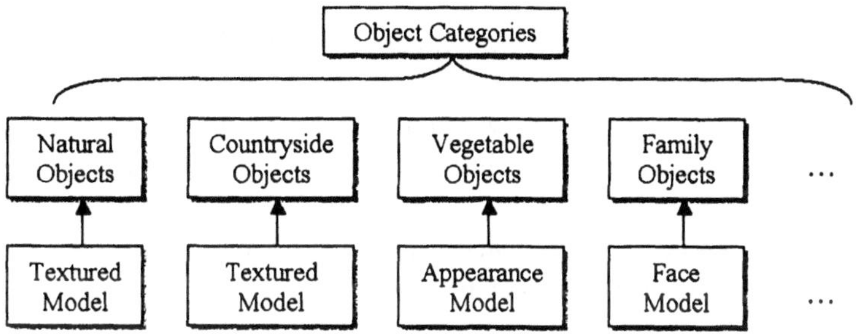

Figure 12.2: Object categories customized for the description of various images.

Each object in an object category is represented by a number of object clusters that correspond to different appearances of that object. The object clusters are created and maintained by fuzzy C-means clustering algorithm. Before applying an object category to an image batch, the user may need to understand what types of objects have been defined in this category and what appearances of each object category have been included. An interactive interface is designed to allow users to browse the object category, which is illustrated in Figure 12.3. Visual appearances presented for each object provide the users with a better linkage between object descriptions and visual features. With the interface, the user can also edit the object category by adding or deleting objects or object appearances.

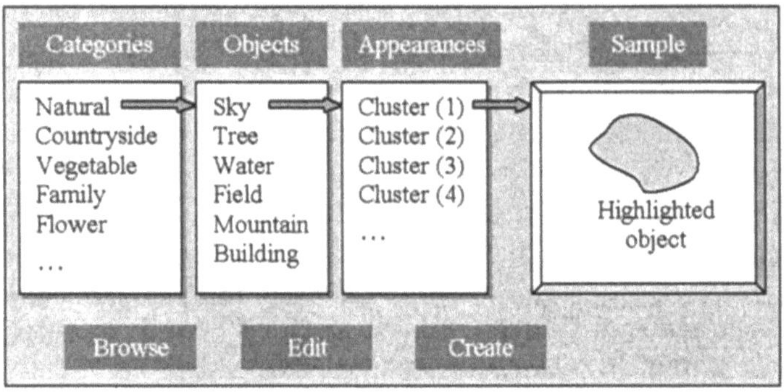

Figure 12.3: The interface for creating, editing, training and browsing object categories.

12.2.2 Object models

The object model here refers to modeling object based image features. The model is very important for successful categorization of image objects. We know image objects have their own characteristics, and require different features for their distinction. In that sense, object model defines effective feature measure to be extracted to distinguish and describe interested objects. The adequacy of the feature measures are also assessed in the model. Following are three object models:

- Textured model: It is for the description of natural objects, such as sky, tree, water, field, mountain, and building, which depend heavily on amount of and types of textures. It consists of three feature components [6]: LUV color component, texture energy component, and texture direction component. The original image is initially segmented into homogeneous regions (based on the LUV color component) by means of the MAP segmentation algorithm [16]. The homogeneous regions are treated as the basic visual units that are represented by a feature vector consisting of the three feature components.

- Face model: It is mainly for the detection and recognition of human faces presenting in images. The hypothetical face regions are firstly segmented by means of skin-color modeling and prior shape knowledge of faces. They are further verified by a set of face templates that can be customized during the processing. The PCA-based method [5] is finally employed to label the identity on each detected face.

- Appearance model: It is mainly for the description of the objects with a few strong color components and relatively fixed spatial distributions of the colors. It may be used for representing a number of vegetables, fruits, toys, etc. Firstly, a few interested regions are segmented from the original image according to the prior knowledge of the color distribution of objects. The color correlograms[13] are computed on the related color regions to confirm the labels of the objects in the image.

12.2.3 System training

After defining the object model, a learning mechanism needs to be developed to accommodate various requirements of particular applications and particular users. Or in other words, it is to incorporate human knowledge into the object models defined in the system by system training. This include:

- Object model specification for object feature extraction and description.
- Establishing links between object categories and visual objects.
- Accumulating knowledge for object category parameters.

We have designed an intelligent interface to accumulate training data from users' interactions for objects categories. Speaking of the system training, many people may relate it to a word "tedious" from their previous experiences. In this design, we try to minimize the users' interactions by employing the normalized fuzzy C-means clustering algorithm. The GUI for the training data acquisition is shown in Figure 12.4. The procedure of the training by example is just as simple as:

- Select the object category (e.g. Natural) that is related to a object model (e.g. textured model).
- Select a sample image. The initial segmentation and labeling results of the image will be displayed on the interface.
- Select a segmented region, and label it with an object label (e.g. Tree). The system will automatically compute the feature vector for the selected region based on the object model, and file it into the data set corresponding to the object label.

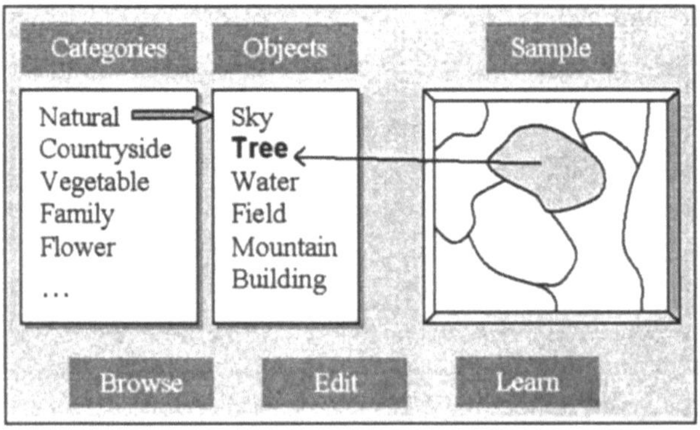

Figure 12.4: The interface for training data acquisition.

We use normalized fuzzy C-means algorithm [8] to compute the object clusters from training data sets. Suppose we have the *original training data sets* $X = \{X_1, X_2, \cdots, X_C\}$ under *O* clusters of the object categories. Each cluster consists of a number of *data members* $X_i = \{x_{i1}, x_{i2}, \cdots, x_{in_i}\}$. The *feature vector* x_{ik} is used to represent a data member.

Assume the distance of two feature vectors v_a and v_b on the first feature component *f* is expressed as $D_f(v_a, v_b)$. The cluster computation is applied to all the training data sets and it is carried on iteratively. Initially, we set the fuzzy membership $U_i = \{u_{i1}, u_{i2}, \cdots, u_{in_i}\}$ for the data sets X_i as 1. The cluster center for X_i can be computed by:

$$v_i = \left(\sum_{k=1}^{n_i} u_{ik}^2 x_{ik}\right) \Bigg/ \left(\sum_{k=1}^{n_i} u_{ik}^2\right) \tag{12.1}$$

The fuzzy membership of the data members in the data set X_i can be computed by:

$$u_{ik} = \frac{C}{C + \sum_{j=1}^{C} \left(D_f(x_{ik}, v_i)/D_f(x_{ik}, v_j)\right)^2} \tag{12.2}$$

where v_i is the cluster center of X_i, and v_j represents the cluster centers of other clusters at the current iteration step. Please note that (12.2) is normalize by the current cluster number C. The new cluster center is then updated by (12.1). The iteration of (12.1) and (12.2) is carried on until:

$$\max_{i,k} |u_{ik} - u_{ik}^*| < \varepsilon \tag{12.3}$$

A threshold T_u is set to evaluate the data member in each cluster. If:

$$u_{ik} < T_u \tag{12.4}$$

the data member x_{ik} will be taken out of the current object cluster to compose a new cluster under the same object category. The iteration of (12.1), (12.2), (12.3) and (12.4) is performed until converging (No new shifting of data member happens between clusters).

Now, a number of clusters may be generated for each object category, expressed as:

$$\{(S_{11}, S_{12}, \cdots), (S_{21}, S_{22}, \cdots), \cdots, (S_{O1}, S_{O2}, \cdots)\} \tag{12.5}$$

Suppose there are C clusters totally for all the objects. To determine the intersection between the cluster $S_{ls} = (x_{ls1}, x_{ls2}, \cdots, x_{lsp}, \cdots)$ under object category l and the cluster $S_{mt} = (x_{mt1}, x_{mt2}, \cdots, x_{mtq}, \cdots)$ under object category m, an indicator $I_{(ls)(mt)}$ is used:

$$I_{(ls)(mt)} = \max\left\{ \max_{q=1}^{Q}\{u_{(ls)(mtq)}\}, \max_{p=1}^{P}\{u_{(mt)(lsp)}\} \right\} \tag{12.6}$$

where,

$$u_{(ls)(mtq)} = \frac{C}{C + \sum_{j=1}^{C} \left(D_f(x_{mtq}, v_{ls})/D_f(x_{mtq}, v_j)\right)^2} \tag{12.7}$$

$$u_{(mt)(lsp)} = \frac{C}{C + \sum_{j=1}^{C} \left(D_f(x_{lsp}, v_{mt})/D_f(x_{lsp}, v_j)\right)^2} \tag{12.8}$$

If,

$$I_{(ls)(mt)} > T_u \tag{12.9}$$

the clusters S_{ls} and S_{mt} are intersected.

We employ the normalized fuzzy C-means algorithm as the training engine in this system, because it has the advantages[11]over other supervised training methods (e.g. neural networks, statistical methods):

- The training data can be minimized[10], if only the user can ensure that the selected training data covers all the interested appearances of the objects. One data member may be enough to be the representative of an object cluster.

- It can be used to maintain the object clusters for different object models, if only the distance functions $D_f(v_a, v_b)$ are available for the object models to measure the difference between feature vectors.
- There is no limit on the number of the clusters maintained for each object if the chosen feature measures are sufficient to distinguish objects among clusters in the category.
- The intersection indicator (12.9) can be given to each intersected object clusters under different object label. That means these objects cannot be reliably labeled due to their similar appearances. By browsing the object appearances in the category, the user is able to decide whether to delete one of the intersected ones or set a higher priority to the more important one.

The system provides the interface to the users to view the training results. The users can have a direct feel of what kinds of appearances of objects have been included and how the system behaves. The system can also tell the user whether the object clusters created are effective or not in terms of the intersection indicator. The friendly interaction makes the system training not boring any more. The system training can be gradually performed. Once new training data is accumulated, and new object clusters are created, the users can choose to update filed images.

12.2.4 Image categorization

Filing images into object categories can be very useful in browsing and retrieving images in the database with a large number of collections. However, it is hard to achieve full automatic categorization of images due to levels of categories. In general, the higher levels we try to categorize images into, the more difficulties we face. For instance, without prior knowledge, it is difficult to tell whether an image of a farm was taken in the UK, or the USA, or Australia. Besides, every user has, normally, his own preference for filing a particular batch of images.

In this approach, an interactive interface is designed to let users create their image stores, as shown in Figure 12.5. An image store can be used to hold a batch of images with any common features, semantic contents, or high level event descriptions. Descriptions of image stores are normally created by users to capture common properties of images, such as Family Photos, Trip to US, Vegetable, etc. It is impossible to derive this kind of high level description from images since there is hardly any global information contained in individual images.

The creation of the image stores is based on the object. An object category is, actually, a collection of objects with certain common properties. It is also related to a certain object model. One single object category can be used to create an image store with the same or different label. The created image store will inherit all the objects defined in the base object category. For instance, the object store "Farm in US" is created based on "Countryside" category, as shown in Figure 12.5. While a batch of images are filing into this image store, the related object model (textured model) will be applied to the images and extract semantic contents in the images (named *plant*, *pond*, *tree*, *soil*, *cottage*, and *sky*).

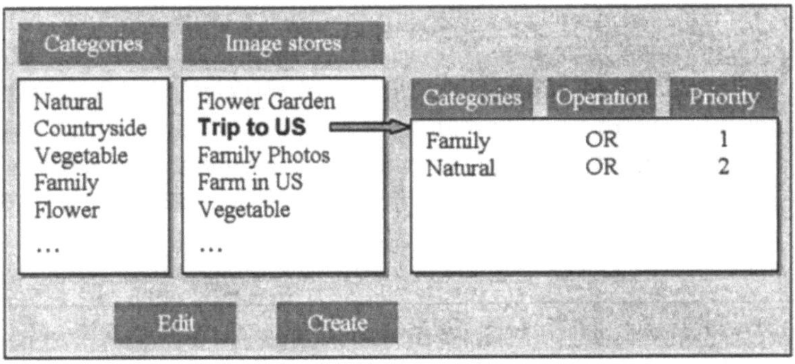

Figure 12.5: The interface for the creation of image stores.

An image store can also be created based on multiple object categories. In this case, the user should set the priorities for each associated object category (as shown in Figure 12.5). Normally, within one object category, the algorithm can ensure reliable object labeling in images, because the system training and object clustering are all performed within the category. However, there may be labeling conflicts (overlapped labels) across object categories, if multiple object models are applied to the same image. When labeling conflicts happen, the object with the highest priority will take over the final label.

While creating an image store, another option the user can set is the operation (AND, OR, NONE) related to the objects category. The operators possess the following meaning:

- AND: If all the objects under the corresponding category can be located in an image, the image can be filed into this image store.
- OR: If one of the objects under the corresponding category can be located in an image, the image can be filed into this image store.

- NONE: The labeling results under the corresponding category will not affect the image's filing direction.

When an image store is created, one or multiple object categories are associated, as shown in Figure 12.5. The object clusters included in the object categories may be trained for general applications or specially trained for previously created object stores. They may not be able to cover all the objects to be extracted from a particular batch of images. In this approach, we design a mechanism for the users to define a special object category attached to an image store, named *private object category*. A private object category is only effective to the attached image store. The same interface, as shown in Figure 12.3, is used to edit, train, and browse the private object category. The newly created private object category will be automatically added into the list of associated object categories (as shown in Figure 12.5), and an operator and a priority will be assigned to it by the user. When required, the user can choose to make a private object category public, such that, other image stores can share the objects defined in the private object category.

Image categorization is automatically carried out according to the semantic objects labeled in the images. The indices for an object store can be automatically created with the same labels as the object labels included in the associated object categories, as illustrated in Figure 12.6. To avoid messy presentation with all the object labels in the indices table, the user is able to delete some useless indices from the list (e.g.: The user has deleted all the object labels generated from "Natural" category, shown in Figure 12.6). With the interface, the user is also able to create new indices based on the semantic object labels available in this image store according to the requirements. In the example shown in Figure 12.6, a new index is created and named as "Family Union". It is created with all the object members in "Family" and all with the same operation "AND", which means the images with all the "Family" members will be filed into this index.

While a user is trying to file a batch of images, he may select one or a few destination image stores available in the system. The images will be directed into various indices created in the selected image stores based on the results of object labeling in images. Therefore, one image may have multiple indexed locations. This can provide the user with ability to create customized indices for efficiency of retrieval. It may happen that some of images are wrongly filed due to mislabeled objects in these images. The reasons for mislabeling objects may include: 1) The object categories are not fully trained. 2) There are overlapped object clusters

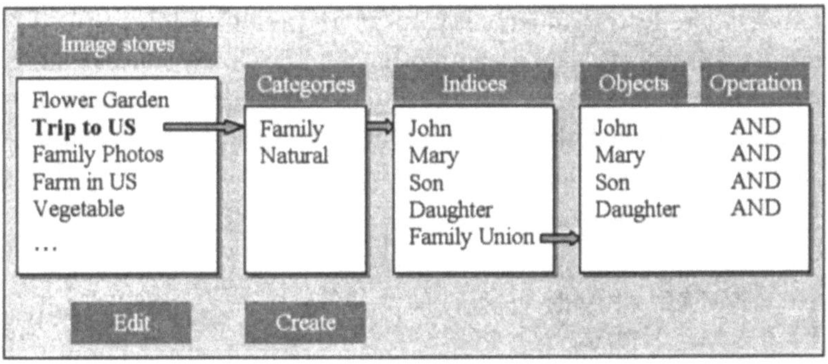

Figure 12.6: The interface for viewing, editing, and creating indices in image stores.

across object categories. 3) The priority settings for the object categories may be only effective to some of their member objects. It is difficult to automatically and completely solve all three problems due to complexity of natural images. Therefore, an interface is designed for fast browsing and redirecting images within one image store, as illustrated in Figure 12.7.

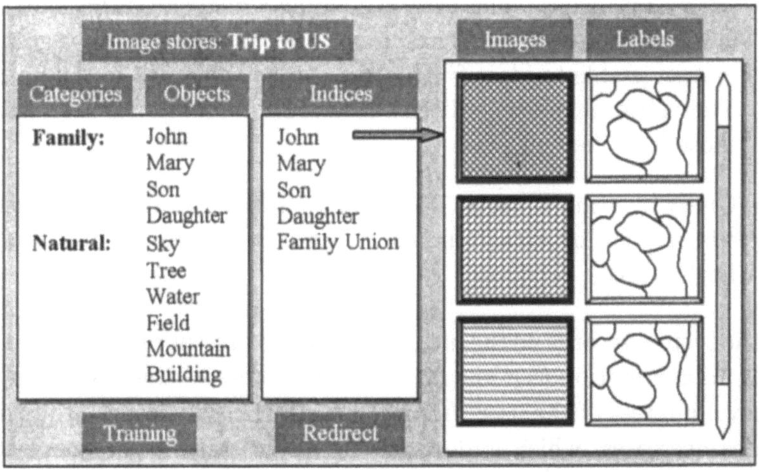

Figure 12.7: The interface for fast browsing and redirecting images in image stores.

With the interface, the user is able to browse the image filing results by each index title (e. g. John in Figure 12.7). On the left column of the display area, the original images are displayed, and on the right column, the corresponding object labeling results are displayed. In an image store, the number of effective objects is limited and relatively fixed (e.g.: there are totally 10 objects in the sample image store shown in Figure 12.7). By assigning a particular color to each object label, it is easy for the user to discover mislabeled objects, especially when the user focuses on only one or a few objects that are related to one particular index title (e.g. John in the example).

12.2.5 Image retrieval

It is assumed that all the images have been pre-filed into the object stores in the system. By understanding the structure of the image stores with related indices, it is easy and efficient for a user to search for desired images. Obviously, the image stores and the related indices are created based on relatively fixed criteria that reflect the user's requirement. The system supports three types of queries:

- Query by descriptions: The user may submit queries by one or a few content descriptions of desired images. The valid descriptions should be related to the object labels in the categories.

- Query by images: The user may submit query by using one or a few image examples. By examining the content of the images, the system is able to identify physical objects contained in the images. The retrieval results will be those images containing the most of those identified objects.

- Query by visual objects: The user may submit queries by picking up one or a few objects from images, which represent specific contents for the image retrieval.

The system records all the interactions of the present retrieval. We have made an assumption that the latest query represents the most desirable retrieval interest of the user. As time passes, the significance of previous queries decreases, which is denoted as "query state". The query state concept is represented by the "state function":

$$\mu_Q = \min(\mu_T, \mu_L) \tag{12.10}$$

where μ_T and μ_L are the state functions related to the query time and query levels, respectively, as shown by Figure 12.8. Therefore, each query is associated with a state function value indicating its query state at present. It will be effective to the image retrieval until $\mu_Q = 0$.

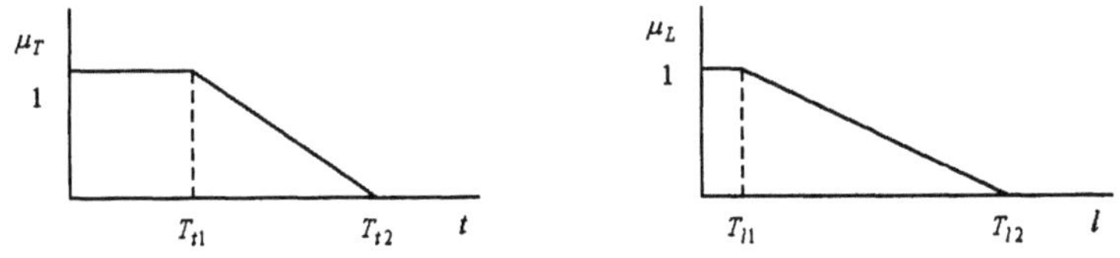

Figure 12.8: The state functions of the query time and query levels.

Visually, the significance of the objects in an image can be approximately represented by their relative sizes, if there is not any object specified. We set a threshold T_S to be a certain percentage of the relative size of an object to the whole image. The weightage μ_S of the object in the image is represented by Figure 12.9.

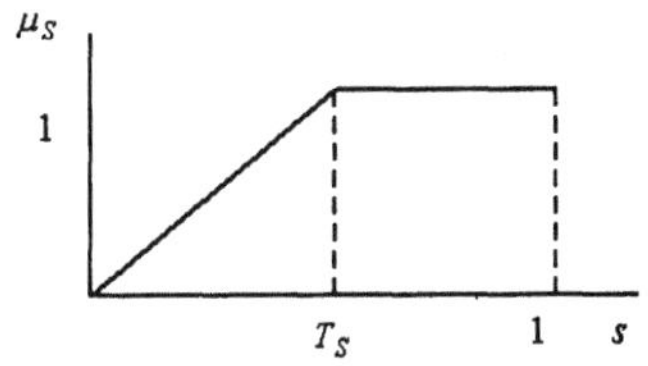

Figure 12.9: The weightage function of an object in a query.

It is often that all the three query methods are used during one query, and we need to sort the query results. Computation of sorting value varies according to query methods. We put three query methods into three columns. Each query is also associated with query state μ_{Qj}.

- Query by visual objects: The related ranking number is set at the first column. The matching number for the column I can be obtained by:

$$\mu_{mI} = \left[\sum_{j}^{J} \mu_{Qj} \left(\sum_{k}^{K} \max_{h}^{H} \mu_{Ojkh} \right) \Big/ K \right] \Big/ \sum_{j}^{J} \mu_{Qj} \tag{12.11}$$

where μ_{Ojkh} represents the matchness for the object k at j query, and H indicates the total number of the query object k in the analysed image.

- Query by images: The related ranking number is set at the second column. The matching number can be computed by:

$$\mu_{mII} = \left[\sum_{j}^{J} \mu_{Qj} \left(\sum_{k}^{K} \mu_{Sjk} \max_{h}^{H} \mu_{Ojkh}\right) \Big/ \sum_{k}^{K} \mu_{Sjk}\right] \Big/ \sum_{j}^{J} \mu_{Qj} \quad (12.12)$$

where μ_{Sjk} represents the significance of the object in the image.

- Query by semantic descriptions: The related ranking number is set at the third column. The computation for the ranking number at this column is made by:

$$\mu_{mIII} = \left[\sum_{j}^{J} \mu_{Qj} \left(\sum_{k}^{K} \max_{h}^{H} \mu_{Sjkh}\right) \Big/ \sum_{k}^{K} \mu_{Sjk}\right] \Big/ \sum_{j}^{J} \mu_{Qj} \quad (12.13)$$

where μ_{Sjkh} represents the significance of the object to be analyzed in the image.

By combining these three query methods, a ranking table can, therefore, be created automatically for the images according to the sorting value computed based on the query methods at the present query state, as shown in Table 12.1. The matching in the first column are, of course, given the highest priority, followed by the second column and the third column. The more details that the user specifies for the desired images, the more relevant the images will be. The refinement of the image retrieval can be achieved progressively.

Query method	By visual object	By image	By semantics
Ranking priority	First	Second	Third
Image 1	μ_{mI}^{1}	μ_{mII}^{1}	μ_{mIII}^{1}
Image 2	μ_{mI}^{2}	μ_{mII}^{2}	μ_{mIII}^{2}
...	...	...	...

Table 12.1: The ranking table for image retrieval.

12.2.6 Experimental results

A prototype system for indexing and retrieval of digital home photos has been implemented with the methods presented in this section. It performs automatic categorization of photos based on the content of photos. It supports three query methods. In the experiments, six object categories are defined: sky, tree, water, field, mountain, and building. Only one image store is created and it is named "Natural Scenery". There are 2400 photos in the database. To train the system, we select 160 photos. The number of the training data items required for fuzzy C-means algorithm is relatively small. In Table 12.2 , we list the statistic figures and the clusters generated . The number of the clusters generated under each object label mainly depends on the variation of the appearances of the object and the similarity to other categorized objects.

Objects	Training data	Number of clusters
Tree	97	23
Sky	82	16
Water	69	31
Field	74	38
Mountain	48	19
Building	83	44

Table 12.2: The statistic figures for training semantic object clusters.

All the images in the database are segmented and labeled based on the object clusters in the object category. The features extracted for the segmented regions are also stored in the database. Based on the image content, the images are categorized automatically. They are also sorted according to the significance values of the objects contained in the images.

To evaluate the effectiveness of the algorithms, we randomly select 160 images in the database. The results of the precision and recall for the six objects defined in this experiments are listed in Table 12.3.

Objects	Precision	Recall
Tree	0.74	0.84
Sky	0.69	0.91
Water	0.63	0.73
Field	0.48	0.55
Mountain	0.69	0.77
Building	0.56	0.70

Table 12.3: The precision and recall for the semantic objects.

The precision and recall of the objects largely depend on the coverage of the training data and the variation of the appearances of the objects. If the system can be trained with the data covering all possible appearances of objects, both precision and recall can be much improved.

We take an example to illustrate the process of object segmentation. The original image is shown in Figure 12.10 (a). The result of the initial image segmentation based on color is displayed in Figure 12.10 (b). After identifying individual regions with the object labels and merging the adjacent regions with the same labels, the complete segmentation is shown in Figure 12.10 (c). Obviously, the result is much closer to human visual perception.

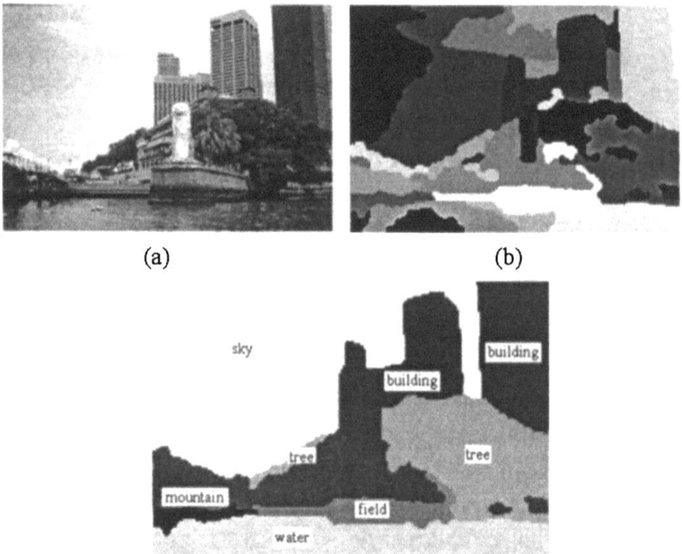

(a) (b)

(c)

Figure 12.10: Semantic object segmentation with the textured object model.

We use an example to show the process of the image retrieval and how the system refines the retrieval results when the user provide more specific requirements for particular images. When a query is made by a description "building", 46 out of 50 retrieved images contain "buildings". We display the first 6 images in Figure 12.11. Then a query is refined by submitting the fourth image. The first 6 retrieved images are shown in Figure 12.12. Among the first 50 retrieved images at this stage, 31 images contain building, sky, water and tree. Another query refinement

Figure 12.11: Retrieval results from a query by a semantic description "Building".

Figure 12.12: Retrieval results from a query by an image.

Figure 12.13: Retrieval results from a query by a specified visual object.

is done by specifying the building in the middle of the first image in Figure 12.12. The first 6 retrieved images are displayed in Figure 12.13. Among the first 50 retrieved images, 28 images contain the buildings that are visually similar to the one specified.

If the user wants more specific images containing some objects with particular visual features, he could just browse the currently retrieved images and point out the special objects in any images step by step. The system is able to refine the retrieval results progressively. By making use of the three designed query methods appropriately, the user could control the retrieval results as expected. For example, a user has a large database. When he locates the specific objects, there may be thousands of images contain the same objects. To refine the retrieval results, he could simply submit one or a few images he likes most.

References

1. KODAK SHOEBOX Photo CD Image Manager, http://www.kodak.com/productInfo/productInfo.shtml
2. Living Album, http://www.clubphoto.com/tools/la_soft.php
3. Ricoh PhotoStudio Application, http://www.ricohcpg.com/support_index.html
4. Apple PhotoFlash, http://www.apple.com/software/
5. A. Pentland, et al., "Photobook: Content-based manipulation of image databases", International Journal of Computer Vision, Vol. 18, No. 3, pp. 233-254, 1996.
6. J. R. Smith, S. F. Chang, "Tools and techniques for color image retrieval", SPIE Proc. on Storage and Retrieval for Image and Video Database IV, Vol. 2670, 1996.
7. J. K. Wu, "Content-based indexing of multimedia database", IEEE Trans. on Knowledge and Data Engineering, Vol. 9, No. 6, pp. 978-989, 1997.
8. D. Hong, et al., "Refining Image Retrieval based on Context-Driven Methods", Proc. of SPIE, Storage and Retrieval For Image and Video Database VII, pp. 581-592, 1999.
9. T. P. Minka, R. Picard, "Interactive learning using a 'society of models"', Special Issue of Pattern Recognition on Image Database: Classification and Retrieval, 1996.
10. James C. Bezdek, et al., "Prototype Classification and Feature Selection with Fuzzy Sets", IEEE Trans. Syst., Man, Cybern, Vol. SMC-7, No. 2, pp.87-92, 1977
11. Bharathi B. Devi, et al., "A Fuzzy Approximation Scheme for Sequential Learning in Patten Recognition", IEEE Trans. Syst., Man, Sybern, Vol. SMC-16, No. 5, pp. 668-679, 1986

12. G. Sheikholeslami, et al., "Semantic Clustering and Querying on Heterogeneous Features for Visual Data", Proc. of ACM Multimedia'98, pp. 3-12, Bristol, UK, 1998
13. J. Huang, et al., "An Automatic Hierarchical Image Classification Scheme", Proc. of ACM Multimedia'98, pp. 219-224, Bristol, UK, 1998
14. A. Jaimes, S. F. Chang, "Model-Based Classification of Visual Information for Content-Based Retrieval", Proc. of SPIE, Storage and Retrieval For Image and Video Database VII, Vol. 3656, pp. 402-414, 1999
15. S. Santini, R. Jain, "Interfaces for Emergent Semantics in Multimedia Databases", Proc. of SPIE, Storage and Retrieval For Image and Video Database VII, pp. 167-175, 1999
16. Y. Linde, A. Buzo, R. Gray, "An Algorithm for Vector Quantizer Design", IEEE Trans. on Communication, Vol. 28, No. 1, pp. 84-95, 1980

Chapter 13

Evaluation of Content-based Retrieval

With the exponential growth of multimedia data comes the challenge of managing this information in a controlled, organized and efficient manner. Content-based multimedia information handling research has therefore proliferated tremendously in the recent past [13]. We can soon expect commercial products which will allow us to handle multimedia information with great ease. This will necessitate the development of commercial solutions for multimedia databases. This will lead to multimedia technologies being adopted both in the professional and commercial world. However, this will require methods that can differentiate between competing multimedia database products offered by rival vendors. Essentially, we need to have a set of objective metrics or benchmarks which can highlight the relative strengths and weaknesses of different multimedia databases. Thus, a customer who is confronted with many choices of multimedia database systems for his particular application, can use these benchmarks to decide which particular system is best suited for his needs. It is instructive to note that there are well known metrics for benchmarking traditional databases either in terms of performance of access methods and query optimization [2] or in terms of transaction throughput power [1].

13.1 Definition of the Problem

As we have seen in the earlier chapters, multimedia database engines can be complex systems. In this section we will first define the types of retrieval mechanisms available and then go on to formulate the definition of the problem of benchmarking multimedia database systems.

13.1.1 Retrieval as a function of data and query

Multimedia databases can contain attribute data, content data and structure data. Let us consider this using a multimedia document on *people of different nations*, as an example. The name of a country, its population, area and GNP are examples of attribute data. The types of terrain, the face images of peoples living in that country, the flag of the country and the trademarks of companies in that country are examples of content data.

Content data are normally expressed in terms of features such as shape, color and texture. Certain types of content data such as a video shot of the terrain may be represented using spatio-temporal features. Structures are used to represent the relationship such as those among the country, its states, their counties, their towns and villages. Structures are also used to define navigation among objects or an object and the information about it.

Queries can be classified as well-formulated or *precise queries* and ill-formulated or *imprecise queries*. Queries expressed in database query languages, such as SQL and similar tools are examples of well formulated queries. Queries that fall under this category are normally those addressing the attribute data or those using the attribute data to get the content or structure data if such pre-defined associations exist.

Imprecise queries consist of two types. The first type of imprecise queries arise mostly because of a user's lack of focus and is prevalent in browsing applications using multimedia data. A typical example of these type of queries arise on the world-wide web when one is navigating through hypermedia documents. The second type of imprecise queries arise either due to the user's inability to express the content data accurately or user's preference to refer to content data using everyday language. Subjective descriptors such as 'beautiful' and 'thin', which are both abstract and relative abound in everyday language.

The retrieval techniques used currently can be related to the nature of query and data. We present this in Figure 13.1.

All the traditional retrieval techniques used for *on-line transaction processing* (OLTP) applications based on their attribute data have collectively been called *database* techniques. A database handles precise queries on precise data sets. Thus, in answer to a query on the names of employees earning a million dollars per month would be null (or a zero set) if no such employee exists. The retrieval techniques used for handling structure data of the first type, i.e. representing relationships such as *part-of* and *is-a*, fall under this category. *Information Retrieval* (IR) techniques,

query type \ data type	precise	imprecise
precise	database	information retrieval
imprecise	links	approximate retrieval

Figure 13.1: Relationship among data, query and types of retrieval

on the other hand, have been addressing collections of text document databases [8]. In such databases, the queries are very precise, they are made up of words and the semantics of the words in a query is very clear. Documents are also made of definitive words. However, the different roles played by the same word in different documents makes the collection of data in the document space less precise. Link based retrieval techniques such as *hypertext* and *hypermedia* [10] have been used to handle the imprecise queries of the first type defined above, to look for precise data. There is as yet no "label" attached to the retrieval techniques that handle imprecise query of the second kind on a collection of data that in itself is imprecise. The popular term in usage is *content-based retrieval.*

However, content based retrieval will also include information retrieval. Content based retrieval covers the right half of the table or the second column in total and not the bottom right quadrant. Therefore we can use the the phrase *approximate retrieval*, (AR) to refer to those retrieval techniques that belong to the bottom right quadrant. We will use the above taxonomy in the following discussions on benchmarking multimedia databases.

13.1.2 Definition of benchmarking of multimedia databases

A multimedia database application could use any permutation and combination of the above four classes of retrieval techniques since multimedia database engines can be complex systems. Clearly, speed of response is an important aspect of benchmarking any database system. This should be assiduously pursued and compiled with respect to different levels of scaling up of data collections.

A second component that has been often used as a measure is the expressive power of a query language. Expressive power, in effect, determines the range of queries that an application can use. This is primarily a metric for the query language and not for a retrieval engine. Thus, even when retrieval engines are capable of handling any type of query, a query language may inhibit certain types of queries due to limitations in either the underlying model (such as relational algebra or calculus), or the syntax and semantics of the query language. Therefore, the range of queries as a measure is not that important since there is now a trend towards using customized *application programming interfaces* (API) for queries as compared to using structured or other query languages. This assumption can only affect the range of ad hoc queries and not API driven queries.

Multimedia database systems introduce a new concept called the *quality of result* to a query. This is due to the necessity of approximate retrieval for multimedia data. This is especially important in the context of the queries on imprecise data collections and assumes an even more important role when the queries are also imprecise. Quality was never an issue in database engines developed for OLTP applications. They simply returned an answer that satisfied the conditionals in the query or returned a null. Hence, the quality dimension was completely ignored. Given the prevalence of imprecise nature of both data and queries in multimedia databases, quality takes on a greater role than speed given that incorrect response however fast it is, will be of little value.

Hence, the benchmark of a multimedia retrieval engine can be thought of as a quality of service metric:

$$\text{QOS} = \text{f (Speed, Quality of answer)}. \tag{13.1}$$

In the rest of the chapter, we will present a measure for QOS and suggest a methodology to evaluate this metric.

13.2 Benchmarking for Content-based Systems

A brief look at the standard metrics for conventional retrieval methods will be followed by a detailed discussion on metrics for links and approximate retrieval.

13.2.1 Benchmarking for database retrieval methods

There are examples of *DebitCredit* [1] and other test standards. These emerged primarily as measures of speed of response for scaled up collections and were typically measured in terms of number of transactions per unit time. The results here will depend on optimization of resources and tools such as buffer management and evaluation of join. The metric for OLTP type of applications T_{DB} is *Transaction per Second*, where transactions are generally speaking, queries. In *DebitCredit*, it is quantified by measuring the elapsed time for two standard batch transactions and throughput for an interactive transaction. A plot of T_{DB} vs. database size will provide the performance of the database engine with respect to database size. Although the database community has considered the *utilization* issue which counts the overhead for generating a useful query result, there has been no benchmark for the quality of retrieval.

13.2.2 Benchmarking of information retrieval methods

An *Information Retrieval* (IR) system returns a set of relevant objects (usually text documents) for any query. The objects not returned are considered irrelevant. Hence an IR system can also be called as a *Boolean* system since any object can either be relevant or irrelevant for a particular query. Assume that we have a database D having n objects (documents):

$$D = \{ o_i \mid i = 1, 2, \ldots, n\} \tag{13.2}$$

where o_i is a database object or a document. For a given query q we have the following:

1. *Ideal System Response*: This assumes that an ideal IR system I exists. The response of this ideal IR system is the *ideal* or the desired response. The ideal response can be considered to be two sets which can be considered as a partition on the database D induced by query q:

$$R_q^I = \{ o_j | (o_j \in D) \wedge (o_j \text{ is relevant})\} \tag{13.3}$$

$$N_q^I = \{ o_k | (o_k \in D) \wedge (o_k \text{ is not relevant})\} \tag{13.4}$$

such that,

$$R_q^I \cap N_q^I = \phi \tag{13.5}$$

$$R_q^I \cup N_q^I = D \tag{13.6}$$

Note that the ideal response can be considered as the *ground truth.* This can be a corpus which is a collection of known objects with known ideal responses to some known queries.

2. *Test System Response*: This is the response actually provided by an IR system E being benchmarked. This system also partitions D for the same query q:

$$R_q^E = \{o_u | (o_u \in D) \wedge (o_u \text{ is relevant according to E})\} \quad (13.7)$$
$$N_q^E = \{o_v | (o_v \in D) \wedge (o_v \text{ is not relevant according to E})\} \quad (13.8)$$

such that,

$$R_q^E \cap N_q^E = \phi \quad (13.9)$$
$$R_q^E \cup N_q^E = D \quad (13.10)$$

Given R_q^I, N_q^I, R_q^E and N_q^E, the IR community has the following two well known measures for benchmarking:

- **Recall**: The *recall* for query q is defined as:

$$\frac{\| R_q^E \cap R_q^I \|}{\| R_q^I \|} \quad (13.11)$$

  where $\| \cdot \|$ indicates the cardinality of the set.

- **Precision**: The *precision* for query q is defined as:

$$\frac{\| R_q^E \cap R_q^I \|}{\| R_q^E \|} \quad (13.12)$$

Relevance of retrieved documents with respect to a query measured in terms of precision and recall have continued to be the commonly accepted metrics. There is, however, a growing disillusionment among the IR community that these two measure somehow do not tell the whole story but there is yet to emerge alternatives to these two measures. Speed of retrieval T_{IR} for IR has to be measured differently from that for database technology. This is primarily because the application environment does not have the same volume of transactions and the retrieval process is more interactive due to the imprecise nature of the data collection.

$$T_{IR} = \frac{\text{No. of query terms}}{\text{Response time}} \quad (13.13)$$

Quality of output from IR systems can be measured as follows.

$$Q_{IR} = W_{PR} * precision + W_{RE} * recall \tag{13.14}$$

where, W_{PR} is the weightage for precision and W_{RE} is the weightage for recall. Then, the overall quality of service can be defined as:

$$QOS_{IR} = T_{IR} * Q_{IR} \tag{13.15}$$

TREC, the annual *Text Retrieval Conference* organized by the *National Institute of Standards and Technology* (NIST) in the United States continues to be the key forum for benchmarking both commercial and academic IR systems [3]. This conference aims to bring IR groups together to discuss their work on a new large test collection. The participants of TREC employ a variety of retrieval techniques, including methods using automatic thesauri, sophisticated term weighting, natural language techniques, relevance feedback, and advanced pattern matching. These methods are run through a common evaluation package in order for the groups to compare the effectiveness of different techniques and to discuss how differences between the systems affected performance.

Thus, the emphasis of this exercise is to benchmark the different IR methods on increasingly large and common collections. It is important to note that these two metrics relate to the quality of the answer to a query. Although TREC participants may record the time taken to get a result, quality measures have assumed a more important role in this benchmarking exercise.

TREC is now considering corpuses in languages other than English. A complementary forum called the *Message Understanding Conference* (MUC) is likely to produce results that may impact information retrieval methods.

13.2.3 Benchmarking links

We have not come across any attempts to benchmark significant sized collections of hyperlinks. We list below the measures that could be used for retrieval methods for links.

Speed as a measure

The time, T_{LI}, to fetch immediate (or next level) information associated with a link is definitely an immediate measure to consider. This measure will be affected by the quality of schemes such as buffer management and cluster management on the disk.

In addition, the time taken to reach distant information, T_{LD}, can also be a measure. This measure will be affected by the design of the information structures. If there are too many levels of nesting before reaching a desired information, then this measure will suffer. It will also be poor when retrieval on structures is not complemented by other retrieval methods. The speed of response, T_L, is defined as:

$$T_L = \frac{W_{LI} * N_{LI} * T_{LI} + W_{LD} * N_{LD} * T_{LD}}{W_{LI} * N_{LI} + W_{LD} * N_{LD}} \tag{13.16}$$

where W_{LD} is the relative importance of distant transactions, N_{LD} is the number of distant transactions, W_{LI} is the relative importance of immediate transactions and N_{LI} is the number of immediate transactions.

Quality as a measure

The ability to find a piece of information is one measure of quality. This can be represented by the ratio Q_L, between the number of successful retrievals of information to the total number of queries.

$$Q_L = \frac{\text{No. of successful retrievals}}{\text{Total No. of queries}} \tag{13.17}$$

No retrieval method employing links can afford to keep all possible links all the time. Hence, it is desirable to generate links when they are not predefined. This is a difficult task and is dependent on the extent of supporting information available to a link retrieval method.

A wholistic measure for link based system

A total quality measure for link based system can be defined as,

$$QOS_L = T_L * Q_L \tag{13.18}$$

13.2.4 Benchmarks for approximate retrieval methods

As benchmarks for the approximate retrieval methods are the least understood or established, we will discuss this topic in detail. The imprecise representation of data will have to be converted into some objective measures represented in terms of numbers or alphanumeric characters. This transformation may employ concepts such as fuzzy mapping, fuzzy set theory, classification using traditional clustering techniques and more recent methods using neural nets, and classification trees.

Speed as a measure

AR methods will in general use data from more than one dimension for retrieval. The features that identify a country from its flag may use color and the spatial location of the different colors as the two features or dimensions for retrieval. The difference between AR and other retrieval methods, more often, lies in the fact that most features take on continuous values. For example, while there are only a finite number of words in a corpus of text, the number of face images in a face database can be very large and the shape feature like "moment invariants" (say for the nose, eyes, mouth and chin) can assume continuous values. Speed of response will continue to be an important measure. However, AR methods may need to be evaluated with greater emphasis on the quality of the response rather than the speed. The speed, T_{AR}, can be measured by:

$$T_{AR} = \frac{\text{No. of features in query}}{\text{Response time}} \tag{13.19}$$

Quality as a measure

Quality of response has been a subject of discussion even as early as 1968 [5]. The measures presented here will apply to the qualitative aspects of an AR system. The ranked list of objects in response to a query (based on some features) is referred to as the *response set*. The objects that are useful and relevant to the query are called *relevant objects*.

To illustrate the importance of quality of result for AR techniques, we will present an example now. This example will also serve as a vehicle to present certain important aspects of the quality of a retrieval result. Assume that we have a database of different trademark shape images. A typical query to this system would be to obtain all images in the database which are *similar in shape* to a query trademark shape image. So it uses an AR technique which utilizes shape similarity computation between two images. It answers any shape-similarity query by computing the similarity between the query trademark shape image and all the trademark shape images in the database and presents them in a ranked list in the decreasing order of similarity to the query image. We also refer to an image (i.e. a trademark shape) as an object. Object i is represented as o_i in the following discussion and in general, it refers to a multimedia object. Assume that the query object o_q is a bird. Let the four objects o_1, o_2, o_3 and o_4 (all of them are stylized versions of birds) be the relevant objects in the database for the query object o_q. Let us also assume that for the four relevant objects, the ith object is expected to appear in i^{th} rank in a response set. So the o_1 is the most similar object to the query bird image, the o_2 is the next-most similar object followed by o_3 and finally o_4 is the least similar relevant object. This also implies that all other objects in the response sets constitute noise and are irrelevant. Figure 13.2 shows the query object o_q, all the relevant objects (o_1 through o_4) and some of the irrelevant objects (o_5 through o_9) in the database. We will use two response sets for our discussions below. The use of two response sets will help illustrate the concepts discussed better than the use of a single response set.

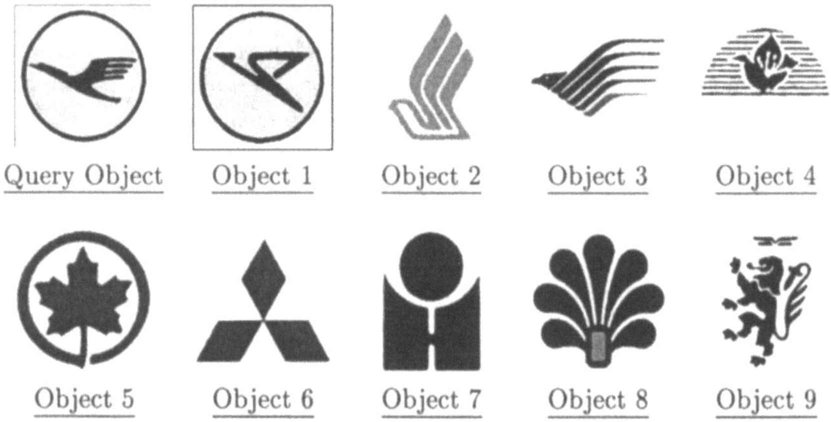

Figure 13.2: Some trademark image objects used in the example

The following observations on relevant objects in ranked response sets obtained for the same query from two different retrieval engines will be used to discuss the new performance metrics (or measures).

- **Observation 1:** The same set of objects may appear in different orders in the two response sets (Order).

  Example 1:

  Response set 1 : $o_1, o_2, o_3, o_4, \ldots$

  Response set 2 : $o_2, o_4, o_3, o_1, \ldots$

  In this example, the first system correctly retrieves the four relevant objects in descending order of similarity. The second system has retrieved the four relevant objects at the top of the list but they have not been retrieved in a descending order of similarity. Hence the quality of the second system is not good as that of the first system.

- **Observation 2:** The same set of objects while appearing in the same order may have different ranks in the two response sets (Rank).

  Example 2:

  Response set 1 : $o_1, o_2, o_3, o_4, \ldots$

  Response set 2 : $o_7, o_1, o_2, o_3, o_4, \ldots$

  In this example, the first system has performed ideal retrieval. The second system has retrieved an irrelevant shape as the most similar shape and the next four objects are the same as in the ideal response. Hence, even though the second system obtains the correct order, the ranks of the individual objects are not correct. Therefore, the second system response is of an inferior quality.

- **Observation 3:**

  The same set of objects while appearing in the same order may have different spreads (Spread).

  Example 3:

  Response set 1 : $o_1, o_7, o_2, o_3, o_4, \ldots$

  Response set 2 : $o_1, o_2, o_8, o_9, o_5, o_3, o_4 \ldots$

  This example shows while the order can be preserved, the number of objects to be considered can vary for all relevant abjects to appear in the response. In this case, both the systems have retrieved the relevant objects in a correct order, but the second system response has more irrelevant objects. Hence the spread of the ranked list which encompasses the relevant objects is larger for the second system which is less desirable.

- **Observation 4:**

  The same set of objects while having the same Spread may have different displacements of individual objects in the two response sets (Displace).

  Example 4:

  Response set 1 : $o_1, o_7, o_2, o_6, o_3, o_4, \ldots$

  Response set 2 : $o_1, o_7, o_6, o_2, o_3, o_4, \ldots$

  Here, the number of objects appearing between the first relevant object and the last relevant object on the ranked list is the same. However, the displacement (from the ideal position) of the individual relevant objects are different. For the first system o_2 is displaced by one position while o_3 and o_4 are displaced by two positions. For the second case o_2, o_3 and o_4 are displaced by two positions each. Hence the response of the second system is of a lesser quality than that of the first system.

Taking these observations in account, we will now classify all types of AR systems into two categories. We will define the measures for a response set and then define the measures for calibrating an AR system.

Types of AR systems

Depending on the type of the response set produced, we can classify AR systems into two categories:

1. **Continuous**: A continuous AR system returns a ranked list of object as the response to any query. Essentially, for any query q, it computes a relevance measure (often a *similarity measure* based on content of multimedia objects) for all the objects in the database and returns the set of objects in a ranked manner where the rank indicates the relative relevance to the query. The first object in the ranked list is the most relevant object for the query (most *similar* object for similarity retrieval) and the last object in the list is the least relevant object. More formally, assume that we have a database D having n objects:

$$D = \{ o_i \mid i = 1, 2, \ldots, n\} \tag{13.20}$$

where o_i is a multimedia object such as text, image, audio or video. For the continuous AR system, we also have a *Relevance Function* $\mathcal{S}$, which for a given query q assigns a relevance measure s_i^q to every every object o_i in the database i.e. it is a function $\mathcal{S} : D \times Q \rightarrow [0, 1]$ such that $\mathcal{S}(o_i, q)$ is the relevance measure of object o_i for query q. Q is the set of all queries. Note that $[0, 1]$ is a closed subset of $\Re$, the set of real numbers. Also note that:

$$\mathcal{S}(o_i, q) = 0.0 \Longrightarrow o_i \text{is totally irrelevant for query } q \tag{13.21}$$

$$\mathcal{S}(o_i, q) = 1.0 \Longrightarrow o_i \text{is totally relevant for query } q \tag{13.22}$$

For a given query q we have the following:

(a) *Ideal System Response*: This assumes that an ideal continuous AR system I which has the associated relevance function $\mathcal{S}^I$ exists. The ideal response to a query q can be considered to be a *ranked* list:

$$L_q^I = (o_1^I, o_2^I, o_3^I, \ldots, o_n^I) \tag{13.23}$$

where L_q^I is a ranked list such that,

$$\mathcal{S}^I(o_1^I, q) \geq \mathcal{S}^I(o_2^I, q) \geq \mathcal{S}^I(o_3^I, q) \cdots \geq \mathcal{S}^I(o_n^I, q) \tag{13.24}$$

Therefore the first ranked element o_1^I is the most relevant object in the database for query q and the last element o_n^I is the least relevant. The ranking is done using the relevance function $\mathcal{S}^I$. Note that $\mathcal{S}^I$ induces a partial order on the objects of D. Most often, this relevance function is a similarity measure based upon some feature of the objects. It is clear that this is the "ideal" or the desired ranking of the objects in the database.

(b) *Test System Response*: This is the response actually provided by an AR system E, with the associated relevance function $\mathcal{S}^E$, being benchmarked. What this system returns is also a ranked list:

$$L_q^E = (o_1^E, o_2^E, o_3^E, \ldots, o_n^E) \tag{13.25}$$

which is ranked in the descending order of relevance by the relevance function $\mathcal{S}^E$. Therefore, $\mathcal{S}^E(o_1^E, q) \geq \mathcal{S}^E(o_2^E, q) \geq \mathcal{S}^E(o_3^E, q) \cdots \geq \mathcal{S}^E(o_n^E, q)$.

Precision and recall are not adequate to capture the performance of an AR system since they cannot account for the *order*, *rank*, *spread* and the *displacement* aspects of response sets. We therefore need new measures for benchmarking AR systems performance. In order to come up with new measures, we adopt the following two principles:

(a) *Principle 1*: If an object is displaced from its "ideal rank" for an AR system, then the penalty is symmetric with respect to moving up or down the list. That is to say that the penalty for displacement around the ideal position is the same whether the displacement increases or decreases the rank.

(b) *Principle 2*: The penalty of an object displaced from its "ideal rank" is directly proportional to its relevancy measure. This is intuitive because given equal displacements, the displacement of an object with a higher relevancy measure is less desirable than for an object with a lower relevancy measure. Also, this is reasonable since the relevancy measure is the *basis* for the ranking.

Based on these two principles, we can use the following two measures:

- **Order:** The *order* of a response set is defined as the size of the longest consecutive subsequence of objects appearing in their ideal order (not the ideal rank). This basically measures one aspect of the quality of the relevance function of the AR system being benchmarked. For a database of size n, the ideal order is n. This measure captures the Order aspect of response sets.
- **Weighted Displacement:** For an object o_i^E, the displacement $d_q(o_i^E)$ for a query q is defined as:

$$d_q(o_i^E) = |(\text{Rank}(o_i^E)\text{in } L_q^I) - (\text{Rank}(o_i^E) \text{ in } L_q^E)| \quad (13.26)$$

The displacement indicates the amount an object has moved from its ideal rank. We define the performance measure *weighted displacement*, ω_q^E, for a query q by weighting the displacement with the ideal relevance measure:

$$\omega_q^E = \sum_{i=1}^{n} \mathcal{S}^I(o_i^E, q) d_q(o_i^E) \quad (13.27)$$

Note that ω_q^E is 0 if the ideal response is returned by AR system E. Also, this measure incorporates the two principles described above. Moreover, it captures the Rank (through $\mathcal{S}^I$) and Displace (through $d_q(o_i^E)$). Note that Spread is not relevant in case of an continuous AR system since the spread will be n for all responses.

2. **Mixed**: A mixed AR system has characteristics of both Boolean IR systems and continuous AR engines. The mixed AR system returns a response set consisting of two subsets – a set of relevant objects and a set of irrelevant objects for any query. Moreover, for the set of relevant objects, it also returns a ranked list of objects based on the relevance function for that query. Again, assume that we have a database D having n multimedia objects:

$$D = \{ o_i \mid i = 1, 2, \ldots, n\}. \quad (13.28)$$

Like in the case of the continuous AR system, we also have a *Relevance Function* $\mathcal{S}$, which for a given query q assigns a relevance measure s_i^q to every every object o_i in the database. It is a function $\mathcal{S} : D \times Q \to [0,1]$ such that $\mathcal{S}(o_i, q)$ is the relevance measure of object o_i for query q. Again, Q is the set of all queries. For a given query q we have the following:

(a) *Ideal System Response*: This assumes that an ideal AR system I exists. The ideal response can be considered to consist of two sets which is as a partition on the database induced by query q:

$$R_q^I = \{o_j | (o_j \in D) \wedge (o_j \text{ is relevant})\} \quad (13.29)$$

$$N_q^I = \{o_k | (o_k \in D) \wedge (o_k \text{ is not relevant})\} \quad (13.30)$$

such that,

$$R_q^I \cap N_q^I = \phi \quad (13.31)$$

$$R_q^I \cup N_q^I = D \quad (13.32)$$

In addition, the set of relevant objects, R_q^I, has an associated ranked list L_q^I:

$$L_q^I = (o_1^I, o_2^I, o_3^I, \ldots, o_x^I) \text{ for some } x \le n, \quad (13.33)$$

such that,

$$\mathcal{S}^I(o_1^I, q) \ge \mathcal{S}^I(o_2^I, q) \ge \mathcal{S}^I(o_3^I, q) \cdots \ge \mathcal{S}^I(o_x^I, q) \quad (13.34)$$

This means that there are x relevant objects for the query q ranked in a descending order of relevance.

(b) *Test System Response*: This is the response actually provided by a mixed AR system E being benchmarked. What this system returns is a ranked list:

$$L_q^E = (o_1^E, o_2^E, o_3^E, \ldots, o_n^E) \quad (13.35)$$

which is ranked in the descending order of relevance by the relevance function $\mathcal{S}^E$. Therefore, $\mathcal{S}^E(o_1^E, q) \ge \mathcal{S}^E(o_2^E, q) \ge \mathcal{S}^E(o_3^E, q) \cdots \ge \mathcal{S}^E(o_n^E, q)$. Now, as far as the relevant and non-relevant sets go, there are two scenarios for the mixed AR system response:

i. **Size Thresholding:** In this case, the relevant number of objects for query q from the response set L_q^E is considered to be ℓ. This means that the top ℓ objects of the ranked list L_q^E are relevant for the query. Formally, the relevant set of objects R_q^E is:

$$R_q^E \;=\; \{\, o_j^E \mid (o_j^E \in L_q^E) \wedge (j \;\leq\; \ell)\} \qquad (13.36)$$

where $\ell \;\leq\; n$. Note that it is reasonable to have $\ell \leq x$ because the ideal system I returns x relevant objects, but this may not always be the case. The set of irrelevant objects N_q^E is defined as:

$$N_q^E \;=\; \{\, o_k^E \mid (o_k^E \in L_q^E) \wedge (o_k^E \not\in R_q^E)\} \quad (13.37)$$

For the case of size thresholding, we can use the following three performance measures:

- **Order:** The *order* of a response set is defined as the size of the longest consecutive subsequence of *relevant objects* (according to I) appearing in their ideal order (but not necessarily possessing the ideal rank). This basically measures one aspect of the quality of the relevance function of the AR system being benchmarked. The ideal order is ℓ if $\ell < x$ and is x if $\ell \geq x$. This measure captures the Order aspect of response sets.
- **Rank**: The *rank* of a response set is defined as the sum of the ranks (positions) of the relevant objects appearing in the system response relevant set. If an object appears in the ideal response set R_q^I but does not appear in the system relevant set R_q^E, it is assumed to have a rank of $\ell + 1$. The ideal rank will be $\frac{\ell(\ell+1)}{2}$ if $\ell < x$. If $\ell \geq x$, then the ideal rank is $\frac{x(x+1)}{2}$.
- **Fill Ratio**: The *fill ratio* is defined to be the ratio of the number of actually relevant objects appearing in R_q^E to the number of objects in R_q^E which is ℓ. Therefore,

$$\text{Fill Ratio} \;=\; \begin{cases} \frac{\|\chi\|}{\ell} & \text{if } \ell < x \\ \frac{\|\chi\|}{x} & \text{if } \ell \geq x \end{cases} \qquad (13.38)$$

  where $\chi \;=\; \{o_j \mid o_j \;\in\; (R_q^I \;\cap\; R_q^E)\}$.

ii. **Object Thresholding:** If some relevant object o_r^I of L_q^I appears at the $\hbar^{\text{th}}$ position of L_q^E and no other relevant object ($\in L_q^I$) appears after this o_r^I in L_q^E, then we threshold L_q^E by $\hbar$. So the response set is thresholded such that the last (ideally) relevant object appears in the set. In other words, the relevant number of objects is $\hbar$ such that the *last* object o_r^I belonging to the ideal response ranked list L_q^I appears in the $\hbar^{\text{th}}$ position of system E's response. So, formally the relevant set of objects R_q^E is:

$$R_q^E = \{ o_j^E \mid (o_j^E \in L_q^E) \wedge (j \leq \hbar)\} \quad (13.39)$$

where $\hbar$ = Rank of $(o_r^I \in L_q^I)$ in L_q^E. The set of irrelevant objects N_q^E is defined as:

$$N_q^E = \{ o_k^E \mid (o_k^E \in L_q^E) \wedge (o_k^E \notin R_q^E)\} \quad (13.40)$$

For the case of object thresholding, these three performance measures can be used:

- **Order:** The *order* of a response set is defined as the size of the longest consecutive subsequence of relevant objects appearing in their ideal order. This again measures one aspect of the quality of the relevance function of the AR system being benchmarked. The ideal order is x. This measure captures the Order aspect of response sets.
- **Spread**: The *spread* of a response set is the threshold at which all the objects in R_q^I appear in R_q^E. In other words, the spread is exactly equal to $\hbar$. This measure captures the Spread aspect.
- **Weighted Displacement:** For an object o_i^E, the displacement $d_q(o_i^E)$ for a query q is defined as:

  $$d_q(o_i^E) = |(\text{Rank}(o_i^E)\text{in } L_q^I) - (\text{Rank}(o_i^E)\text{in} L_q^E)| \quad (13.41)$$

  The displacement indicates the amount an object has moved from its ideal rank. We define the performance measure *weighted displacement*, ω_q^E, by weighting the displacement with the ideal relevance measure:

  $$\omega_q^E = \sum_{i=1}^{n} S^I(o_i^E, q) d_q(o_i^E) \quad (13.42)$$

  Note that ω_q^E is 0 if the ideal response is returned by RLIR engine E. This measure incorporates the two principles described earlier. It also captures the Rank and Displace.

Quality measures for calibrating an AR system

Measures for calibrating an AR system will assume the existence of an ideal AR system that produces the Expected Response Set (ERS). ERS is the ideal answer to a query. Hence ERS will become the reference result against which, results from all other AR systems will be evaluated. Such evaluations can then be used to calibrate the AR system under test. We can define relative measures which show how well a system E performs with respect to a particular measure against the ideal system I. We define the relative measures in the range $[0, 1]$. A relative measure closer to unity indicates a better (more "ideal") response and hence is of better quality. We have defined the new measures in the previous section. We will now show how to compute the relative measure for each of the type of AR system:

1. **Continuous AR System**:

   - **Order**: Since the ideal order for a database of size n is equal to n (the largest possible), the relative order for a query q can be defined as:

   $$\text{Relative Order}_{\text{q}} = \frac{\text{order of Engine } E \text{ for query } q}{n} \tag{13.43}$$

   - **Weighted Displacement**: Since the ideal weighted displacement is 0, the relative weighted displacement for a query q can be defined as:

   $$\text{Relative Weighted Displacement}_{\text{q}} = \frac{\omega_q^E}{\Omega} \tag{13.44}$$

   where,

   $$\Omega = \begin{cases} \frac{n^2}{2} & \text{if } n \text{ is even} \\ \frac{n^2-1}{2} & \text{if } n \text{ is odd} \end{cases} \tag{13.45}$$

   for a database of size n. Note that it can be proved that Ω is the largest weighted displacement possible assuming all objects have the highest weight of unity.

2. **Size Thresholded Mixed AR System**:

   - **Order**: Since the ideal order for a database of size n is equal to ℓ, the relative order for a query q can be defined as:

   $$\text{Relative Order}_{\text{q}} = \begin{cases} \frac{\text{order of } E \text{ for query } q}{\ell} & \text{if } \ell < x \\ \frac{\text{order of } E \text{ for query } q}{x} & \text{if } \ell \geq x \end{cases} \tag{13.46}$$

   - **Rank**: This can be computed as the ratio of the ideal rank to the engine rank:

   $$\text{Relative Rank} = \frac{\text{Rank}(R_q^I)}{\text{Rank}(R_q^E)} \tag{13.47}$$

- **Fill Ratio**: Since the fill ratio of the ideal system is 1 and that of the system response is less than or equal to 1, the relative fill ratio is equal to the fill ratio.

3. **Object Thresholded Mixed AR System**:

- **Order**: Since the ideal order for a database of size n is equal to x, the relative order can be defined as:

$$\text{Relative Order}_{\text{q}} = \frac{\text{order of } E \text{ for query } q}{x} \tag{13.48}$$

- **Spread**: The relative spread is the ratio of the spread of the ideal response to that of the system response:

$$\text{Relative Spread}_{\text{q}} = \frac{\| L_q^I \|}{\hbar} \tag{13.49}$$

- **Weighted Displacement**: Since the ideal weighted displacement is 0, the relative weighted displacement can be defined as:

$$\text{Relative Weighted Displacement}_{\text{q}} = \frac{\omega_q^E}{\Omega} \tag{13.50}$$

where,

$$\Omega = \begin{cases} \frac{n^2}{2} & \text{if } n \text{ is even} \\ \frac{n^2-1}{2} & \text{if } n \text{ is odd} \end{cases} \tag{13.51}$$

for a database of size n.

Overall measure for AR method

The measures defined earlier can be combined to derive an overall figure of merit by using a weighted combination of the individual measures. The quality *AR* of an AR system can be computed as:

$$Q_{AR} = \frac{\sum(W_i * M_i)}{\sum W_i} \qquad for\ i = 1...N \tag{13.52}$$

where M_i is the appropriate relative measure i (e.g. for an object-thresholded mixed AR system, it will be relative order, relative spread and relative weighted displacement), W_i is the relative importance of the measure i and N is the total number of measures appropriate for that AR system. Then the overall quality of service can be defined as:

$$QOS_{AR} = T_{AR} * Q_{AR} \tag{13.53}$$

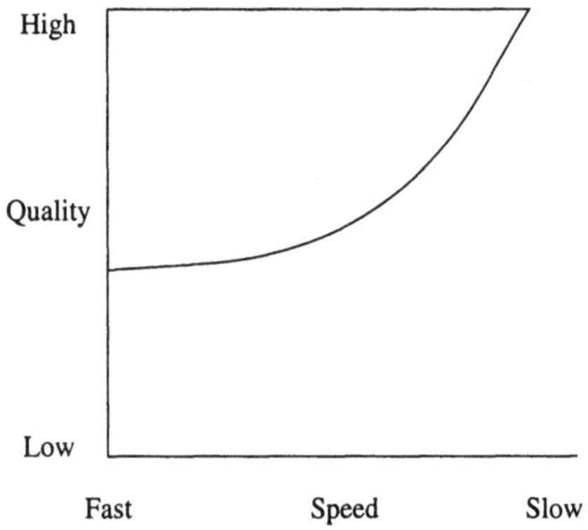

Figure 13.3: Desired region in Quality-Speed plane.

13.2.5 Complete benchmark for multimedia databases

The combination of retrieval methods may be used either independently or in some interdependent manner. The independent combination will use the different retrieval method to get the answers to different parts of a complex query. The results are usually collated into different parts of the response to a query. The overall benchmark for such an application will be,

$$QOS_{MMDB} = \frac{W_Q * \prod(Q_i)}{W_T * \max(T_i)} \tag{13.54}$$

where W_T is the importance of time of response, W_Q is the importance of quality, Q_i is the quality measure of the ith retrieval technique, T_i is the speed measure of the ith retrieval technique. The simplest form of interdependent usage may be to use the results from one retrieval method as the input to another retrieval method. In such a case, the overall benchmark may be represented as follows.

$$QOS_{MMDB} = \frac{W_Q * \prod(Q_i)}{W_T * \sum(T_i)} \tag{13.55}$$

The graph in Figure 13.3 shows the desired region into which we would like to see the systems fall.

13.3 Testing Multimedia Databases

The benchmarking of multimedia databases use the time and quality measures on a multimedia database engine. Such an engine may be just one of the four types of retrieval methods or some permutation and combination of the four types.

13.3.1 Scalability with respect to time

This is a fairly straightforward method. One can start with certain number of records in the database and then scale up using multiples of same quantity. Then a plot of time (or speed) of response versus the database size for the same query will give us a good idea of scalability of the engine with respect to time.

13.3.2 Scalability with respect to quality

Database technology

Since quality has not been a factor for consideration in database technologies used in OLTP applications, we do not suggest any methodology.

Information retrieval

TREC has been attempting to set up testing standards and hence we will keep our discussion on this topic to a minimum. The following quality related tests may be desirable in addition to what TREC has been carrying out. It would be desirable to construct corpuses containing different roles of words capable of playing multiple roles, and to set up the queries corresponding to each of these roles. The different parts of speech will be the set of roles that words can assume.

The corpuses, roles and queries will be determined by the type of applications. For example, applications using corpuses containing name databases would be interested only in those words that play the role of noun phrase. Applications using corpuses containing sports information would be interested in noun phrases and verbs.

The method for such testing can be designed using an iterative two step process. We will first define the two step process.

The first step will be to choose a word that plays the most types of roles and to generate documents and queries corresponding to each of these roles. This will give the different IR algorithms and methodologies an opportunity to refine themselves against this test data. The second step would be to choose additional words that play the same set of roles and corresponding documents and queries to test the IR methods against this "scaled up corpus"

Later iterations of this two step process should increasingly bring in other words, documents and queries that correspond to other types of roles as dictated by the type of application. The testing can be said to be completed when sufficient corpus and queries have been generated and tested corresponding to all the common (and necessary) roles.

Links

Benchmarking the links for quality can be set up as a test set of information to be retrieved against queries on links and then computing the quality measure.

Approximate retrieval methods

The benchmarking of quality of retrieval from AR methods can be set up in two steps: evaluation of individual features, and overall testing. Evaluation of approximate retrieval is application-type dependent. It must be done against a given set of objects – the *test data set.* The sample data set specifies a sequence of objects which should be retrieved for every given sample. To define a test data set for approximate retrieval, let us define the ideal retrieval. It must be clearly understood that for any AR query, there is a "context" associated with it. This context can vary from person to person and perhaps it can vary with time for the same person. The response to a query can then vary depending on the context. So for AR, the 'right answer' to a query can vary depending on the context. This makes the task of evaluating an AR system very difficult. Therefore, in order to benchmark various AR systems, one needs to fix a context for every query and then obtain a corresponding *ideal retrieval result.* For any given sample, the ideal retrieval result should exactly follow designer's expectation of similarity – all similar data items must be retrieved and be ordered from the most similar to the least similar. In order to perform a fair evaluation, it is necessary to have a large set of queries, contexts and the associated ideal retrieval results. These are in turn driven by the specific application area which the AR system purports to address. Moreover, for ideal approximate retrieval, the test data set should consist test data (and associated queries) for both individual features and the overall retrieval. The system should be tuned using individual features and then tested for overall retrieval. The test data should be used to evaluate the measures. We give a brief description of the use of this methodology for real applications in the appendix.

Combined retrieval techniques

The individual retrieval techniques should be first tested to obtain their individual performance measures. The results can be used to tune the different retrieval techniques. Once the individual retrieval techniques are tested, then they will remain unaltered unless the range of values of the individual features change. The next step is to change the weights for combining the results obtained from each of the component retrieval techniques. The combined result is the overall benchmark and can be used to modify the weights until the desired performance levels are obtained.

13.3.3 Examples of testing and evaluation

FACE application

The FACE application was reported in [11]. It used image features and text descriptions as the two dimensions. The image features were defined both as crisp sets and fuzzy sets on six facial features: chin, eyes, eyebrow, nose, mouth, and hair. A set of artificially composed facial images are created to form a test data set. In the test data set, there are faces with one, two, or more different facial features. The test is conducted in two steps: Firstly, quality of retrieval is tested against individual facial features. For example, to test retrieval on eyes, a subset of test image data set with different eyes are used. Samples for the test is arbitrarily chosen from the set. Retrieval results are evaluated subjectively by several (10 in our test) people.

The second step is the overall test. It is conducted against all facial features. Figure 13.4 gives an example of a set of faces with change in one or more features. On the bottom-right side, there is a "similarity retrieval" panel to control the weightage among facial features. Here, all weightage are equally set to 10. The nine images on the left are retrieval result with the first being the sample. Comparing with the sample, the differences of other eight images are listed in Table 13.1, where "small" "medium" stand for "small difference" and "medium difference".

Such test sets were used for refining the image database engine used in the system. The fuzzy retrieval engine also used similar tests except that the membership of a feature was not limited to one set only. These engines are of the *AR type.* The text retrieval engine used in the system was tested along the quality measures. The text retrieval engine uses the *IR method.* The iconic browsing uses the *link method.*

	eyes	eyebrow	nose	mouth	chin	hair
1	same	same	same	small	same	same
2	medium	same	same	small	same	same
3	same	same	small	small	same	same
4	medium	same	small	same	same	same
5	same	medium	same	small	same	same
6	same	medium	small	small	same	same
7	medium	medium	same	same	same	same
8	medium	medium	small	same	same	same

Table 13.1: The differences of the images with the sample image.

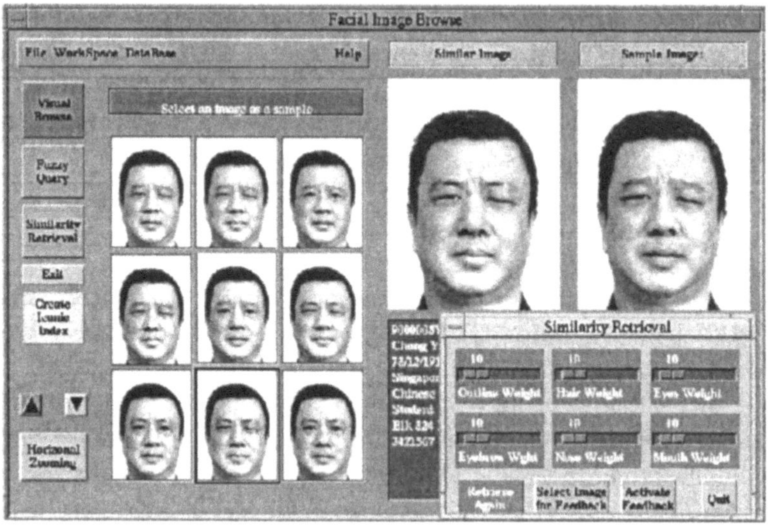

Figure 13.4: Testing of quality of retrieval for facial images.

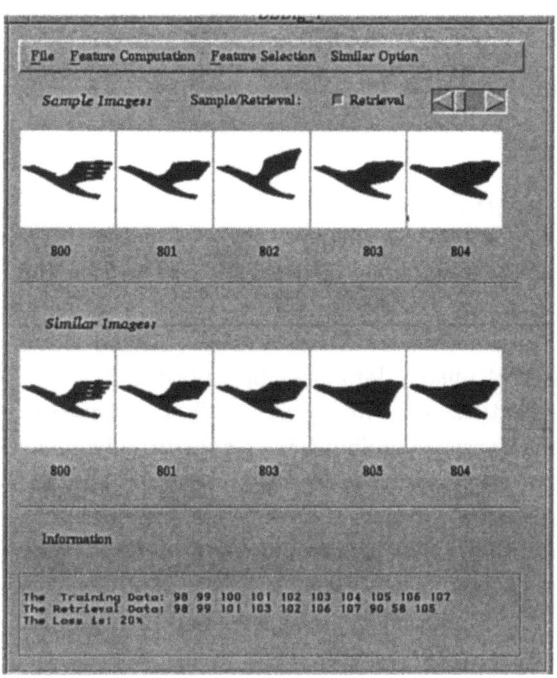

Figure 13.5: Evaluating the shape retrieval for trademarks.

Trademark application

The trademark application consisted of device mark (local and global shape measures) retrieval, phonetic retrieval, word-in mark retrieval and retrieval by meaning. The retrieval engines used in this application are reported in [12, 13]. While we have different engines for using color as a feature [6], we have not yet integrated this into the present trademark application. The device mark uses the *AR method.* The phonetics retrieval, word-in mark retrieval and the retrieval by meaning are all based on the *IR method.*

To test the quality of retrieval for device mark shape, three levels of test data sets have been created: mathematically created geometric patterns, actual device marks and their variations, complicated device marks. In the first class of test patterns, the variations can be exactly controlled by the program used to create these patterns. For example, one series of geometric patterns consists of a circle, an octagon, a hexagon, a pentagon, a square, and a triangle. Figure 13.5 shows the test results using the second class of test patterns. The images shown in the first row belong to one test series with the first as the sample for retrieval. Neighboring images are more similar than distant ones. The second row shows retrieval result. By comparing these two rows, different quality measures are computed.

13.4 Conclusion

We have provided a taxonomy of retrieval methods in this chapter and defined the measures for benchmarking each of the methods and combinations of these methods. We have also outlined a methodology for benchmarking multimedia database applications.

We believe that there are further research opportunities in refining the quantitative measures and defining the test environments for benchmarks. We also believe that there is a real need for some international body to work towards MREC (Multimedia Retrieval and Evaluation Conference) along the lines of TREC, which would essentially try to establish benchmarking data and standards for multimedia databases. A good starting point may be the MIRA effort being undertaken in the EC which works on evaluation frameworks for interactive multimedia information retrieval applications [4]. We strongly feel that the multimedia database community should have standard test data sets, standard queries and the *ideal* retrieval output for each of these queries. Perhaps one database will not be enough, several would be needed for the different types/features of multimedia data and also for overall combined retrieval in various applications. In the long run, standard data sets, queries and known ground truth will be the only way to judge the accuracy and utility of different retrieval engines. Moreover, common collections for each type of multimedia data type should be built up. Commercial vendors should be encouraged to report the benchmark evaluation metrics for their products.

References

1. Anon et. al, "A Measure of Transaction Processing Power", Readings in Database Systems, edited by M. Stonebraker, Morgan Kaufmann Publishers, Inc., San Mateo, CA, pp. 300-312, 1988
2. D. Bitton and C. Turbyfill, "A Retrospective on the Wisconsin Benchmark", Readings in Database Systems, edited by M. Stonebraker, Morgan Kaufmann

Publishers, Inc., San Mateo, CA, pp. 280-299, 1988

3. http://potomac.ncsl.nist.gov:80/TREC/
4. http://www.dcs.gla.ac.uk/mira/
5. F.W. Lancaster, "Information Retrieval Systems", John Wiley, 1968
6. B. M. Mehtre, M. S. Kankanhalli, A. D. Narasimhalu, C. M. Guo, "Color Matching for Image Retrieval", Pattern Recognition Letters, Vol. 16, pp. 325-331, 1995
7. A. D. Narasimhalu, M. S. Kankanhalli, J. K. Wu, "Benchmarking Multimedia Databases", Multimedia Tools and Applications, Vol. 4, No. 3, pp. 333-356, May 1997
8. G. Salton and M. J. McGill, "Introduction to Modern Information Retrieval", McGraw-Hill Advanced Computer Science Series, Auckland, 1983
9. G. Salton, "The State of Retrieval System Evaluation", Information Processing and Management, Vol. 28, No. 4, pp. 441-449, 1992
10. P. Wright, "Cognitive Overheads and Prostheses: Some Issues in Evaluating Hypertexts", Proceedings of Third ACM Conference on Hypertext, pp. 1-12, San Antonio, Texas, 1991
11. J. K. Wu, Y. H. Ang, C. P. Lam, H. H. Loh, A.D. Narasimhalu, "Inference and Retrieval of Facial Images", ACM Multimedia Journal, Vol. 2, No. 1, pp. 1-14, 1994
12. J. K. Wu, B. M. Mehtre, Y. J. Gao, P. C. Lam, A. D. Narasimhalu, "STAR - A Multimedia Database System For Trademark Registration", Applications of Databases, Lecture Notes in Computer Science, Proc. First International Conference on Applications of Databases, Vol. 819, pp. 109-122, 1994
13. J. K. Wu, A. D. Narasimhalu, B. M. Mehtre, C. P. Lam, Y. J. Gao, "CORE: A Content-based Retrieval Engine for Multimedia Databases", ACM Multimedia Systems, Vol 3, pp. 3-25, 1995

Index

MIX
Papier aus verantwortungsvollen Quellen
Paper from responsible sources
FSC® C105338

If you have any concerns about our products,
you can contact us on
ProductSafety@springernature.com

In case Publisher is established outside the EU,
the EU authorized representative is:
Springer Nature Customer Service Center GmbH
Europaplatz 3, 69115 Heidelberg, Germany

Printed by Libri Plureos GmbH
in Hamburg, Germany